THE
REMAKING
OF
EVANGELICAL
THEOLOGY

Also by Gary Dorrien
from Westminster John Knox Press

The Word as True Myth:
Interpreting Modern Theology

THE
REMAKING
OF
EVANGELICAL
THEOLOGY

Gary Dorrien

Westminster John Knox Press
Louisville, Kentucky

Book design by Jennifer K. Cox
Cover design by Pam Poll
Cover photograph © 1998 PhotoDisc, Inc.

First edition
Published by Westminster John Knox Press
Louisville, Kentucky

This book is printed on acid-free paper that meets the American National Standards Institute Z39.48 standard. ∞

PRINTED IN THE UNITED STATES OF AMERICA
98 99 00 01 02 03 04 05 06 07 — 10 9 8 7 6 5 4 3 2 1

Library of Congress Cataloging-in-Publication Data

Dorrien, Gary J.
    The remaking of evangelical theology / Gary Dorrien.
        p.   cm.
    Includes bibliographical references and index.
    ISBN 0-664-25803-4
    1. Evangelicalism.   I. Title.
BV3790.D65   1998
230′. 04624—dc21   98-23573

For Mike and Eric

*the "little boys" who grew
beyond me in many ways*

Contents

Introduction: What Is Evangelicalism?   1

    Claiming the Gospel Message
    Defining the Scripture Principle

1. Antimodernist Modernizers:
    The Making of Fundamentalist Evangelicalism   13

    Luther, Calvin, and Protestant Scholasticism
    Scholastic Certainty: Princeton Realism as Reformed
       Orthodoxy
    Dividing the Word: Dispensationalism
    Princeton Orthodoxy in the Fundamentalist Movement
    Defending and Splintering Fundamentalism
    Fundamentalism without Inerrancy

2. "Needing Prestige Desperately": Fundamentalism
    Reformed   49

    Reforming Fundamentalism: The Founders
    Carnell's "Sack Full of Arguments"
    The Limits of Apologetics: Clark and Van Til
    Is Rationality Enough?

Managing Fuller Theological Seminary
Personalizing Apologetics
Representing the New Evangelicalism
The Battle for Fuller Seminary

3. The Evangelical Crossroads: Rethinking Infallibility   103

Carl Henry and Evangelical Epistemology
Upholding Inerrancy Evangelicalism
Refiguring Word and Spirit: Bernard Ramm
Fundamentalism Reconsidered: Clark Pinnock
Rethinking Infallibility
Taking the Barthian Option

4. Arminian and Catholic Options:
   Opening Up Evangelicalism   153

Upholding the Wesleyan Difference
Word and Spirit in the Wesleyan Traditions
Appealing to the Great Tradition: Catholic Evangelicalism
The Arminian Turn
A Wideness in God's Mercy

5. Postconservative Evangelicalism:
   Dialogues in Search of a Generous Orthodoxy   185

Authorities in Dispute: Liberalism and Evangelicalism
Evangelicalism Beyond Modernity: Donald Bloesch's
   Catholic (Neo)Orthodoxy
Opening the House of Authority: Progressive Evangelicalism
Revelatory Narrative: Engaging Postliberal Theology
Taking Culture Seriously: New Horizons in Hermeneutics

Notes   211
Index   249

Acknowledgments

Grateful acknowledgment is made to HarperCollins Publishers, Clark Pinnock, Simon & Simon, and Cambridge University Press for permission to quote, respectively from Clark Pinnock's *The Scripture Principle* (San Francisco, Calif.: Harper & Row, 1984), copyright © 1984 Clark H. Pinnock, used with permission by Harper Collins Publishers; Pinnock's article "Three Views of the Bible in Contemporary Theology" in *Biblical Authority*, ed. Jack Rogers (Nashville: Word Publishing, 1977); E.J. Carnell's *Christian Commitment,* reprinted with permission of Scribner, a Division of Simon & Schuster, from *Christian Commitment* by Edward John Carnell. Copyright © Edward John Carnell 1957; and Rudolf Nelson's *The Making and Unmaking of an Evangelical Mind* (Cambridge: Cambridge University Press, 1987), copyright © 1987 Cambridge University Press. Reprinted with the permission of Cambridge University Press. Thanks as well to my editors at Westminster John Knox Press, Stephanie Egnotovich and Catherine Carpenter, and copyeditor Joanna L. Mullins. As always, I am grateful for the friendship and support of numerous colleagues at Kalamazoo College, especially Conrad Hilberry, Pam Sotherland, Christopher Latiolais, Jan Solberg, Paula Pugh Romanaux, Jimmy Jones, and Gregory Mahler.

My gratitude to my wife, Brenda Biggs, has been expressed in some of my previous books, but this occasion is special. This present book was written over a two-year period in which the unlikely blessing of each additional day lived together in this life was cherished with ineffable thanksgiving. May God's light continue to shine through her.

Introduction:
What Is Evangelicalism?

Most books on evangelicalism are written by evangelicals; most of the rest are written by secular academics and journalists. Though evangelical thinkers have paid considerable attention over the past half century to the writings of liberal, neoorthodox, and liberation theologians, the favor has not been returned. The kind of theology produced at Harvard, Vanderbilt, and most "mainline" seminaries rarely acknowledges the existence of evangelicalism, except to criticize the baleful influence of the "Christian Right" on American politics. The fact that many evangelicals are not politically conservative is rarely noted in so-called mainstream theology. The notion that evangelicals are producing theology worth taking seriously is considered even more rarely. Except for its role in buttressing certain segments of the politicized Christian Right, evangelical theology attracts little academic attention outside evangelicalism, despite the fact that this world includes tens of millions of Christians in the United States alone.

Most theologians today dismiss evangelical theology on the assumption that it prescribes belief in unbelievable things. On this account, evangelical theology is assumed to be hostile toward and incompatible with modern science, historical and cultural criticism, and intellectual freedom. Though scholars generally allow that *evangelicalism* and *fundamentalism* are not interchangeable terms, the impression persists that modern evangelicals are merely fundamentalists with better manners. Unfortunately for evangelicals, such preconceptions have a considerable basis in the history of American fundamentalism and evangelicalism. Modern evangelical theology forged its early identity by saying no to modern biology (especially evolution), modern historical criticism (especially higher criticism of the Bible), and modern culture. In the late nineteenth century, conservative church leaders organized a powerful antimodernist movement that defended biblical "inerrancy" as a fundamental doctrine of the faith and that sought to gain control over the established Protestant churches.

By the time this movement acquired its name in 1920, "fundamentalism" already bore more than its share of undesirable connotations. "Sectarian" and "anti-intellectual" were prominent among them. By 1930, after the movement lost its battle to gain control of the major denominations, fundamentalist leaders had begun to wear these labels proudly. Some argued for separation from unbelievers only. Others required separation also from believers who refused to separate from unbelievers. Others taught that associating with mainline Christians was permissible as long as one tried to convert them. The differences among these positions emerged as quite significant when a group of nonseparating fundamentalists set out to reform fundamentalism in the 1940s, but most fundamentalist leaders during this period made separatism a badge of honor. They built an extraordinary subcultural network of alternative institutions and gave up on the dominant culture. Fundamentalism lost its movement character and turned inward.

The close association of modern American evangelicalism with this religious heritage has caused most theologians to dismiss evangelical theology. The very existence of a continuing tradition of evangelical theology goes unacknowledged in most modern theology. Even neoorthodox theologians have generally ignored evangelical theology or, like Emil Brunner, ridiculed its continued existence. One reason Protestant evangelicalism still exists, however, is that it keeps alive a spiritually potent and redemptive form of the gospel message. A second reason is that it contains a wide diversity of theologies and institutional forms, some of which bear little relation to the evangelicalisms of the fundamentalist reaction. Sociologist of religion James Davison Hunter begins to account for this variety by identifying four major types of evangelicalism: the Baptist tradition, the Holiness-Pentecostal tradition, the Anabaptist tradition, and the Reformational-Confessional tradition. In this schematism, the individualistic congregational Baptist tradition is the dominant form of evangelicalism; the second type includes all groups from the Wesleyan and other "Holiness" traditions that emphasize spiritual sanctification, moral perfectionism, and/or ecstatic gifts of the Spirit; the third type, the Anabaptist tradition, includes the communal Anabaptist peace churches, such as the Mennonites, Amish, and Church of the Brethren; and the Confessional type includes the churches of the Reformed and Lutheran (and arguably, Anglican) traditions.[1]

Other typologies focus on attitudinal factors or precise differences in theological emphasis. Evangelical historian Richard Quebedeaux argues that the fundamental distinguishing factors in evangelicalism are predispositions pertaining to openness, separatism, confessionalism, and identification with the organized evangelical establishment. Evangelical theologian Robert E. Webber delineates fourteen kinds of evangelicalism that differ according to their emphasis on speaking in tongues, dispensationalism, separatism, and the like.

My approach is closer in spirit to the kinds of historical typologies offered by ethicist Max Stackhouse and the evangelical historians Donald W. Dayton and Timothy P. Weber. These interpretations distinguish three dominant paradigms in evangelical history. The first paradigm derives from the confessional and dissenting movements of the sixteenth-century Reformation. Stackhouse calls this type "Puritan" evangelicalism, and Weber, more appropriately, calls it "classical" evangelicalism. I shall call it *classical evangelicalism,* while taking care to distinguish between its Reformationist and post-Reformationist (scholastic) phases as well as between its confessional and Anabaptist forms. The second paradigm, *pietistic evangelicalism,* derives from the eighteenth-century German and English Pietist movements and, in the United States, from the Great Awakenings. The third paradigm, *fundamentalist evangelicalism,* derives from the modernist-fundamentalist conflict of the nineteenth and twentieth centuries.[2]

From this interpretive standpoint, the crucial question is how any particular form of evangelical thinking relates to these three dominant contexts out of which most evangelical thinking has been formed. The first kind of evangelicalism is grounded in and seeks to sustain the doctrinal heritage of the continental Reformationist traditions, especially the Reformed tradition. The second kind, pietistic evangelicalism, deviates substantially from the languages of absolute divine sovereignty, forensic justification, and literalistic inerrancy developed in the Reformed and Lutheran traditions, giving heightened evangelical emphasis to experiences of conversion, sanctification, spiritual regeneration, and healing. Though evangelicals from the Pietist traditions generally see themselves as belonging to the heritage of the Reformation, they also tend to follow the eighteenth-century Pietists and Puritans in viewing the "classical" tradition as experience deprived. American evangelicalism in the nineteenth century was dominated by groups in this category, especially various Baptist and independent church groups, Methodists, Wesleyan Holiness groups, Oberlin perfectionists, Campbellite restorationists, and New School Presbyterians. Fundamentalist evangelicalism, the third paradigm, is a product of the fundamentalist reaction against theological modernism. It often emphasizes an apocalyptic premillennialist reading of scripture and always emphasizes the absoluteness of certain "fundamental" beliefs impugned by modernist criticism.

These categories are more permeable than Hunter's sociological types; some conservative Methodists, for example, might plausibly claim inclusion in all three categories. At the same time, the historical paradigms approach implicitly accentuates the basic disagreements that exist within evangelicalism without cutting these differences too finely. Webber's typology is too unwieldy to be usable, and it gives little sense of the historical origins of evangelical pluralism. A plausible argument could be made for separating the Anabaptist groups from the Lutheran, Reformed, and Anglican churches of the "magisterial" Reformation, but in this book I pursue different issues from those that might illuminate important differences between these sixteenth-century traditions.

The irony of evangelicalism is that while it contains an essentially contested family of theologies, it has been poorly suited to affirm pluralism of any kind. The evangelical impulse is to insist that only one religious tradition can be true, but evangelicalism itself contains several disparate traditions. The fact that evangelicalism contains very different kinds of Christianity has prompted some evangelicals to worry that the term is becoming meaningless in the process of being claimed by too many parties. Dayton suggests that the term should have been reserved for groups in the pietistic category; evangelical theologian David F. Wells insists that genuine evangelicalism is linked exclusively to the Augustinian confessionalism of the magisterial Reformationist churches; many others urge that belief in biblical inerrancy is the bedrock of true evangelicalism.

In each of these cases, the clear implication is that many people who call themselves evangelicals should be calling themselves something else. Dayton regrets that the fundamentalist founders of Fuller Theological Seminary reclaimed the term for their position. Since the term is now claimed by all manner of fundamentalists, dispensationalists, Pentecostals, Barthians, conservative confessionalists, black churches, Adventists, Holiness movements, and others, he argues, it has become too confused to be useful. While sharing his sense of its deeply conflicted nature, I do not accept Dayton's verdict (which even he fails to practice) that use of the term *evangelicalism* should therefore be discontinued. Rather, I use the term in a way that carefully bears in mind the different kinds of gospel Christianity that evangelical Protestantism has engendered.[3]

CLAIMING THE GOSPEL MESSAGE

The word *evangelical* derives from the Greek *euangelion,* which means "gospel" or "message of good news." In the root sense of the term, an evangelical is anyone who accepts the good news of the gospel that Jesus is Savior and Lord. For this reason, there is an element of presumption in the attempt by any group to claim the term exclusively for itself. All authentically Christian theology is rooted in the gospel proclamation of the incarnation, saving death, and resurrection of Jesus Christ. By definition, all genuinely Christian theology is evangelical. The modern tendency to associate evangelicalism only with theologically conservative forms of Protestantism slights the presence of gospel faith in other forms of Christianity. Numerous Christian traditions justifiably claim the right to an evangelical identity. Historically and theologically, conservative Protestants have no more right to an exclusive claim over the term *evangelical* than to the word *Christian.*

Yet the conservative Protestant claim to ownership of evangelicalism does signify something worth naming. It cites certain points of theological distinction that are religiously significant. Luther and Calvin judged that the gospel message of salvation by faith through grace was obscured, if not fatally subverted, by the paganizing tendencies of the Catholic Church of their time. These included especially the development of an ecclesiastical system in which extrabiblical functions were recognized as sacraments, the sacrament of Holy Communion was understood to be a priestly sacrifice, and the Pauline doctrine of salvation by faith was blended with a doctrine of works righteousness. By accommodating the gospel message to paganizing theological and ecclesiastical motifs, the Reformers argued, Roman Catholicism distorted the distinctive "evangelical" message and character of biblical faith. To be *evangelisch* in this continental sixteenth-century context was to be a protester. The Reformers summarized the evangelical message in the great Latin slogans of the Reformation: *sola gratia* (salvation only through divine grace), *sola fide* (justification by faith alone), and *sola scriptura* (scripture as the single rule of faith and practice). Evangelical Christianity is defined by its faithfulness to these inclusive but distinguishing biblical motifs, the Reformers insisted.

The Lutheran and, especially, Reformed emphasis on salvation as an unmerited gift of grace, bestowed by an absolutely sovereign God through faith in Christ, gave rise to highly forensic understandings of the gospel message. Post-Reformation orthodoxy assiduously protected this message from any creeping Catholic influence. Lutheran and Reformed confessional statements emphasized the themes of double predestination, absolute divine sovereignty, and salvation by grace through faith. Right doctrine not only trumped all concerns with the spiritual life but sharply limited any possible claims about the sanctifying work of the Holy Spirit. The spiritual coldness and troubling moral implications of Protestant orthodoxy gave rise to the first glimmerings of a different kind of evangelicalism in seventeenth-century England and Germany. In England, Puritans such as William Ames (1576–1633) prefigured a movement away from the creedal intellectualism of Reformed orthodoxy, arguing for a more spiritually integrative understanding of Christian faith. Ames's influential work *The Marrow of Theology* emphasized that theology should be devoted to the "teaching of living toward God" in a way that makes an appeal to one's entire heart, soul, and mind.[4] In Germany, Philipp Jacob Spener (1635–1705) and other Pietists launched a more explicit and far-reaching protest against the spiritual limitations of Lutheran orthodoxy. Spener urged that Christianity cannot be believed and is not redemptive without being practiced. His movement subsequently recovered dimensions of the biblical witness pertaining to spiritual regeneration and sanctification that engendered a new kind of evangelicalism.[5]

Without challenging the basic Reformationist preoccupation with individual salvation, the German Pietists and, later, the evangelical followers of John Wesley and George Whitefield lifted up the biblical themes of holiness, good news, and new life in the Spirit. They claimed that Christians are not only justified from without but also given a new life of Spirit-filled holiness through their saving faith in Christ. The point of Christian life is not merely to acknowledge God's merciful grace and wrathful jealousy, they urged; it is also to experience the joyful and life-giving new birth in Christ that the gospel promises. They objected that if God has predestined everything that happens in life, including the salvation and damnation of all people, it is difficult to see how Christianity could be spiritually or even morally inspiring. What is the point of biblical morality if everything is predestined? How can the moral and spiritual commands of scripture mean anything if human beings possess no power of moral or spiritual choice? Wesley pressed the ultimate question sharply: How can God be loving and merciful if God condemns most people to eternal torment? Wesley replied that he could not believe such a doctrine. "So ill do election and reprobation agree with the truth and sincerity of God!" he wrote. "But do they not agree least of all with the scriptural account of his love and goodness: that attribute which God peculiarly claims wherein he glories above all the rest?" Wesley judged that the unconditional-predestining God of classical Protestantism was a product of speculative reason, not of biblical faith.[6]

To the descendants of German and English Pietism, the so-called Holiness movements of the eighteenth and nineteenth centuries were simply the means by which the full spiritual heritage of gospel evangelicalism was finally recovered.

They were the true evangelicals. The differences between classical and Pietist evangelicalism were strong enough that in Germany, Pietists were never called *evangelisch* but were (and still are) referred to as *Pietismus* or as followers of "the awakening movement" (*Erweckungsbewegung*). Only Lutherans qualified as true evangelicals. In the modern period, a third Protestant configuration with highly variable, often tenuous connections to these earlier movements has also claimed the mantle of evangelical faith. Modern evangelicals routinely invoke the *sola* claims of the Reformation, but many of them do so in a way that reflects their rootage in the fundamentalist reaction of the late nineteenth and early twentieth centuries. Fundamentalist evangelicalism identifies above all with a list of literalistic tests for determining what it means to submit to the sole authority of scripture.

The rise of an evangelical movement that speaks so insistently about the "perfect errorlessness" of the Bible was prefigured in the scholastic apologetics of seventeenth-century Protestant orthodoxy, but in its modern context, fundamentalist evangelicalism is a by-product of the rise of modern historical consciousness. In the nineteenth century, conservative theologians were pressed to explain how traditional claims about the infallibility of scripture could be squared with the conclusions of biblical source criticism, early versions of form criticism (especially as practiced by Ferdinand Christian Baur and the later Tübingen School), Darwinian evolutionary theory, and the like. How could biblical authority be defined and secured in the light of modern scientific, historical, and philosophical criticism? The answer that emerged from what came to be called the fundamentalist movement was that biblical authority cannot be secured at all apart from the affirmation of biblical inerrancy. If the Bible contains any errors, it cannot be God's Word; and if it is not literally God's verbally inspired Word, it cannot be a secure source of religious authority. With unsurpassed intellectual energy and spiritual passion, the descendants of Old School Reformed orthodoxy at Princeton Theological Seminary defended this position at the outset of the fundamentalist reaction and thereby established the defining basis of fundamentalist evangelicalism.

I argue not only that the classical, pietistic, and fundamentalist movements produced different kinds of evangelicalism but also that a progressive fourth kind is conceivable. Timothy Weber speaks vaguely of a possible fourth paradigm that would incorporate elements from earlier evangelicalisms while going beyond them in the areas of theology, biblical criticism, and ethics.[7] In the closing chapters, I explore this possibility of a *postconservative* or even *progressive evangelical theology*. Because thinkers in the Reformed-fundamentalist tradition have dominated modern evangelical theology, my early chapters focus mainly on this tradition. At the crucial turn in the book's narrative, however, I argue that some of the most creative and promising developments in contemporary evangelicalism are coming from other sectors. Modern evangelical theology has been dominated by third-type fundamentalists, many of whom have called for a restoration of first-type confessional orthodoxy; but much of the creative ferment in evangelical theology today is being stirred by thinkers from the Pietist traditions.

The modern origins of the possibility of a postconservative evangelicalism can be traced to a cluster of thinkers who began the process of rethinking evangelicalism a half century ago. In the mid-1940s, Carl F. H. Henry and Edward J. Carnell committed themselves to the task of reforming American fundamentalism. Both men were Baptists and young academics. Both knew from close acquaintance that the intellectual heroes of fundamentalist Christianity were ignored at America's elite universities. Thinkers such as Reuben A. Torrey, Benjamin B. Warfield, and J. Gresham Machen were not taken seriously enough even to be dismissed. It was as if their writings did not exist, barely twenty years after they waged an epochal struggle for control of America's mainline churches. Henry and Carnell were keenly aware that in the succeeding generation, *fundamentalist* had become a term to be used only derisively in educated circles. Their judgment that some of this contempt was deserved prompted them to criticize the reactionary spirit of their tradition.

Henry and Carnell set out to rehabilitate the intellectual foundations of evangelical fundamentalism and make it worthy of respect. Theologically, they harkened back to a classical Protestant orthodoxy that was shorn of millennialist apocalypticism and separatist ecclesiology. As Baptists, they looked especially to their Reformed Puritan heritage, but always in a way that interpreted this heritage through the lens of the ongoing fundamentalist battle against modernism. With Harold J. Ockenga and other founders of Fuller Theological Seminary, they embraced the term *neoevangelicalism*—later shortened to *evangelicalism*—to mark their claim that something new was happening in conservative American Protestantism. A generational retreat from the world was being called off.

The process of evangelical self-criticism that Henry, Carnell, and others set into motion ultimately carried well beyond the boundaries of their fundamentalism, however. By drawing attention to some of the unexamined cultural and philosophical presuppositions that American fundamentalism typically assigned to biblical faith, the first neoevangelicals opened the door to critical evangelical perspectives that undermined their own doctrinal fundamentalism. This process was accelerated by evangelical thinkers who pressed the distinction between the doctrine of strict biblical inerrancy and the doctrine that scripture is infallible in all that it affirms about faith and morals. Other forms of evangelical thinking were opened up by theologians who appropriated arguments by Karl Barth and other so-called neoorthodox theologians. Theologians from Wesleyan and other Holiness traditions, who opposed the Reformed orientation of the evangelical establishment, offered other kinds of evangelical thinking. Most recently, in conversation with postmodern critics of epistemological foundationalism, another group of evangelicals has been aided by the "postmodern" character of much of Barth's theology in rethinking the philosophical assumptions of traditional evangelical theology. While some evangelicals bemoan the loss of the cultured scholastic orthodoxy that was fueled, for several generations, by its intellectual opposition to modernity, a new generation of evangelicals is seeking to rethink the claims of gospel faith apart from the countermodernist assumptions of past evangelical theologies.

What is at stake in the evangelical encounter with postmodern criticism? How far can evangelicals appropriate neoorthodox, liberationist, and postmodern modes of thought and remain evangelical? Is evangelical theology necessarily committed to the concept of propositional revelation and the doctrine of scripture as God's infallible written Word? How should evangelical theology respond to the host of historical problems raised by the presence of myth in the biblical witness? Is evangelical theology compatible with any form of hermeneutical demythologizing? How should evangelical theology deal with evangelical pluralism? How should it deal with world religious pluralism? Is evangelicalism necessarily a movement that proclaims the primacy of particular doctrines about scripture and salvation? If the question of biblical authority can be opened up in evangelical theology, what about the doctrines of God and salvation? This book will pursue these questions as it interprets the history and prospects of evangelical theology.

I do not claim or pretend that there exists any golden thread that links all the groups that call themselves evangelical. Though *evangelical* means "message of good news," there is no precisely defined belief about this message that evangelicals distinctively emphasize or agree on. Classical evangelicals from the Reformed and Lutheran traditions tend to emphasize the saving death of Christ crucified as the heart of the gospel, but this assertion of the centrality of substitutionary blood atonement is disputed in other evangelical traditions, especially the Holiness groups. Many evangelicals have tried to make biblical inerrancy the crucial test of evangelical conviction, but prominent evangelical thinkers have disputed this claim for more than a century, and it is now widely rejected.

The recent histories of evangelical theology and American fundamentalism further confuse even the muddled ways of speaking about these movements that their proponents and observers have typically adopted. For example, one of the chief definitional features of fundamentalism has been its separatist impulse. The tendency to associate fundamentalism with a sectarian politics and ecclesiology always raised difficult problems for historians who sought to account for the many fundamentalists who never left the "mainline" churches. It raised equally perplexing problems for those who tried to explain the existence of fundamentalist currents in such conservative denominations as the Christian Reformed Church, the Lutheran Wisconsin and Missouri Synod churches, and the Southern Baptist Convention. Because these churches never drove their fundamentalists into exile, they did not reproduce the exile-and-separation pattern of other fundamentalist groups. Even among the large fundamentalist groups that did take the separatist route, however, a determination to make an impact on the dominant culture has become evident in recent decades—to put it mildly.

In the 1970s, Jerry Falwell's Moral Majority movement propelled a critical mass of formerly separatist fundamentalists into partisan politics. Today, a potent new form of politicized Christianity is expanding on the gains of the Moral Majority movement, especially by attracting conservative Pentecostals to the cause. No Christian movement has ever been more politically mobilized, media savvy, or culturally engaged than the current Christian Coalition movement led by Pat Robertson, which contains a strong fundamentalist core while also embracing conservative evangelicals, Pentecostals, and Catholics. With the rise of this highly public-oriented social phenomenon, it is hardly appropriate any longer to define fundamentalism primarily by its separatism. Because much of the leadership of this movement is postmillennialist in its eschatology, the traditional association of American fundamentalism with dispensational theology or vaguer forms of premillennialism has also been weakened considerably. The apocalyptic approach to politics and history assumed by premillennialist fundamentalism hardly suits a movement led by figures with ambitious political aims.[8]

"Fundamentalism" is thus more elusive as a concept than popular usage implies, and by comparison, "evangelicalism" is almost impossibly elusive. This is not only because evangelicalism includes so many traditions but also because these traditions are rooted in disparate historical paradigms, including the paradigm of fundamentalist reaction. Classical evangelicalism is different from the evangelicalism of the Wesleyan Holiness movements, and both are considerably different from the antimodernist fundamentalism that the Fuller Seminary evangelicals first sought to reform. With careful regard for the problems that these differences pose for any definition of evangelicalism, evangelical historian George Marsden has described it as a Christian movement that emphasizes the Reformation doctrine of the final authority of scripture, the real historical character of God's saving work recorded in scripture, salvation to eternal life based on Christ's redeeming death and resurrection, the importance of evangelism and missions, and the importance of a spiritually transformed life.[9] Even this definition may be weighted too much toward the Reformed side, but like Marsden's work in general, it usefully holds in view the variety of evangelicalisms while assuming a Reformed center. It is carefully vague on key points without being meaningless and thus gives appropriate content to my favorite definition of an evangelical, which is "anyone who likes Billy Graham." I shall therefore use the term in a way that assumes Marsden's general description.

The problem is that these factors do not distinguish evangelicalism from fundamentalism. This is not a serious problem for Marsden, since his work seeks only to account for the historical development of modern evangelicalism. Historically, modern fundamentalism and its "evangelical" corrective have shared a common theological foundation. So-called evangelicalism has adopted a more respectable style than fundamentalism while retaining the doctrinal core of fundamentalist belief. The first neoevangelicals blasted the anti-intellectualism and sectarianism of the fundamentalist movement, but their writings left the structural core of fundamentalist theology virtually intact. They repeated the same slippery-slope warnings that Warfield and Torrey used to defend biblical inerrancy. If evangelicalism is to become something more than fundamentalism with good manners, however, it must become clearly distinguished from fundamentalism in its approach to core theological issues, especially concerning the nature and authority of scripture. Without a clear difference of kind with regard to theological authority, there is no such thing as evangelicalism. Evangelicalism cannot seek merely to repristinate the theologies of Luther or Calvin, but no such thing as evangelicalism can exist if evangelicals do not make a clean break with scholasticist and fundamentalist notions about what it means to affirm "the Reformation doctrine of the final authority of scripture."

DEFINING THE SCRIPTURE PRINCIPLE

I argue that this process of delineating clear, substantive differences from fundamentalism is occurring today in evangelical theology, though not without strong resistance from the fundamentalist evangelical establishment. The most appropriate definition of *fundamentalism* still focuses on its commitment to a list of literally interpreted "fundamental" doctrines that are founded on a doctrine of precise biblical inerrancy. Fundamentalism contains a narrow range of debates about the degree to which precise factual accuracy of either the original scriptural "autographs" (the biblical books in their first form) or the received text must be affirmed, but in all cases, the fundamentalist position is defined by its insistence that at least the scriptural autographs contained no errors of any kind. Fundamentalists at the liberal edge of their tradition maintain that the attribution of errorlessness refers only to authorial intention (recognizing that "error" holds different meanings in different literary forms), but most fundamentalists hold out for a more literal and univocally precise understanding of inerrancy.

For the past half century, most of the evangelical movement has remained theologically fundamentalist in this foundational sense of the term. In recent years, however, mainstream evangelical theology has begun to show signs of becoming not only different in degree or style from fundamentalism but also different in kind. Regarding the nature and authority of scripture, many evangelical thinkers have moved to some form of "infallible teaching" model, in which scripture is held to be infallible only in the affirmation of its message. This infallible message is variously construed as all matters of faith and practice, or all matters pertaining to salvation, or the overall message of scripture, or the essential message of scripture. I call this infallible-teaching model of scriptural authority the *neoevangelical* position, while bearing in mind that this "new" model has deep roots in the Reformationist and Pietist traditions. In the context of modern evangelicalism, the neoevangelical model stands as a variable mediating position between the *neoorthodox* and regnant *fundamentalist* models. In speaking of neoorthodoxy as a position at the left edge of the modern evangelical continuum, I define this position primarily as a theological perspective in which scripture is regarded not as revelation itself but as a witness to revelation that can *become* the Word of God through the movement of God's Spirit. In each case, therefore, I distinguish fundamentalist evangelicalism, infallible-teaching neoevangelicalism, and neoorthodox evangelicalism primarily by the ways in which these models differently address the question of the nature of scriptural inspiration and authority.

These are ideal types. Evangelicalism would be far less perplexing than it is if it actually broke neatly into fundamentalist, neoevangelical, and neoorthodox models. The question of whether the neoorthodox understanding of biblical authority qualifies as an evangelical perspective has been debated extensively for much of the past century. Today, some evangelical theologians are seeking to shade the differences between the fundamentalist and neoevangelical approaches to biblical authority, sometimes on the ground that while belief in absolute inerrancy is defensible and desirable, it is not mandatory. Another, perhaps larger, and certainly younger group of evangelical theologians is seeking to blend aspects of the neoevangelical and neoorthodox approaches, sometimes with appeals to postmodern arguments that undermine traditional evangelical assumptions about the correspondence theory of truth and the character of propositional revelation. These fundamental debates within evangelical theology about the nature of biblical authority have generated a host of related disputes about the nature of revelation, the purpose of theology, the narrativist character of scripture and theology, the meaning and scope of salvation, the challenges of social injustice and feminist criticism, and the mission of the church. They have also seriously raised the question of whether evangelical theology has been working with the right hierarchy of topics. I address all of these issues.

These are not the debates that the first "new evangelicals" were seeking a half century ago, when they set out to reform fundamentalism. The creative ferment taking place in evangelical theology today is to some degree a symptom of present theological and philosophical confusion, as many evangelical fundamentalists lament. At the 1989 Consultation on Evangelical Affirmations, cosponsored by the National Association of Evangelicals and Trinity Evangelical Divinity School, the intellectual guardians of the conservative evangelical establishment denounced all attempts "to limit the truthfulness of inspired Scripture to 'faith and practice,' viewed as less than the whole of Scripture, or worse, to assert that it errs in such matters as history or the world of nature."[10] Former Dallas Theological Seminary president John F. Walvoord similarly complains that "while right-wing evangelicals have tended to hold fast to orthodox theology, left-wing evangelicals have openly affiliated with the world church movement, have first questioned and then abandoned inerrancy, and now have become leading advocates of neoorthodoxy."[11]

To fundamentalist evangelical leaders, the rethinking of evangelical claims currently under way is a disaster. I argue for a different reading of the recent history of evangelicalism, however, suggesting that the creative ferment presently taking place in evangelicalism is a sign of health and vitality in a postmodern situation. As an Anglican social gospeler and dialectical theologian, I am viewing evangelicalism from outside, but not as a stranger. Evangelical theology is a product of the Protestant house of authority and is thus prone to biblicism. It is also prone to produce mean-spirited social movements that sacralize religious authoritarianism and male chauvinism. In their resolve to rethink the basis and character of Christian faithfulness, however, evangelical theologians such as William J. Abraham, Rodney Clapp, Stanley Grenz, Rebecca M. Groothuis, Henry H. Knight III, J. Richard Middleton, Nancey Murphy, Clark Pinnock, Miroslav Volf, and Brian J. Walsh are developing compelling understandings of the gospel as an open-ended communal message of saving grace, conveyed through the freedom of God's Spirit.[12] With help from its Barthian and postmodern interlocutors, evangelical theology is casting off some of the more dubious vestiges of its scholastic and fundamentalist inheritance, reminding the church today, as John Robinson assured his Puritan followers, that God still has more light and truth to break forth from his Word.

Antimodernist Modernizers:
The Making of Fundamentalist
Evangelicalism

In 1899 *Record of Christian Work,* a Moody Bible Institute publication, asked a number of prominent American evangelists to describe Christ's attitude toward those who held erroneous doctrines. The dean of American evangelists, Dwight L. Moody, characteristically replied that Christ's teaching was unfailingly constructive and loving. "His method of dealing with error was largely to ignore it, letting it melt away in the warm glow of the full intensity of truth expressed in love," he assured. "Let us hold truth, but by all means let us hold it in love, and not with a theological club." The response of Moody's chief associate, Reuben A. Torrey, was equally characteristic: "Christ and His immediate disciples immediately attacked, exposed and denounced error. We are constantly told in our day that we ought not to attack error but simply teach the truth. This is the method of the coward and trimmer; it was not the method of Christ."[1]

The contrasts were telling. In 1899, Moody was still a giant figure in American religion and one of the two most influential evangelists produced by nineteenth-century American revivalism. Behind him lay the immense cultural influence of the past two centuries of revival preaching, which included the two Great Awakenings, Charles G. Finney's "protracted meeting" evangelism of the mid–nineteenth century, and the "layman's revival" of 1858. In the later decades of the century, Moody's preaching drew enormous throngs in the United States, Canada, and England. Though lacking almost any formal education, he was admired by modernist academics and pastors, many of whom he counted as friends. Through his annual summer conferences in Northfield, Massachusetts, he helped build a multistranded evangelical movement that welcomed various kinds of premillennialists, Pietists, Holiness revivalists, mainline confessionalists, and others. His theology, to the extent that he had one, was a minimalist patchwork of Wesleyan and Keswick themes tempered by dispensationalist eschatology. In essence, it called individuals to make a decision for Christ and gain "victory over sin." This message was based on what he called the three R's: "Ruin by sin, Redemption by Christ, and Regeneration by the Holy Ghost." Moody emphasized God's love for sinners and pointedly avoided the themes of hellfire and divine wrath. He also avoided controversy. In a calm and mildly sentimental style, he preached evangelistic sermons that featured inspiring anecdotes, stories of tender pathos, and a closing appeal to make Christ the Lord of one's life. "I look upon this world as a wrecked vessel," he famously remarked. "God has given me a lifeboat and said to me, 'Moody, save all you can.' "[2]

But even as his revival preaching made him a towering figure in American religion, his movement took on a more aggressive and militantly doctrinal posture. In the 1880s, Moody's pietistic emphasis on love and his opposition to controversy became increasingly alien to the new kind of evangelical movement that his preaching helped build. Unwittingly, he was a bridge figure. His great forerunner in mass evangelism, Charles Finney, was an abolitionist and postmillennialist who viewed revival as a way of building the kingdom on earth. But in the aftermath of the Civil War, Moody had no illusions that his revivals would spread righteousness throughout the earth. He hoped only to save as many souls as he could before the Antichrist overtook history. His massive revival campaigns gave influential support to the premillennialist view that history is doomed to destruction. At the same time, though he popularized the dispensationalist premillennial writings of J. N. Darby and C. H. Mackintosh, Moody opposed the preoccupation with doctrine that dispensationalist teaching engendered. He pleaded against the in-house doctrinal hairsplitting that consumed many of his colleagues and also spoke against the heightening warfare between modernists and conservatives that consumed the churches in his later lifetime. Moody warned repeatedly that the latter conflict was impeding the church's evangelical mission to save souls. He urged both sides to go back to the practical work of soul winning. "People are tired and sick of this awful controversy," he observed in one of his last sermons. "I hope the motto of the ministers of this country will be, 'quit your fighting and go to work and preach the simple gospel.' "[3]

The simple gospel was enough for Moody. His preaching of it brought thousands of souls to Christ and created a vast network of evangelical institutions. By 1899, however—the year of his death—Moody's irenic Holiness revivalism belonged to a bygone era. His kind of evangelicalism was giving way to a more disaffected, creedal, culture-fighting evangelicalism. Moody cultivated friendships with liberal church leaders, but his operatives at Moody Bible Institute and various big-steeple churches were committed to outright warfare with the liberal modernizers. To them, his pleadings for a ten-year truce were pitifully softheaded. An epochal battle for control of the churches was already raging. One side was bound to win the battle and drive out the other side. The question was not whether this divisive faction fight could be avoided but whether conservatives would win it. A new kind of evangelicalism was emerging barely in time to fight off the spiritual subversion of a well-positioned enemy. Hence, while Moody pleaded for a ceasefire and called unbelievers to accept God's loving embrace, his chief associates called for a purgative war of reaction. They waged a factional struggle to seize control over denominational mission boards, seminaries, and administrative offices that were being lost to modernist forces. They committed Christian orthodoxy to a lengthy list of literally interpreted fundamentals while debating among themselves the details of Darby's dispensational schematism.

In 1875 a group of hard-line conservatives had organized the founding convention of what would later be called the annual Niagara Bible Conference. This summer resort meeting became the prototype for hundreds of Bible conferences at which evangelicals gathered for two weeks to preach and defend the fundamentals. The Niagara conference was not overwhelmingly dispensationalist at the outset, but it quickly became so. Darby-style premillennialists such as the Presbyterians Nathaniel West, James H. Brooks, William J. Erdman, and Henry M. Parsons and the Baptist A. J. Gordon all urged that the doctrine of Christ's premillennial second coming be included among the fundamental doctrines of Christianity. By 1878 their position prevailed; the Niagara conference that year put premillennialist eschatology on the same level as the doctrine of Christ's incarnation. Some conservatives protested that the Niagara conferences overemphasized premillennialism, but these complaints soon backfired as dispensationalists organized other conferences that excluded all other views. The heavily dispensationalist character of early American fundamentalism is illustrated by the fact that the Bible conference movement on which fundamentalism was mainly founded was dominated by dispensationalists. Over the next generation, dispensationalist fundamentalism was championed by such Moody associates as Erdman, Gordon, Torrey, James M. Gray, C. I. Scofield, George Needham, and A. C. Dixon. American fundamentalism is a product of the protest movement that these men and others waged against the perceived apostasy of the established churches in the closing decades of the nineteenth century.[4]

The fundamentalists gained their name from their defense of "fundamental" beliefs of Christian orthodoxy that they charged were being betrayed by the established churches. At the Niagara conference of 1878 they listed fourteen such beliefs, beginning with biblical inerrancy and ending with the doctrine of Christ's premillennial return to earth. This list was reaffirmed at various conferences afterward, notably the Niagara conference of 1895, but some Presbyterian fundamentalists objected that the idea of a core or essential belief was undermined by the identification of so many beliefs as fundamental. In 1910, in an effort to censure modernist currents in the Northern Presbyterian church, the church's General Assembly reduced the list to five points. It declared that the fundamental beliefs of Christianity are the inerrancy of scripture, the virgin birth of Christ, the atonement of Christ, the resurrection of Christ, and the miracle-working power of Christ.[5]

The Northern Presbyterian church was too deeply rooted in the confessional tradition of Reformed orthodoxy to make premillennialist eschatology a fundamental article of the faith, even though some premillennialist leaders were Presbyterians. Moreover, with only five fundamental points, an alliance between conservative Presbyterians and other conservative Protestants was conceivable. In later years, fundamentalism was identified routinely with the defense of these five beliefs. The movement's adoption of this common-ground approach, however, was possible only during the period when most of its leaders were members of the established denominations. Gray was a Reformed Episcopalian; Torrey was a Congregationalist; Dixon, J. Frank Norris, and William B. Riley were Baptists;

many other fundamentalist leaders were Presbyterians. Their awareness that the modernizers were winning drove them to make alliances across denominational lines. In 1916, while announcing the formation of the World's Christian Fundamentals Association, Riley and Torrey declared that "the time has come for a correlation of the orthodox conservative forces yet found in the churches." Nothing less than a militant united front would prevent the modernists from completely taking over the churches, they warned. Though most of the movement's leaders were dispensationalists, most of them were sufficiently alarmed by the seriousness and immediacy of the crisis to set aside doctrinal disagreements over eschatology. The stakes were too high to afford divisive conservative battles over the interpretation of biblical prophecy.[6]

This resolve to emphasize common fundamentals was displayed in the movement's most famous self-presentation. The fundamentalist revolt produced a sizable literature and galvanized immense popular resistance to any form of theological modernism. In 1909 two wealthy Christian laymen, brothers Lyman and Milton Stewart, enlisted Dixon to produce fundamentalism's signature defense of traditional Protestant teaching, titled *The Fundamentals*. Between 1910 and 1915, Dixon, Torrey, and Louis Meyer (a Jewish-Christian evangelist) secured contributions to this twelve-volume series from a formidable array of conservative American and British scholars, including Gray, Torrey, George Frederick Wright, William Caven, James Orr, and Benjamin B. Warfield. Several million copies of *The Fundamentals* were given eventually to pastors, academics, missionaries, and church officials. Though the series gained little notice at first from academic or church periodicals, it later became the defining symbol of the fundamentalist movement. More than half of its contributors were dispensationalists or premillennialists, but eschatology was rarely mentioned. A number of writers defended Keswick-style Holiness teaching—a movement that took a mediating position between traditional Wesleyan and Reformed understandings of sanctification—but this was not yet a sharply divisive issue in American fundamentalism.

For the most part, the editors maintained a united-front strategy. The series hammered repeatedly on the theme that modernist theologians and pastors were betraying fundamental Christian beliefs. Torrey, Caven, and Gray inveighed against the destructive errors of biblical criticism, especially critical scholarship on the opening chapters of Genesis. Wright criticized the Graf-Wellhausen documentary hypothesis (which distinguished among "Yahwist," "Elohimist," "Deuteronomic," and "priestly" literary strands in the Pentateuch) and defended the doctrine of the Mosaic authorship of the Pentateuch; Caven emphasized that Jesus accepted the authority of Hebrew scripture; Gray reaffirmed the doctrine of the plenary and verbal inspiration of the Bible; Warfield argued that the doctrine of the deity of Christ is a control belief that impinges on all lines of critical inquiry. These conservative thinkers sought to protect Christian belief from outside criticism by defending the doctrines of biblical inerrancy, verbal inspiration, and propositional revelation, as well as the literal interpretation of scripture.[7]

They also maintained a higher tone and a more rigorous standard of argument than the movement that succeeded their labors. Until 1925, the trajectory of American fundamentalism was upward. The fundamentalist "five points" were reaffirmed by the Northern Presbyterian church in 1916 and 1923; during this period, after resigning as Woodrow Wilson's secretary of state, William Jennings Bryan devoted his immense energy and prestige to the fundamentalist cause in the Presbyterian Church. In the early 1920s, fundamentalists nearly seized control of the Presbyterian and Northern Baptist churches, receiving crucial intellectual support from academics at Princeton Theological Seminary. The movement also supported Prohibition and sought to stop the teaching of evolution in American public schools. In 1925, however, the movement's outward progress stopped. Bryan was humiliated at the Tennessee evolution trial, and fundamentalists lost virtually every key battle that they waged in the established churches. In a remarkably short period of time, this formidable mass movement gave up its defining struggle to save the churches. Much of the movement descended swiftly into sectarianism. American fundamentalists built up a substantial network of countercultural Protestant schools, publishing houses, radio ministries, and revival conferences in the 1930s and 1940s, but they gave up the dream of reclaiming the churches and universities that earlier generations of Bible-believing evangelicals had created. A critical mass of the fundamentalist movement coped with its defeat by turning inward.[8]

The mid-century founders of Fuller Theological Seminary evangelicalism were products of this historical turn. They took for granted the existence of an extensive fundamentalist subculture, but they refused to accept their movement's subcultural status. They sought to create a new kind of fundamentalism that would engage the dominant culture and make conservative Protestantism worthy of respect. They saw themselves as reformers of what had become a strangely distorted and uprooted Protestant orthodoxy. By contrast, the modern theologians whom they admired most had never thought of themselves as the "first fundamentalists" or the first anything. Charles Hodge and his theological successors at Princeton Theological Seminary had regarded themselves strictly as custodians of a confessional tradition. They had aspired only to carry on the received doctrines of traditional Reformed orthodoxy, which included the doctrine of biblical infallibility. In the late nineteenth century, however, the Princeton theologians had made common cause with the founders of modern fundamentalism largely on the basis of their vigorous defense of biblical infallibility and other "fundamentals." Some of their key arguments in this cause were more novel than they had acknowledged.

Charles Hodge summarized his understanding of classical Reformed teaching on biblical authority by asserting that because the Old and New Testaments were written under the inspiration of the Holy Spirit, they are "infallible, and of divine authority in all things pertaining to faith and practice, and consequently free from all error whether of doctrine, fact, or precept." This conception of biblical infallibility as perfect errorlessness was carefully refined and developed by Hodge's son, A. A. Hodge, in the 1850s, in close collaboration with his father. A. A. Hodge's *Outlines of Theology* (1860) taught that the "original autographs" of scripture were "absolutely infallible when interpreted in the sense intended, and hence are clothed with absolute divine authority." Crucial to this formulation was the qualitative distinction between the scriptural autographs and all copies of these hypothesized texts. The orthodox doctrine of divine inspiration applies directly only to the inspired autographs, the Hodges taught; it does not apply directly to surviving texts that are subject to scribal error. "The Church has never held the verbal infallibility of our translations, nor the perfect accuracy of the copies of the original Hebrew and Greek Scriptures now possessed by us," A. A. Hodge explained. "The Church has asserted absolute infallibility only of the original autograph copies of the Scriptures as they came from the hands of their inspired writers."[9]

Like most of the old Protestant dogmatists, the Hodges recognized that scripture contains various apparent discrepancies and other factual problems. Charles Hodge called these troublesome passages "specks of sandstone" in a marble edifice. With his soon-to-be Princeton Seminary colleague Benjamin B. Warfield, A. A. Hodge conceded in 1881 that the biblical writers "were in large measure dependent for their knowledge upon sources and methods in themselves fallible." He and Warfield further allowed that textual variations among the existing copies of scripture "embarrass the interpretation of many details." The Princeton theologians advised that some apparent discrepancies in the Bible can be explained as errors in the process of transcription and that others can be harmonized. In other cases, they counseled, apparent problems in the text must simply remain problems for believers in biblical inerrancy.[10] But, they exhorted, the one thing that orthodox Christians must never do is accommodate the doctrine of perfect inerrancy to any inductive problem or group of problems. The Bible that we possess may contain various troublesome passages, but the original scriptural autographs were perfectly free from error. In the early 1880s, Warfield and A. A. Hodge fervently warned the Northern and Southern Presbyterian churches not to concede anything to critics of perfect inerrancy doctrine. Presbyterians must hold fast to what the Reformed tradition has always claimed regarding scripture, Hodge declared, which is that "all the affirmations of Scripture of all kinds, whether of spiritual doctrine or duty, or of physical or historical fact, or of psychological or philosophical principle, are without any error, when the *ipsissima verba* [exact unaided words] of the original autographs are ascertained and interpreted in their natural and intended sense."[11]

Hodge had assumed his father's chair in systematic theology in 1877. Nine years later, Warfield succeeded him in the position. By then, this position played a special leadership role in the struggle to resist modernist trends in the Northern Presbyterian church. Warfield embraced this calling with extraordinary zeal, emerging as the church's leading proponent of perfect inerrancy doctrine. He denied that the doctrine of inerrancy requires a dictationist view of inspiration or that the Reformed tradition had ever taught a mechanical understanding of inspiration, "though dishonest, careless, ignorant or overeager controverters of its doctrine have often brought the charge." The church's teaching is that every word of scripture is the Word of God communicated through the language and personalities of the biblical writers, he explained. Charles Hodge's *Systematic Theology* provided the authoritative explication of biblical inspiration for the Princeton theologians. "When God uses any of his creatures as instruments, He uses them according to their nature," he wrote. "He uses angels as angels, men as men, the elements as elements." Hodge acknowledged that the church fathers and Protestant scholastics often spoke of the biblical writers as pens in the hands of the Spirit, but this was merely a colorful way of illustrating their conviction that scripture is God's inspired Word. "The Church has never held what has been stigmatized as the mechanical theory of inspiration," he insisted. "The sacred writers were not machines. Their self-consciousness was not suspended; nor were their intellectual powers superseded. Holy men spake as they were moved by the Holy Ghost."[12]

So-called Princeton theology was thus merely a reaffirmation of sixteenth- and seventeenth-century Reformed orthodoxy, which had never taught a "mechanical" or dictationist view of the divine nature of scripture. Warfield and the Hodges insistently denied that their version of Reformed orthodoxy contained any novel elements or that it marked any significant departure from the spirit of early Calvinism. The Princeton theologians protested too much, however. They obscured the differences between Reformationist and post-Reformationist orthodoxy, as well as their own revisions of Reformed orthodoxy. Warfield and the Hodges treated post-Reformationist scholasticism as fully continuous with Calvin, partly because their own version of Reformed theology owed more to this tradition than to Calvin. Princeton theology was a form of Reformed orthodoxy that rarely quoted Calvin. The Princeton theologians were more at home with the systematized neo-Aristotelianism of Protestant scholasticism than with the Augustinian dialectics of Luther and Calvin. For this reason, they were militantly determined to preserve the doctrine of perfect inerrancy in some form, even though they no longer held out for the dictationist theory of inspiration from which it logically and historically arose.

LUTHER, CALVIN, AND
PROTESTANT SCHOLASTICISM

Luther and Calvin both referred to scripture as an "infallible" or "unerring rule" of faith, but for them the attribution of infallibility to scripture referred to its trustworthiness in all things necessary for salvation, not the precise accuracy of its historical or phenomenal accounts. Both emphasized the dynamic unity of Word and Spirit and, with Augustine, the priority of faith over reason. Luther freely acknowledged various factual inaccuracies and contradictions throughout the Bible. He judged that the prophets often erred in their predictions, that various prophecies in Isaiah were scrambled together, and that Moses "mixed up his laws" in a confused and disorderly way. He taught that Chronicles contained numerous inflated accounts: "When one often reads that great numbers of people were slain—for example, eighty thousand—I believe that hardly one thousand were actually killed." He noted that the Gospel writers often gave conflicting accounts of the same event, such as the denials of Peter, the time at which Jesus purified the Temple, and other details of the Passion. Luther doubted that the book of Esther belonged in the Bible (because it does not mention God), and he famously judged that the book of James ("an epistle of straw") was defective in its treatment of jus-tification. Neither could he find any trace of evidence that the book of Revelation was inspired, because "Christ is neither taught or known in it." With less than com-plete accuracy, he maintained against Revelation that "the apostles do not deal with visions." "My spirit cannot accommodate itself to this book," he declared, though he declined to require the Lutheran Church to exclude Revelation or James from the New Testament canon. Luther appreciated the witness to the priestly of-fice of Christ contained in the letter to the Hebrews, but he judged that Hebrews 6:4 taught false doctrine in denying a second repentance. Overall, he found that Hebrews "mixed together" a good deal of "wood, straw, or hay" with its gold and jewels. With biting sarcasm, he protested that no German prince, burgher, or peas-ant could possibly be expected to abstain from eating geese, doe, stag, sausage, or other delicacies proscribed in Acts 15:29.[13]

In all of these cases, Luther judged the spiritual worth of scriptural texts by the relative force and directness of their witness to Christ. To him, the "true kernel and marrow" of scripture was contained in those books that showed "how faith in Christ overcomes sin, death, and hell and gives life, righteousness and salvation." The gospel message is the key to Christianity, he taught, and the gospel is essen-tially oral in character. It is never to be equated with the scriptural text itself. Luther noted that Christ wrote nothing and gave no command to record his words or deeds. The very existence of a New Testament became necessary only after the Holy Spirit's presence weakened in the early church. He placed only one of the Gospels among the "true and noblest books of the New Testament," arguing that the gospel message was presented most directly in John, 1 John, Romans, Gala-tians, Ephesians, and 1 Peter. Luther's conception of scriptural authority was so firmly tied to his understanding of scripture as a book about Christ's salvation of sinners that he could retort to his opponents that if they alleged scripture against Christ, he was prepared to allege Christ against scripture.[14]

Calvin was generally more cautious than Luther in dealing with scriptural texts, and more respectful of the early church's judgments pertaining to the biblical canon. He was more stringent than Luther in opposing allegorical exegesis, and he rejected Luther's dogmatic schematism of law and gospel. Calvin acknowledged as plainly as Luther, however, that the biblical writers were not strongly concerned with precise accuracy and that their worldview often prevented them from making accurate statements. He noted that Genesis describes the moon as being larger than Saturn and that Matthew's account of the journey of the wise men probably misidentifies a comet as a star. He regarded such passages as evidence that the Holy Spirit accommodated the ancient worldview of the biblical writers in inspiring scripture. Elsewhere, Calvin observed that the Gospel writers "were not scrupulous in their time sequences, nor even in keeping to details of words and actions." The evangelists "had no intention of so putting their narrative together as always to keep an exact order of events," he remarked. Calvin explained that the Gospel writers were moved by a deeper spiritual concern than factual accuracy. This concern was their commitment to "bring the whole pattern together to produce a kind of mirror or screen image of those features most useful for the understanding of Christ."[15]

Calvin urged that it was pointless to quibble over the details of scriptural texts or to treat the Bible as a sourcebook for rational proofs or arguments. Just as the prophets and apostles did not fuss with details or proceed by arguments, he argued, "we ought to seek our conviction in a higher place than human reasons, judgments, or conjectures, that is, in the secret testimony of the Spirit." To Luther and Calvin, what was crucial in scriptural narrative was not its precise facticity or its rational persuasiveness but its capacity to convey the significance of Jesus Christ through faithful reading illuminated by the movement of the Holy Spirit. This capacity to bring faithful readers to saving knowledge of Christ was, to them, the heart of what it means to affirm that scripture is God's infallible Word.[16]

Within Calvin's lifetime, however, the Protestant followers of Luther and Calvin were pressed to defend Protestant teaching by making putatively "higher" claims for the nature of scripture and its authority. In the generation after the Reformation, Lutheran and Calvinist theologians had to cope with the reforms of the Council of Trent (1545–1563) and the polemics of Counter-Reformationist critics. Many of them adopted the methods of their adversaries in reaction. Luther and Calvin were both influenced by Latin-tradition scholasticism, especially in their theorizing on the doctrine of atonement, and on various occasions, Calvin referred to miracles and fulfilled prophecies as confirming evidence of the truth of Christianity. On other occasions, he and Luther spoke of biblical inspiration as dictation. The second and third generations of Reformers expanded considerably, with systematizing precision, on statements of this kind.

As early as 1531, Philipp Melanchthon's *Apology of the Augsburg Confession* defended Protestant reasoning about morality by appealing to Aristotle.[17] Protestant dogmatists afterward increasingly adopted the Aristotelian-Thomist modes of argument that their Catholic opponents employed. Scholasticism was methodologically question-oriented, its aim was knowledge (*scientia*), and its educational process was rationalistic. Many of those who assumed the post-Reformation burden of defending Protestant theology against Catholic criticism took for granted the intellectual superiority of this approach. Over the course of the later sixteenth and seventeenth centuries, the guardians of a new Protestant orthodoxy increasingly embraced a rationalistic approach to scripture and the problem of faith's relation to reason. They treated scripture as a storehouse of revealed propositions and dissolved the tension between reason and faith, presenting Protestant teaching as the highest form of science. Lutheran dogmatists Johann Gerhard (1582–1637) and Johann Andreas Quenstedt (1617–1688) maintained that Holy Scripture passes all of Aristotle's tests for scientific veracity. The very title of Quenstedt's dogmatics, *Theologia didactico-polemica,* reflected the sense of theology as rationalistic tournament that pervaded Protestant orthodoxy. Quenstedt insisted that scripture contains "no lie, no falsehood, not even the smallest error either in words or in matter." Every word of scripture is precisely accurate, he explained, "whether it be a matter of dogma or of morals or of history or of chronology or of topography or of nomenclature." Gerhard was generally more moderate as a dogmatist and polemicist, but through the influence of his twenty-three-volume *Loci theologici,* the Christian doctrine that scripture is God's Word became, in Lutheran orthodoxy, not an article of faith but the foundation of other articles of faith.[18]

Reformed dogmatists such as Johannes Wollebius (1586–1629) and Francis Turretin (1623–1687) reinterpreted Calvinist teaching along similar lines. Wollebius's *Compendium theologiae Christianae* (1626) reformulated Christian theology as a system of propositions; his follower, Turretin, developed a full-scale scholastic system that employed the Thomist method of question-answer-objections-refutation. Like most of the early Protestant scholastics, Turretin still spoke of the correlation of Word and Spirit; following Calvin, he retained (at least formally) the distinction between the words of the Bible and the revelatory divine wisdom embedded in the Bible. His system marked a highly influential step on the road to a thoroughly rationalized orthodoxy, however. It stoutly defended biblical inerrancy and maintained that "before faith can believe, it must have the divinity of the witness." Turretin's three-volume *Institutes of Elenctic Theology* was published between 1679 and 1685. In the succeeding generation, his son Jean-Alphonse Turretin became a significant proponent of the kind of Calvinist orthodoxy that made no appeal to the testimony of the Spirit at all. Reformed orthodoxy in its totally rationalized phase turned Francis Turretin's somewhat hedged apologetic arguments into full-scale apologetic systems. More important, later Reformed orthodoxy based its entire doctrinal structure on a Turretin-style argument for the necessity of strict biblical inerrancy. "The prophets did not make mistakes in even the smallest particulars," Turretin assured. "To say that they did would render doubtful the whole of Scripture."[19]

The Princeton theologians later lauded his system as the best summary of Reformed teaching, but Turretin repudiated the very autograph resort in which Warfield and the Hodges later took refuge. He insisted that it was not enough to claim that only the original autographs of scripture were inerrant. Nothing could be "more derogatory to God" than to assert that God permitted the books containing his doctrine to be corrupted. Why would God dictate the words of scripture to succeeding generations of sacred writers without bothering to preserve them? Allowing for occasional minor textual variations, Turretin countered that "the original texts of the Old and New Testaments [must have] come down to us pure and uncorrupted." No other verdict is consistent with the biblical doctrine of divine providence, he argued. In his judgment, the deity of Christ was equally at stake in this matter, since Christ would not have passed over in silence the problem of textual corruption if it had existed, "nor could he bear to use corrupted books."[20]

Turretin's view of biblical inspiration was mechanical enough to commit the Reformed churches under his influence to defend the inspiration of the Hebrew Bible's vowel points. At his urging, the four Protestant cantons of Zurich, Basel, Bern, and Schaffhausen issued the Helvetic Consensus Formula of 1675, which proclaimed its belief in the divine inspiration of the "Hebrew Original of the Old Testament." This summary of Reformed teaching asserted that scripture is inspired "not only in its matter, but in its words." And what does it mean to confess that the words of scripture are literally God breathed? The Helvetic Formula spelled out the logic of its claim that biblical words equal God's Word. Divine inspiration is to be found not only in the consonants of the Hebrew scriptural words, it asserted, but also in the vowels of the words, "either the vowel points themselves, or at least the power of the points."[21] This unfortunate piece of scholastic logic failed to comprehend that the pointing of the Masoretic text of the Old Testament could not have belonged to the original autographs, since Hebrew has no vowel points.

Unlike many of his followers, Turretin was not oblivious to the problem. He knew that recent textual scholarship by Brian Walton, Louis Cappel, and others had begun to expose the developmental history of Hebrew punctuation and the problems of textual variation. He was aware that Walton had ridiculed the English Puritan John Owen when Owen insisted on the necessity of believing in the divine inspiration of the vowel points. Owen persisted afterward that "whoever weighs up the matter seriously and without bias will find the pointing to be perfect, divine, and absolutely complete, like all the other works of God, from which nothing may be taken away, and to which nothing may be added."[22] Turretin was nearly as categorical in pressing the same verdict. He warned that the doctrine of biblical authority could not withstand the judgment "that the punctuation was a merely human invention." This conclusion would make parts of scripture purely human and would thus make God's Word dependent on mere tradition. It would negate the "certain and constant sense of the Holy Spirit" in Holy Scripture. If the Hebrew vowels were not represented in their present form in the autographs, Turretin argued, they must have been represented by "some marks in place of points." He was relieved by Walton's surmise that some kind of marking system must have been used by the biblical writers. Turretin's extremism in defense of verbal inspiration was trimmed by his nineteenth-century followers, who then denied that their tradition had ever taught a dictationist view of inspiration.[23]

The Princeton theologians relinquished the language and the most extreme implications of dictation theory, but these implicit concessions did not move them to attribute any substantive material significance to the human component of scripture. Their wedge between the inspired autographs of scripture and its later copies helped them cope with the advances of nineteenth-century textual criticism. It also helped them avoid various inductive problems peculiar to the doctrine of existing material inerrancy. It is enough to say that the unavailable autographs were protected from human fallibility, they argued; the principle of biblical authority does not require a similar claim about the entire process of biblical transcription. But in the rationalistic spirit of their tradition, the Princeton theologians maintained that the Bible can be no authority at all if it contains any errors on anything it affirms. In effect, their conception of the human component of scripture was barely distinguishable from Turretin's. For them, as for Turretin, the notion that the human component of scripture might open the Bible to any kind of factual error was ruled out categorically. Christian faith falls apart if it is not held together by a perfectly inerrant witness.

Two centuries after Turretin's death, his dogmatics remained the principal textbook on theology at Princeton Seminary. Unlike Calvin, for whom the divine character of scripture was unknowable apart from Spirit-inspired faith, Reformed scholasticism sought to ground the authority of scripture in reasons prior to faith. Calvin taught that scripture is self-authenticating by the testimony of the Spirit. He explained that even if scripture "wins reverence for itself by its own majesty, it seriously affects us only when it is sealed upon our hearts through the Spirit." The mark of faithful theology is that it remains open to the Spirit. Faithful theology seeks no proofs, he insisted, "no marks of genuineness upon which our judgment may lean."[24] A century later, the Westminster divines who composed the Westminster Confession of Faith (1647) retained enough of Calvin's spirit to emphasize the dynamic role of the Holy Spirit in making scripture God's living Word. The Westminster Confession declared that our assurance of the "infallible truth and divine authority" of scripture must derive ultimately "from the inward work of the Holy Spirit, bearing witness by and with the Word in our hearts." One of its authors, Samuel Rutherford, inveighed against a rising rationalistic orthodoxy by warning that the Bible is not a rule "in things of Art and Science . . . to demonstrate conclusions of Astronomie." Scripture is rather a rule of faith "in fundamentalls of salvation," he urged. By the time that Rutherford and the Westminster divines composed the Westminster Confession, however, the scholastic trend in Reformed orthodoxy was a stronger force. Reformed and Lutheran scholasticism did not appeal to the paradoxical unity of scriptural Word and the word of the Spirit. These triumphant orthodoxies ceased even to speak of the *testimonium Spiritus Sancti*. They did not require the actual movement of God's Spirit to possess revealed teaching, for they already possessed God's univocal Word in the words of a perfect, self-interpreting text.[25]

SCHOLASTIC CERTAINTY:
PRINCETON REALISM AS REFORMED ORTHODOXY

This assurance inspired Protestant scholastics to make novel claims to intellectual certainty. Though he was careful to repeat Calvin's assertion that the witness of the Spirit is the ultimate ground of faith, Charles Hodge in his *Systematic Theology* taught that the role of the Holy Spirit is restricted to the application of the rule of faith, not to its shaping. In the spirit of later Reformed orthodoxy, he loaded the faith with scholastic formulations about the divine infallibility and doctrinal unity of scripture, the universal order of nature, and the reliability of reason. Both of the Hodges opened their dogmatic systems with rationalistic proofs of the Christian worldview before moving to the "true knowledge" of faith acquired through the witness of infallible scripture. Charles Hodge emphasized that the truths of reason and faith claimed by Christian theology cannot be secured without assuming a realist theory of knowledge. The form of epistemological realism to which he subscribed was the school of Scottish "common sense" philosophy pioneered by Thomas Reid. Hodge insisted that the Christian worldview necessarily assumes the real existence of objects of knowledge perceived by the human senses. All other accounts of how the mind intuits or orders objects of sense data leave the reality of our knowledge in doubt, he warned. The witness of scripture is useless if one does not assume the reliability of authorial witnesses through human texts and the reality of an objective world outside the human mind. Epistemological realism *must* be true if the truth of anything is to be claimed as a certainty.[26]

This belief in the necessity and unique reasonableness of epistemological realism was a Princeton tradition. The first president of the College of New Jersey (later Princeton College), John Witherspoon, was a prominent proponent of commonsense realism. A generation later, with the founding of Princeton Theological Seminary, Archibald Alexander taught that Witherspoon's realism was the only theory of knowledge fully compatible with Christian orthodoxy. Hodge's dogmatics endorsed and heightened these claims. He asserted that every theology is ultimately a form of philosophy, for "to understand any theological system, we must understand the philosophy that underlies it and gives it form."[27] Even the doctrine of biblical infallibility cannot keep theology true if one does not assume the correspondence theory of truth, the universality of common sense, and the possibility that God's revelation to humanity has been given in propositional form. Christian thinking must begin with the presupposition that all knowledge begins in common sense and is reliably objectified and categorized by the mind, Hodge taught. The incongruity between this trust in the reliability of common sense and the Reformed doctrine of universal human depravity gave him little pause. Hodge warned that we have no reliable knowledge at all, including any knowledge of God, if we cannot assume that ordinary sense perception is trustworthy.

It followed for Hodge, as for his tradition, that scripture should be understood primarily as the answer to an epistemological question. Just as the chemist or astronomer uses reason to interpret nature scientifically, he taught, so the theologian uses reason to interpret the Bible, which is "his store-house of facts," scientifically. Scientific study of scripture discloses truths about God in the same way that scientific study of nature discloses truths about the natural world. In both cases, the author of the object of investigation is God, but scripture bears a special character because it is through scripture that God makes himself known to us. More precisely, the Bible exists because God has chosen to make himself known to us through its witness. "What He reveals is made known," Hodge explained. "We apprehend it as it truly is. The conviction that what God reveals is made known in its true nature, is the very essence of faith in the divine testimony." If we were unable to receive God's truth as it really exists, he contended, it would be pointless for God to reveal himself to us. But because our minds apprehend the real as it is in itself, and because our ideas of God are founded on the testimony of God's inerrant Word, we can be certain that these ideas "correspond with what He really is, and constitute true knowledge."[28] True knowledge is univocal, not analogical or symbolic. Against the Augustinian principle that God cannot be the direct object of univocal God-language, the Princeton theologians thus claimed to know God directly as God is in himself. Only true knowledge about the divine will can deliver God's assurance of salvation to us, but our capacity for true knowledge and our possession of it in infallible scripture ascertain that all biblical testimony to God and everything else is true.

With its assurance that commonsense experience is reliable and certain, Scottish realist epistemology provided the philosophical undergirding that orthodox theology required. Hodge never tired of cautioning that it was not "his" theology; he was merely a transmitter of Reformed orthodoxy. His reliance on Scottish-school realism merely refined the philosophical worldview that Turretin and the Westminster divines took for granted. Near the end of his career, Hodge boasted that no theological novelty was ever taught during his fifty-plus years at Princeton. His successor at Princeton, Francis Patton, later affirmed that the seminary never contributed anything to the modern modifications of Calvinism. "She went on defending the traditions of the Reformed Theology," Patton explained. "You may say that she was not original: perhaps so, but then, neither was she provincial. She had no oddities of manner, no shibboleths, no pet phrases, no theological labels, no trademark." From Alexander to the Hodges and Warfield to Patton, Princeton simply transmitted the same scholastic version of Reformed orthodoxy without modification. "There has been a New Haven theology and an Andover theology, but there never was a distinctively Princeton theology," Patton observed. "Princeton's boast, if she have reason to boast at all, is her unswerving fidelity to the theology of the Reformation."[29]

Hodge counseled that this record of theological fidelity could be sustained only by holding fast to the doctrine of biblical inerrancy and the realist assurance that ordinary sense experience apprehends the real. He warned that underneath the fatal accommodationism of liberal theology lay the philosophical skepticism of David Hume and Immanuel Kant. If one cannot assume that the mind apprehends external objects as they are in themselves, he contended, there is no escape from the kind of cognitive relativism that creates a new liberal theology every few years. Hodge was a sharp observer of liberal trends. He studied under Friedrich Schleiermacher at the University of Berlin in the 1820s and maintained a running (if shuddering) debate with the liberal tradition throughout his career. Against liberal theologians he insisted that if one does not assume that scripture is God's infallible Word, Christianity has no basis for teaching anything. Scripture describes Jesus Christ as being "the same yesterday, today, and forever" (Heb. 13:8). Theology can remain faithful to its unchanging Lord, he admonished, only if it believes that its source of knowledge is without error and only if it adopts the worldview of supernaturalistic realism presupposed by the biblical writers.[30]

Hodge died in 1878, just as fundamentalism was beginning to emerge in America as a protest against modernizing trends in the churches. In the early 1880s, Warfield and Hodge's son assumed the polemical burden of defending Princeton orthodoxy from modernist criticism. After the younger Hodge died and Warfield assumed the systematic theology chair at Princeton, Warfield declared that "though the power of Charles Hodge may not be upon me, the theology of Charles Hodge is within me." His vocational desire was merely to teach Hodge's theology to the next generation of Reformed seminarians. By then, Warfield was deeply embroiled in a more contentious theological scene than Charles Hodge had experienced, however, and temperamentally he lacked much of Hodge's personal power. Hodge was a gregarious and well-traveled churchman who made friends easily and who zestfully debated all manner of theological, cultural, and political concerns. Warfield was a far less engaging or exuberant personality and not as well suited to play a leading role in partisan church struggles. Hodge helped his church cope with the ravages of the Civil War, which broke the Northern and Southern Presbyterian churches apart, but Warfield was compelled to fight for the church's very survival against a more insidious enemy. His career took on a more embattled factional cast than Hodge's as a consequence.[31]

His chief concern was to restate the case for Reformed orthodoxy against various forms of modernist theology and biblical criticism that were making inroads in the Presbyterian churches. In the 1880s and early 1890s, Warfield carried out highly publicized debates over biblical infallibility with fellow Presbyterians Henry Preserved Smith (of Lane Seminary) and Charles Briggs (of Union Theological Seminary) that dramatized the crisis of belief in American seminaries. He vigorously defended biblical inerrancy, condemned higher criticism of scripture, and charged that Smith and Briggs were heretics for disputing inerrancy. His opponents countered that Warfield's standard of orthodoxy was inflated and that the Westminster Confession was on their side. Like the confession, Smith and Briggs affirmed that scripture is the only infallible rule of faith and practice. In their view, this principle was violated by Warfield's insistence on pressing the test of infallibility to matters of science and incidental historical details. In separate proceedings, however, the church found both Smith and Briggs guilty of heresy and suspended them from the ministry. Against Briggs, the church declared in 1892 that the "inspired Word, as it comes from God, is without error, and the assertion to the contrary cannot but shake the confidence of the people." This verdict against Briggs led to the termination of the Northern Presbyterian church's relationship with Union Theological Seminary, after Union refused to fire him. The American fundamentalist tendency to make strict inerrancy the superbadge of orthodoxy has its origin in Warfield's antimodernist writings of this period, which, in effect, set up an imaginary Bible as the supreme test of orthodoxy.[32]

It was not only the liberal modernizers who posed a serious threat to the religious authority of Reformed orthodoxy. Warfield also confronted the spectacle of a rising conservative reaction that added various novel and eccentric elements to traditional Protestantism. With painstaking persistence, he tracked the rising popular tide of assorted premillennialist, perfectionist, and Pentecostal movements and sought to refute them. Pentecostalism was a separate case in Warfield's lifetime; it arose in 1907 from the Azusa Street revival in Los Angeles and was largely excluded from the fundamentalist movement. To Warfield, Pentecostalism was merely the most misguided offshoot of a wayward American revivalism. He was appalled that Finney-style perfectionism, Keswick Pietism, the Higher Life movement, and other Holiness traditions were so prevalent in American Protestantism. He attacked all of them with scholarly Calvinist disapproval. He also inveighed against the extraordinary popularity of premillennialist dispensationalism and pretribulationist "rapture" doctrine (sometimes called the "two-stage return" of Christ). Warfield was incredulous that Presbyterians and Baptists were flocking to the dispensationalist and (milder) Holiness movements. He countered that

traditional Reformed theology should be enough. It is no improvement on orthodoxy to claim that God is working miracles again, he lectured, for the age of miracles ended with the death of the last apostle. Nor is orthodoxy enhanced by novel
apocalyptic schemes, promises of deliverance from the human condition, or
promises of a "secret rapture" from history itself.[33]

DIVIDING THE WORD:
DISPENSATIONALISM

Such promises were plentiful in the premillennialist currents of British and
North American revivalism. At its core, premillennialism is the belief that Christ
will someday (if not soon) return to earth and establish an earthly kingdom. Most
of the Puritans who settled New England were premillennialists, but they were, for
the most part, not especially doctrinaire about the details of millennial prophecy.
The new millennialist movements of the nineteenth century were distinctive in this
respect. Central to the outlook of these movements was the view that history is
doomed to destruction. People may be saved in history, but history itself has no
future and is not worth saving. In the nineteenth century, this sense of the futility
and darkness of the world fueled an explosion of apocalyptic millennialist movements that included the Shakers, the Millerites (who believed the world would end
in 1844), and the followers of John Nelson Darby. Though all claimed otherwise,
all these movements in effect made a detailed eschatological doctrine the heart of
their creed and cult. For all of its world-weariness and preaching of doom, the Darbyite movement met with spectacular success.[34]

J. N. Darby (1800–1882) was a widely traveled Irish sectarian whose teaching
emphasized the doctrine of the secret rapture of the church in an "any-moment
coming," as well as the doctrine of a qualitative dichotomy between Jewish and
Christian truth in scripture. His system of dispensations served to explicate these
fundamental teachings. Though he was clearly influenced by other millennialist
movements of his time, Darby insisted that his version of premillennialist doctrine
was both original and derived from scripture alone. He acknowledged no dependence on other, current forms of millennialist prophecy or even a connection between these and his prophetic vision. Nor did he take much instruction, except
negatively, from established church traditions. Like many premillennialist leaders, he combined a Calvinist view of history as entirely predetermined by God with
decidedly non-Calvinist views of biblical interpretation and ecclesiology. Historian Ernest Sandeen remarks that his ecclesiology seems to have been devised by
reversing nearly every position held by the Church of Ireland. Darby's intolerant
temperament and his supreme confidence in the directing movement of the Holy
Spirit in his life caused him to spurn relations with like-minded Christian groups.
These qualities also made him a formidable sectarian leader. In the 1860s and
1870s, he traveled extensively in the northeast and midwest United States and converted the existing Plymouth Brethren movement to his spiritual vision. This vi-

sion emphasized the corruption of existing Christianity, the necessity of the restoration of Jews to Palestine, and the hope of raptured deliverance for the faithful Christian remnant that awaited Christ's imminent return.[35]

Darby-style dispensationalism was a variant of the popular premillennialist belief that world conditions will inevitably degenerate until Christ returns to establish his millennial kingdom from an earthly Jerusalem. It was distinctive in its doctrine of the any-moment secret rapture and its insistence that God has two completely different plans operating in history. Darby argued that according to scripture, God has one plan for an earthly people (Israel) and a separate plan for a heavenly people (the church). To read the Bible rightly is to "rightly divide" it between these two programs, interpreting every passage literally in terms of its dispensational context. Though his deepest concern was to teach the doctrines of the any-moment secret rapture and the dichotomy between Jewish and Christian truth, it was Darby's dispensational interpretation of scripture that made possible his extraordinary influence on subsequent American fundamentalism. Not all dispensationalists agreed about such points of interpretation as the precise timing of the rapture or the points at which dispensational lines should be drawn in interpreting scripture. After dispensationalism became a constitutive part of a rising fundamentalist movement, especially among Baptists and Presbyterians, many dispensationalists indignantly denied that their theology had any connection to Darby. Like Darby, however, all of them ascribed great importance to the interpretive project that Darby and C. I. Scofield called "rightly dividing the Word of Truth." This project hinged on a literal-projective reading of Revelation 20 (the only text in scripture that explicitly mentions a future millennium) and a handful of other texts, especially Daniel 2:1–49, Daniel 9:24–27, and 1 Thessalonians 4:16–17. Because the Word of God contains right divisions, Scofield famously declared, "any study of that Word which ignores those divisions must be in large measure profitless and confusing."[36]

With this, a considerable spiritual heritage was dismissed. According to Darby's schematism, which was elaborated by such influential followers as Scofield, Torrey, C. H. Mackintosh, W. E. Blackstone, James H. Brookes, and Arno C. Gaebelein, God has tested humanity through a distinct plan of salvation described in scripture. Each era ends with a catastrophic divine judgment for humanity's failure to meet the ascribed test. The first dispensation ended with the human fall from sin and expulsion from Eden, the second with the Flood, the third with the Tower of Babel, the fourth with the end of the Hebrew exodus from Egypt. The fifth comprised the period of the law, from Exodus 12 to Acts 1 (Pentecost), and the sixth is the age of the church, in which we live. The seventh dispensation will be the millennial reign of Jesus in Jerusalem.

The impact of dispensationalist teaching was threefold. First, it turned the Bible into a kind of secret code containing divine messages about the future of the world. Second, it decentered the incarnation, death, and resurrection of Christ by consigning these events to the period of the law. Third, it nullified the previous nineteen centuries of biblical interpretation. The concept of scripture as a schematic guidebook to world-sundering future events overtook traditional ways of reading scripture and relating to it. To read the Bible truly meant to crack its code, perceiving, for example, that a seemingly obscure passage, Daniel 9:24–27, actually contains a precise prediction of the end of the fifth dispensation, the inauguration and entire history of the church, and the arrival of the future messianic age. Daniel 9:24–27 refers to a period of seventy weeks that must be completed "to put an end to sin and to atone for iniquity" before the inauguration of the kingdom. Dispensationalist theology calculates that seventy weeks actually means seventy weeks of years (that is, 490 years, or seventy "sevens"). With a bit of strenuous figuring, dispensationalism teaches that the first 483 years of this period (seventy weeks and sixty-two weeks) were taken up by the latter stage of the fifth dispensation, specifically, the period that fell between the rebuilding of Jerusalem described in Ezra and Nehemiah and the saving death and resurrection of Christ.

One problem with this interpretive scheme is that Jesus did not return seven years after his death to establish his kingdom. Dispensationalism deals with this difficulty by appealing to a "postponement theory" that stops the clock between the sixty-ninth and seventieth "week." A historical interval between the sixty-ninth and seventieth weeks not clearly foreseen by the Old Testament prophets begins after the completion of the last 483 years of the fifth dispensation. This interval is the sixth dispensation, which is the entire age of the Christian church. The church has no prophecies of its own but exists in a kind of time warp, or "great parenthesis," that interrupts the fulfillment of God's promise to Daniel.

Because God works with only one people at a time, Darby taught, the church has to be removed from the scene before God can resume his dealings with Israel; this, he argued, is what Paul's seemingly strange remark in 1 Thessalonians 4:16–17 was about. The church will escape the great tribulation of Daniel 9:24–27 by being raptured from the earth to meet Christ in the air. Since the church exists in nonhistorical time, the pretribulational rapture could occur at any moment. Before the tribulation, Christ will come to rescue his saints; after the tribulation, he will return with his saints to defeat the Antichrist and establish his millennial kingdom. The beginning of the tribulation marks the resumption of Daniel's seventieth week. That is, biblical history resumes with the climactic seven-year countdown to the inauguration of Christ's millennial kingdom. Numerous prophecies from Daniel and Revelation must be fulfilled during this period, including the appearance of the "anti-Christ" (often identified as the pope, in dispensationalist teaching); the rise of the nation-uniting beast foretold in Daniel 2:1–49; the return of the Jews in unbelief to Palestine; the conversion of some of the Jews; the terrible persecution of converted Jews during the first three and one-half years of the great tribulation; and the triumphant return of Christ to earth foretold in Revelation 19:11–21.[37]

Dispensationalists debated various points of interpretation and chronology in this scheme, especially the doctrine and timing of the secret rapture. These debates were often bruising and sharply divisive. Disputes between Robert Cameron's postribulationist party and the Scofield-Gaebelein pretribulationist party led to the demise of the Niagara Bible Conference series in 1901. By the turn of the century, however, the pretribulationist view that Christ would rapture the church before the great tribulation was clearly dominant among dispensationalists. This influence was sealed by the enormous success of the Scofield Reference Bible, first published in 1909, which provided an accessible guide to scripture from a Darbyite standpoint. Featuring an extensive system of annotations and cross-references, the Scofield Reference Bible made the case for a dispensationalist division of biblical and Christian history, the doctrine of the any-moment second coming, and the pretribulationist secret rapture in a manner that made dispensationalism seem self-evident to millions of Bible readers afterward. It also canonized Keswick Holiness teaching on the gradually appropriated sanctity of the Spirit-filled "victorious life" in Christ.[38]

The ascendancy of this kind of theology in American evangelicalism was disheartening to the guardians of Reformed orthodoxy at Princeton Seminary. Warfield and his chief successor, J. Gresham Machen, shook their heads at the popularity of dispensationalism among Baptists and Presbyterians. The fact that even some of the faculty and students at Princeton embraced some form of dispensationalism or Holiness Pietism or both meant the problem could not be ignored. Warfield tried and failed to restrain these impulses in conservative American Protestantism, emphasizing several points. He argued that the reference to Christ's thousand-year reign in Revelation 20:1–15 was obviously a symbol for the peace of eternal life, enjoyed by those who are saved in Christ. He chided the Holiness movements for displacing the centrality of Christ's saving death with appeals to personal experience. He denounced the "heretical" understanding of divine providence that led faith-healing movements to dissociate God's purpose from the processes of nature. Physical healing through medicine is no less godly than the healings claimed by charismatics and Christian Scientists, he maintained, since God works in and through the processes of nature.[39]

Dismayed at the fundamentalist tendency to make strange or mistaken teachings central to Christianity, the Princeton theologians held out for the sufficiency of Reformed orthodoxy. Their eschatology was generally amillenial, with occasional suggestions of the postmillenial view that Christ will return after the church has spread righteousness throughout the world. Warfield disapproved of the Darbyite proof-texting method of scriptural exegesis taught by the fundamentalist Bible colleges and institutes. Though he admired Torrey's spiritual seriousness and even judged that Torrey was capable of producing "thoughtful Bible-readings," he judged that, as biblical theology, Torrey's work was "incomplete, insufficient and occasionally erroneous."[40] As biblical theologians, Torrey and Scofield persuaded thousands of impressionable readers that scripture scholarship consisted mostly of categorization and proof-texting. Warfield was anxious to explain why this method was not to be confused with Princeton-style scientific exegesis. Charles Hodge may have described theology as a scientific, or "taxonomical," method of gathering and classifying facts, but the dispensationalists applied this method reductionistically to the biblical text, with no regard for the historical context of biblical meaning.

The fundamentalists' view of the Bible as a mere sourcebook of proof texts inevitably produced superficial understandings of scriptural teaching and literary forms. Warfield grasped the irony of fundamentalist activism. Despite its emphasis on restoring biblical authority, he noted, the fundamentalist movement was contributing greatly to the decline of biblical literacy in the church as a whole. In his judgment, the extraordinary influence of dispensationalism in the fundamentalist movement was symptomatic of the movement's failure to interpret scripture according to its total historical context. Instead of reading scripture inductively to determine its meaning in its widest historical and canonical contexts, the dispensationalists based their understanding of Christianity on a few apocalyptic texts, ripped out of context and applied literally to the near future. In the name of recovering fundamental full-gospel Christianity, they promoted bad exegesis and displaced the biblical Calvary-centered plan of salvation with a bizarre schematism only remotely derived from scripture. On top of these defects, Warfield complained, "Mr. Torrey still teaches his Arminianizing theory of redemption, and his Keswick doctrine of the Baptism of the Spirit, as well as his burning, evangelical blood-theology." The laudable impulses of American fundamentalism were thus being led astray by Christian leaders who did not understand their tradition or the principles of responsible biblical interpretation. Warfield and Machen despaired at the triumph of Scofield-style premillennialism and Holiness revivalism over most of the fundamentalist movement. Commenting on the work of young Lewis Sperry Chafer, who later became the chief systematizer of this blend of theologies, Warfield pronounced that dispensational fundamentalism was "at once curiously pretentious and curiously shallow."[41]

PRINCETON ORTHODOXY IN THE FUNDAMENTALIST MOVEMENT

Although the Princeton theologians were sharply critical of the rising fundamentalist movement, this did not prevent them from linking themselves to it. Despite their withering judgments on the deracinated sectarianism of American fundamentalism, Warfield, Machen, and others made alliances with it on the basis of their desire to defend "the fundamentals" of the faith. They were uniquely valuable to the movement as spokesmen for the bedrock fundamental. The Princeton theologians defended biblical inerrancy with an assurance and intellectual authority that was inspiring to many who did not share their class privileges or Puritan heritage. With typical straightforwardness, Charles Hodge condemned Darwinian evolutionary theory as contrary to scripture, ungodly, and therefore impossibly mistaken. Whatever its scientific pretensions, he argued, at its root Darwinism was a form of atheism, masquerading as an objective account of the origins and history of the natural world.[42] Fundamentalists who had little regard for the tradition of Reformed othodoxy nevertheless cited Hodge's judgment on evolutionary theory for decades afterward.

Not all Princeton fundamentalists joined in Hodge's categorical denunciation of evolution as anti-Christian and impossible. Warfield believed that the Genesis creation narrative was compatible with a theory of theistic evolution; and at the height of the struggle between fundamentalists and modernists for control of the mainline churches, Machen also maintained that there was no reason for fundamentalists to oppose a theistic understanding of evolution. He referred inquirers to Warfield's writings on the subject and pointedly declined to take part in the Scopes evolution trial in Dayton, Tennessee.[43] Machen's alliance with the fundamentalist movement was based on his devotion to biblical inerrancy and his belief that liberal Protestantism was teaching a non-Christian doctrine of salvation. The centrality of the question of biblical authority in fundamentalism is illustrated by the fact that such a figure as Machen could play such an epochal role in fundamentalist history.

Machen was the product of a privileged, devout, and intellectually serious family. His father was a prominent Baltimore lawyer, and his mother, to whom he was extremely devoted, was a highly literate, strong-willed, and emotionally complex woman who read Victorian poetry and hosted numerous university presidents, including Woodrow Wilson. Machen took his undergraduate training in classics at secular Johns Hopkins University, studied theology under Warfield at Princeton Seminary, and undertook postgraduate studies at Marburg and Göttingen before joining the faculty at Princeton Seminary in 1906. He nearly lost his orthodox faith while studying under Wilhelm Herrmann, Adolf Jülicher, and other liberals in Germany, an experience that chastened him for the rest of his life. Machen's student career at Princeton was rather desultory, by his account. He complained that the seminary was "run like a boarding school," questioned the spiritual sincerity of his teachers and classmates, and doubted the intellectual integrity of Princeton theology.

These misgivings prompted Machen to make a fresh start in 1905 at Marburg, one of the strongholds of German theological liberalism, where he was immediately attracted to Herrmann. The liberal historicism of Ernst Troeltsch and the new *Religionsgeschichtliche Schule* (History of Religions School) was in the ascendancy at the time, and Herrmann was the leading German proponent of an antihistoricist liberal theology. His blend of liberal, evangelical, and antihistoricist elements had considerable influence on young Karl Barth and Rudolf Bultmann during the same period. On first meeting, Machen was nearly overwhelmed by the spiritual force of Herrmann's personality. He wrote to his father in October that "my chief feeling with reference to him is already one of the deepest reverence." He told his mother that Herrmann possessed the most "overpowering personality" he had ever encountered. Herrmann's brilliance and his deep piety nearly converted Machen to theological liberalism. In December of 1905, Machen remarked that "Herrmann has shown me something of the *religious* power which lies back of this great movement, which is now making a fight even for the control of the Northern Presbyterian church in America."[44]

But Machen never quite relinquished his suspicion that Herrmann's Christ was an imaginative fiction. He greatly admired the intellectual and spiritual force of Herrmann's classic work *The Communion of the Christian with God* (1892), but he questioned whether its appeal to the "inner life of Jesus" was truly Christian.[45] Though he readily granted that liberal German scholarship was superior to conservative scholarship, he doubted the plausibility of Herrmann's attempt to separate Jesus' spirituality from the church's traditional christological claims. Machen reasoned that while the Christ of Christian orthodoxy is based on the Gospels and elaborated in Christian tradition, liberal Christianity ultimately seemed to be based on the desires and prejudices of modern religious consciousness. The issue pressed on him after he resumed his studies in Göttingen, at a safe distance from Herrmann's personal influence. Machen began to cast his seminary training at Princeton in a more favorable light, recalling in particular that William Park Armstrong had lectured with impressive erudition on the history of New Testament criticism. During his last months at Göttingen, Machen began to consider that Armstrong, committed to providing a stronger scholarly grounding for traditional Christian belief, might be a better role model for him than Herrmann. In July 1906, Armstrong also disclosed that he wanted to hire Machen as a junior colleague at Princeton.

Thus, barely a year after he had left behind a rather unsatisfying career as a seminarian, Machen returned to Princeton as a New Testament instructor. He became the junior colleague on whom Warfield, Patton, and Armstrong pinned their hopes for the future of Princeton orthodoxy. The fact that he had come so close to exchanging his orthodoxy for a modern substitute frightened him greatly. If *he* could be duped into nearly following a Christ of the modern liberal imagination, he reflected, what chance would others who did not share his orthodox background and training have? The experience fueled his animus against theological liberalism for the rest of his life. It convinced him that the crucial battleground for the modern church was the field of higher education. In his later career, he warned repeatedly that no amount of stirring preaching would have much effect on a civilization that undermined the credibility of Christianity in its institutions of higher learning.[46]

Machen was slow to relinquish some of his original misgivings about the ethos of Princeton Seminary. He continued to find the institution self-satisfied and provincial. He complained bitterly about the laziness and anti-intellectualism of his students, and his courses attracted few of them. He defended the seminary's traditional curriculum against student demands for a more practical, ministry-oriented curriculum, but Machen worried that the seminary itself was too mediocre to heighten its intellectual standards or even sustain its prevailing standards.

With the outbreak of the Great War in Europe, Machen became alienated from many of his colleagues and students in other ways. He was inclined to sympathize with Germany in its conflicts with England and Russia. (France was a separate case.) He believed that Germany had every right to become a major commercial power and that the chief cause of the war was England's determination "to crush the life out of a progressive commercial rival." Thus he did not share the fervent patriotism and anti-German militarism that pervaded Princeton Seminary in the early years of World War I. He lamented that the prevailing jingoism at Princeton made him feel "like a man without a country." Machen condemned President Wilson's subsequent conscription order as a "brutal interference of the state" in the lives of families and individuals; but after America entered the war, he volunteered for a tour of duty as a Young Men's Christian Assocation (YMCA) functionary,

telling his mother that "to remain behind in an easy life, and loaf as I am now doing would throw me into the depths of skepticism." He spent slightly more than a
year helping manage various army canteens in France before returning to Princeton in 1919, this time to assume the mantle of leadership of an embattled Reformed
orthodoxy.[47]

After the war, the conflict over fundamentalism escalated to new heights of faction fighting and confrontation, partly as a consequence of charges and counter-
accusations that had accumulated throughout the war. In the early years of World
War I, most liberal Protestant leaders opposed military preparedness, but most also
fervently supported America's intervention in the war once one of their spiritual
brethren had taken America into it. Social gospel leaders such as Shailer Mathews,
Lyman Abbott, and Henry Churchill King endorsed Wilson's insistence that the
cause of Christian democratic civilization was at stake in the world-historical
struggle against German tyranny. The war was a great crusade to make the world
safe for (Christian) democracy. With significant exceptions, notably Walter
Rauschenbusch, most liberal church leaders thus accepted that the fight to extin-
guish German despotism was indissolubly linked to their own social-gospel struggles to "Christianize" American society and the world. Some of these leaders
charged that fundamentalists were too lacking in patriotism and democratic idealism to be counted as allies in this effort. Because fundamentalists did not support
America's Christian mission to democratize the world, they explained, it was not
possible to trust fundamentalists as allies in America's war against Germany. In
response, fundamentalists replied that it was the liberal Protestants who were
undermining Christian civilization in America and importing German philosophy
and biblical criticism into American universities and churches. The fundamentalists argued that they were the true patriots, struggling to defend the remains of
a Christian civilization while liberal church leaders eroded America's inner
strength.[48]

When Machen returned home to this church-rending dispute, he could hardly
have struck anyone as a prospective leader of the fundamentalist cause. In many
respects, he was far from a typical fundamentalist. Like Warfield, he opposed faith
healing, revivalism, Holiness teaching, Pentecostalism, and any form of Christian
doctrine or practice that smacked of anti-intellectualism. Politically, he was a lib-
ertarian who belonged to the Democratic Party. He believed that the very idea of
Christian America was a terrible mistake that undermined the capacity of the
churches to be Christian. He opposed most forms of government interference in
public life and nearly all forms of church involvement in politics. He therefore opposed Prohibition, military conscription, the registration of aliens, jaywalking
laws, child labor laws, and the creation of a federal Department of Education. He
also opposed Bible reading in schools and school prayer. He was open to evolutionary theory and refused to join any fundamentalist organization that professed
adherence to dispensationalist theology. He was repulsed by the aesthetic crude-
ness of fundamentalist preaching, hymnody, and public manners. Revival music
especially repelled him.

Yet, on the strength of his commitment to biblical authority and his alarm that liberal Protestantism had abandoned the Christian understanding of salvation, Machen gave his voice to the fundamentalist movement and became the chief symbol of its rise and marginalization. "Do you suppose that I do not regret my being called by a term that I greatly dislike, a 'Fundamentalist'?" he later remarked. "Most certainly I do. But in the presence of a great common foe, I have little time to be attacking my brethren who stand with me in defense of the Word of God. I must continue to support an unpopular cause." Like Warfield, he disliked the modern "ism" in fundamentalism. His loyalty was not to any modern movement but to Reformed orthodoxy, which, he believed, was too rich to be reduced to five or six fundamentals. Much of the historical literature on fundamentalism plays up certain parallels between the forms of resistance that Victorians and fundamentalists put up against a rising cultural modernism between 1912 and 1925, but even here, Machen defies conventional categorizing. Though his mother epitomized the social type, he was not a defender of the "genteel tradition." Machen blasted nineteenth-century Victorian manners and values with nearly the same withering disregard that he showed for revival music. On various cultural and political fronts, he had more in common with cultural modernists such as H. L. Mencken and Ezra Pound than he had with fundamentalists or his mother's polite society friends. These conflicting loyalties weighed heavily on him. He had no home beyond his idea of what Reformed orthodoxy should be, and he greatly disliked the culture of fundamentalism. In the closing months of Warfield's life, however, Machen began to accept that he was fated, like his mentor, to make common cause with the fundamentalist movement.[49]

Machen revered Warfield for his clear and faithful scholarship and admired his courage in addressing controversial topics. He was deeply grateful for Warfield's supportive, almost fatherly interest in him. Near the end of Warfield's life, Machen told him that he longed for "a great split" in the Presbyterian Church that would separate true Christians from the modernists, but Warfield warned him that "you can't split rotten wood." Warfield's position on biblical authority had been upheld for the past forty years by various church adjudicatories, yet by 1920 he realized that most of the church's leaders did not believe in inerrancy. He judged that the church was already so infected by antisupernaturalist modernism that intrachurch battles were useless. Machen shared Warfield's reading of the situation but not his fatalistic response to it. After Warfield died, Machen told friends that he felt "very blank without him" and that he was pained to realize Warfield would never read his forthcoming first book. "With all his glaring faults he was the greatest man I have known," Machen declared. As a loyal caretaker of his invalid wife, Warfield had rarely ventured more than a few blocks from his study; but in the year of his death, his successor's career turned a corner that would leave him constantly embroiled in national church politics for the rest of his life.[50]

Machen's early involvement in church politics was spurred by his opposition to one of the chief outgrowths of liberal theology, the modern ecumenical movement. In 1920 he opposed a proposed Plan of Union to create an interdenominational organization called the United Churches of Christ in America. It is difficult to imagine any ecumenical movement that Machen might have supported, but he complained that the theology behind the existing ecumenical movement was hopelessly liberal. He charged that ecumenism was conceivable only as a movement that began by relativizing fundamental doctrines of the faith. The next year he published his first book, a scholarly monograph titled *The Origin of Paul's Religion*. The book's language was carefully modulated, but Machen's message augured factional polemics to come. He argued that the Pauline theology of Christ's death and resurrection was central to the faith of the early Christian church.

This was hardly an innocuous argument, as Machen understood. Between the lines, the book repudiated the ethical-experientialist Christologies favored by liberal Protestantism. Liberal theology sought to salvage a normative center for Christian faith that was not vulnerable to historical criticism, finding this center in the redeeming influence or moral example of Jesus. From Schleiermacher to Herrmann, Christ became the exemplar of a religious or moral ideal. Machen countered that this strategy was the invention of a compromised culture-faith that no longer believed in the gospel. Liberal Protestantism set the "religion of Jesus" against Paul's theology of the cross and resurrection. Machen argued, in response, that so-called Paulinism was actually the heart of any authentic Christianity. For Paul, Jesus was a divine being who vicariously atoned for human sin through his death on the cross. This understanding of the gospel is as old as Christianity itself, Machen contended. It followed for him that any theology that would dilute or displace this central biblical understanding of salvation forsook its connection to genuine Christianity. Though his first book never quite drew out the polemical implication of this thesis, the seed of the argument that soon made him famous was already there: The difference between liberal theology and true Christianity was not a matter of degree but a question of different religions.[51]

Then came the firestorm. In 1922, liberal Baptist preacher Harry Emerson Fosdick set off a nationwide ecclesial explosion with a provocative sermon titled "Shall the Fundamentalists Win?" The next year, Machen published a primer on true and counterfeit Christianities titled *Christianity and Liberalism*. Although the book mentioned Fosdick only once, many people read it as a rejoinder to Fosdick's modernizing sermons and his warnings about fundamentalism.

Like Machen, Fosdick was not a likely candidate for a factional leadership role. Theologically he was a liberal, but in church politics his impulses were moderate. It was not his intention to drive fundamentalists out of the mainline churches, though those he offended often described him otherwise. In 1922, Fosdick's chief concern was simply to warn liberals and moderates that their churches were in danger of breaking apart. The modernist-fundamentalist controversy had already driven the Northern Presbyterian and Northern Baptist churches to the brink of schism. Fosdick believed that extremists on both sides of the conflict were allowed to dominate too much of the debate. He sought to awaken liberals and especially church moderates to a brewing disaster. He later recalled about his sermon, "If ever a sermon failed to achieve its object, mine did," for his purpose was to inspire like-minded moderates to hold the churches together, not to give fuel to those on both sides who wanted the churches to split.

Nonetheless, in the process of warning that the fundamentalists "are giving us one of the worst exhibitions of intolerance that the churches of this country have ever seen," Fosdick raised the specter of a fundamentalist rout. It was a chilling picture, for reasons he elaborated plainly. Like most liberal pastors, he did not believe in the historicity of the virgin birth, the inerrancy of scripture, or the second coming of Jesus from the skies. But if the fundamentalists gained control over the churches, he warned, they were sure to move against every devout person who did not adhere to their beliefs on these matters. "The Fundamentalists propose to drive out from the Christian churches all the consecrated souls who do not agree with their theory of inspiration," Fosdick cautioned. "What immeasurable folly!"[52]

His implicit warning was that the fundamentalists were winning. The fundamentalists were fired by a righteous cause, they were skilled in ecclesiastical faction fighting, and their maneuvers to gain control over church institutions were supported by a burgeoning mass movement. Meanwhile, most Protestants were leaving the struggle against fundamentalism to a handful of radical-liberal ideologues who wanted the churches to split. Fosdick's candid portrayal of the battleground sparked an enormous controversy over the goals of fundamentalist leaders and the creedal limits of liberal belief, which in turn forced pastors across the country to take sides.

Machen was eager to make them choose sides. In 1916 he had heard Fosdick speak at a Madison Avenue church in New York and had been appalled. "Fosdick has a great vogue—especially, I believe among college men," he observed. "And he is dreadful! Just the pitiful modern stuff about an undogmatic Christianity." It frightened Machen to realize that prominent clergy and church leaders were reducing Christianity "to such insignificant dimensions."[53] Machen's primer on historical Christianity sought to remind Americans that the genuine thing made no apology for its supernaturalism. In the great debate of the present day, he argued, the fundamentalist side stood with Jesus and Paul. He insisted that liberal Christianity was not a modern version of the Christian faith, as its theologians supposed. It was rather an alternative religion that rejected the authority of the Bible, substituted self-flattering Christ consciousness for Christ's sacrificial atonement, and blathered endlessly about love and compassion while denigrating the faith of traditional believers. "Modern liberals are never weary of pouring out the vials of their hatred and their scorn," he claimed. For all their self-congratulating talk about sensitivity, the liberals were grossly insensitive to the feelings of believers who followed Christ as Lord and Savior. They used "every weapon of caricature and vilification" to deride the doctrine of Christ's atoning death. They spoke with disgust, Machen observed, "of those who believe 'that the blood of our Lord, shed in a substitutionary death, placates an alienated Deity and makes possible welcome for the returning sinner.'"[54]

This quote was from Fosdick, who contended that the doctrine of penal substitution was crude anthropomorphism that turned God into an avenging tyrant. Liberal theology sought to relieve Christianity of such unfortunate misunderstandings, however anciently rooted. Machen countered that this was a perverse form of moral sensitivity. Speaking with contempt about the doctrine of Christ's atoning sacrifice, he remarked, the liberals "pour out their scorn upon a thing so holy and so precious

that in the presence of it the Christian heart melts in gratitude too deep for words."
The ironies were galling to Machen: Liberals abandoned and derided genuine
Christianity on account of their presumed moral superiority, but "it never seems to
occur to modern liberals that in deriding the Christian doctrine of the Cross, they
are trampling upon human hearts."[55] In plainspoken but highly charged language,
in *Christianity and Liberalism* he made the case for a traditional Protestant understanding of God, humanity, Christ, the Bible, and the church. Machen warned that
because of sin, we cannot be saved by the discovery of eternal truth, for the discovery of truth only brings us to the truth of our hopelessness. Even if all the ideas
of Christianity were to be discovered in another religion, he remarked, there would
be no genuine Christianity in that religion, for Christianity does not depend on any
particular complex of ideas. The truth of Christianity depends rather on the narra-
tion of an event. Without this event, humanity is consumed by an overpowering ag-
gressor, the kingdom of sin and death. "But a blessed new face has been put upon
life by the blessed thing that God did when He offered up His only begotten Son,"
Machen explained.[56] This is the heart of gospel faith that makes the gospel "good
news."

And how do we know the gospel proclamation is true? Machen made a passing reference to various evidences, including arguments for early dates for the
Gospels, the evidence for apostolic authorship, the historical credibility of the
Gospel narratives, and the testimony of Christian experience, but he cautioned that
all these arguments are merely supporting claims for faith, and not the ground of
Christian certainty. Apologetics can provide evidence that reinforces Christian belief, but faith is ultimately grounded on the certainty that God has communicated
to us through the words of scripture. "The doctrine of plenary inspiration does not
deny the individuality of the Biblical writers; it does not ignore their use of ordinary means for acquiring information; it does not involve any lack of interest in
the historical situations which gave rise to the Biblical books," he explained.
"What it does deny is the presence of error in the Bible."[57] The doctrine of inspiration proposes that the guiding presence of the Holy Spirit in their writing saved
the biblical writers from any kind of error. Everything depends on the fact and implications of this claim. "Christianity is founded upon the Bible," Machen urged.
"It bases upon the Bible both its thinking and its life. Liberalism on the other hand
is founded upon the shifting emotions of sinful men."[58]

It was not altogether implausible in 1922 that the fundamentalists might win
their struggle for hegemony in the churches. They nearly controlled the Northern
Presbyterian and Baptist churches. Disagreeing with his revered teacher Warfield,
Machen judged that a successful purge was possible. He therefore ended *Christianity and Liberalism* with a ringing call to drive the liberals out. He and Fosdick
became famous in the mid-1920s as symbols of the modernist-fundamentalist crisis. Both repeatedly gave their names and voices to the struggle. A Northern Baptist, Fosdick was forced out of his Presbyterian pulpit in 1927 (after prolonged
legal maneuvering to avert this fate) as a consequence of a fundamentalist campaign against him waged in the Northern Presbyterian church's General Assembly. His ouster was orchestrated by William Jennings Bryan, who dominated the

General Assembly of 1923 and then, two years later, took up the cause of the state of Tennessee's anti-evolution law.

Despite appearances, however, the fundamentalists were not winning. After reaching its highest point of influence and outward-moving mass energy in 1925, the movement lost nearly all of its succeeding battles. Bryan's humiliation at the Scopes trial was devastating to the movement's ambitions and public image; Fosdick became an eminent figure in American religion as pastor of Riverside Church (built by his friend John D. Rockefeller Jr.); modernist forces gained decisive control over the Northern Presbyterian and Baptist churches; Princeton Seminary underwent a bitterly contested reorganization in the late 1920s that consigned fundamentalists to a minority status in the faculty and administration; and, as a whole, fundamentalism went into retreat.

Machen's later life exemplified the pathos of this historical turn. In 1926 he was named by the Princeton Seminary board to a prestigious chair in apologetics and ethics, but this appointment sparked a protest (mostly from evangelical moderates) that brought the seminary under investigation by the church's General Assembly. Machen made a poor impression on the church's examiners, while various seminary officials complained to them that he was responsible for a spirit of discord at the institution. Seminary president J. Ross Stevenson told the investigators that Machen was a constant source of "suspicion, distrust, dissension, and division."[59] As a result of the church's investigation, the seminary's government was reorganized to ensure a wider range of theological perspectives, and Machen resigned in disgust. Having failed to preserve old Princeton, he led a group of defeated faculty and students out of the seminary to form Westminster Theological Seminary in Philadelphia. The faculty included Cornelius Van Til, Oswald T. Allis, and Robert Dick Wilson; the students included Harold Ockenga, Ned Stonehouse, and Carl McIntire.

The closing years of Machen's life were consumed by his dogged legal and factional maneuvers to oppose liberalism in the Northern Presbyterian church. He battled against the church's foreign mission agencies and organized an independent board of foreign missions that supported conservatives only. Machen's refusal to obey the church's directive to resign from this board led in 1936 to his expulsion from the Presbyterian Church in the U.S.A. With another small group of followers, he promptly founded the Presbyterian Church of America, but he died of pneumonia barely six months later while trying to recruit members in North Dakota. His fledgling denomination numbered fewer than six thousand members at his death, and a few years afterward it split into the Orthodox Presbyterian Church and the Bible Presbyterian Church.[60]

DEFENDING AND
SPLINTERING FUNDAMENTALISM

Machen's excommunication was instructive to fundamentalists who had wavered on whether to "come out" from the mainline churches. For some, the fact that Machen had been driven into sectarianism answered the question. As a social phenomenon, fundamentalism became increasingly marginalized in the 1930s as a consequence of its loss of influence in the mainline churches. A chain of schisms related to Westminster Seminary exemplified the larger fundamentalist pattern. Having arisen as the consequence of a schism at Princeton Seminary, Westminster was soon divided by a group that left to form Faith Seminary, which was itself later split by a group that founded Covenant Seminary, which was later split by a group that founded Biblical Seminary in Hatfield, Pennsylvania. Fundamentalists split repeatedly over Arminianism (the theology of Dutch thinker Jacob Arminius, characterized by opposition to Calvin's doctrine of absolute predestination), dispensationalism, the boundaries of separatism, and a host of lesser issues. In his last years, Machen was pressed hard by J. Oliver Buswell and other dispensationalists to make room in his movement for premillennial fundamentalists, but Machen firmly refused, calling premillennialism "a very serious heresy" that compromised the doctrinal integrity of Reformed orthodoxy. By then, American fundamentalism had fragmented into many groups that retained little or no connection to their ecclesial heritage. Fundamentalist leaders such as Buswell, Carl McIntire, John R. Rice, and Bob Jones committed their followers to a strict doctrine of biblical inerrancy and ecclesial separatism, turning separatism into an article of faith. Having failed to capture a single major denomination, fundamentalists organized a substantial network of alternative institutions, including the Independent Fundamental Churches of America, and settled for subcultural status.[61]

Fundamentalist thinking and piety were by no means restricted to movements that broke away from the established churches during the battle over modernism. Despite the attempts of McIntyre and others to identify orthodoxy with fundamentalist separatism, many fundamentalists remained in the mainline Protestant churches and fought the liberalization of mainline teaching. Many others belonged to conservative denominations that identified or sympathized with the fundamentalist reaction but sustained their ties to older traditions of Protestant conservatism. In confessional traditions such as Missouri Synod and Wisconsin Synod Lutheranism, the Christian Reformed church, and the Reformed Episcopal church, modernist inroads were kept to a minimum by maintaining old-style dogmatic systems. Nonconfessional denominations such as the Southern Baptist Convention and various churches from the Anabaptist and Holiness traditions also kept modernist inroads to a minimum by maintaining a strict understanding of biblical inspiration and a carefully nurtured opposition to higher criticism of scripture. In all of these cases, however, the rise of evangelical fundamentalism exercised a larger influence over the language and thinking of "traditional" Christian groups than their theologians typically acknowledged. Conservative Lutherans rarely called themselves *fundamentalists,* mainly because the term carried negative connotations but also because they regarded themselves as participants in a classical orthodox tradition that predated fundamentalism. This self-understanding was not unwarranted, but it did somewhat shield conservative Lutherans, Calvinists, and Anglicans from confronting their own stake in the modernist-fundamentalist conflict. While keeping their distance from the increasingly pitiable fundamentalists, conservative confessionalists often failed to acknowledge that their own core doctrinal claims were indistinguishable from and often influenced by fundamentalist evangelicalism.[62]

One highly significant network of traditionalist theologians made a notable exception to this pattern, however. In the generation after Machen's death, figures such as Van Til, Allis, Ockenga, Gordon Clark, Clarence Macartney, John Murray, E. J. Young, and Francis Schaeffer insisted that the fundamentalists had been right to wager everything on the doctrine of biblical inerrancy.[63] They accentuated the connection between the old orthodoxy and modern fundamentalism. All these theologians were associates or disciples of Machen. Some, especially Ockenga, devoted themselves in the 1940s to the construction of a transdenominational evangelical movement; others remained in the Orthodox Presbyterian Church (OPC) and shunned organizational ties with non-OPC evangelicals. But for all these theologians, the key to the survival of Reformed orthodoxy was the fundamentalist doctrine of perfect errorlessness. They saw no reason not to acknowledge that contemporary Reformed orthodoxy was a form of Christian fundamentalism. Young's classic defense of inerrancy doctrine made the case for Reformed fundamentalism. "In all its parts, in its very entirety, the Bible, if we are to accept its witness to itself, is utterly infallible," Young declared in *Thy Word Is Truth*. To call the Bible the Word of God is precisely to affirm that scripture is "free entirely from the errors which adhere to mere human compositions." It is not merely with regard to the Bible's affirmations on faith and conduct, Young explained, but with regard to all its statements of fact that scripture is divinely inspired and therefore inerrant. The divine inspiration of scripture is plenary and extends to the very words of every biblical text. "It is, to state the matter baldly, a verbal inspiration," he wrote. "We cannot have the blessed life-giving doctrines of Holy Writ apart from the words in which they are expressed."[64] The notion that any other view of scripture can be held by a Christian is a product of modern liberal theology, which, he assured, is not Christian.

This is the bedrock claim of a continuing theological tradition. Allowing for minor variations in definition, the doctrine of strict biblical inerrancy is aggressively defended today by such organizations as the Evangelical Theological Society and the International Council on Biblical Inerrancy. Its major proponents include such theologians and biblical scholars as Gleason Archer, James M. Boice, Edmund P. Clowney, Norman Geisler, John Gerstner, Kenneth S. Kantzer, James I. Packer, Robert D. Preus, and R. C. Sproul.[65] With less scholarly acumen but greater popular influence, Harold Lindsell made the question of inerrancy unavoidable for evangelical thinkers in the 1970s and 1980s. He argued that inerrancy is the crucial dividing issue for evangelicalism today, and that no evangelicalism worthy of the name can deny or evade the inerrancy claim. Any Christian movement that gives up its claim to an inerrant scripture will soon lose the gospel altogether, he warned: "It will result in the loss of missionary outreach; it will quench missionary passion; it will lull congregations to sleep and undermine their belief in the full-orbed truth of the Bible; it will produce spiritual sloth and decay; and it will finally lead to apostasy."[66] Like most defenders of inerrancy,

Lindsell insisted that Christian orthodoxy has always claimed to possess a divinely inspired and therefore inerrant scripture: "For two thousand years the Christian church has agreed that the Bible is completely trustworthy." To be sure, he allowed, Holy Scripture is not a textbook on chemistry, astronomy, philosophy, or medicine, "but when it speaks on matters having to do with these or any other subjects, the Bible does not lie to us. It does not contain error of any kind."[67]

This claim has become so deeply constitutive to fundamentalist evangelicalism that the possibility of a fundamentalist alternative to it has been defined out of existence. Fundamentalist evangelicals repeatedly insist that their commitment to inerrancy is the only position that maintains continuity with the orthodox Christian past. Inerrancy is the only orthodoxy. It is the only view of biblical authority that orthodox Christianity has ever held because it is the only view that secures genuine biblical authority.

FUNDAMENTALISM WITHOUT INERRANCY

The thesis that Christian orthodoxy has always upheld biblical inerrancy does not hold true even for modern fundamentalism, however. The identification of orthodoxy with inerrancy in recent fundamentalist history not only distorts premodern Christian history but erases an important chapter of early fundamentalist history; for in its early years, the fundamentalist movement was open to evangelicals who plainly rejected the doctrine of biblical inerrancy.

The eminent Scottish theologian James Orr was a notable example. Orr studied philosophy and theology at the University of Glasgow in the early 1870s, just in time to witness the eclipse of commonsense realism as a dominant philosophical system. Though he sided closer to his realist mentor at Glasgow, John Veitch, than to his other principal instructor, the Hegelian Edward Caird, Orr was never as dogmatic as old Princeton about the necessity of assuming epistemological realism. He regarded Christian orthodoxy as a distinctive worldview without claiming that this worldview necessarily required a realist epistemology. The crucial issue was the truth of biblical supernaturalism, he explained, not the plausibility of its philosophical handmaiden. His major work, *The Christian View of God and the World* (1893), defended the thesis that the incarnational theism of Christian faith contains a uniquely adequate and coherent interpretation of reality. That is, orthodox Christianity presents the most compelling account of how the world works, and its incarnational theism uniquely explains the human capacity to apprehend rational and moral truth. As he explained, "Though Christianity is neither a scientific system, nor a philosophy, it has yet a world-view of its own, to which it stands committed, alike by its fundamental postulate of a personal, holy, self-revealing God, and by its content as a religion of Redemption." Part of the work of theology is to compare the Christian worldview to alternative worldviews, for like all serious theological and philosophical systems, Christianity has "its own way of looking at, and accounting for, the existing natural and moral order."[68]

Orr's concern to present Christian orthodoxy as the system that best explains reality was taken up sixty years later by Edward J. Carnell and Carl Henry as a crucial corrective to fundamentalist anti-intellectualism.

In his own time, Orr's concern to compare the incarnational supernaturalism of Christian faith with other worldviews brought him into sustained debates with modern liberal theology, especially the dominant Ritschlian theology. Albrecht Ritschl accepted the strictures on metaphysical reason prescribed by Kant's *Critique of Pure Reason* and also followed Kant in assigning religious claims to the realm of moral (practical) reason.[69] Ritschl argued that religious claims do not properly explain anything in the world of fact but consist of value judgments about reality. Science describes the way things are or appear to be through disinterested pure reason, but religious knowledge is never disinterested; it describes the way things should be, in the language of value judgments. As Ritschl explained in his dogmatics, religion is about the moral worth and depth of things: "Religious knowledge moves in independent value-judgments, which relate to man's attitude to the world, and call forth feelings of pleasure and pain, in which man either enjoys the dominion over the world vouchsafed him by God, or feels grievously the lack of God's help to that end."[70] The goal of true religion is the attainment of the highest possible personal and social good.

Ritschl's proposal was a variation on the liberal quest for a secure home for religion. Kant, Schleiermacher, and Hegel all proposed strategies to rehabilitate theology by giving theology its own distinctive work and operative sphere.[71] To many theologians, Ritschl's moralistic historicism was an especially attractive variation on this theme, since it recovered much of the language of biblical Christianity for liberal theology and also urged the church to carry out a social mission of reform and renewal. His theological adoption of the Kantian disjunction between pure and practical reason gave liberal theology immunity from further conflicts with modern science. Moreover, by replacing all forms of metaphysical reasoning in theology with a combination of historical and moral-religious argument, the Ritschlian approach made an appealing claim to a recovery of original gospel faith. For these reasons, Ritschlians such as Herrmann and Adolf von Harnack dominated liberal theology in Orr's time.

Orr appreciated the appeal of this strategy to a battered theological establishment. He recognized that the religion-science conflict over evolution alone was causing terrible damage to the Christian cause. Nevertheless, he urged, it would be a terrible mistake for orthodox churches to take refuge in the Ritschlian approach, because this strategy saved "Christianity" by giving up the Christian worldview. Instead of showing the relevance and coherence of Christian supernaturalism to a disbelieving academic establishment, the Ritschlians tried to rescue a remnant of Christian language by restricting theology to value judgments. This so-called solution to the science problem stripped Christianity of its capacity to explain anything, Orr objected: "Instead of using their principle of faith as a check against the inroads of destructive criticism—as, if it has any worth, they ought to do—they make concessions to opponents which practically mean the cutting away of the bough they themselves are sitting on."[72] For Orr, as for Ritschl, faith was a means of knowing, but Ritschl's restriction of the realm of faith's knowledge to value judgments abandoned the gospel claim to knowledge of the inner coherence of all things. By turning away from all metaphysical reasoning in theology, it dissociated liberal theology from the incarnational Athanasian confession that Christ is of one being with the Father. Faith and reason are distinct, Orr conceded, but they also have points of contact in the life of a Christian, and ultimately, in God's kingdom, they must come together. "It is not sufficiently recognized by Ritschl and his school that religion itself, while in the first instance practical, carries in it also the impulse to raise its knowledge to theoretic form," he remarked. "Faith cannot but seek to advance to knowledge—that is, to the reflective and scientific comprehension of its own contents."[73] Orr's deep sense of the unity of all knowledge in the divine Logos inspired a later generation of evangelicals to use Christian reason to find the hidden wholeness of things. For fundamentalist evangelicals such as Carnell and Henry, his presentation of Christianity as a biblically grounded supernatural worldview offered an exemplary model of how orthodox Christianity might climb out of its bunker and challenge the world with its truth.

The first neoevangelicals found another aspect of Orr's theological legacy less exemplary, however. Orr was conservative enough to be a three-time contributor to *The Fundamentals*.[74] He was an unabashed defender of biblical supernaturalism and a leader of the evangelical opposition to the Graf-Wellhausen documentary hypothesis.[75] He embraced the traditional orthodox view that scripture is divinely inspired and therefore fundamentally reliable for its specific religious purpose. But he defined this biblical goal as "the discovery of a gracious purpose of God's love for the redemption and blessing of mankind."[76] The goal of inspiration is the communication of *life,* he explained, not knowledge. Princeton-style scholasticism made the doctrine of divine inspiration foundational; it began with inspiration and then drew its account of revelation from this posited foundation. But this procedure misrepresented and distorted the actual process of revelation, Orr objected. The proof that scripture is inspired "is to be found in the life-giving effects which that message has produced, wherever its word or truth has gone." To profess that scripture is inspired is to claim that through the witness of the Holy Spirit, the Bible "leads to God and to Christ; it gives light on the deepest problems of life, death, and eternity; it discovers the way of deliverance from sin; it makes men new creatures; it furnishes the man of God completely for every good work."[77]

This is the revelatory claim that scripture makes for itself. The charter biblical texts on inspiration do not speak about inerrancy, Orr observed; rather, they speak about the inspired power of scripture to bring people to a saving union with Christ. Paul says that the purpose of inspired scripture is "to instruct you for salvation through faith in Jesus Christ." He explains that scripture is useful "for teaching, for reproof, for correction, and for training in righteousness" (2 Tim. 3:15–16). The biblical way of speaking about inspiration covers everything that is crucial to Christian belief and life, Orr noted. What it does not include is the claim that scripture is inerrant in all that it affirms. Orr believed that inerrancy is neither a necessary nor a desirable inference from the doctrine of the divine inspiration of scripture. Instead of strengthening or supporting the doctrine of inspiration, he argued, the claim of inerrancy subjects biblical faith to absurd tests.

Orr was critical of Princeton-style scholasticism throughout his career, but his opposition to inerrancy became more outspoken at the turn of the century as he witnessed the burgeoning antimodernist movement increasingly identifying itself with inerrancy doctrine. He sought to dissuade the fundamentalist movement from committing genuine Christianity to this test. The presupposition that biblical authority requires the protection of inerrancy, he observed, "is a violent assumption which there is nothing in the Bible really to support."[78] Far from protecting biblical authority for Christian faith, he urged, the claim of inerrancy imposed a disastrously unbelievable dogma on top of the Christian worldview. It made faithful people afraid to open their Bibles, lest they find the single error that would destroy their faith. In effect, the Princeton theologians told them that they *should* be afraid to open their Bibles. Warfield repeatedly claimed that a single error in the Bible would bring down the house of biblical authority. He explained that "a proved error in Scripture contradicts not only our doctrine, but the Scripture claims and, therefore, its inspiration in making those claims." Warfield and A. A. Hodge usually added that, of course, any such proof would have to show that the error existed in an autograph. Since no autographs are available, no errors can be proven.[79]

To some leaders in the antimodernist evangelical movement, the effect of the entire Princeton line of argument was to place Christian faith at perilous and unnecessary risk. Orr's eminent Scottish Reformed colleague James Denney echoed his objection that the trend toward inerrancy in the evangelical movement was gravely mistaken. In the United States, leading Baptist evangelicals such as Augustus H. Strong and Robert Stuart MacArthur concurred that inerrancy doctrine was indefensible and strategically misguided. Even the Baptist conservative who coined the term *fundamentalist,* Curtis Lee Laws, maintained that inerrancy doctrine applied an inappropriate (scientific) test to biblical truth. He judged that those who defended the authority of scripture in terms of a "verbal mechanical" doctrine of inspiration were as far from Christian truth as the followers of Schleiermacher's experiential liberalism.[80] Speaking for many evangelicals, Denney argued that the doctrine of biblical infallibility referred only to the infallible power of the biblical witness to save souls. "If a man submit his heart and mind to the Spirit of God speaking in it, he will infallibly become a new creature in Christ Jesus," he wrote. This is what the early church and the biblical writers themselves believed about the authority of scripture. Moreover, Denney contended, this statement describes the only kind of infallibility that is worth believing today: "For a mere verbal inerrancy I care not one straw," he declared. "It is worth nothing to me; it would be worth nothing if it were there, and it is not."[81] Orr remarked that proponents of biblical inerrancy always urged that "unless we can demonstrate what is called the 'inerrancy' of the biblical record, down even to its minutest details, the whole edifice of belief in revealed religion falls to the ground. This, on the face of it, is a most suicidal position for any defender of revelation to take up."[82]

It was suicidal for theologians to claim that Christianity must be false if any of the Bible's statements on matters of science, history, or geography should turn out to be factually inaccurate. When a later generation of fundamentalist evangelicals sought to rethink the understanding of biblical authority that they inherited from American fundamentalism, some of them looked back to Orr as the symbol of an evangelicalism that wisely refused to read inerrancy into the doctrine of divine inspiration. Others looked further back to the Augustinian Calvinism of the Westminster divines, who taught that only the Spirit of Christ in faith can bring Christians to the authority of the Word and rightly guide their understanding of it.[83] In both cases, a strong view of the divine character of scripture was upheld without turning the Bible into a source of information on astronomy or plant biology.

One instructive example of the effort to rethink fundamentalism grew out of the effort merely to reform fundamentalism that is represented by the founding of Fuller Theological Seminary in 1947. In that year, Ockenga and radio evangelist Charles Fuller set out to establish a new kind of fundamentalist institution. The fundamentalist movement of which they were products had long since descended into reactionary sectarianism. In 1942, Ockenga had cofounded the National Association of Evangelicals (NAE) as an ecumenical evangelical alternative to the Federal Council of Churches. The NAE became best known for its sharp attacks on the liberalism, if not apostasy, of the mainline churches; but its very existence also had the effect of distinguishing evangelical fundamentalists from separatists to their right, represented institutionally by McIntire's American Council of Churches. The founding of Fuller Seminary accelerated this process of delineation. Fuller and Ockenga wanted Fuller Seminary to hold fast to biblical inerrancy while taking a constructive approach to the dominant culture and the mainline churches. To Ockenga and most of the faculty he hired, including Henry and Carnell, the ideal of a reformed fundamentalism was old Princeton.[84]

This ideal had its problems from the outset, not least because the new institution could hardly afford to identify with the amillennialism or scholasticism of old Princeton. Charles Fuller's base of support was too deeply premillennialist to allow his seminary to disparage premillennialism or even, at first, to criticize the Darbyite theory of dispensational ages. Half the institution's original faculty were strongly committed to dispensational theology, and the other half subscribed to a broader premillennialism. The first neoevangelicals soon discovered that their ideal of intellectualized fundamentalism had deeper problems than this, however. In the process of working out what it means to be evangelical but not fundamentalist, the Fuller theologians and other evangelicals of their generation opened the door to religious currents that today are raising the prospect of a paradigmatically different kind of evangelicalism.

"Needing Prestige Desperately": Fundamentalism Reformed

The claim that American evangelicalism is overdefined by its cultural and intellectual opposition to modernity is not new, even among evangelicals. The seeds of the creative ferment taking place in evangelical theology today were sown a half century ago, when a handful of academics and church leaders associated with the newly founded Fuller Theological Seminary began to talk about the need for a "new evangelicalism." These thinkers had a very conservative idea of the religious reform that was needed. Though some of them strongly criticized the separatist anti-intellectual spirit of existing American fundamentalism, all of them were fundamentalists. They identified with the aims of the early fundamentalist movement and held fast to its primary doctrinal claims. Further, though some of the early fundamentalists may not have subscribed to biblical inerrancy, all of the Fuller Seminary evangelicals did. The seminary's intellectual architects conceived their principles for reform as a recovery of the high-minded Protestant orthodoxy that the previous generation of fundamentalist sectarianism and anti-intellectualism had obscured.

American fundamentalism at mid-century was hardly promising territory for a reform movement. Most of its institutions were defensive and provincial; much of its literature was barely literate; all of its reigning public images were negative. To mention fundamentalism was to call up memories of Billy Sunday's gymnastic altar calls, the embarrassing performance of William Jennings Bryan at the Scopes evolution trial, the (fictional) snake-oil evangelism of Elmer Gantry, and Carl McIntire's bitter screeds against the mainline churches. Fundamentalists were ignored by the major media and excluded from teaching at most American universities outside the South. The lack of respect from academe was especially disturbing to the fundamentalists who founded Fuller Theological Seminary in 1947. All of them accepted Machen's dictum that the crisis of modern Christianity was, above all, a crisis of intellectual credibility and respect.

Outside the Deep South, fundamentalists were invisible on university faculties and in most of the mass media. The national radio networks gave Sunday-morning time to liberal Protestants from the ecumenical Federal Council of Churches, especially Harry Emerson Fosdick, but they spurned fundamentalists. Throughout the 1930s and 1940s, however, fundamentalist leaders built a sprawling subculture of parachurch organizations, and one of them commanded a huge international radio audience. Every week, millions of Americans listened to Charles Fuller's broadcast of the *Old Fashioned Revival Hour* on the Mutual Broadcasting System, which offered a message of warm-hearted devotion to Christ in the familiar Moodyesque tones of old-time revivalism.[1]

Fuller preached that every word of scripture was literally God's Word, and that Christ would soon return to establish a millennial kingdom in Jerusalem. A former student of R. A. Torrey at the Bible Institute of Los Angeles, Fuller's idea of a good seminary was Dallas Theological Seminary, the stronghold of fundamentalist dispensational theology. His sermons occasionally plunged into the esoteric details of dispensationalist typology, and his organization distributed tracts that charted the fulfillment of biblical prophecies. At the heart of his ministry, however, was an evangelistic appeal to personal faith in Christ as the redeemer of sin. His immensely popular radio program began with a ringing chorus of "We have heard the joyful sound, Jesus saves, Jesus saves." This old-fashioned anthem set the tone ("spread the tidings all around . . . shout salvation full and free") for an intimate program of gospel singing, testimony, and revival preaching. Thousands of people wrote heartfelt letters to the Fullers every week, and on each program, Fuller's wife, Grace, read a half dozen of the most "precious" letters in a warm, maternal, perfectly inflected voice.[2]

Most American Protestants were descendants of a now-marginalized revival tradition, with or without the dispensationalism. *The Old Fashioned Revival Hour* made a straightforward appeal to their (mostly secondhand) memory of a Christian America and a more personal religion. Charles Fuller ended every sermon with a call to repentance and salvation:

"Now at this Christmas season I know there are some out in radio land who perhaps do not know just where to turn or what to do. I am going to ask the choir to sing a favorite number of mine, 'He's the One,' a song I'm sure you love. Give me a song book, Mr. Miller, and I want you to notice the words of the first verse as I read them." Fuller recited the opening verse and the chorus of this gospel-song testimony to the friendship and unfailing love of Jesus, and then declared:

"Listen, my friend, out in radio land tonight. You have tried a thousand ways to find peace and comfort. Perhaps your heart is breaking tonight with a load, with trouble—you are in despair and disheartened. I want you to know that in all the eternal realm, there is only One throughout eternity that you can trust. You can trust Him right now, and He is willing to come in and be a friend, an advocate, a paraclete, one who stands by—Jesus will become your friend. I want you to know that through the many, many trials Mrs. Fuller and I have gone through—that God has graciously permitted us to go through—and we have rejoiced in them—we have found time after time how sweet it is just to turn to Him, to go to Him, and He strengthens, cheers, comforts, guides, and directs."[3]

The Old Fashioned Revival Hour had the largest network radio audience in America in 1942 and 1943. After Mutual Broadcasting cut back its prime-time access for Fuller in 1944, he pitched the program to a vast assortment of independent radio stations and raised its weekly worldwide audience to more than 20 million. Like most American evangelists, Fuller had little connection to any denomination and took little part in any institution apart from those he founded. In the early 1940s, as he approached the age of sixty, his lack of a means to perpetuate his ministry began to trouble him. Would any part of his far-reaching ministerial operation or legacy survive after he retired? What should he do to ensure that his evangelistic ministry continued?

The question gnawed at Fuller throughout the early 1940s, partly because he already had the beginning of an answer to it. In November 1939 he had awoken with the strong feeling that God was calling him to create a training school for missionaries. Specifically, he later recalled, God's Spirit pressed on him the need for "a Christ-centered, Spirit-directed training school, where Christian men and women could be trained in the things of God, to become steeped in the Word, so as to go out bearing the blessed news to lost men and women." Though he was neither an academic nor an administrator and not even much disposed to fund-raising, for several years afterward Fuller could not shake the sense that God wanted his radio ministry to produce a college of missions or perhaps a seminary. To one prospective leader of the school he wrote in 1946, "Oh, brother, God has laid so heavily on my heart the need of this type of school for training men for the preaching of the Gospel in these terrible days, but I am not qualified to plan such a curriculum. I see this great need, but I am not an educator. I must have the help of men of like vision."[4]

Fuller and Harold Ockenga were not close friends, but they knew and admired each other as leaders in the world of transdenominational fundamentalism.[5] Both were renowned among fundamentalists for their commitment to world missions and evangelism. In 1946 they began to talk in earnest about establishing a school, and Ockenga agreed to serve as a consultant for it. The next February, after Fuller showed him a beautiful five-acre estate in Pasadena that he had purchased for the school, Ockenga agreed to help organize and serve on the board of trustees of a school to be called Fuller Theological Seminary. They talked about the kind of faculty that a postgraduate theological school would require, and Fuller's wife, Grace, questioned whether such people existed. Were there enough fundamentalist scholars in the country to start a seminary? Would Fuller Seminary be able to attract them?[6]

Ockenga was a cofounder and president of the newly established National Association of Evangelicals (NAE), which fashioned itself as a fundamentalist evangelical alternative to the Federal Council of Churches. In the mid-1940s he convened several informal seminars and two sizable summer conferences on the need for a new, inerrancy-claiming, more sophisticated evangelical literature. His guests at the 1945 Plymouth Conference for the Advancement of Evangelical Scholarship included young academics such as Carl Henry, Merrill Tenney, and Burton Goddard, as well as established evangelical scholars Everett F. Harrison, Allan MacRae, and Cornelius Van Til. Ockenga's belief that Fuller Seminary could succeed derived partly from the recent establishment of the NAE and especially from the discussions that took place at his summer conferences. With soothing confidence, he assured both Fullers that they would be able to choose from among more than a dozen qualified scholars.[7]

REFORMING FUNDAMENTALISM:
THE FOUNDERS

When Fuller Theological Seminary opened its doors later that year, Ockenga was its president (serving in absentia from Boston). The original faculty that he recruited consisted of Everett F. Harrison in New Testament, Wilbur Smith in apologetics, Carl Henry in theology and the philosophy of religion, and Harold Lindsell as registrar and acting professor of missions.

Since Henry's specialty was actually apologetics, Smith was qualified to teach only apologetics, and apologetics expert Edward John Carnell joined the faculty in 1946, the original Fuller curriculum was rather long on apologetics, especially in light of the fact that it offered no courses in Old Testament or Hebrew and barely took a pass at church history. Though Harrison was a Machen protege, he was also a Dallas Seminary dispensationalist who, at mid-career, was looking for a new start. Smith was past mid-career and also looking for a new start, having spent most of his life associated with the dispensationalist Moody Bible Institute. Smith's father had been converted by Dwight Moody and later served for many years as a board member of the Moody Institute, where Wilbur's maternal grandfather was R. A. Torrey's assistant. Smith was thus born and raised in the fundamentalist movement; he knew all its leaders personally. Though he never earned a college or seminary degree, by the 1920s he was a popular fundamentalist writer and Presbyterian pastor; though he was a militant dispensationalist, he made alliances with Machen and other old Princeton fundamentalists in the battle against modernism.

To Smith, Charles Fuller was a family friend and fellow proponent of Torrey-style dispensationalism. Like Fuller, however, Smith was eager to see if a new kind of fundamentalist seminary could be created. He judged that the Moody Institute was comfortable in its mediocrity, Westminster Seminary was amillennialist and spiritually frosty, and Dallas Seminary was thoroughly dispensationalist. In the past generation, fundamentalist movements on both sides of the millennialist divide had splintered repeatedly over small matters of doctrinal disagreement, as well as over the larger question of ecclesial separatism. Smith had straddled more than one fence as a major player in this turbulent history. As a nonseparating Presbyterian fundamentalist, he opposed the fundamentalist tendency to make separatism an article of faith; but he had no real home in the Presbyterian Church either. Like many fundamentalists who joined the NAE instead of Carl McIntire's American Council of Christian Churches, he favored independence over either McIntire's reactionary separatism or the liberal ecumenism of the Federal (later National) Council of Churches. He identified most with various ministries that kept their independence within the fundamentalist network.[8]

More than any other founder of Fuller Seminary, Smith also represented the bunker-mentality, apolitical spirit of existing fundamentalism. His writings presented a dispensational, otherworldly gospel as the only serious answer to the specter of rising Communist power. While painting the threat of Soviet communism in lurid colors, he insisted that the faithful church must spurn political involvement and keep itself spiritually pure in anticipation of the imminent return of Jesus.[9] His writings on this dual theme soon exercised considerable influence over young Billy Graham, who relied on Smith's readings of biblical prophecy and called him "the greatest evangelical leader of our day."[10] By the mid-1940s, however, Smith was weary of the factional splintering and anti-intellectualism of his movement. He felt keenly the lack of a worthy literature in fundamentalist theology, biblical studies, church history, and apologetics. In his influential book *Therefore Stand* (1945), he challenged evangelicals to develop "a new body of evangelical literature" and, if possible, "a truly great journal established for the defense of the faith," and even a new "seminary for advanced studies."[11] Fuller Theological Seminary seemed made to order.

The symbol of Ockenga's hope that Fuller Seminary could create a new fundamentalism was Carl Henry, the young philosophical theologian from Northern Baptist Theological Seminary in Chicago who was then completing his doctorate in philosophy at Boston University. In June 1947, Ockenga published a scathing assessment of the fundamentalist movement, deriding its "fragmentation, segregation, separation, criticism, censoriousness, suspicion, [and] solecism." These vices were "the order of the day for fundamentalism," he claimed.[12] Shortly afterward, only a few weeks before Fuller Seminary opened its doors, Henry published a manifesto for a new fundamentalism that echoed this perception of the fundamentalist crisis. *The Uneasy Conscience of Modern Fundamentalism* depicted existing American fundamentalism as a marginalized retreat from the gospel mission to spread righteousness throughout the world. Henry observed that fundamentalist pastors virtually never preached against "such social evils as aggressive warfare, racial hatred and intolerance, the liquor traffic, exploitation of labor or management, or the like." They ignored the heritage of Christian teaching and replaced the great hymns of the Christian past with "a barn-dance variety of semi-religious choruses." In fidelity to their premillennialist understanding of the coming kingdom, they turned the redemptive, world-changing gospel of Christ into "a world-resisting message."[13]

Henry countered that a more authentically Christian fundamentalism would reclaim the social mission of the gospel, discard those elements of contemporary fundamentalism that "cut the nerve of world compassion," and rethink the importance and nature of eschatological hope in Christian faith. He disclosed that his own eschatology was "broadly premillennial" and nondispensationalist but urged that it was crucial for fundamentalists to stop elevating their precise position on the kingdom to ultimate significance. Though he did not share the dispensationalist preoccupation with discerning prophetic signs of the end time in present history, Henry proposed a truce between the premillennialists and amillennialists, "who together form the largest segment in modern Fundamentalism." It would be enough for these camps to oppose the postmillennialist fantasy of a Christianized world, he suggested. The notion that the kingdom will come about through the life and work of a faithful church must be ruled out, but in a way that does not negate the church's socially transformative mission. The gospel is relevant to every world problem until the Lord's return. "The main difference between the kingdom of God *now* and the kingdom of God *then* is that the future kingdom will center all of its activities in the redemptive King because all government and dominion will be subjected to Him," Henry explained. "This difference overshadows the question, however important, whether the future kingdom involves an earthly reign or not."[14]

Ockenga read this tract with excitement. He felt that Henry's theology was firmly fundamentalist but outward moving and sophisticated, his balanced approach to the millennialist problem was exactly right, and his tone had perfect pitch for the needs of the day. "If the Bible-believing Christian is on the wrong side of social problems such as war, race, class, labor, liquor, imperialism, etc., it is time to get over the fence to the right side," Ockenga declared. "The church needs a progressive Fundamentalism with a social message."[15] Henry's earlier book, *Remaking the Modern Mind* (1946), had argued that modern Western culture was disintegrating on account of its lack of a stable or sustainable basis. All the humanist presuppositions of modern culture regarding the inherent goodness of humanity and the inevitability of human progress were thoroughly discredited after a half century of genocidal warfare, he observed. Henry urged that only Christian orthodoxy could provide a stable and regenerative basis for Western civilization.[16] To Ockenga, the externally directed energy and boldness of Henry's spiritual vision were deeply confirming. Henry's ambitions for a revitalized fundamentalism matched Ockenga's own. When he asked Henry to commit himself to the establishment of a new seminary, Henry readily accepted and convinced Ockenga to hire Lindsell as well.[17] He needed little persuasion that Fuller Seminary was needed or possible.

Ockenga's own ministry exemplified the kind of ecumenical, scholarly fundamentalism that he was seeking to institutionalize. As a student, he had arrived at Princeton Seminary just in time to become enmeshed in its modernist-fundamentalist schism. He was the son of a Chicago transit worker and graduate of a Holiness Methodist college, but at Princeton he was attracted to Machen's conservative Presbyterianism. He took Machen's side in his fight against reorganization and then faced a daunting decision when Machen's group lost the battle and left Princeton Seminary: Should he follow his mentor to Westminster Seminary? Was he obliged to give up the prestige of a Princeton degree for a degree from a seminary with no history or accreditation? With some trepidation, Ockenga resolved that he could not agree with Machen and remain at Princeton. A year later, he was ordained to the Presbyterian ministry as a member of the first graduating class of Westminster Seminary. Machen spoke at his installation service at Point Breeze Presbyterian Church in Pittsburgh and praised Ockenga for putting ambition aside "to stand without hope of preferment of what this world can give."[18]

Ockenga nevertheless was filled with ambition for the revitalized fundamentalist movement that he imagined. In his early career, he groomed himself to lead such a movement. He apprenticed with the conservative Presbyterian leader Clarence Macartney, married into a social class considerably higher than his own, and earned a doctorate in philosophy at the University of Pittsburgh. In the early 1930s, the limits of his loyalty to Machen were tested again in the controversy over Machen's antimodernist activities in the Northern Presbyterian church. Machen, Carl McIntire, Charles Woodbridge, and others organized a competing mission board that diverted funds from the denomination's official mission board. In 1935 the church's General Assembly declared Machen's board to be unconstitutional and ordered its members to be tried by local presbyteries. Machen's followers were forced to take sides: Should they follow Machen into ecclesiastical separatism?

Unlike McIntire, who had been his classmate at Princeton and Westminster, Ockenga sided with the denomination. He did not accept Machen's verdict that the Northern Presbyterian church was hopelessly apostate. Moreover, he distrusted the increasingly harsh and unwelcoming spirit of Machen's movement. His suspicion that it was acquiring some of the worst characteristics of a sect was confirmed within weeks of the Machenite schism, when Machen's tiny group broke into a bitter faction fight for control of the movement against a more dispensationalist-oriented group led by McIntire and Wheaton College president J. Oliver Buswell.[19]

The spectacle of an increasingly isolated fundamentalism was chastening to Ockenga in the 1930s and tempered his admiration for his mentor Machen. At the same time, he was appalled by the failure of the mainline churches to hold fast to the fundamentals, especially the doctrine of biblical inerrancy. The issue of biblical authority always meant more to Ockenga than any issue that divided Protestant denominations from one another. In 1936, he became pastor of the prestigious Park Street Congregational Church in Boston (later renamed Park Street Church) and became widely known for his preaching eloquence and vigorous church leadership, especially in promoting missions.

Ockenga made use of his increasing prominence by seeking to create a genuine third force in American Protestantism. The abysmal state of existing fundamentalism and the liberalizing trend in the mainline churches moved him to call for new evangelical institutions and a new evangelical literature. The formation of the National Association of Evangelicals and the establishment of Fuller Seminary laid part of the foundation for this neoevangelical third force. His ambitions for the seminary were grandiose. At its inaugural convocation in 1947, he declared that the mission of Fuller Seminary was to spark the "revival of Christian thought and life" that was needed to rethink "the principles of western culture" and "rebuild the foundations of society." He later recalled that when Fuller was founded, twelve members of Park Street Church were students at Princeton Seminary. "They reported that authoritative Scripture was not taught at Princeton, and they felt the effect of it upon their own faith," he wrote. "We needed a highly academic theological institution founded upon an infallible Scripture. After discussion and seasons of prayer together, Dr. Fuller agreed to furnish the funds if I would direct the seminary."[20]

Ockenga never quite fulfilled his end of this agreement. Though seminary advertisements announced that he would serve as president in absentia for three years, he stretched this arrangement to five years and then reneged on a promise to move to Pasadena as the seminary's full-time president. His action led to the naming of Edward Carnell as president, a move that proved disastrous for Carnell. Then, a decade later, as board chair of *Christianity Today,* Ockenga engineered the peculiar firing of Carl Henry as editor, after Henry had built the magazine into an evangelical institution.[21] Nevertheless, Ockenga was a figure of singular importance in the origins and development of the new evangelicalism. He cofounded most of the movement's flagship enterprises, including *Christianity Today,* and defined its original commitments and spirit. "Neo-evangelicalism was born in 1948 in connection with a convocation address which I gave in the Civic Auditorium in Pasadena," he later recalled, missing the date by a year. "While reaffirming the theological view of fundamentalism, this address repudiated its ecclesiology and social theory. The ringing call for a repudiation of separatism and the summons to social involvement received a hearty response from many evangelicals."[22]

Fuller Seminary never actually did much in the way of social involvement. Its leadership in the 1950s was unfailingly conservative on political issues, when it was not invisible. The seminary did nothing to challenge its country's imperial maneuvers in Southeast Asia, Central America, or Africa; it did not question America's rationale for the cold war or criticize America's maldistribution of wealth; it gave no voice to the struggle for racial justice when Martin Luther King Jr. called for support from the churches. Though Fuller professors occasionally allowed in print that race was a major problem in American life, the differences between their institution and more right-wing fundamentalist seminaries regarding race and other social justice issues were barely perceptible in the 1950s. The seminary supported Billy Graham's integrated crusades and practiced integration to some degree in its admissions policy, but for all its early words about needing to make fundamentalism more progressive on social justice issues, it made few actual gestures in this direction.[23]

The defining concerns and creative energy of the institution were instead focused elsewhere. Fuller Seminary was established on the premise that American fundamentalism could become intellectually respectable and participate in the dominant culture. Its founding was, in part, a pitch for status recognition. Ockenga and Henry were especially anxious to change the negative image of fundamentalism that pervaded higher education. Nothing wounded them more deeply than the repeated snubs they received in the seminary's early years from mainline church leaders, committees, and pension boards, especially those associated with the Northern Presbyterian church. Fuller administrators and faculty struggled for years to convince mainline church leaders that they were civil, well meaning, and deserving of recognition. When Edward Carnell joined the seminary in its second year of its existence, Henry gained a colleague who matched his burning desire to make fundamentalism intellectually and culturally respectable. Together these men epitomized the spirit of the new evangelicalism and became its leading intellectual proponents.

The similarities between Henry and Carnell were striking, especially in light of their considerable differences in temperament. Both attended Wheaton College in the late 1930s; both were greatly influenced at Wheaton by the Calvinist philosopher Gordon Clark; both specialized in modern philosophy of religion in their graduate studies; and both earned doctorates under personalist philosopher E. S. Brightman and liberal theologian Harold DeWolf at Boston University, completing their oral exams on the same afternoon in May 1949. The month after commencement, they celebrated their degrees by sharing Ockenga's pulpit at Park Street Church. By then, they were well-established colleagues at a seminary where three of the five professors were specialists in apologetics.

If it seemed to Ockenga in the seminary's first year that Fuller needed to hire someone other than another apologist-theologian, Carnell helped him see the matter differently. He lobbied for a position at Fuller as a member of Ockenga's church, just before Fuller Seminary opened its doors. "From my years of friendship with you I have discovered that our world-views coincide almost jot for jot and tittle for tittle," he wrote to Ockenga. "You combine a happy appreciation of Reformation Christianity with a love for the Fundamentalists of our present day." Then he offered himself as the solution to a problem that Ockenga might not have perceived. Carnell observed that Henry was presently slated to teach systematic theology and philosophy of religion at Fuller, and, he suggested, this was not a sustainable arrangement. Sooner or later, Henry would have to decide whether he wanted to teach theology or philosophy of religion. Carnell pressed for an early verdict, since he was ready to teach whichever field Henry did not. "I have had equal training in systematic theology and philosophy of religion," he explained. "Collaboration with Dr. Henry could mean the publication of a series of contemporary volumes of great worth."[24] With Henry's strong support, Carnell thus became the fifth member of Fuller's teaching faculty and soon surpassed Henry as the symbol of its ambition.

Carnell was six years younger than Henry and, in certain respects, better prepared than Henry for a theological career. Henry's father was Lutheran and his mother Roman Catholic, but neither was religiously observant. The Henrys were German immigrants who settled in New York; after the Great War broke out, they changed the family name from Heinrich. Their son converted to evangelical Christianity at the age of twenty, while working as a journalist. Two years later he enrolled at Wheaton College, where he was older and more worldly-wise than his classmates. As a student, he covered the Wheaton area for the *Chicago Tribune,* wrote for the local Wheaton newspaper, and taught typing and journalism at the college. His journalistic endeavors also concerned college officials who were anxious about their image and unaccustomed to aggressive undergraduates.[25]

Carnell was closer to the norm. His father was a conservative Baptist pastor, who brought the family to Albion, Michigan, after failing as a salesman. Herbert Carnell was a strict disciplinarian and fundamentalist preacher. In later life, he portrayed himself as a mediator between moderates and fundamentalists in the denominational faction fights of the 1920s, but his son remembered their household as an example of "the tyrannical legalism of fundamentalism."[26] Edward Carnell spent his entire adult life defending and struggling against this inheritance. The burden of belonging to a poorly educated religious minority weighed heavily on him. As a young man he was moody, undisciplined, indifferent to school, and seemingly uninterested in religion. He performed poorly in high school and professed no interest in college but got into Wheaton on the strength of his father's ministerial standing.

It was Wheaton College and, in particular, the philosopher Gordon Clark who inspired Carnell to become an intellectual defender of his heritage. Clark seemed a bit out of place at Wheaton. He was an Old School Calvinist who drilled his students in the history of philosophy and sought to convert them to his style of rationalistic Reformed orthodoxy. An eccentric, enthusiastic teacher, he taught at Wheaton during the brief period when his decidedly nonrevivalist form of evangelicalism could be endorsed by the administration. The heritage of Wheaton was Arminian and interdenominational, but in the 1930s, under the leadership of Calvinist theologian J. Oliver Buswell, the college raised its national profile dramatically and expanded its enrollment and faculty.

Wheaton also became enmeshed in the controversies spawned by the Presbyterian schism. Buswell was a prominent member of the Machenite opposition to the Northern Presbyterian church, but shortly after the church's schism in 1936, he and McIntyre fought with Machen for control of the new Presbyterian Church of America. Buswell became a symbol of the kind of fundamentalism that sought greater inclusivity through separatism. He wanted to build a fundamentalist movement that broke off all connections with the modernizing churches while also embracing theological and cultural currents that Machen's Old School confessionalism opposed. In 1936, at the height of the controversy over the future of the Machenite reaction, Buswell lured Clark from the University of Pennsylvania to the Wheaton faculty.

Clark immediately provided the star power that Buswell was seeking. His writings brought attention to Wheaton, and he attracted a cultish following among its brightest students, including Henry, Lindsell, Edmund Clowney, Clair Davis, Paul Jewett, Lars Granberg, Glenn Barker, James Tompkins, and Robert Rudolph. Though not a follower, Billy Graham was also influenced by Clark during this period. Clark's brand of Calvinism made him an outsider to both sides of the struggle over Wheaton's religious identity in the 1930s. He criticized the college's revivalist heritage and openly derided the long, emotional chapel services that cut into class time. He urged his students to identify more with the tradition of Reformed orthodoxy than with the poorer tradition of American fundamentalism. Though he came to Wheaton on Buswell's invitation, he remained an ardent Machenite in the denominational fight between Machen and Buswell. Buswell encouraged Wheaton graduates to get their seminary training at Faith Theological Seminary—the separatist institution organized by the McIntyre-Buswell group—while Clark guided his students to Westminster Seminary. Carnell became one of this latter group after his graduation in 1941.[27]

Many Wheaton board members and alumni were disturbed by the extent to which their school was dragged into divisive Presbyterian church politics in the

1930s. Though Wheaton boomed under Buswell's fourteen-year leadership, it also lost much of its broad, interdenominational fundamentalist identity. Buswell's movement and others like it (especially the General Association of Regular Baptists) increasingly made separatism an article of faith, a development that distressed many Wheaton officials and alumni. The fact that Buswell brought Clark to Wheaton also did not endear him to many Wheaton donors, who charged that Clark created a spirit of arrogant intellectualism among his followers and, more important, that his emphasis on predestination undermined the college's historical commitment to mission work and evangelism. These complaints led to Buswell's firing in 1940 and to Clark's dismissal three years later. Wheaton replaced Buswell with a revival-tradition missionary who opined that philosophy never saved anyone. Both departures were ugly, and Clark's required a trial for heresy; after he was dismissed, Wheaton College replaced his required philosophy courses with courses on Bible memorization and evangelism.[28]

This was the background music to Carnell's experience at Wheaton. Though he was oblivious to much of the factionalism that consumed his teachers during this period (Henry's journalistic activities made him more aware of it), he keenly grasped the significance of Clark's outlook in the Wheaton environment. His attraction to Clark was based on this recognition. Unlike most of those who specialized in Clark's courses and followed him around, Carnell was not an especially strong student at Wheaton; his overall undergraduate performance was mediocre. But Clark's intellectually commanding discourses on the history of philosophy and on the objective truth of Christianity awakened Carnell to an unsuspected vocation.

Clark described Christianity as the true universal worldview. His insistence on the necessity of logical precision in defending this position awakened Carnell's interest in the life of the mind, inspiring him to become a Christian apologist. Carnell delighted in Clark's assurance that liberal theologians cowered in the face of a scientific worldview that they knew nothing about. He embraced Clark's thesis that special revelation contains a rationality that surpasses scientific rationality on account of its divine character.[29] What was needed in Christianity was not to retreat from critical reason, Clark asserted, but to embrace the transcendent rationality contained in the biblical revelation. "In matters of religion, where a knowledge of God is desired, experimentation cannot hold a dim candle to the sunburst of special revelation," Clark taught.[30] His insistence that Christian orthodoxy provided the most rational explanation for the existence and nature of the world was inspiring to bright young fundamentalists who smelled surrender in the fideism of revivalist religion.

Carnell was a student at Westminster Seminary by the time his revered teacher was fired at Wheaton. He later remarked that while he learned more at Westminster than at Wheaton, it was Clark who taught him how to think. One incident from his college days illustrates the state of mind that he maintained afterward. One evening, as a member of a Wheaton gospel-witness team that conducted street meetings off campus, an onlooker asked Carnell a question that he could not answer. The experience disturbed him greatly. He told his friend David Roberts that he would not put himself into that situation again until he knew the answer to every possible question. Roberts replied that a Christian can never know all the answers; the obligation of a Christian is to witness to Christ, he argued, not to refute every possible objection. But Carnell was adamant. If Christianity is true, he reasoned, there must be a right answer to every possible objection to it. The obligation of the apologist is to find and explicate all the answers.[31]

It followed that the purpose of a seminary education was to find as many of these answers as possible. Carnell chose to attend Westminster Seminary because he judged (under Clark's influence) that the Machenites defended the gospel with greater scholarly and apologetic seriousness than anyone else. Before long, he despaired that Westminster was also a spiritual wasteland; the right-thinking intellectualism of Machen's successors seemed to negate any sense of the joy or beauty of Christian life. To his surprise, Carnell became nostalgic for Wheaton's Pietism in the face of the spiritual coldness of the Machenites.[32] While Carnell was personally unhappy at Westminster, however, his Calvinist teachers reinforced his overriding desire to find all the answers. Under the instruction of Cornelius Van Til and John Murray, he gained a deep grounding in the thought forms of presuppositionalist Reformed scholasticism, earning two predoctoral degrees. Then he tested his faith and intellect in two doctoral programs simultaneously at two bastions of the modernizing liberal Protestant establishment—Harvard Divinity School and Boston University.

Carnell was unaware that Harvard had a rule forbidding candidacy for two degrees at the same time. Near the end of his Harvard program, he was embarrassed to learn about this policy from a stunned Harvard dean, who questioned his honesty and wondered how he could have managed two doctoral programs at once. Part of the answer was that Harvard's program at the time was not very rigorous. Carnell worked with two prominent philosophers of religion (Edgar S. Brightman and Peter Bertocci) at Boston University, but Harvard employed only one professor of theology during Carnell's time there, and he was not a theologian.[33] While neoorthodoxy ruled the field elsewhere, Harvard clung to its long-entrenched liberal humanism and barely taught theology at all. Carnell wrote his Harvard dissertation on Reinhold Niebuhr's theology and his Boston dissertation on the problem of verification in Søren Kierkegaard's philosophy.[34] His compulsion to overachieve was undoubtedly accelerated in the early 1940s by the fact that his country was at war. Like many seminarians, he felt pressed to justify his 4-D deferment status.

Carnell hardly required any extra motivation or guilt compulsion to throw himself headlong into the work of defending the faith, however. Henry later recalled that as a graduate student, Carnell drove himself relentlessly to acquire greater faith-defending knowledge. Henry and Carnell barely knew each other at Wheaton, but during their years in Boston, they often took long walks together and talked about intellectual problems. Except for odd moments of humor, Henry recalled, "Carnell was almost always serious and intellectually engaged; he wrestled speculative problems as personal inner tensions and pressed for precision." As Clark's disciple, he blended an unswerving commitment to biblical inerrancy with an acute mindfulness of what Clark and Henry both called "the epistemic importance of presuppositions." Theology was never an academic game to Carnell "but a matter of life and death for evangelical theism."[35]

CARNELL'S "SACK FULL OF ARGUMENTS"

Carnell's Harvard dissertation measured and criticized Niebuhr's departure from orthodoxy, while his Boston dissertation similarly exposed the problem of verification in Kierkegaard's existentialist dialectics. In both cases, the young fundamentalist censured modern theology for retreating from the problem of objective religious truth. Clark's fundamental "either-or" pervaded both works. Just as Clark distinguished between revealed Christianity and everything else in categorizing thought systems, so Carnell argued that everything in life and thought depends on one's relation to special revelation. To accept special revelation (the words of scripture) is to make sense of the world from the perspective of its divine author; to begin with any other presupposition is to be swallowed by nihilism. Carnell cautioned that there was no such thing as "neoorthodox" or "modern" Christianity. Niebuhr's "neoorthodox" appropriation of "biblical myth" built a religious way station on shifting sand. It made no sense and would not survive. One must choose between orthodox Christianity and the void, Carnell asserted. Niebuhr tried to claim a little bit of Christianity and a little bit of empiricism, but he offended logic in both cases.[36]

The only serious choice was between the authority of divine revelation and the authority of scientific reason. One of these explanatory systems must prevail over the other. If the Bible is not true in all that it affirms about nature, history, and geography, Carnell insisted, there is no point in attempting to save some remnant of Christian belief from the reach of scientific rationalism. Christianity is either the true philosophy of life or a futile gesture against the void.

Carnell's dissertations employed the Clarkian either-or to show that modern theology leads to nihilism, but neither defended Christian orthodoxy in Carnell's own constructive voice. The limitations of the dissertation form prevented him from developing his own constructive position. But this was what his life was supposed to be about. Just as one doctorate was not enough for the young graduate student determined to make fundamentalism intellectually respectable, neither was it enough for him to complete two degrees while beginning his teaching career at Gordon College. In the midst of his exam preparations, therefore, "hip-deep in sticky academic problems as a graduate student," Carnell composed a major 350-page work, *An Introduction to Christian Apologetics,* which won the 1948 Eerdmans Evangelical Book Award Competition.[37]

He often told acquaintances that he had "a sack full of arguments" to defend Christianity. *An Introduction to Christian Apologetics* nearly emptied his sack. The book's style was aggressive and opinionated, yet inviting. In the manner of his scholastic forebears, Carnell ranged widely over a long list of questions and objections, disposing of many with two-sentence reminders about the importance of beginning with correct presuppositions. Like Clark, he emphasized that Christianity is logically consistent; like both Clark and Van Til, he emphasized that all systems presuppose unprovable axioms; like Machen and his Machenite teachers, he assumed that faith is based on rational knowledge. Carnell conceived apologetics as the task of arranging answers to current objections against Christian belief. In the preface to the book's fourth edition, he disclosed that the apologetic function of theology was crucially important to him personally because "my heart cannot believe what my mind rejects as false."[38] Following Machen, he therefore defined faith as "a resting of the soul in the sufficiency of the evidence."[39]

Though he was often interpreted afterward, even by followers, as a straightforward knowledge-before-faith apologist, Carnell denied that his commitment to Machen-style verificationism committed his theology to the position that reason is temporally prior to faith. He distinguished between evidentialist "generic" faith and the particular form of faith in which a person holds to the saving person and work of Jesus Christ. Saving faith is invested in Christ and is formed of knowledge, assent, and cordial trust, he taught; nonsaving faith pertains to matters outside the sphere of salvation and follows the evidence. But in both cases, Carnell maintained, genuine faith engages the entire soul of a person. It is never a matter of rational proof alone. One can know and love a person at the same time. Just as Machen taught that faith is never "independent of the knowledge upon which it is logically based," so Carnell insisted that faith and reason are intrinsically linked.[40]

He repeatedly contrasted this "whole-person" objectivist claim to the "feeling theologies" of modern liberalism, urging that theology is not *about* anything if it cannot explain anything known to science. The liberal fear that science will refute Christianity if Christianity comes into conflict with science is unfounded, Carnell asserted, for if Christianity is true, "the heart has nothing to fear."[41] By contrast, if Christianity is not true, there is no point in trying to salvage some part of it for spiritual or moral purposes. The heart should look elsewhere. Liberal theology is weak and sentimental, but Christian orthodoxy is strong, tough-minded, and unafraid of the truth. In this respect, Carnell's apologetic was linked to the modern Reformed orthodoxy of James Orr, who blasted liberal theology for its subjectivist reductionism. "A religion based on mere feeling is the vaguest, most unreliable, most unstable of all things," Orr instructed. "A strong, stable, religious life can be built up on no other ground than that of intelligent conviction."[42]

Like Orr, Carnell regarded faith as, in part, a type of knowledge and believed that Christianity must be accepted or rejected on the basis of its capacity as a worldview to explain the world. "Christianity's coherence is its power to explain history as well as its ability to maintain logical self-consistency," he wrote. "The Christian would prefer to be erroneously labeled a 'rationalist' rather than give up his faith in a rational God, who made a rational universe with rational minds in it, in favor of a religious immediacy where all universality and necessity is lost."[43] But Carnell went beyond Orr in insisting that the fundamental problem of any religion, including Christianity, is the problem of verification. "Faith without objectively verifiable truth is comparable to the sort of certainty which goes along with snake-handlers, sun-adorers, and esoteric faith-healing cults of sundry species," he asserted. No scientist would ever take seriously the kind of report that claims to know something it cannot express or measure. Serious theology is no different. "Faith must be founded in objectively verifiable metaphysical theories even if they fail to provide perfect demonstration," Carnell declared. "Apart from this, theology *has* no logic."[44]

Carnell's preoccupation with the need for secure knowledge drove him to a deeper epistemological dogmatism than Orr's and propelled him well beyond Orr's position on biblical authority. In claiming to possess univocal knowledge of divine reality, he sided with Hodge and Clark against most of the classical tradition. Carnell noted that much of the classical tradition from Augustine onward spoke of God's essence as unknowable or mysterious. Against Thomas Aquinas in particular, he countered that Christianity has no right to claim any knowledge of God at all if its claims are merely analogical. Aquinas argued that we know God as God appears in his works, not as God is in himself. Since God's being transcends all human knowledge, including knowledge derived from revelation, theology must speak of God in the form of analogical, not univocal, expression.[45] Carnell objected that if we cannot know God as God is in himself, we cannot know who or what it is that appears in the saving acts of biblical history. How can we claim to know that God exists if we cannot know what "God" is? Classical theism begs the question of its ultimate referent, he insisted. If we do not know God's essence as it is in itself, we cannot speak of it at all, for we cannot say *what* it is that we are talking about.[46]

Carnell warned that there is no truth without meaning, "for truth is systematically consistent meaning." Without some means of ascertaining the univocal meaning of the word *God,* it does no good to speak of God's essence as "mysterious" or anything else. The referent is missing. It is pointless and contradictory to assert that something exists but cannot be known, Carnell objected, echoing Clark. If something cannot be known, how can it be known to exist?[47] Carnell pressed this objection against all theologies that denied any claim to univocal knowledge of divine reality. He judged that any theology that concedes God cannot be known as God is in himself relinquishes any serious claim to knowledge at all. Without a definite referent, the analogical language of Catholicism, Eastern Orthodoxy, and liberal Protestantism amounts to so much haze and mystification: "If we can continue to talk of God whose essence we do not know, we can also talk of snark, gobble-de-gook and splinth, whose essences are also mysteries."[48]

Following his teacher Clark, Carnell appealed to the argument from the *cogito* as the starting point of a stronger theological discourse. This argument from the soul's thinking about thinking linked him not only to Warfield, Hodge, and Calvin but ultimately to Augustine. Augustine was greatly concerned to refute the skeptical claim that because all existence comes from flux sensations, no changeless truth can be known. In his debates with skeptics he always asked, "Do you exist?" If they said no, Augustine concluded that nobody was present to dispute his position. If they conceded that they did exist, Augustine countered that this admission refuted their skepticism. Not only were they admitting to know something, but they were also admitting to possess a truth that is not derived from sense perception. The truth known in self-awareness is an internal, ineffable experience that makes all other reasoning and use of sense experience possible, Augustine argued. Even to say, "I do not know if I exist," is to betray through self-reference the self-awareness that one does exist.[49] On the strength of the assurance that it is impossible not to know that we exist, Warfield argued that "many other things are certain along with it, and the confident denial of this is only another way of demonstrating it."[50]

Carnell founded his prerevelationist claim to univocal knowledge of God on this argument. Through self-awareness we know what knowing is, and we know undeniably that we know it. This knowledge of the truth is the fundamental basis of our knowledge of God apart from revelation, for God *is* truth. God is the "perfect consistency" in whom all life and being consist, Carnell explained. Just as logic must be used to prove logic, God must be assumed in order to account for God. Without God, there is no ground of truth, but since we know truth, we know also that God is. For Carnell, the Augustinian form of the ontological argument was a bulwark not only against skepticism but against all theologies that stopped short of making univocal predications about God. He avoided the slippery debates over Anselm's form of the argument, which claims that God exists on account of God's being a part of the definition of the kind of thing God is.[51] Carnell reasoned that because God's existence is the indispensable condition for all demonstration, God cannot be the object of any demonstration of divine reality. But in knowing ourselves, we know truth; and in knowing truth, we know God, for God is truth. God is the presupposition of the very question of God. Put differently, Carnell argued, God is not the object of the question of truth but its basis. The *cogito* allows us to make univocal predications about God, "for we are not limited in our *rationes* [changeless rational criteria] to those which can be abstracted from sensation."[52] One can deny the existence of truth only in the name of truth, which is a contradiction. The Christian alternative is to give the only consistent explanation for the undeniable existence of truth, which is that God exists.

Carnell followed Calvin in taking this argument a crucial step further. Calvin taught that without the aid of sensation, the knowing subject is aware not only of its bare existence but also of its finitude, dependence, and misery. The self's knowledge of God as the correlative ground of primal human experience is based on this latter form of prereflective awareness. In Calvin's formulation, the impression of one's infelicity implies and drives one toward the ground of infinity, independence, and felicity. To know oneself as dependent is to be driven toward that on which one is dependent. God is the absolute Being on whom we depend and to whom we are responsible. From bare self-awareness of our finite sinful condition, we know not only *that* God is but also a good deal about *what* God is. In Calvin's words, God is the immediately knowable ground of "true wisdom, solid strength, perfect goodness, and unspotted righteousness."[53]

This constellation of arguments from the Augustinian and Calvinist traditions was crucial to Carnell's purpose. He assumed that a Christian apologetic must demonstrate the credibility of the Christian worldview before it preaches the

Christian gospel. It must appeal to Christian truths that are open to rational assessment by all people—he called these truths "natural revelation"—before making any claim to special revelation. Carnell persistently presented Christianity as the worldview that makes more sense than any alternative. Though he defended the literal historicity of scriptural narratives nearly without exception, his work gave little attention to historical issues. For him, metaphysics always trumped history. He took it for granted that the crucial questions had to be answered long before any worthwhile consideration of historical problems could be taken up.

Carnell recognized that his absolute either-or presuppositionalism worked against his apologetic desire to establish common ground between Christians and non-Christians. He acknowledged the problem while insisting that the rationality of the Christian worldview provides a substantial basis for apologetic argument. Though Christians share no epistemological common ground with non-Christians in regard to absolute presuppositions, he explained, the Christian apologist can use reason to persuade unbelievers that the world makes sense only on Christian presuppositions. Without a divine ground of truth, there is no truth at all, and the value of rationality is destroyed. Science needs Christianity to secure its own belief in rationality. Plato observed that the best one can do in the absence of a Word of God is to make a raft from the best available theories and try to sail through life on it, knowing that the raft may fail.[54] Carnell posed the same alternatives in contending for the reality of a credible divine alternative to Plato's *bricolage*.

The apologist works up to the claims of special revelation only after laying the groundwork provided by natural revelation, Carnell taught. The light of nature is enough to bring rational inquirers to a knowledge of God, but the fullness of Christian truth is disclosed to the mind only through special revelation. In making the transition from arguments based on natural revelation to arguments derived from scripture, the apologist does not bifurcate epistemology. The whole field of Christian apologetics properly operates under the single epistemological premise that the divine subject of biblical testimony exists. Carnell maintained that "we are not exchanging reason for faith, as did Thomas; rather we are seeking to strengthen the faith which we already have, for faith is a resting of the heart in the worthiness of the evidence."[55]

It followed, then, that the primary function of scripture is to provide more evidence. Apologetics does not abandon the spirit of demonstration and verification when it turns to the Bible, Carnell instructed. Special revelation is obliged no less than natural revelation to make sense of the world. "Truth is systematically construed meaning, and if the Bible fulfills this standard, it is just as true as Lambert's law of transmission," Carnell maintained. "Any hypothesis is verified when it smoothly interprets life."[56] In classic scholasticist fashion, he presented the Bible as the answer to an epistemological question and affirmed that scripture is inerrantly inspired by God: "In other words, the entire corpus of revelation was preserved free from logical and historical mistakes."[57] With unusual directness, he addressed the problem of the lost autographs. If God was so concerned to entrust his literal words to the church, why didn't God admonish anyone to preserve them? If it was so important to God to give his Word continually to inspired writers over a period of more than a thousand years, why were all of the autographs lost? Carnell replied that the good is what God does, and God elected not to preserve the autographs. "God was under no antecedent compulsion to give man a revelation in the first place; so why should there be any external force upon Him to preserve this revelation inerrant?" he reasoned. Besides this appeal to divine sovereignty, Carnell observed in passing that humankind "is too depraved to be trusted with holy things."[58] God may have anticipated that any surviving autograph would be turned into a relic, and the history of relic worship offers ample evidence that humankind is too depraved not to turn sacred objects into instruments of corruption.

Though he insisted that the doctrine of biblical inerrancy must be defended against modern biblical criticism, Carnell gave little attention to biblical criticism. He gave extensive treatment to such classical philosophical questions as the problem of evil, the possibility of miracles, and the ethical problem of the one and the many, but his defense of biblical revelation operated at a level of abstraction that rarely dealt with specific biblical texts or critical problems. He conceded in passing that a few biblical texts are hard to fathom, such as Paul's admonition that women must wear veils because of the angels (1 Cor. 11:10), Paul's reference to the baptism of the dead (1 Cor. 15:29), and the reference in Jude 9 to a struggle between Michael and the devil for the body of Moses. He excluded so-called lower criticism from censure, explaining that modern textual criticism was bringing Bible readers closer to the inspired autographs. And, for the rest of his career, Carnell tried to explain to fundamentalists why the new Revised Standard Version was closer than their beloved King James Version to God's original Word.

But the specific problems for biblical authority raised by recent form criticism and other historical-critical methodologies rated no attention in Carnell's defense of biblical credibility. Carnell readily disposed of higher criticism on presuppositional grounds. He argued that "the Christian" and "the higher critic" were separated not by "the facts of Scripture, but [by] two different philosophies of reality." On one side, the Christian struggles to comprehend "how anybody can be so conceited as to try to solve the problems of history without resorting to revelation." On the other side of the presuppositional divide, the higher critic tries to fathom the feeble-mindedness of believers in revelation. Carnell cautioned that there was no way to bridge the chasm between Christians who accepted God's revelation and unbelievers who challenged the biblical account of creation, the historicity of the biblical narratives, the credibility of the biblical miracle stories, and the predictive aspects of biblical prophecy. Either one struggles with the biblical text under the premise that it is God's Word or one does not, he explained. The all-determinative issue is a conflict of absolute presuppositions.[59]

Charles Hodge observed at the beginning of his dogmatics that scripture is no more a system of theology than nature is a system of chemistry or mechanics. "We find in nature the facts which the chemist or the mechanical philosopher has to examine, and from them to ascertain the laws by which they are determined," he explained. "So the Bible contains the truths which the theologian has to collect, authenticate, arrange, and exhibit in their internal relation to each other."[60] Carnell invoked this analogy to explain the close relation between Christian and scientific modes of reasoning. "As Christianity assumes that all in the Bible is supernatural, so the scientist assumes that all in nature is rational and orderly," he observed. Neither hypothesis is based on all the evidence, but each appeals to the evidence "for the most part." Science presupposes that nature is mechanical, despite the indeterminacy of the electron and the Heisenberg uncertainty principle. Since regularity in nature seems to obtain for the most part, the smoothest hypothesis for science to adopt as a fundamental presupposition is that nature is uniform.

This is exactly how the faithful Christian looks on scripture. "The Christian carefully surveys the facts in the Bible and discovers that the regular and consistent witness of Scripture is that it is from God, wholly without error, and sufficient for faith and practice," Carnell explained. "Therefore, constrained by the convergence of this uniform testimony to Scripture's supernaturalism, the Christian adopts the hypothesis of the uniform supernaturalism of the whole of the Bible, although, *de facto,* there are minor patches of Scripture which may not at times seem to fit into this pattern."[61] The fact that the biblical deposit of revelation contains troublesome passages does not deter the Christian from treating scripture as God's Word.

Carnell believed that most of the apparent problems of interpretation were attributable to the insufficient knowledge or interpretive comprehension of modern readers. He did not believe that Bible-believing Christianity was obliged to oppose all forms of evolutionary theory. He judged that orthodox Christianity could accommodate what he called a theory of "threshold" evolution that pictured far-reaching changes within "kinds" originally created by God.[62] For him, the crucial point was that no theory of creation, evolution, or anything else should displace the authority of the Christian presupposition that scripture is God's Word. Just as science does not relinquish its presupposition of the uniformity of nature when some evidence fails to fit the pattern, so Christianity is not obliged to relinquish the doctrine of biblical inerrancy merely because there are some inductive problems with it.

Carnell urged that this tough-minded belief in the *truth* of Christianity distinguished orthodox Protestantism from liberal "feeling" religion and most forms of revivalism. Most modern religious alternatives to orthodoxy reduce the faith to states of subjective feeling, desire, and wholeness, he asserted, but orthodoxy focuses on the wholeness of biblical truth. Because it assumes that truth is propositional correspondence to the mind of God, it accepts the challenge of the most rigorous test for truth: systematic consistency. Just as science and philosophy are possible because the mind makes judgments—and all judgments are hypotheses— the Christian claims the right to appeal hypothetically to the authority of scripture. Moreover, Carnell explained, the Christian hypothesis of biblical inerrancy is as justified as the scientific appeal to the law of gravity, "for each is an inference based upon the observation of specific facts." The validity of the Christian hypothesis is proven in the same way that science proves the law of gravity. If it produces a self-consistent philosophical system that makes peace with the law of contradiction and fits the facts of life, the hypothesis is vindicated. In this case, the truth that is witnessed to is the very ground of truth, the divine Logos, or mind of God, who is "the synthesizing principle and true meaning of all reality."[63] Christians are brought to the wholeness of truth by being faithful to the Word of the author of truth.

The bold either-ors of Carnell's first major work were inspiring to a rising generation of new-style fundamentalists. Carnell was hardly the only fundamentalist of his generation to earn a religious studies doctorate at Harvard and become a respected scholar. More than a dozen others during this period took the same career path, including Merrill Tenney, Gleason Archer, John Gerstner, Harold Kuhn, Paul Jewett, George E. Ladd, Glenn Barker, Samuel Schultz, Kenneth Kantzer, Burton Goddard, Terelle Crum, Roger Nicole, and Jack Lewis.[64] Like Carnell, most were already married, employed, and seminary-educated when they arrived at Harvard. Several taught at one time or another at Gordon College Divinity School, and most became acquainted with Ockenga. For a time, Archer was Ockenga's assistant. Jewett, Ladd, Barker, and Archer later joined Carnell on the faculty at Fuller Seminary.

But it was Carnell who gained attention for the new fundamentalism and became the symbol of its hopes. His vigorous presentation of arguments that he learned from the Machenites earned a wider and more respectful audience than his teachers ever attained. William Hordern later praised him for breaking American fundamentalism out of its intellectual ghetto; with a sharper edge, Roger Shinn referred to him as "one of the new generation of brainy fundamentalists who have studied at Harvard in order to learn the arguments they will spend the rest of their lives attacking."[65] In fact, Carnell learned more from Clark than from Harvard, but his graduate school experiences were formative for him in two crucial respects. First, the fact that nobody at Harvard or Boston bothered to read the Hodges or Warfield or Machen, much less Gordon Clark, was disturbing to him. The realization that his religious tradition had no standing whatsoever at the elite universities troubled him greatly and fueled his intellectual ambition. Second, though Carnell was slow to acknowledge or assimilate the influence, his doctoral programs exposed him to modes of thinking that later filtered into his apologetic.

THE LIMITS OF APOLOGETICS: CLARK AND VAN TIL

Without drawing attention to the critical either-ors, Carnell took sides on a cluster of issues that seriously divided his two major teachers. Clark and Van Til were both strong Calvinist fundamentalists, but they sharply disagreed over the relation of rationality to faith as well as the comprehensibility of divine knowledge. In the mid-1940s, these disagreements fueled a bitter dispute in the Orthodox Presbyterian Church. For Clark, the purpose of apologetics was largely but not exclusively, negative. Like Van Til, he used the Aristotelian law of contradiction to expose the deficiencies of all non-Christian thought systems, but he further claimed that the superiority of Christianity could be demonstrated by the same test. As a system of thought, Christianity alone passed the crucial philosophical test of noncontradiction. Moreover, Clark insisted, the supposed "qualitative difference" between human and divine knowledge posited by classical theology was erroneous. He asserted that there must be some univocal point of contact between human knowledge of God and divine reality as it is in itself; otherwise, theology leads to skepticism.[66]

Van Til countered that while this position gives the appearance of orthodoxy, it is actually heretical because it implicitly denies the doctrine of the incomprehensibility of God. The claim to univocal knowledge of God inevitably commits the sin of hubris, if not idolatry, he maintained. In God's being, possibility is identical with reality and potentiality is identical with actuality. Human beings can never know the depths of their own reality, much less the depths of God's being, but there is no possibility or actuality that God's being does not already know and subsume. Divine knowledge is therefore "wholly different from ours," he argued. The finite mind cannot understand how God can have complete knowledge of all reality without predetermining this reality "in such a way as to make it meaningless." To Van Til, this kind of "problem" only exposed the chasm between the finite mind and God's mind. Because God's knowledge is original and wholly determinative of all existence, he asserted, human knowledge of God can never be more than subordinate and analogical. That is, because God is glorious, holy, and transcendent while human beings are limited and thoroughly depraved, human understanding of divine reality is necessarily limited to scriptural forms of expression known through human experience. The Christian mind beholds a revelation that cannot be grasped as it is in its essence but only analogically from the side of a fallen creature. To claim more than this is heresy.[67]

Van Til contended that the same heresy lurked behind Clark's notion that Christian truth could be subjected to some kind of philosophical test. To use the law of contradiction as a criterion for establishing the truth of Christianity was to subject God's Word to the authority of human reason, he objected. It was to require Christianity to possess a rational foundation defined by a pagan philosopher. Van Til countered that the rational basis of Christianity was provided by revelation and tested only by revelation: "The only 'proof' of the Christian position is that unless its truth is presupposed there is no possibility of 'proving' anything at all." Revelation is its own basis. A faithful orthodoxy does not subject revelation to nonbiblical tests or claim any common epistemological ground with unbelievers apart from revelation. Apart from the self-disclosing activity of a God who sustains all reality as a system without extinguishing human individuality, there is no rational ground for truth at all. "But such a God must really be presupposed," Van Til insisted. "He must be taken as the prerequisite of the possibility and actuality of relationship between man's various concepts and propositions of knowledge. Man's system of knowledge must therefore be an analogical replica of the system of knowledge which belongs to God."[68]

Like both his teachers, Carnell emphasized the determinative significance of correct presuppositions, the revelational basis of Christianity, and the negative use of the law of contradiction. Like them, he also strenuously opposed any resort to paradox, irony, or dialectic in theology. He insisted that Christianity must be rational if God is the ground of all truth. On the key issues that divided his formative teachers, however, Carnell, in his first major work, clearly sided with Clark and mentioned Van Til only once. Like Clark, Carnell believed that Christianity must claim some sure point of discursive contact with God, since merely analogical knowledge makes a weak defense against skepticism, and that Christianity cannot claim to be rational if it is not "rational" in the ordinary sense defined by Aristotelian logic. For the rest of his career, Carnell repeatedly described the law of contradiction as "the most perfect philosophical argument ever devised." Like Clark, he could not imagine believing anything that failed the test of noncontradiction; and even more than Clark, he was passionately committed to the apologetic task of defending the faith in the public sphere. He therefore rejected Van Til's categorical presuppositionalism because of its fideistic implications. In his view, Van Til's approach left the gospel undefended in the public sphere. Though his apologetic made its own distinctively Calvinist claim to rationality, Van Til assumed the superiority of Christianity and thus left the impression that this assumption could not be rationally defended or demonstrated.[69] Van Til later recalled that Carnell believed, "as he told me during a whole day we spent together discussing these matters, that since I did not do justice to Aristotle's fourth book of the *Metaphysics,* my faith must be a blind faith. He was sure I could make no intelligible contact with the unbeliever."[70]

This verdict was not completely fair to Van Til, who practiced a negative, or "apagogic," form of apologetics that defended Christianity by logically refuting various alternatives to Christian belief. The function of apologetics, he argued, is to show that all non-Christian thinking is contradictory and futile, and he urged that this project can be carried out only by meeting non-Christian opponents on their own ground. The apologist does not properly defend the truth of Christianity on alien philosophical ground, he explained, but apologetics can demonstrate the futility of all alternatives to Christianity on rationalist non-Christian grounds. This emphasis on the apagogic function of apologetics was embraced by Clark, who passed it on to Carnell and Henry; but Clark also insisted that apologetics must have a constructive dimension. His form of presuppositionalism placed revelation first, without driving a wedge between faith and reason. It presupposed the same conservative Calvinism that Van Til presupposed but treated orthodoxy as a hypothesis that must be subjected to verificationist tests. Clarkian rationalism sought to show not only that all non-Christian systems fail the test of noncontradiction but also that Christianity is uniquely self-consistent.[71]

Carnell's early work embraced Clark's apologetic program and expanded on it. Carnell argued that apologetics must demonstrate not only that Christianity is uniquely self-consistent but also that it "fits the facts of life" better than any alternative system. The Christian apologist must begin with the Christian presupposition that a personal, all-powerful divine reality exists, he explained, but must also be prepared to show why the Christian worldview is true. The starting point for this task is not an unexamined presupposition (the deductivist approach) or a purportedly objective description (the empirical or inductivist approach) or an un-mediated religious insight (the mystical approach). Rather, the apologist begins with an interpretive hypothesis—the Christian worldview—and then seeks to demonstrate that this worldview is singularly true. Christianity is not only uniquely coherent but true as an all-embracing account of all objective and sub-jective reality.

Carnell sought to carry out this apologetic assignment for the rest of his intel-lectual career. He persistently maintained that revelation and reason go together. Because God is the author of all truth, he reasoned, it cannot be necessary for the-ology to denigrate rationality, especially the law of contradiction. His writings rarely mentioned Karl Barth or neoorthodoxy without blasting the "irrationalism" of neoorthodox theology. Throughout his career he sternly censured Barth, Niebuhr, and others for indulging in the language of paradox, myth, and metaphor. Neoorthodoxy described God as the unknown source of revelation and the incar-nation of Christ as an absolute paradox. It abounded in dialectical descriptions of time and eternity that seemed to treat paradox as a criterion of truth. It identified the gospel message with oxymorons such as "impossible possibility." Niebuhr used this phrase to characterize the perfectionist ethic of Jesus; Barth used it to de-scribe the metaphysical reality of the devil. Carnell countered that such language was "plain 'weasel-wording.'" The neoorthodox affinity for paradox and myth was leaving Christianity undefended, rationally speaking, in the very institutions of higher education where reason was supposed to be exalted. In the real world, he observed, nobody accepts a reply such as "It is an impossible possibility" as any kind of answer to a serious question. Theology should be no less serious in its demands, for it is no innocent matter to violate the law of contradiction.[72]

IS RATIONALITY ENOUGH?

But Carnell was too introspective and complicated to sustain Clark's belief that only the rational is real. During his early career at Fuller, he theorized that fol-lowing Clark's view to its logical conclusion, an electron machine that perfectly employed the law of contradiction would be able to grasp the truth of the Bible.[73] Carnell's inward turn began with his recognition that something was seriously lacking in this account of Christian truth. His apologetic compelled him to explain what he called "the facts of experience," but he recognized that Clark's rational-ism barely scratched the surface of important aspects of Christian experience that Kierkegaard explored deeply. The contrast both disturbed and instructed him. Un-der Kierkegaard's influence, Carnell increasingly accepted that not all the "facts" of Christian experience can be reduced to either-or propositions, and that Chris-tian existence is not merely the outcome of a logical argument. His philosophy dis-sertation had accused Kierkegaard of seducing modern theology into an existential never-land of paradox and inwardness, but Kierkegaard had hooked him more deeply than he let on.

The first crack in Carnell's rationalistic certainty showed up in *A Philosophy of the Christian Religion* (1952), which sought to reestablish the boundary between orthodox Christian rationalism and its various pseudo-Christian rivals. Carnell acknowledged at the outset that he found "very strange about Christianity" the fact that scripture does not present or develop a coherent philosophical system. "Whereas the great philosophic systems are fortified by immense arguments to justify both their procedure and their goal, the Scriptures start off point-blank to discuss some of the profoundest topics conceivable to man: God, creation, the relation between time and eternity, the nature and destiny of man," Carnell observed. "The procedure seems almost naive in our eyes, we are so used to proceeding along other lines of method."[74] To the apologist who evaluated world religions on the basis of their logical consistency, it was strange that scripture did not begin by defining its major and minor premises. Why does God's inspired Word speak about profound topics in such an apparently naive fashion? How should one explain the fact that divine revelation is less rigorous in its arguments than a respectable undergraduate philosophy paper? Carnell's answer was that scripture addresses the whole person, not merely the intellect.

"Man is not simply *nous*," he remarked. "He happens to be a complexity of intellect, emotions, and will—plus a lot more. Whole truth must satisfy the whole man." In its unblinking realism, Carnell reasoned, scripture seeks not merely to inform but also to inspire, judge, challenge, and comfort the human subject. Scripture assumes and assures that "the most lasting and abiding joys in life are never so purely rational that they engage only the mind. The lasting pleasures are whole pleasures: friendship, love, devotion to truth, devotion to goodness."[75] The Bible transcends philosophy not only because of its divine character but also because it is deeply concerned with the religion of the heart; scripture captures the "abiding experiences of the race." Carnell cautioned that he was not suggesting that biblical revelation ever contradicts reason, for in scripture, the insights of heart religion "may never be separated from rational consistency." Biblical religion is never irrational; it does not resort to paradox or otherwise violate the laws of right reason. The biblical writers failed to include a section on formal logic only because they took it for granted that human beings are rational: "They were so absorbed in revealing the richness of fellowship with God that the labor of listing the laws of formal logic was left to others. And it was upon Greeks in particular that the responsibility of defining (but not inventing) the canons of rationality fell." With the publication of *A Philosophy of the Christian Religion,* however, Carnell began to allow that biblical heart religion is "not univocally identified" with rationality.[76]

This inward turn drove him into disturbing territory. Carnell's passion for logic was, in part, a defense against inner disorder. For most of his adult life, he suffered from depression and acute insomnia. He was nervous, painfully shy, compulsive, and extremely achievement-oriented. Carnell was an excellent teacher and a devoted husband and father, but apart from family, he was never comfortable in one-on-one conversations. Though he possessed a wry sense of humor, he was nearly always serious and preoccupied with intellectual problems. These qualities are vividly displayed in the correspondence that he took up with his mentor after he began to take account of inner religious truths that his intellectual training had stifled. Clark loved to argue, especially with Carnell; their friendship (which later soured) easily survived Carnell's early misgivings about his rationalism. But Clark must have found his former student's inward turn unsettling. In friendly but unsparing language, Carnell told him that he sensed a "scholarly sterility" in Clark's position. The law of contradiction is much more limited than you imagine, he scolded Clark, and moreover, on the question of the divine inspiration of scripture, "inspiration is far more dynamic than you are willing to concede." Carnell judged that there was a significant difference between biblical truth and Clark's philosophy of biblical truth. "On your view a person can have the infallible assurance that the chronologies in the Old Testament or the dimensions of the temple or the endless Levitical laws are true, and then yawn and go to sleep; on my view this truth must be probed until it blesses the heart, moves, and convicts: *then* inspired truth has been found," he explained. "Our consolation in the Bible is more than that which comes from a rational assurance that it is infallibly true; it is a spiritual response based upon a source of life."[77]

This was far from a disavowal of Clark's rationalism. Carnell still believed that spirit rests in truth only when the knower is satisfied that the evidences are sufficient. In pointed opposition to Kierkegaard, he denied that time-eternity relations stand outside the logic of rational coherence, explaining, "If rationality does not form a univocal bond of meaning which significantly relates these two orders of being, not only is the venture of faith made difficult; it is rendered impossible."[78] Carnell maintained that we cannot trust God for our salvation if God is not rationally related to us. If the existentialists are right, he argued, Christians have no way of understanding God's will and no way of knowing whether God will act on it. Moreover, existential theologies share the problem of all fideism, which is that no *reason* for the crucial choice, or "leap of faith," can be given. Why should one follow Christ? Why should one even believe in God? By consigning time-eternity relations to the realm of faith, Carnell protested, existential theologians deprived Christianity of its rational basis. Besides their praise for the "passionate inwardness" of true faith, they offered no case for the truth of Christian faith. Carnell rejected the Kierkegaardian claim that reason, while useful in practical affairs, is harmful to true faith. "We do not think dialectically when we do geometry, operate a battery of drill presses, drive our automobiles, or converse with friends," he observed. Why should we switch to irrationality when we read scripture or seek fellowship with God?[79]

For Kierkegaard, the doctrine of the incarnation symbolized the essentially paradoxical nature of Christianity. This doctrine embraces and proclaims an absolute contradiction: Time and eternity are brought together in the supreme paradox of faith that in a remote Mediterranean village, the infinite, eternal God became a finite individual without ceasing to be divine. To Christian faith, Christ is simultaneously fully God and fully man. "The paradox consists principally in the fact that God, the Eternal, came into existence in time as a particular man," Kierkegaard wrote.[80] With ferocious dialectical force, he ridiculed all apologetic attempts to drain the offense out of this religious claim. Apologists sought to make the offensive paradoxes of Christianity sound reasonable, he observed. To the extent that they succeeded, they eliminated the very possibility of true faith, for faith requires risk. Faith is a form of daring. It is not about intellectual certainty but about the subjective risk of will: "If passion is eliminated, faith no longer exists, and certainty and passion do not go together."[81]

Apologists sought to make Christianity seem reasonable, but they could do so only by eliminating its offensive character, thus negating the faith itself. Kierkegaard judged that it was better to lock up the churches or turn them into recreation centers than to take the offense out of Christianity.[82] As it was, he complained, the apologists were making Christianity easier to accept by killing it. "They sought by reasons to prove the truth, or to adduce reason in support of it. And these reasons—they begat doubt, and doubt became the stronger. For the proof of Christianity really consists in 'following.' That they did away with. So they felt the need of reasons; but these reasons, or the fact that there are reasons, is already a sort of doubt—and so doubt arose and thrived upon the reasons."[83]

Carnell's response to this critical blast was surprisingly weak. Against Kierkegaard's suggestion that the incarnation presents the absolute or highest imaginable paradox of faith, he observed that more extreme possibilities were surely imaginable—the church might have claimed that God became half a man or perhaps that God became a worm. Surely, a God-worm would have heightened the offense to reason and thus heightened the risk and purity of faith. This rejoinder scored against Kierkegaard's extremism, but it failed to explain how the doctrine of the God-man might be squared with the law of contradiction. Carnell offered that "there could be no lovelier garment for God to robe himself with than unfallen human nature, a nature replete with righteousness, knowledge, and holiness of the truth." Since humankind is made in the image of God, "the intellect is *not* completely offended to learn that God has taken on his own image." But these objections begged the issue. Is there no paradox in claiming that Jesus Christ is both fully divine and fully human? Carnell responded only that "the incarnation may be received by rational minds without self-betrayal." The orthodox mystery of Christ's dual nature "is not to be confused with objective paradox," he asserted, without explaining why. It could not be that the central Christian doctrine contains a paradox, for paradoxes are irrational and God's truth excludes irrationality. "Whatever guidance we may glean from Kierkegaard, we must draw the line at that point where reason is betrayed," Carnell declared. "The result of setting faith against logic is the loss of a test for error."[84]

Kierkegaard betrayed reason, yet he also brilliantly used reason to explore the psychodynamics of Christian experience. Carnell blasted his betrayal of the rationality of faith, but he was also moved by Kierkegaard's intellectual and spiritual power. He gained insight into his own spiritual struggle from Kierkegaard's religious writings, especially *Works of Love*. Carnell therefore concluded *A Philosophy of the Christian Religion* with a call for a Christian spirituality that integrated "the subjective and objective *loci* of truth." As a reaction against a sterile and spiritually corrupted objectivism, he judged, Kierkegaard's protest was needed but, unfortunately, one-sided. In contrast to Kierkegaard, "a *healthy* inwardness must be guided by, and proportioned to, objective evidences."[85]

Classical theology from Augustine to the Protestant scholastics had been taught by Greek philosophy to respect the demands of ontological and propositional truth. Carnell proposed that the kind of apologetic that was needed would hold fast to these demands while affirming with Kierkegaard that Christianity also contains another kind of truth. Kierkegaard described it as a kind of truth that comes into being only as one is transformed by ethical decision. The truth-seeking work of theology is not completed by full application of any system of propositional thought, he argued; in fact, the main work of theology lies elsewhere. Carnell rejected Kierkegaard's polemic against the uses of philosophical reasoning in theology, but he took to heart the Kierkegaardian thesis that there is a personal type of knowing that transcends the limitations of knowledge by acquaintance and inference. Objective truth is not enough. With this corrective to his self-protecting rationalism in mind, Carnell turned his intellectual energy toward the task of explaining what a "healthy inwardness" would mean for Christian apologetics. He confidently told his classes that his next book would be his best work thus far, and that it would change the way apologetics was done. Carnell was living a different life by the time that *Christian Commitment* was published, however—a life for which he was poorly suited. The book that was supposed to make his major contribution to modern theology instead marked the beginning of his intellectual and personal decline.

MANAGING FULLER THEOLOGICAL SEMINARY

The founding faculty of Fuller Seminary had all taken their jobs believing that Ockenga would take up residence after three years. The seminary was growing, and it needed a full-time administrator–fund-raiser–educational leader. In 1954, after Ockenga backed out of a second agreement to move to Fuller, Carnell began to lobby discreetly for the job. He told Ockenga that the next president needed to be an academic leader who would "perpetuate your own ideals of Christian scholarship, spiritual deportment, and world-wide cultural and academic integration."[86] He confided that he feared his faculty colleagues were small-minded and mediocre. The seminary needed a strong, thoughtful educator who would stand up to the faculty and challenge them to aim higher. By implication, Carnell was already dissociating himself from them. There was some talk on campus of luring Ockenga to Pasadena by securing a local pastorate for him, but Carnell cautioned him that the Fuller presidency was "sufficiently demanding in obligations and sufficiently replete with prestige to be an end in itself." He confided that he harbored serious concerns about the emotional health of various faculty members and also let Ockenga know that he was helping an older colleague with his personal problems. He strongly advised Ockenga not to name an outsider to the presidency but urged him rather to "cast about for one here at the Seminary who can be your understudy in learning the techniques of running this institution."[87] The only solution was to groom an inside successor, and nobody else was qualified.

Ockenga resolved at first not to take this alternative. Having realized that the seminary could not afford his vacillation any longer, in the summer of 1954 he tried for the last time to commit himself to the Fuller presidency. Announcements were made that he would soon move to Pasadena, but a strong show of affection by his congregation persuaded him to renege again. This time, a full-time successor had to be found, but Carnell had second thoughts. At a faculty retreat at which Ockenga's resignation was announced, each faculty member gave his view of the seminary's current situation and future. Carnell was appalled by what he heard. His sense of isolation from the faculty magnified. He reported to Ockenga that they apparently wanted an evangelical Dale Carnegie, who would spin good public relations for Fuller, shake down the rich, and, on the side, publish "world shaking literature."

Carnell could hardly see himself as a smooth-talking money-raiser, and it galled him that his faculty colleagues expected their president to outperform them as a scholar. It was *their* job to make evangelicalism intellectually respectable again, he complained to Ockenga, yet none of them was doing it: "Has it not occurred to them that in the seven years they have had to show deeds rather than words, that not one man on this faculty has published as much as one article in a scholarly journal; let alone publishing a book with a major house." For a group with such meager accomplishments, he reflected disapprovingly, "this faculty has an amazing sense of its own virtues. If I were president, I would only irritate them."[88] If his alienation from the faculty had earlier made him want to be president, now it repelled him from accepting the post.

A few days later, Ockenga and Fuller met with Henry to discuss the seminary presidency. Henry recommended Frank Gaebelein, the headmaster of Stony Brook School on Long Island. When they asked about a possible inside candidate, Henry recommended the Machenite church historian and militant fundamentalist Charles Woodbridge. Then Ockenga asked him what he thought about Carnell as a candidate for the post. Henry quickly reeled off five reasons that Carnell should not be president: he was too valuable as a teacher, he was too valuable as a scholar, he had no administrative experience, he had no fund-raising experience, and he had little pastoral experience. An awkward pause followed, and then Ockenga informed him that they had already selected his junior colleague to be the seminary's next president.

Henry was stunned and embarrassed. His own credentials for the presidency were stronger. He was older than Carnell, and he had more teaching experience. He had served as the first acting dean of the seminary and had performed many other administrative functions in Ockenga's absence. Though he had published little in recent years, he was still a promising scholar. He was also much more gregarious than Carnell and knew more about journalism and public relations. He later recalled that he would have said nothing to Ockenga and Fuller if he had known they had already chosen Carnell.[89] Yet his list of objections was generous and incomplete. He was right that the post would be harmful to Carnell's theological career, and from his long acquaintance with him, Henry surely knew that Carnell's personality was wrong for such a socially and administratively demanding position.

Carnell was not oblivious to the personal risks he was taking. He told the faculty that he considered himself a sacrifice for the school: "For the first time in my life I have done something really sacrificial," he declared. "Up until now I have been guarding my own interests." He explained to Clark that he took the post only because "I simply could not sit back and watch the school go into the wrong hands by default." He feared that the presidency would go to someone like Lindsell or Woodbridge if he did not accept it. Fuller Seminary would settle for Bible-institute mediocrity. "To see this school fall into the hands of those who would let it develop into a mediocre, fundamentalist institution, would be more than I could stand," he told Clark.[90] Carnell therefore took the post. Despite the seminary's shaky financial structure, over the next five years he strengthened its curriculum, secured its academic accreditation, expanded its student enrollment, recruited new faculty—and burned himself out in the process.

His relations with certain faculty, especially Smith and Woodbridge, were tenuous to begin with, and Carnell promptly gave them fresh reasons to distrust him. His inaugural presidential speech, "The Glory of a Theological Seminary," made no reference to the fundamentals or even to the word *evangelical*. Along the lines of his forthcoming book on the third kind of knowing, he emphasized the primacy of the law of love in Christian living and Christian higher education. A faithful Christian seminary must embrace the truth of Christ and hold fast to Christianity as the best explanation of the facts of life, he affirmed; but beyond these commitments, it must also deal honestly with all the evidences, "damaging as well as supporting." Fuller Seminary needed to struggle faithfully and critically with difficult issues. To be the kind of place in which teachers and students faithfully struggled together to find more of God's truth, Carnell exhorted, a seminary had to cultivate a special collective virtue. The crowning glory of any good Christian seminary was its spirit of tolerance in seeking truth.[91]

His older colleagues sharply objected that this was not what Fuller Seminary was about. Smith and Woodbridge fumed immediately that Carnell's speech gave no voice at all to Fuller Seminary's distinctive educational mission. Henry and Lindsell joined their protest, claiming that Carnell's tone and substance betrayed the school's fundamentalist evangelical identity. Carnell later recalled that his confrontations with Smith, Woodbridge, Henry, and Lindsell gave him a lump in his stomach "that didn't leave the entire time I was president." To its fundamentalist militants, Fuller Seminary was supposed to be a high-powered fundamentalist institution, and Carnell a fundamentalist apologist. This meant that it was his role to emphasize biblical inerrancy and propositional revelation at every apologetic opportunity. As David Hubbard later explained, when Carnell made love a touchstone of Christian apologetics, "it was as if the seminary was being basically changed in their eyes."[92]

Carnell soon confirmed this impression when he acted on a key and highly sensitive issue. Fuller Seminary's statement of faith officially committed it to premillennialist eschatology, and Charles Fuller often assured his supporters, with enthusiasm, that "every professor on our faculty is premil." However, shortly after Carnell took office and maneuvered to have his friend Paul Jewett appointed to his former theology position, Carnell took aim at the seminary's official eschatology. Jewett's career trajectory was similar to Carnell's—Wheaton to Westminster to

Harvard as a student, before a teaching position at Gordon Divinity School. Now he was following Carnell to Fuller, where he promptly joined George Eldon Ladd, Dan Fuller, and Carnell in seeking to remove the premillennialist commitment from the seminary's statement of faith. Carnell told Ockenga that Fuller Seminary would never be able to take a prophetic position on any major social issue as long as the school was officially committed to premillennialism. He also noted that the seminary's statement of faith would have disqualified Calvin, Warfield, Hodge, and Machen from teaching there.

The hard-core premillennialist fundamentalists outnumbered Carnell's group among the faculty, but Dan Fuller, his parents' only child, tipped the balance of power to the revisionists. Together, they went to work on Dan's father. To Charles Fuller, dispensational premillennialism was part of the core gospel faith; it was unthinkable to him to break his seminary's link with the past century of dispensationalist revivalism. Carnell and Dan Fuller therefore took a longer-range tack. They persuaded Fuller to sign a private statement that voided the seminary's premillennialist clause on the occasion of his death. The intent was not to repudiate premillennialism, they convinced him, but rather to repudiate the fundamentalist notion that premillennialism was the only orthodoxy. Technically, Charles Fuller was right: Every Fuller Seminary professor was premillennialist, in the broad sense of the term. All of them believed, as the statement of faith declared, that "the Lord Jesus will return bodily, visibly, and personally to conform believers to His own image and to establish His millennial Kingdom."[93]

This formulation made room for Carnell's belief that the kingdom of Christ would not be based on earth. At the same time, most of the seminary's hard-core fundamentalist wing (Lindsell, Smith, Woodbridge, and Gleason Archer) was not only dispensationalist but pretribulationalist. They believed that just prior to the calamitous world events that would usher in the millennium, Christian believers would be secretly raptured out of the world "to meet the Lord in the air" (1 Thess. 4:17). Though not a strict fundamentalist, Harrison was also a dispensational pretribulationalist, and Henry, though not a dispensationalist, also believed that rapture doctrine was part of the gospel faith. When Ladd directly attacked the biblical basis of pretribulationalism in his book *The Blessed Hope* (1956), he was careful to declare his belief that Christ would personally return to set up a millennial kingdom.[94] In the prevailing fundamentalist evangelical context, it was perilous enough simply to call for a more open-ended premillennialism. Carnell's group took a longer view, however. Though all of them were premillennialists of some kind, they were committed to opening Fuller Seminary to other possibilities. To them, it was not tolerable for the long term to teach at an institution that would have disqualified Calvin and Warfield as colleagues.

PERSONALIZING APOLOGETICS

Carnell published his watershed work *Christian Commitment* (1957) midway through his five-year term as president. His expectations for the book were enormous; his belief in its originality and wide appeal was exaggerated; and his disappointment when it generated little reaction was immense. Carnell's inflated estimate of the book's importance was partly a result of the failure of his previous book. *A Philosophy of the Christian Religion* received lukewarm reviews in the evangelical press and almost no attention elsewhere. He complained bitterly to Henry that the book received nowhere near the acclaim it deserved. His explanation for the book's underwhelming reception was that American evangelicals were extremely parochial. Since most evangelicals weren't interested in serious scholarship, and since nobody else took evangelical theology seriously enough to read it, he explained to Henry, it was nearly impossible for a serious evangelical thinker to gain much of an audience. Carnell took this response by the evangelical market as a personal challenge, however. He explained to Henry that the only solution to the cultural dilemma of evangelical theology was to produce superior, attention-getting work. He was convinced that what evangelical Protestantism needed most was a thinker who produced such a profound body of work that readers across the theological spectrum would be compelled to take notice. For this reason, he vowed to "withdraw" from evangelical provincialism in order to produce the kind of apologetics that would realign the entire theological field. "I want to command the attention of Tillich and Bennett," he told Henry. "Then I shall be in a better place to be of service to the evangelicals. We need prestige desperately."[95]

This was his frame of mind as he wrote *Christian Commitment*. Carnell proposed to lift the veil from his experience "in order that others might be guided into a more accurate understanding of their own," but most of this fateful book fell considerably short of the standard. He observed at the outset that most philosophers and theologians were poorly equipped to interpret the crucial influence on their thinking of the moral and spiritual environments in which they lived. Few religious thinkers even took a pass at interpreting life "from within the center of their own perspective as individuals." But this was precisely the home of all interest, insight, intellectual energy, and creative conflict, Carnell protested. The abstract "man" posited in philosophy and theology textbooks does not exist; there are only individual men (and women), who struggle variantly with the fact of their mortality and apparent meaninglessness. "What it means to be held in a moral and spiritual environment can only be learned as one acquaints himself with the realities that already hold him from existence itself," he argued. "This pilgrimage into inwardness is a painfully personal responsibility, for only the individual himself has access to the secrets of his moral and spiritual life."[96]

Carnell's point was not to downgrade the importance of rationally attainable, objective, universal truths for Christian apologetics. He observed that ontological truths express the reality or participation of something in being and are known by the method of acquaintance. The idea of ontological truth assumes that the real is the true; whatever is, is true. Ontological truths are established by direct experience, he explained, for in the kind of knowledge that is made known through acquaintance, the mind passes to a conclusion without the aid of a middle premise. By contrast, propositional truth is known through rational inference. In propositional truth, the mind is brought into touch with reality and forms a conclusion with the aid of a middle premise. Carnell allowed that this process can be construed in different ways. In some philosophical systems, the ideas themselves are conceptualized as the real; in other systems, the ideas are held to correspond to the real. Similarly, different philosophical systems impose different tests for the verification of propositional truth. Some systems appeal to systematic consistency, some to correspondence, some to coherence, some to pragmatic utility. But in each case, he observed, the philosopher assumes that the *proposition* is the receptacle of truth, and that truth is established through rational inference. Knowledge by acquaintance directly introduces the mind to reality, but knowledge by rational inference conceptually houses the real by means of symbols and words.

Carnell assured that both ways of knowing are indispensable to Christian apologetics; it would be ridiculous for an apologist to try to work without one or the other. But, he asserted, there is another way of knowing that Western philosophy has simply ignored, aside from Socrates, Pascal, and Kierkegaard. Except for these figures, Carnell asserted, Western philosophy has routinely ignored "the moral and spiritual realities that already hold man as a creature made in the image of God." These establishing "moral and spiritual realities" form the key to the third way of knowing, which Carnell called "truth as personal rectitude."[97]

He gave a rare and revealing personal example to describe this way of knowing. "Although I have always been reasonably healthy, insomnia has plagued me from adolescence until now," he disclosed. "Only those who are unable to sleep at night can appreciate the distressing toll this ailment takes on one's life: the omnipresent sense of fatigue, the susceptibility to irritation, and the grossness of an unrefreshed mind." Carnell recalled that during his graduate school career, he struggled daily "against a never ending torpor, mental and animal. Each night the disquiets of mind prevailed over weariness." The ill effects of insufficient sleep were heightened by the mounting tension he experienced from the demands of two sets of degree requirements. One afternoon, as he prepared for spring language exams, he exploded emotionally: "My mind was like a mass of live rubber: continually expanding, it threatened to divide down the center." He threw a stack of German idiom cards against a wall and stomped out of the house, heading down the railroad tracks leading out of town.

As he walked hurriedly away from campus into a less-manufactured environment, he was struck by the contrast between the serenity of the natural world and his inner turmoil. Carnell yearned to identify with the natural harmony of the grass and trees, but he also reflected that he could experience such harmony only by relinquishing everything that comprised the essence of his freedom. This flash of recognition that he could not and should not have the sense of oneness with nature that he seemed to desire left him with an overpowering sense of his finitude. "I could *consider* an ant, but I could not be one; and the more I tried to be one, the more I used moral freedom as an escape from the perils and responsibilities of moral freedom," he recalled. "Everything I conceived became a burden; every anticipated obligation threatened to impale me. Even so ordinary a responsibility as conversing with others overwhelmed me with consternation."

He thought about killing himself, but another thought struck him forcefully. As he stood on the railroad track, it occurred to Carnell that "one's ability to see reality is somewhat conditioned to the tone of one's affections." For the first time, he reflected on the drastic alteration that his loss of sleep was causing in his perception of reality and his capacity to relate to others. The world grew ugly and threatening; his will to live decayed; he became snarling and sarcastic with others. This was his reality. "But after a powerful sedative, I see things in a different light," he reflected. "The harmony of nature is restored; I am patient with others; the zest for creative living revives."[98]

This recognition was a breakthrough for Carnell, giving him a more complicated and intuitive sense of truth than the rationalistic orthodoxy that filled his writings. Though his insight into the subjectivity of truth was too subversive to be assimilated into his early apologetics, Carnell could not repress it indefinitely. By the time he wrote *Christian Commitment,* he also knew that sleeping pills are addictive. Ten years later, he would die from an overdose of barbiturates. It was this experience on the railroad track, however, that drove him to the realization that human beings are committed by existence itself to accept certain realities. Despite all the rhetoric about relativism that fills higher education, he reasoned, the "absolute truth" is that no human agent is the author of his (or her) own existence: "When one is threatened with a nervous breakdown, he has no difficulty acknowledging his own limitations. He spiritually reckons with the fact that forces other than his own are in control of his destiny. No further proof is needed."[99]

The truth of our dependence cannot be formally demonstrated, yet it is no less absolute than the law of contradiction or the axioms of geometry. It is also the first clue to the personal mode of knowing, Carnell proposed. Like Friedrich Schleiermacher, who taught that contingency is not merely an object of thought but must be felt, Carnell began his own apologetic from the experience of contingency, though without noting the parallel.[100] "We do not know the significance of 'dependence' until a mental awareness of this relation fructifies in a whole-souled adjustment to its claims," he observed. Just as guilt implies the feeling of culpability, dependence implies the feeling of subordination. It is therefore impossible rightly to apprehend the nature of dependence until one conforms oneself to this relation. "The necessity of this conformity is included in the relation itself," Carnell explained. "If an individual *professes* to be dependent, while he lives as if he were self-sufficient, he deceives himself and the truth is not in him. His proud life shows that his admission is academic and formal, not moral and spiritual."[101]

Each of us lives in a moral and spiritual environment that is as binding in its own sphere as the law of contradiction. If someone violates our sense of fairness or dignity or fellow feeling, our sense of moral order is offended. We seek in some way to restore an existing moral order that we did not create. Two questions about this moral reality drive us to God, Carnell observed. The first is how we should account for the existence of the moral law within; the second is why we should care about it or respond to its call. He recalled that as a graduate student, he was awed by the technical rigor of Kantian moral theory. Kant's ethic of the categorical imperative described the existence and requirements of the inward moral law with impressive precision. It appeared to salvage a strong, rule-producing universal ethic without appealing to any authority beyond the authority of reason. But, Carnell argued, the self-contained rationalism of Kant's moral theory is actually its fatal weakness: The Kantian system seeks to acquaint the mind with moral duty through a rational demonstration of duty, but it never explains why anyone should care about the moral requirements of rationality. That is, Kantian ethics is devoid of moral power. "I was mentally challenged by Kant, but not spiritually convicted," Carnell recalled of his experience. "Unless one is already held by an antecedent moral obligation to be rational, a statement of duty is spiritually powerless to communicate a sense of duty."[102]

Kant was not oblivious to the problem; he believed that religion had a vital role to play in providing and nurturing the idea of a divine guarantor of moral existence.[103] Kant's moral religion was too reductionist for Carnell to take seriously, however; Kant salvaged the idea of God without recognizing God as a personal, active authority. Carnell countered that the idea of a moral law within must drive the thinker beyond Kant's pale deism to the Creator-Lord of the universe. "The very manner of our existence commits us to the reality of a God who is occupied with what is vastly more dignified business than eternal self-knowledge," he asserted. "God is the author of the moral and spiritual environment; he is the sleepless monitor of our dignity; he completes the moral cycle by answering to the judicial sentiment. He is, in short, our only reason for believing that human values, and the ultimate values of the universe, are metaphysically continuous; and that we are not alone in our moral stand."[104]

Our judicial sentiments are part of a moral cycle that is real, but which can be real and efficacious only in relation to a supervisory metaphysical ground. God is the necessary author of a reality that we know through moral and spiritual experience. That is, God is necessary to moral experience and is known through it as the administrator of justice. Carnell denied that he was trying to prove the existence of God through moral experience. He pointedly denied that his argument contained any resort to a proof that passed from the idea of God to the existence of God. His argument was not a moral reformulation of the Anselmian claim that God exists of necessity. Carnell countered that this was one of the implications of recognizing a third kind of truth. The apologist who begins with the reality of moral experience and then proceeds to God as the necessary ground of this reality does not invest importance in rational proofs of divine reality.

This marked a significant shift for Carnell. He had learned from Clark to be dubious of the Anselmian form of the ontological argument, but his later apologetic devalued rationalistic proof making altogether. He cautioned that even the demons believe in God. What is needed in apologetics is not any kind of rational proof that God exists, he asserted, but a "spiritual approach to God" that exercises and holds together one's rational *and* spiritual faculties: "A wretched man can intellectually assent to God's existence, but only a man of character can spiritually approach God's person." It followed for him that the purpose of apologetics was not to prove the existence of a supernatural reality outside the self but to delineate a procedure "by which one acquaints himself with the realities that already hold him."[105] The third way of knowing is a method, not a proof. But the reality that it explicates includes and is authored by God, he explained, for God is the reality in whom we live and move. To assert that God exists of necessity is not to ground Christian faith on any form of the ontological argument, he cautioned, since the assertion of God's necessity is far more certain than Anselm's claim that the existence of God can be proven by the very reality of the idea of God.[106]

Carnell's argument from necessity assumed (with Aquinas and Kant) that if *anything* exists, something exists of necessity. He was no longer interested in establishing that divine necessity can be proven through reason alone, for God can be *known* only by means of a method that combines rational and spiritual factors. In and through the third way of knowing, he explained, the ground of moral and spiritual experience is made known as perfect rectitude. God is the necessary moral guarantor who completes the cycle of moral necessity by defending our dignity. It is God who responds to the God-given judicial sentiment in human beings by acting out of a divine inner necessity. "To argue otherwise would be repugnant to truth," Carnell argued. "Were we to assert that God is *not* held by a necessity to judge those who mistreat us, we would obscure the clearest element in our moral experience; for our reliance on God is woven into the very fabric of existence itself."

In more traditional language, God judges the reprobate through those who are in fellowship with him. Though believers are never to arrogate to themselves the right of divine judgment, Carnell cautioned, it is not possible for those who are in fellowship with God to have fellowship with wicked people. Believers are vessels "through which a duly authorized moral tribunal works." God is God, and God's moral character is known to us through its presence in our own moral personality. "Just as we need not thank God for his existence, so we need not thank him for completing the moral cycle," he reasoned. In completing the moral cycle of justice, God acts out of a necessity that resides in the divine nature.[107]

This apologetic strategy was less novel and inspiring than Carnell anticipated. Though he claimed to have left behind his earlier preoccupation with rationalistic proof making, *Christian Commitment* was crammed with metaphysical arguments about the necessity of God's existence and moral character. Though his focus on moral experience represented a new apologetic approach for Carnell, this strategy had an ample history in Christian theology. Carnell made little contact with it, undoubtedly because so much of it was liberal Protestant. But a related yet deeper problem was exposed in the book's discussion of salvation. In Carnell's hands, the "third method" apologetic broke down as soon as his discussion turned to specifically Christian themes. With no warning and little explanation, he noted that he could not describe the nature or effects of Christ's saving death without making "a radical shift in method." The Christian doctrine of salvation through Christ cannot be explicated appropriately from the field of moral and spiritual experience, he tersely assured. Claims of this kind belong exclusively to the dogmatic propositional language of orthodoxy.[108]

The example of liberal theology from Schleiermacher on undoubtedly deterred Carnell from explicating the specific claims of Christian faith from a third-method perspective. It was one thing for him to analogize his own moral experience to the character of a divine moral guarantor; it was another matter to explain the meaning of Christ's redemption through the prism of his moral experience. Liberal theology specialized in this kind of anthropocentric reversal, but Carnell was not prepared to claim that he could carry it out in a way that met orthodox tests for right belief. Though he wrote that his switch to received dogma was to be understood as a "literary convention," the reason for it was surely deeper. At the crucial turn in his argument, the only truth came from above: The doctrine of forensic justification is a datum derived from revelation, not from everyday experience.

Carnell feared that third-method Christologies invariably turned Christ into a moral exemplar (as in liberal Christianity) or a projection of religious desire (as in Pietism and revivalism). He thus claimed to offer the new apologetic that evangelicalism needed, while allowing that it could deal only with secondary issues. He joined a sprawling patchwork of philosophical arguments and claims from experience to a dogmatic exposition of gospel teaching that made no attempt to work out the relation between these modes of discourse. And while Carnell repeatedly asserted that one of the two chief duties of the Christian apologist is to demonstrate that Christianity is consistent "with the broad facts of history and nature," in his closing pages he confessed that the book made no such demonstration.[109]

Christian Commitment thus arrested Carnell's upward trajectory and raised questions among some conservatives about his orthodoxy. His attempts to realign the field of theology ended with the silence that greeted the book's publication. His disappointment over its failure to attract attention coincided with the last two years of his presidency, when he was forced to grow accustomed to charges from fundamentalist leaders that Fuller Seminary was accommodating modernism and neoorthodoxy in its quest for respectability. Carnell endured a steady barrage of these charges from fundamentalists outside and within the institution. Smith and Woodbridge repeatedly complained that he was too eager to gain respect from modernists and too polemical in his attacks on fundamentalism. Carnell's contribution to the *Handbook of Christian Theology* offered a case in point; he defined fundamentalism as "an extreme right element in Protestant orthodoxy" and, with more than a hint of ridicule, criticized its provincialism, separatism, and anti-intellectualism.[110]

Though Fuller Seminary expanded and matured as an institution under his leadership, Carnell never grew comfortable with the social or administrative demands of his position; nor did he ever really understand the financial maneuverings that kept the institution afloat after some of Charles Fuller's oil investments went bad. The strains of managing the seminary were debilitating, and in 1957 he tried to resign from the presidency. Ockenga talked him out of resigning, not realizing that Carnell was addicted to barbiturates and heading toward an emotional breakdown. On doctor's orders, Carnell tried to cut back on both stress and sleeping pills but was overwhelmed by the demands of his position. Finally, he cabled Ockenga in April 1959 that "the present financial war of nerves is more than I can suffer" and that his health was in danger of being ruined permanently. He resigned from the presidency and took an eight-month sabbatical to recuperate.[111]

But Carnell never recovered. In 1960 he suffered a severe emotional breakdown and began psychiatric treatment for depression. The next year he was hospitalized for depression and subjected to electroconvulsive therapy. Over the next six years, he received perhaps forty more shock treatments, underwent intensive neo-Freudian psychotherapy, and suffered from severe dependence on barbiturates, all the while managing to teach full-time at Fuller. He repeatedly assured Ockenga and others at the seminary that none of this was their fault. "My anxieties were brought to a head by the fears which I faced in the presidency, of course, but I want you to know that I am fully aware that the root of my anxieties goes back to childhood," he told Ockenga, with the assurance of someone who has done a lot of therapy. "I am a minister's son who was raised in a highly legalistic and emotionally erratic atmosphere. The scars of these early childhood experiences remain with me."[112] He died in 1967 from an overdose of barbiturates; the coroner ruled his death "undetermined whether accidental or suicidal."

REPRESENTING THE
NEW EVANGELICALISM

Carnell gave up his dream of publishing "world-shattering" literature in the last years of his life. Under the pressure and confusion of what he described as a recurring "black cloud" of depression, he struggled simply to teach effectively in a new field, theological ethics.[113] Ironically, it was during this period that he found much of the audience that he had craved in his early career. The success of the new evangelicalism as a socioreligious movement brought notice to Carnell, who was its leading intellectual voice. During Carnell's presidency at Fuller, Billy Graham became a member of the seminary's board of trustees and a popular symbol of the existence of a new evangelicalism. Graham and Charles Fuller, the two leading evangelists of the current and passing generations, joined together to bring a critical mass of the fundamentalist movement into the mainstream of American life. As evangelicalism acquired an increasingly respectable reputation in the dominant culture through Graham's ministry and the establishment of new evangelical institutions, Carnell gained increasing attention as a kind of unofficial academic spokesman for the movement. He wrote several articles for the *Christian Century,* participated in an ecumenical group dialogue with Karl Barth at the University of Chicago, and wrote a volume on evangelicalism for a widely noted Westminster Press series on major theological perspectives. These ventures into the religious mainstream considerably heightened Carnell's renown, if not his influence, in American theology—and continued his controversy among evangelicals.

The Case for Orthodox Theology (1959) gave particular offense. As the most prominent evangelical thinker of his generation, Carnell defended the evangelical perspective in a three-volume series that also included William Hordern's case for neoorthodoxy and Harold DeWolf's for theological liberalism. (DeWolf was one of Carnell's former teachers at Boston University.) Both of these respected theologians offered clearly written and compelling defenses of their theological positions.[114] To be linked with these figures as the spokesman of a major theological tradition was an honor for Carnell, which he gratefully accepted. Neither of his fellow theologians had to cope with the demands of a seminary presidency or the misery of Carnell's inner turmoil, however, nor were they subjected to the kind of pressure that he felt to make a good showing. Carnell made it clear that he did not wish to be held to the term *evangelicalism* or even *neoevangelicalism*. His position was that of Reformed orthodoxy. He also turned down the opportunity to know who would be writing the other volumes. It was enough to know that he would be judged harshly by many evangelicals and fundamentalists if he failed to make the best possible case for their position in this showcase forum.

Carnell begged for mercy on the first page. He confessed that his case for orthodoxy made a "heavy draft" on the Reformed tradition that nearly amounted to plagiarism, explaining that Reformed orthodoxy was the only tradition that he knew well enough to speak for. He hoped this limitation would "not seriously depress the value of my work," but even his prose style was depressed. Carnell no longer counted on his ability to dazzle readers with his intellectual energy or brilliance. "A poor showing at this point does not imply a deficiency in classical orthodoxy," he cautioned. "It implies only that I am a poor apologist."[115]

The challenge was daunting, perhaps impossible. Carnell felt pressured to make the strongest possible case for the evangelical cause, but he was deeply alienated from much of American evangelicalism. Though his doctrinal position was still fundamentalist in most respects, he believed that most American fundamentalism was legalistic, anti-intellectual, and prone to mean-spiritedness. For Carnell, it was terribly important that no reader mistake him for the wrong kind of fundamentalist. He therefore reserved his harshest criticism for the fundamentalist sector of his own group, while ostensibly seeking to persuade nonevangelical readers to convert to conservative Christianity. *The Case for Orthodox Theology* reaffirmed Carnell's core convictions about the inerrancy of scripture and the interrelation of faith and reason, but this time he emphasized various difficulties that he found in holding fast to these beliefs.

He made it clear that his wing of the Reformed tradition was the scholastic-rationalist wing. Carnell allowed that there were many otherwise good Calvinists (such as Abraham Kuyper) who drove a deep wedge between faith and knowledge, but he countered that no claim to Christian belief could be intellectually credible that did not submit to outside tests of rationality.[116] If Christian claims are to be taken seriously, he insisted, they must be grounded in the sufficiency of evidence, just like any other serious truth claim. Aristotle taught that the mark of an educated person is the achievement of the capacity to judge the variable degree of verification that should be expected in different fields of inquiry. If it is true that theology (unlike mathematics) cannot be expected to achieve sufficiency at the level of demonstration, Carnell maintained, theology must at least be no different from history or philosophy in being required to submit to ordinary rules of evidence. Any theology that makes a special exemption for faith makes faith invulnerable by making it meaningless.[117]

His discussion of "science versus Scripture" leaned heavily on the distinction between ultimate and proximate causes. Carnell noted that scripture speaks of ultimate causes, as when it says that God rained "fire and brimstone" on Sodom and Gomorrah; moreover, it uses optical language in its descriptions of nature, as in its references to the rising and setting of the sun. These are not scientific statements, he allowed; scripture does not present scientific explanations of nature but rather employs appearance-language in the manner of an untrained observer. Its judgments are therefore true (God did destroy Sodom and Gomorrah), but not as science. Moreover, the notion that science has "disproved" the possibility of miracles is ridiculous, he asserted. The question of miracle occurrence is always a matter of history, not science, for the limits of possibility in nature are revealed only through whatever actually happens in history.

He reasoned that biblical teaching is not incompatible with evolutionary theory as long as the biblical doctrine of divine creation and inbreathing is upheld. Since the biblical account of creation is not a form of scientific explanation, Carnell maintained, it is wrong to set the biblical description of the process of creation against the scientific description. For this reason, it is wrong for orthodox Christians to maintain that evolution cannot be true, even though evolutionists have not yet proved their case. The biblical account implies that God made the world through an act of immediate creation, but it also implies that the world came into being through divine action over the course of six literal days. "Since orthodoxy has given up the literal-day theory out of respect for geology, it would certainly forfeit no principle if it gave up the immediate-creation theory out of respect for paleontology," he observed. The two cases are parallel, and no biblical principle is at stake in either case. Scripture requires only that evolution be viewed as a process of divine action, and that humanity be viewed as specially ensouled through an act of divine inbreathing.[118]

Carnell thus assured that evangelical orthodoxy is capable of accommodating most of the challenges that science appears to pose for it. Orthodoxy is committed to the worldview of sacred scripture, he affirmed, but this outlook is more open to reinterpretation than its critics and even many of its proponents often assume. Orthodoxy does not claim to know how God ensouled the human race or to what extent the genealogies of scripture compress the actual history of humanity. It does not claim to understand why there is no geological evidence for a universal flood. These were problems for Christian apologetics, but orthodoxy faced worse problems elsewhere. The real minefield was biblical criticism. Carnell dismissed most higher criticism of scripture as illegitimate and destructive, but he also recognized that in modern academia, biblical criticism, far more than science, was damaging the credibility of evangelicalism. In seeking to explain the basis on which he gave short shrift to modern biblical scholarship but also struggled to cope with problems that are readily apparent in the biblical text, Carnell sought a middle ground, as on other issues, between Orr and Warfield.

Orr taught that biblical criticism is legitimate as long as it does not replace a clear biblical affirmation with a contrary claim. As long as no clear biblical assertion is contradicted, he explained, orthodoxy does not desire "to tie up honest inquiry on any question of author, origin, date, or mode of composition of the

Biblical books."[119] Warfield, however, denied that higher-critical methods could ever be legitimately applied to the Bible. He insisted that higher criticism was inherently unacceptable as applied to scripture, because it presumed to correct the divine mind on the basis of human reason.[120] Carnell suggested that a middle ground between these positions needed to be worked out by contemporary evangelicals. "Orthodoxy can repudiate destructive higher criticism and still claim to be honest before the facts," he asserted without elaboration.[121]

He was far afield in this area. Carnell had little training in form criticism or other historical-critical techniques. He was therefore in a poor position to demonstrate how evangelicalism could cope with developments in biblical scholarship. He quickly shifted the discussion to more familiar ground, arguing that the kind of biblical criticism with which evangelicals needed to struggle had nothing to do with modern form or redaction criticism. The crucial problems for evangelicalism fell under the general category of biblical criticism, he explained, but one need not be acquainted with higher-critical techniques to find them. Instead, the key problems are plainly evident in the text of scripture. The church fathers and Reformers knew most of them very well. Christian orthodoxy teaches that scripture is inerrant on account of its divine inspiration, Carnell observed, but the Bible is filled with "all sorts of troublesome passages," many of which cannot be attributed to scribal error.

He recalled that Warfield's debate with Henry Preserved Smith cast a spotlight on several key examples. Like most debates of its time over the credibility of inerrancy doctrine, this exchange took place within a larger debate over what it means to say that scripture is divinely inspired. In seeking to dissuade a rising fundamentalist movement from committing itself to strict inerrancy, Smith had drawn attention to the speeches of Eliphaz in the book of Job and to various contradictions between parallel accounts in 1 and 2 Samuel, 1 and 2 Kings, and 1 and 2 Chronicles. Carnell's treatment of the same issue drew on this debate, which, in his estimation, the past half century of evangelical scholarship had not advanced.

Smith had noted that some of the speeches in Job teach nonbiblical doctrine and that numerous differences in detail between parallel accounts in 2 Samuel and 1 Chronicles or between 1 Kings and 2 Chronicles are readily apparent. His point was not that these are the most troublesome passages in scripture but that both sets of texts (Job and the historical books) presented undeniable problems for the claim that divine inspiration means "God says." Following Smith's example, Carnell used the same examples to drive a wedge into the old Princeton doctrine of inspiration. For Warfield and the Hodges, the biblical expression "it is written" always meant "God says." Warfield defined inspiration as "that extraordinary, supernatural influence (or, passively, the result of it) exerted by the Holy Ghost on the writers of our Sacred Books, by which their words were rendered also the words of God, and, therefore, perfectly infallible."[122] But what, Carnell asked, is "infallible" about the speeches in Job, some of which are contrary to biblical teaching? And how do we account for the nearly habitual tendency of the Chronicler to inflate or otherwise adjust earlier figures pertaining to the number of David's horsemen and chariots, the number of chariots he destroyed, the number of Solomon's horse stalls, and so on?

Carnell noted that the pattern of differences between Chronicles and Samuel or Kings is too uniform to make a credible appeal to repeated scribal error. As Smith had explained, the Chronicler lived several centuries after the time of David, and he clearly held an exaggerated idea of what his country's wealth and power must have been during its days of glory. He therefore revised earlier accounts to satisfy his own sense of realism. Moreover, with regard to the book of Job, Smith had maintained that "biblical inspiration" could not mean that false doctrine presented in scripture is inspired. In his judgment, the doctrine of inspiration merely demanded that the writer of Job "was inspired to give a true account, first of what the men said, and then of what God said."[123]

Carnell judged that Smith's solution was a shrewd and perfectly orthodox response to problems of this kind. The problem with Smith's alternative, however, was that it saddled orthodoxy "with a very troublesome expedient," for the upshot of Smith's conception of biblical inspiration was that it ensured no more than an infallible account of error. Even the phrase "it is written" became no protection against error on Smith's approach, for the phrase occurs in one of the speeches of Eliphaz. Faced with inductive problems of this kind, Smith had accommodated his doctrine of biblical inspiration to the problems. That is, he took the very expedient that Warfield disallowed. Warfield did not deny that scripture contains numerous inductive problems; what he categorically denied was that Christians have any right to accommodate the doctrine of biblical inspiration to its problems. The crucial issue for Christian theology is always "the perennial old question, whether the basis of our doctrine is to be what the Bible teaches, or what men teach," he insisted.[124] This presuppositional either-or must be settled before the reader sets out to consider any inductive problems that scripture may present. It followed for Warfield that Smith's failure to put himself on the right side of the either-or presupposition placed him outside genuine Christianity. He explained that Smith had "more confidence in his own historical judgments than in Scriptural statements, and prefers to harmonize the Scriptural statements with his opinions."[125] By definition, Warfield countered, Christian orthodoxy trusts in the infallibility of scriptural statements rather than in the infallibility of historical criticism.

Carnell still felt the lure of this apologetic strategy. For old Princeton, the overriding issue was the question of the norm by which doctrine is established, not any inductive problems that the norm may appear to contain. This was Carnell's tradition. Most of his work elaborated on its claims. He had no desire to venture far from it. But he could not ignore the fact that Warfield and the Hodges gave woefully inadequate attention to inductive problems. They responded to questions about troublesome passages by restating the primacy of the norm in a louder voice. Carnell countered that this would not do for an orthodoxy that prized its credibility: "If orthodoxy is to command the respect of scholarship, it must become more artistic and imaginative when it relates the doctrine of inspiration to wider claims of Scripture."[126]

Was there such a thing as an evangelical orthodoxy that upheld a high view of inspiration and revelation but also took seriously the various problems that any attentive reading of scripture discloses? Carnell pointed to James Orr as an exemplar of such an orthodoxy. For Orr and his "English school" evangelical followers, he noted, biblical inspiration was linked not with propositional truth but with power to communicate life in Christ. Inspiration was conceived not as the answer to an epistemological question but as the dynamic work of bringing people to saving faith in Christ. In the charter text of biblical inspiration, Paul says that God's inspiration of scripture confers on it the property of being able "to make wise unto salvation through faith which is in Christ Jesus" (2 Tim. 3:15, RSV). Carnell observed that this dynamic work is communicated in scripture through the forms of poetry, history, and propositional revelation. Each form is mediated differently: Poetry is mediated by religious experience, history is mediated by documentary evidence, and doctrinal writings are mediated by direct revelation. Carnell reasoned that this is why doctrinal writings such as Romans and Galatians are more important than the rest of scripture. Because scripture is filled with various kinds of language, he explained, some interpretive key to the whole of scripture must be identified. This is the key that Paul's letters to the Romans and Galatians provide in teaching the doctrine of justification by faith. The doctrinal passages of Romans and Galatians are uniquely important because they teach the saving message of scripture in language that is explicitly didactic, systematic, and direct. However, Carnell cautioned, orthodoxy must never fail to emphasize that the Bible contains only one theology. God's Word is a singular unity in a pluralism of forms: "While the *whole* Bible is inspired, inspiration is pluralistic in substance; and it is pluralistic because in the single work of drawing men to Christ, various kinds of evidence are used. Poetry charms, history informs, and doctrine binds."[127]

This is how Orr and his tradition of evangelicalism looked at scripture, though not always with Carnell's precise hermeneutical rules. To old Princeton, "it is written" always meant that scripture must possess the same precise facticity for us that it possessed for Jesus. It meant that the Bible must be "incapable of being broken" in all matters "of doctrinal truth, of practical duty, of historical fact and of verbal form."[128] But to Orr and the English school, this deductionist form of intellectualism missed the point and beauty of God's multiform Word. Inspired scripture is not fundamentally about propositional truth, Orr insisted, but about the power of Christ to save sinners.[129] Carnell observed that because he was armed with a richer understanding of biblical inspiration, Orr was not threatened by the apparent errors and contradictions that scripture contains. He did not sweep them under the rug of tradition or authority.

Orr accepted Matthew Henry's explanation that the Chronicler was seeking to acquaint the Hebrew captives, who were returning from the Babylonian exile, with their heritage. This purpose was accomplished by drawing on the books of the Kings of Israel and Judah and similar sources. The Holy Spirit used these documents as they were, without correcting their revised accounts or figures. Orr remarked that inspiration has nothing to do with correcting bad information, despite the presumptions of those who read inerrancy into inspiration: "The records of the Bible have only to be studied as they lie before us to show that this is an entire mistake." One of the forms that biblical revelation takes is history, he noted, and in historical matters "it is evident that inspiration is dependent for its knowledge of

facts on the ordinary channels of information—on older documents, on oral tradition, on public registers, on genealogical lists, etc."[130] Scripture mentions many of
these sources, including the book of Samuel the Seer, the book of Nathan the
Prophet, and the book of the Chronicles of the Kings of Israel. Orr observed that
inspiration clearly did not lift the biblical writers above the "lacunae, or blots, or
misreadings of names, or errors of transcription" that these sources contained.[131]
Since the purpose of inspiration is to communicate the reality of Christ's saving
death and resurrection, he reasoned, this purpose is fulfilled throughout scripture
whether or not the biblical writers knew enough to correct their sources.

Carnell added that scripture raises similar questions whenever it expresses human feelings or confessions. To what extent should the imprecatory psalms be
taken as expressions of the divine mind? When Jeremiah says, "Cursed be the day
on which I was born" (Jer. 20:14), how should this be understood as a sentiment
inspired by God? This is what orthodoxy should be talking about, Carnell asserted;
but the descendants of Warfield and Orr had become too fearful and defensive
even to raise the right questions. "The fountain of new ideas has apparently run
dry, for what was once a live issue in the church has now ossified into a theological tradition," he lamented. Orthodoxy was reduced to a set of loyalty tests, fixed
to frozen positions. "As a result a heavy pall of fear hangs over the academic community," he remarked with knowing regret. "When a gifted professor tries to in-
teract with the critical difficulties in the text, he is charged with disaffection, if not
outright heresy. Orthodoxy forgets one important verdict of history: namely, that
when truth is presented in a poor light, tomorrow's leaders may embrace error on
the single reason that it is more persuasively defended."[132]

Carnell seemed to want a new debate, if not a fresh defense of Orr's alternative. He believed that Protestant orthodoxy had come to a dead end. He clearly believed that Princeton-style inerrancy doctrine was indefensible on the inductive
level. His argument seemed to call for an orthodox rethinking of inspiration that
updated the Scottish Reformed orthodoxy of Orr and James Denney. He praised
Orr for capturing the dynamic character of inspiration while holding fast to a high
view of biblical revelation. He claimed to identify with Orr's willingness to address at least certain kinds of inductive problems in scripture. But at the crucial
turn in his case for evangelical orthodoxy, Carnell stepped back from the force of
his argument. He could not make a clean break from inerrancy fundamentalism.
He sought instead to claim a rhetorical middle ground between Warfield and Orr.

If it is evident that scripture does contain errors, Carnell reasoned, this does
not necessarily refute the doctrine of inerrancy, even if one makes little resort to
the autograph–scribal error argument. It might simply mean that inerrancy
should be defined in a way that shifts the conception of its referent. "Orthodoxy
works itself into excessive difficulties by artlessly defining the relation between
assertion and the thing signified," he observed. In what way does poetry communicate divine truth? Is scripturally recorded religious experience normative
for Christians living in a later time and culture? Moreover, what is the standard
for error in biblical history to which the doctrine of inerrancy is obliged to answer?

Carnell left the first question hanging and made a brief case for partial relativism on the second question. To him, the crucial question was the third one. He embraced Henry Preserved Smith's answer to it, but in the name of upholding biblical inerrancy. To call biblical history inerrant is not necessarily to claim that every statement in the biblical text is true, he reasoned. In the case of some biblical accounts, inerrancy does not have to refer to anything more than the assurance of an infallible account of whatever was said or recorded. That is, Carnell opted for the "very troubling expedient" of claiming that inspiration ensures at least an infallible account of error. Just as the inspired author of Job gave infallible accounts of Eliphaz's speeches, he explained, so the inspired writers of the historical books gave infallible accounts of whatever they found in the public registers and genealogical lists. "At first blush this may seem like a very desperate expedient, but it actually implies no more than a strained use of procedures already at work in orthodoxy," he remarked. "If Hodge and Warfield had honored this as a possibility, they might have avoided their lofty disregard for the inductive difficulties. And if Orr had done likewise, he might have avoided his perilous admission of historical errors in Scripture."[133]

Evangelicalism could not abide Orr's rejection of inerrancy doctrine, even if it followed his argument up to that point. Carnell thus resolved to call the Bible's historical errors something else. He undoubtedly feared that he would be excommunicated from the evangelical movement if he gave up the inerrancy claim altogether. As it was, he was pilloried by many evangelicals for devoting so much of his case for evangelicalism to its problems. Carnell backed away from the force of his argument on the lodestar fundamentalist issue, but his critique of the movement's history and character virtually invited fundamentalist outrage.

This critique was encapsulated in his charge that "fundamentalism is orthodoxy gone cultic." Carnell observed that fundamentalist evangelicalism went awry by failing to root itself in the creeds and history of the early church and sealed its fate by cutting itself off from past traditions of Christian orthodoxy. Because fundamentalist evangelicalism never managed to develop into a serious form of orthodoxy, it never acquired any protection from degenerating into cultism. Fundamentalism became a mere "mentality" dominated by ideological thinking, which he characterized as "rigid, intolerant, and doctrinaire." Carnell noted that the ideological mentality sees principles everywhere, "and all principles come in clear tones of black and white; it exempts itself from the limits that original sin places on history; it wages holy wars without acknowledging the elements of pride and personal interest that prompt the call to battle; it creates new evils while trying to correct old ones."[134]

Fundamentalist dispensationalism made the details of eschatology into a fundamental test of Christian fellowship, for example, but Carnell observed that this had nothing to do with Christian orthodoxy. It was, rather, a significant example of "straight-line cultism." He reported from close acquaintance that to the fundamentalist ideologue, it was second nature to banish any serious consideration of internal problems, since to admit a problem implies a lack of faith, "and a lack of faith is sin." Carnell's chief example of the distorted fundamentalist mind-set was more surprising, however, and offended not only those fundamentalists who were not his friends but also many of his closest allies. The fundamentalist mentality sometimes shows up in surprising places, he cautioned, "and there is no better illustration of this than the inimitable New Testament scholar, J. Gresham Machen."[135]

Carnell granted that on most counts Machen was not a typical fundamentalist but argued that this fact highlighted his point. Machen disliked fundamentalism, yet he came to epitomize its ideological mentality, Carnell observed, "for he took an absolute stand on a relative issue, and the wrong issue at that." By setting up his own mission board and then defying the church's order to abolish it, Machen showed contempt for the courts of the Northern Presbyterian church. The church had no choice but to expel him, Carnell judged. Presbyterianism is a federal system; it cannot succeed without vesting supreme judicial power in a highest court. Machen claimed to be a Presbyterian, but his ideological preoccupation with the evils of modernism made him oblivious to the seeds of anarchy and destruction that his own group had sown. Because he knew he was right, Carnell explained, Machen took no moral responsibility for the destruction that he caused: "Ideological thinking prevented Machen from seeing that the issue under trial was *the nature of the church,* not the doctrinal incompatibility of orthodoxy and modernism."

In response to Machen's claim that the presence of modernists within the church's leadership made the Presbyterian Church apostate, Carnell replied that this was cultist thinking, not Reformed ecclesiology. Because Machen embraced Reformed theology but not the Reformed doctrine of the church, he therefore threatened the church with anarchy and reproduced the sectarian cultism of the fundamentalist movement at its worst, all in the name of Christian orthodoxy. He thought he was founding what he called "a true Presbyterian church," but within weeks of the schism, many of his separatist brethren turned on him. "Since Machen had shaken off the sins of modernists, but not the sins of those who were proud they were not modernists, the separatists fondly imagined themselves more perfectly delivered from heresy than the facts justified," Carnell explained. "This illusion spawned fresh resources of pride and pretense. The criteria of Christian fellowship gradually became more exacting than Scripture, and before long Machen himself was placed under suspicion."[136]

To Carnell, this was the key to the fundamentalist mistake. In the *Christian Century,* he described the fundamentalist movement as a form of "cunning pharisaism." Fundamentalism began as an often-justified revolt against modernist theology, he explained, but it soon degenerated into a movement that confused right doctrine with virtue. It replaced the biblical test of Christian discipleship, which is works done in love, with assent to a list of doctrinal fundamentals. This fundamental distortion of orthodoxy was epitomized by the Machenites, who enlisted the doctrine of the church in their quest for doctrinal purity and convinced themselves that only they were pure enough to form the body of Christ.[137] Carnell countered that the church's nature must never be measured by the doctrinal maturity of its membership. Sinners are justified by faith and repentance, not by doctrine. Moreover, doctrinal immaturity is remedied by sanctification, not by justification.

By making justification dependent on correct doctrine, he charged, fundamentalism recapitulated the Catholic heresy of works righteousness. Carnell allowed that these were elementary New Testament themes, "but to one reared in the tyrannical legalism of fundamentalism, the recovery of a genuine theology of grace is no insignificant feat." As a child of fundamentalist cultism, he disclosed, he was intimately familiar with the "serious illness" from which it suffered, since he was presently struggling to rid himself of this affliction. He assured liberal readers of the *Christian Century* that virtually all educated evangelicals shared his diagnosis: "I know of no enlightened conservative who wants to perpetuate the ethos of fundamentalism."[138]

Fundamentalist leaders were predictably outraged by Carnell's attacks on their history and theology. Woodbridge, Jack Wyrtzen, John R. Rice, and others made blistering counterattacks on Carnell's character and faith, often drawing Fuller Seminary into the line of fire. Rice's nationally distributed newspaper *Sword of the Lord* bitterly accused Carnell of being "very anxious to please modernists" and demanded to know what Fuller Seminary planned to do about him. "I do not believe that out-and-out Bible believers can safely send students to Fuller Seminary or send any money to support the seminary as long as Dr. Carnell and men like him are in places of authority and responsibility in the school, and as long as they openly repudiate the great principles and doctrines and standards dear to Bible believers," Rice declared.[139] Carnell had already measured the cost of alienating out-and-out fundamentalists such as Rice, however. He declared that he was prepared to be censured by "those who are too sure of their own perfection." Of deeper concern to him and his closer colleagues was the fact that his critical blasts against fundamentalism also offended many conservative evangelicals. Ockenga chided him for forgetting that "our real enemy is the modernist." He reported that many evangelical leaders—"people who are our friends"—were outraged by Carnell's recent writings. At a recent Inter-Varsity Christian Fellowship convention in Paris, he disclosed, virtually everyone had agreed "that you are lost to the evangelical cause."[140]

Fuller Seminary could ill afford to antagonize conservative evangelical groups such as Inter-Varsity, Young Life, and Campus Crusade for Christ. To all evangelicals who expressed concern about the seminary's apparent direction, Carnell replied that evangelical orthodoxy needed to become a genuine third-way alternative to fundamentalism and theological liberalism. The evangelical movement that is needed will not be bound by its recent history, he argued; it must rather identify with the tradition of classical Protestant orthodoxy that precedes and transcends the fight over modernism. "The struggle between fundamentalism and modernism may have been unavoidable, but this is no reason why elements in the modern church should be locked in prejudice."[141]

With ample warrant, Carnell claimed to carry forward the original idea and implications of Fuller Seminary neoevangelicalism. As an intellectual and academic leader, he worked diligently to win respect for Fuller Seminary in the American theological establishment, at the same time struggling to hold on to the seminary's patchwork of fundamentalist-leaning constituencies. Despite his considerable personal problems, which cut his life short, he believed that his writings and academic career exemplified the kind of balanced, scholarly, and faithful witness to the gospel that the cause of Protestant orthodoxy required.

THE BATTLE
FOR FULLER SEMINARY

But it was Carnell's fate to become the chief symbol of the contradictions in Fuller Seminary evangelicalism. He redefined inerrancy to accommodate the existence of biblical errors while insisting on a priori grounds that scripture contains no historical errors. Having aligned himself with the younger generation of post-fundamentalist faculty at Fuller Seminary, he was in a poor position after he resigned the presidency to oppose their demands for further change. *The Case for Orthodox Theology* and his articles for the *Christian Century* exposed the seminary to a barrage of damaging criticism that made even many of its friends suspicious about the seminary's direction. The fact that Carnell had just resigned his presidency when the book came out heightened the controversy over the seminary's future. Was Fuller Seminary still committed to real biblical inerrancy? Would Carnell be allowed to keep his teaching position? Would he be replaced as president by a strong proponent of inerrancy?

These questions were fielded by three institutional caretakers who definitely believed in strict inerrancy. Ockenga reassumed his role as interim president after Carnell resigned; Lindsell managed the institution's day-to-day affairs as a newly appointed vice president; and Archer served as acting dean of the faculty while Dan Fuller completed his doctorate in Basel. Together, the three launched an aggressive public relations campaign that assured Fuller constituents that the seminary was still impeccably orthodox. All the seminary's publicity and correspondence emphasized that all faculty members and trustees signed the statement of faith every year. More than thirty thousand copies of the statement of faith were distributed between 1960 and 1962. For his part, Carnell repeatedly assured inquirers that having written this confessional statement in the first place, he could still sign it in good conscience. He was still committed to all the fundamentals, including the Fuller confession that the biblical autographs were "free from all error in the whole and in the part."[142]

He thus ended up on the conservative side of the faction fight that changed Fuller Seminary in the aftermath of his resignation. His closing years were filled with irony, for at the critical turn in the seminary's history, Carnell was the figure most responsible for making it the object of controversy. His attacks on fundamentalism and his participation in the Barth symposium at the University of Chicago made many evangelicals wary that Fuller was "going neoorthodox." During his presidency, he had supported the progressive faction on the faculty, which included Jewett, Ladd, Dan Fuller, and William LaSor. Most of these colleagues thought of him as belonging to their side. He clearly respected them more than he respected the Smith-Lindsell group.

But Carnell belonged to neither side. He embodied the contradictions that fueled the seminary's rival factions. Like his Fuller colleague Everett Harrison, he believed that the seminary's combination of doctrinal fundamentalism and intellectual ambition was sustainable. Though he favored the progressive group on most issues, on the crucial issue he was still a fundamentalist. As president he had mediated the differences between a divided faculty, but when his resignation opened up the question of the seminary's creedal future and the progressive group made it clear that they opposed the existing creedal commitment to inerrancy, Carnell sided with the fundamentalists. With all its problems, biblical inerrancy was still nonnegotiable.

The borders of permissible dissent had been tested for several years. The conservatives allowed that discrepant accounts in the biblical narratives could be recognized as discrepancies; what was not permitted was the judgment that apparent contradictions pointed to error. Smith, Lindsell, and Archer all specialized in the old Princeton art of harmonizing discrepant accounts. While Archer was a more accomplished scholar than either Smith or Lindsell, in the old-school scholastic style, his four-hour senior course on Old Testament apologetics featured one-by-one answers to questions about specific passages raised by textual and higher criticism. Since God would never inspire any kind of error, he taught, Christian scholarship is obliged to find rational explanations for all the Bible's apparent contradictions, historical errors, and the like.[143]

Some of Archer's colleagues doubted this was the best way to defend the doctrine of inerrancy. In 1958, in a statement that prefigured the seminary's shifting position, Harrison gently questioned the evangelical obligation to defend the precise facticity of scripture. Like Carnell, Harrison sought to find an acceptable middle ground between Warfield and Orr, but he took a significantly more open-ended tack in this pursuit than Carnell's rationalism could allow. Harrison argued that evangelicals were bringing overloaded assumptions to the biblical text about the meaning of the attribution of inerrancy. He affirmed that the Bible teaches its own inspiration and that the notion of biblical inerrancy is "a natural corollary of full inspiration." The problem is that scripture does not confirm any of the standard evangelical assumptions about the meaning of inerrancy; the Bible does not say that its truth confers literal inerrancy on its statements pertaining to historical details, geography, and the like, he observed. The assumption that inerrancy applies to such matters is brought to the text by evangelicals, rather than found within it. Harrison proposed that in their consideration of the implications of inerrancy, evangelical theologians needed to leave behind their customary preoccupation with noncontradiction and literal meaning. "We may have our own ideas as to how God should have inspired the Word, but it is more profitable to learn, if we can, how he has actually inspired it," he urged. Scripture is no less God's Word when it apparently violates the canons of logic or science or modern historiography.[144]

This position played a key role in opening up the seminary's discussion of inerrancy. Though Harrison's proposal smacked too much of Barthianism to assuage any of the conservatives, it soon provided the rationale on which certain Fuller professors, and for a brief time the seminary itself, claimed to adhere to inerrancy.

It allowed some faculty members to sign the statement of faith each year in tolerably good conscience. But Harrison's attempt to change the terms of the inerrancy debate did not prevent his institution from breaking apart over the issue. In 1960, at the height of the furor over *The Case for Orthodox Theology,* Ladd and Jewett argued at a faculty meeting that some discrepant accounts in scripture are impossible to reconcile with the doctrine of inerrancy. If two accounts of the same event give plainly contradictory information, they argued, at least one of them must be in error. To resort to harmonization in many cases only makes the problem worse. Ladd protested that it was not possible to produce good scholarship or maintain a healthy educational atmosphere when such elementary problems could not be addressed honestly. He worried aloud that he would be fired for speaking openly about the issue. He and Jewett pointedly refused, briefly, to re-sign the statement of faith for the seminary's Christmas publicity mailing.[145]

The conservatives quickly grasped that their position would be routed from the field if they did not immediately take steps to get rid of the backsliders. A fight for control of the seminary was on. Lindsell and Archer warned Ockenga that some faculty colleagues were signing the statement of faith in bad conscience. They urged him immediately to fire Ladd, Jewett, and anyone else who could not sign it in good conscience. Ockenga replied that, in effect, he had no stomach for such a purge, but he privately chastised the progressives and warned them that a crackdown might be necessary; meanwhile, he organized a massive public relations campaign to assure evangelicals that Fuller Seminary still adhered to inerrancy.

This was the battleground to which Dan Fuller returned in November 1962, after completing his doctorate with Barth. It took only one faculty and board meeting two days before his installment as dean of the faculty to set off the explosion that had been building at Fuller for several years. Jewett had been pressing the seminary to adopt a new statement of faith, along classical evangelical lines, that eliminated fundamentalist tests concerning inerrancy and eschatology. When Ockenga questioned whether the seminary actually needed a new creed, Fuller, the only person in the room with job security, told him frankly that the present creedal statement on biblical inerrancy was indefensible. "Dr. Ockenga, there are errors which cannot be explained by the original autographs," he declared. "It is simply not historically feasible to say that these errors would disappear if we had the autographs."[146]

His alternative was Orr's position, coupled with a selective appeal to inerrancy. "Inerrancy" makes sense only as a claim about the revelational teaching of scripture, Fuller urged. It refers only to those things that bring one to a saving relationship with Christ. With regard to incidental matters, pertaining to history or geography, for example, it is plainly evident that God accommodated himself to the imperfect standards of ancient times in speaking his Word to the world. The Bible contains numerous incidental errors, as any attentive reader must recognize, Fuller maintained. The crucial matter is not the existence of these errors but rather that they do not hinder God's revelational purpose in inspiring the biblical writers. Scripture is infallible in all that it affirms about matters of faith.[147]

This was the moment the conservatives had dreaded. For years they had fretted about Fuller's influence on his parents and his friendship with Jewett. They worried that he would return from his doctoral studies with Barth as a Barthian. In fact, Fuller's position turned out to be significantly different from Barth's. He rejected Barth's revelational fideism and insisted that theology must defend its claims about historical events on the basis of historical evidence. Moreover, in a more univocal sense than Barth, he apparently regarded the scriptural text as God's Word written. Nonetheless, the fact that he remained some kind of evangelical while rejecting traditional inerrancy doctrine made him a more threatening opponent than if he had returned home a Barthian. Ockenga replied with icy indignation, "Well, what are we going to do then? Dan Fuller thinks the Bible is just full of errors."[148] Lindsell, Archer, Geoffrey Bromiley, and others also weighed in against Fuller, sometimes with equal exaggeration. The most impassioned defense of Old School inerrancy doctrine, however, came from Carnell.

His opening statement was both assuring and withering. He scolded Fuller that he did not need to be lectured about biblical discrepancies. "My laundry list of difficulties that biblical Christianity has with empirical facts is longer than any other list in this room of 120 people, including yours, Dan Fuller," he announced. Carnell knew better than Fuller where to find the troublesome passages of scripture. He had agonized over them for many years. But the question of the truth of scripture cannot be settled on inductive grounds, he lectured. One does not work up to biblical truth by making judgments about apparent biblical problems. The only way to hear the truth of God's Word is to begin with the hypothesis that all of scripture is God's Word and therefore without error. To begin with this approach to scripture is to acquire some unresolved inductive problems, he conceded, but the payoff is that one enters the circle of God's inspired truth. Moreover, Carnell concluded, if we approach the Bible as God's inspired and therefore inerrant Word, we find ourselves in possession of a system that contains fewer problems of any kind, including inductive problems, than any alternative system.[149]

In the end, he appealed to the answers he had learned in Clark's philosophy classroom. Throughout this period of personal and institutional crisis, Carnell insisted, he had remained a faithful proponent of Clarkian-style conservatism, notwithstanding his personal falling-out with Clark. The previous April, Carnell had roused himself from a deep depression to take part in a public symposium with Barth at the University of Chicago Divinity School. There, he had asked Barth how he could regard scripture as the Word of God if scripture contains errors, but he had not pressed any objections to Barth's explanation that scripture is an inspired *witness* to revelation. In the audience, Clark had fumed at Carnell's failure to argue with Barth. The next morning at breakfast, Clark had informed Carnell that he could never forgive his derogatory remarks about Machen, and to various acquaintances elsewhere he criticized Carnell's performance at the Barth seminar. Instead of challenging Barth's inadequate doctrine of biblical authority, he complained, Carnell confessed his own doubts and tried to ingratiate himself with Barth and a liberal audience.[150] Carnell was wounded at being denounced by his teacher. He later explained that at the Barth seminar, he chose not to infringe on the designated time of other panelists, and that with regard to Machen, he obviously did not share Clark's opinion "that Saint Machen could do no wrong."[151] Elsewhere, he explained that he regarded Barth as a great proponent of the evangelical faith who was unfortunately, perhaps tragically, inconsistent in his appeal to the authority of God's inscripturated Word.[152]

But despite all his purported failures to defend the faith with sufficient rigor and self-confidence, his caveats about the law of love and the personal mode of knowledge, and his disappointment at being disowned by his teacher, Carnell remained an inerrancy rationalist to the end of his life. He repeatedly affirmed and defended his adherence to inerrancy on Clarkian presuppositionalist grounds. In the early 1960s, he taught the parts of Jewett's course on systematic theology that dealt with the doctrine of scripture, partly to protect Jewett from heresy hunters but also to make sure that Fuller students were given the best arguments for inerrancy. His willingness to play this role exemplified his later career at the seminary and in evangelicalism as a whole. Near the end of his life, he wrote in *Christianity Today* that theology must begin either with the Bible's view of itself or with some non-Christian presupposition. "We are free to reject the Bible's view of itself, of course, but if we do so we are demolishing the procedure by which we determine the substance of *any* Christian doctrine," he warned.[153] We cannot hear scripture as God's revealed Word if we do not work with the hypothesis that it is God's Word. At the time of his death, he was working on a book that defended the doctrine of inerrancy.

After Ockenga declined for the last time to assume full-time presidential duties at Fuller Seminary, Charles Fuller named David Hubbard to the post. Hubbard was a Fuller graduate from a dispensationalist background, who made impressive claims to his belief in biblical inerrancy; but the conservatives quickly perceived that his appointment marked their defeat. A few years earlier, Hubbard and Robert Laurin had cowritten a draft survey of the Old Testament that incorporated numerous historical-critical conclusions, including a late date for the book of Daniel and a characterization of Genesis 1 – 11 as nonhistorical. Though Hubbard later dissociated himself from the manuscript's historical-critical elements, the conservatives at Fuller Seminary correctly surmised that he was not on their side. Shortly after Hubbard assumed the presidency, he and Dan Fuller reorganized the curriculum and discreetly encouraged conservatives to look elsewhere for teaching opportunities.[154]

Having lost the battle for control of the seminary, Carnell's allies on the right swallowed their defeat and departed. Smith was the first to leave, taking a position at Trinity Evangelical Divinity School in Chicago, which fashioned itself as the new home of intellectual fundamentalism. Lindsell took an editorial position at *Christianity Today,* which Henry had cofounded several years earlier. After Hubbard and Fuller eliminated all topical courses in biblical studies, including Archer's course on Old Testament apologetics, Archer also moved to Trinity and protested that Fuller Seminary was abandoning the cause of biblical inerrancy. Debates over Hubbard's character and the tactics of the Jewett-Fuller group soon became a favorite indoor sport among evangelicals. For the old-style conservatives, Hubbard's assurance that he still believed in an infallible-teaching model of inerrancy merely added insult to injury. While making allowances for faculty who clearly disavowed inerrancy doctrine, the seminary remained officially committed to a minimalist understanding of inerrancy until 1970, when Hubbard told alumni that the term was too precise and mathematical "to describe appropriately the way in which God's infallible revelation has come to us in a Book." Fuller Seminary subsequently adopted a new statement of faith that described scripture as the divinely inspired Word of God, "the only infallible rule of faith and practice."[155]

By then Carnell was dead, and the seminary's identity was decidedly postfundamentalist. Having, as president, half-unwittingly paved the way to this transposition, Carnell spent his last years as a beloved but often pitied figure. Though he was only in his mid-forties, his ravaged health and his old-style theology made him seem quaint to many students. His prodigious memory was obliterated by the shock treatments and drugs; in class, he would often lapse into confused silence for two or three minutes before finding his train of thought. In the mid-1960s, he was invited to speak at Stanford University by Robert McAfee Brown, who later provided a chilling account of the event: "His speech was halting, with long pauses between words, and he was obviously under a very heavy tension and pressure. I think he was getting a very bad kind of pressure from his right-wing constituents during that period. One wanted to pull the words out of him, so great was the difficulty in articulation. What he said was good, but it was produced with tremendous effort. A student asked him some question that was particularly difficult to answer from an ultraconservative Biblical viewpoint, and he responded something like 'That's . . . one . . . of those . . . questions . . . I . . . have . . . in a folder . . . marked "Unsolved . . . Problems."' He was clear that there were problems, and he was not trying to duck them. But the price of his intellectual honesty clearly took a heavy toll."[156]

Carnell coped as best he could during his last years, while lamenting deeply that he could not fulfill his life's vocation. Though he maintained good relations with colleagues and achieved a degree of magnanimity that eluded him during his achievement-oriented early career, he felt keenly the loss to evangelical theology that his illness caused. The evangelical movement was growing and gaining respectability on many fronts: Fuller Seminary was flourishing, Billy Graham's evangelistic campaigns drew huge crowds, *Christianity Today* was a major success, and new evangelical institutions were being created. But no one was providing the kind of high-powered, attention-getting intellectual work that Carnell believed was crucial to evangelical success. The knowledge that he could not provide it cut him deeply. Over the years, he had often expressed to Henry and others his sense of a calling to make a major contribution to modern evangelical theology. Evangelicalism needed prestige desperately, he had said. The present generation needed its own Warfield or Hodge.[157] Though he respected Henry's achievement in making *Christianity Today* a highly successful magazine, Carnell clearly did not expect Henry to complete the major-scale apologetic project that he had assigned to himself. Henry was smart, energetic, and creative, but not a disciplined scholar—or so it seemed.

But it was Henry who defined and defended evangelical orthodoxy to a mass audience in the late 1950s and afterward. In the critical period of the movement's consolidation and takeoff, Henry and Bernard Ramm became the major intellectual leaders of American evangelicalism. Later, it was Henry who made the seminal apologetic case for propositional revelation and inerrancy that Carnell had expected to produce. Long after Fuller Seminary had given up on Old School inerrancy doctrine, and when even Ramm had adopted a form of neoorthodoxy, Henry provided intellectual leadership for an evangelical movement that was anxious not to lose its basis of religious authority. He directly addressed every divisive theological and social issue of his generation, while working to build lasting evangelical institutions. For many, he defined what it meant to be an evangelical. Carnell worried that there was no theology-reading evangelical public to support evangelical theology, but more than any other figure, Henry labored to create such a public. Whether his work defines what it means to be an evangelical or only one, somewhat outmoded form of evangelicalism is a critical question in this book.

The Evangelical Crossroads: Rethinking Infallibility

For a movement that has always claimed to be merely recovering a neglected orthodoxy, American evangelicalism has been remarkably preoccupied with the problem of finding an identity. In 1967, Carl Henry warned in *Evangelicals at the Brink of Crisis* that American evangelicalism was in danger of becoming "a wilderness cult in a secular society." Nine years later, while *Newsweek* proclaimed the "Year of the Evangelical" and much of the mass media gave unprecedented attention to the growth and prospects of a burgeoning evangelical movement, Henry delivered a more troubled assessment titled *Evangelicals in Search of Identity*. "It is time that the evangelical movement sees itself for what it is: a lion on the loose that no one today seriously fears," he declared.[1]

Henry had not changed. He still believed that only a great revival of Protestant orthodoxy could prevent Western civilization from rotting to death. He still dreamed grand visions of a re-Christianized America. In the 1940s and 1950s, Henry and a handful of others had struggled to create the kind of seminary that exemplified and sustained this vision. In the 1950s and 1960s, he had labored with another handful of evangelicals to create a mass-circulation magazine that gave voice to evangelical hopes for a spiritually regenerated America. In the 1970s, having built *Christianity Today* into the chief organ of a growing evangelical movement, he gave his counsel and encouragement to politicized currents within the movement. Henry lauded the rise of an ascendant Christian Right and sought to influence the character of its political activism. He exhorted evangelicals to struggle for a regenerated America in which a righteous evangelical movement would no longer be reduced to "Christian countermoves in a decadent culture."[2]

Having devoted so much of his career to the creation of a culture-forming evangelical movement, however, Henry found himself without an institutionalized leadership position within it at the moment of its political ascendancy. Having lost his editorship of *Christianity Today,* he became a lecturer at large for World Vision International, speaking at seminaries and conferences throughout the world. More significant, having lost his editorial influence over the day-to-day concerns of an ascending evangelical movement, he was given the opportunity, albeit against his wishes, to return to the scholarly interests he had left behind as a young academic. In the 1970s and early 1980s, Henry seized the opportunity to pursue scholarly research. His intellectual labors produced a massive six-volume apologetics that fulfilled Carnell's hope for a definitive defense of modern conservative evangelicalism. To judge from his writings, Henry never found the grace to accept the roundabout blessing that came from his self-perceived mistreatment at *Christianity Today;* his autobiography seethed with resentment at the various slights and insults he had received from what he called "the evangelical establishment." In reality, however, the bruising dismissal he endured at the height of the magazine's influence made possible the achievements of Henry's later career.

From his standpoint, his situation at the magazine was never sufficiently stable or professional. *Christianity Today* was founded in 1955 by Billy Graham, Sun Oil millionaire J. Howard Pew, and Graham's father-in-law, Nelson Bell, as an outreach vehicle to liberal clergy. All three founders remained deeply involved in the magazine's editorial and financial affairs for many years, but from the outset, it was Bell's personal ministry and passion. The fact that Bell and Graham wanted the magazine to reach out to liberal clergy made Graham doubt at first that Henry was the appropriate editor. Graham admired Henry, but he worried that Henry was too fundamentalist and too intellectual to be able to address their target audience, the kind of searching or confused liberal ministers who read the *Christian Century.* Bell and Graham wanted *Christianity Today* to provide a Bible-believing alternative to mainline pastors who might be open to a skillfully presented evangelical message.

While Graham also believed that the new magazine should promulgate its theological position only gradually, Henry warned against this approach from the outset. He argued that the magazine needed to take its readers and itself seriously enough to present the gospel truth from the outset, for the crisis of belief in contemporary Protestantism left no other choice. The ecumenical tide in America was running high; fully half of all churchgoing American Protestants were in favor of a united Protestant church, and nearly 40 percent of the clergy believed that scripture contained legends and myths. This was the crisis to which a new evangelical magazine must speak, Henry urged. American Christianity needed an assertive new voice that presented a vigorous evangelical alternative to the modernizing secularization of mainline Protestantism.

He won the magazine's editorship by converting its founders to his vision.[3] Henry announced in the inaugural issue that the magazine "has its origin in a deep-felt desire to express historical Christianity to the present generation." *Christianity Today* would present the true gospel of an often-maligned movement: "Neglected, slighted, misrepresented, evangelical Christianity needs a clear voice to speak with conviction and love, and to state its true position and its relevance to the world crisis. A generation has grown up unaware of the basic truths of the Christian faith taught in the Scriptures and expressed in the creeds of the historic evangelical churches." Henry thus committed the magazine "to be both salt and light in a decaying and darkening world."[4]

Though he quickly attracted an audience for the magazine that outstripped its founders' expectations, Henry was regularly reminded that it was their magazine, not his. His editorial authority was often undermined by various board members, especially Pew, who insisted on the right to preview all editorials and controversial articles, especially articles about capitalism. Henry resisted these encroachments on his editorial freedom, but Bell mollified Pew and other key supporters by passing advance galley proofs to them. Bell's ability to play this role was the heart of the problem for Henry. Bell wore too many hats in the organization. He worked on the magazine's staff as executive editor while also serving as secretary-treasurer of the board. The latter position gave him a seat on the board's executive committee (chaired by Ockenga) and thus gave him considerable power over Henry, who complained that this arrangement was not only unfair but destabilizing to the magazine's professional structure.[5]

The founders countered that Henry was not personable enough to handle the social and fund-raising aspects of an executive editor's duties. Despite the magazine's extraordinary success, they repeatedly suggested that he was insufficiently collegial and that he published too many academic articles. In later years, they also complained that Henry was more committed to both lecturing and his own writing interests than to the magazine. These conflicts of interest and temperament finally cost Henry his position in 1967. With no warning or consultation, the executive committe maneuvered him into resigning, partly by leaking the information that *Christianity Today* was looking for a new editor. "After ten years of service [actually twelve], my relationship to the magazine was not only summarily ended without consultation or reason, but in the absence of a resignation and without agreement on public announcement," he observed at the time. Several weeks afterward, while admitting that the committee's maneuverings (especially Ockenga's) had hurt him deeply "after twelve years of sacrificial labor," Henry remarked that the worst part of the episode was that it left him without any chance of obtaining a better position "while I still had a prestigious base." Before Ockenga turned him into a lame duck, he later recalled, he might have landed a position at a state university, directed the religion division of a major publishing house, or at least returned to seminary teaching.[6]

Only after his resignation was Henry informed that the board was willing to keep him if he agreed to reduce substantially his outside speaking engagements and other activities. His feelings were wounded especially by the fact that Graham shared the board's reading of his situation and his legacy at the magazine. "Not faced was the need for professionally skilled aides, and the importance of creative interaction and dialogue that advanced evangelical penetration," Henry noted. He felt betrayed by the evangelical establishment. Like Carnell, Henry fretted that the provincialism and small-mindedness of America's evangelical leaders prevented the evangelical movement from fulfilling its regenerative cultural mission.

Almost twenty years later, in 1986, he reported that he still dreamed of "the movement's profound potential," but he admitted that it was becoming increasingly difficult for him to distinguish his dream of an evangelical Christendom from a hallucination. "I remain profoundly convinced that evangelicals are now facing their biggest opportunity since the Reformation, and yet are forfeiting it," he warned.

"Unless soon enlarged, the present opening, at least in the United States, may not long remain."[7] He predicted that in the closing years of the twentieth century, evangelicals would either mobilize their energies to transform the world or be driven by the world into a reactionary ghetto. Holding on to the status quo was not an option. In the face of a post-Christian and increasingly decadent culture, evangelical Christianity would either "penetrate" the modern world or be defeated by it.

At the same time, Henry warned that deep conviction and mobilized spiritual fervor would not be enough. He never doubted that Carnell was right about the crucial inadequacy of American evangelicalism. The movement needed prestige desperately. It needed to be taken seriously by the academic establishment; and at the very least, it needed to be respected by religious scholars at the elite universities. Having preached these themes for twenty-five years while claiming that modern nonevangelical theologies were discredited, Henry set out to show why evangelical orthodoxy explained the world better than rival worldviews.

He had laid the basis for this project in sabbatical work done in 1963, which had set into motion various complaints that he was not giving first priority to the magazine. Henry had been granted a nine-month leave from magazine deadlines. His idea of relaxation was to arrange interviews with European theologians. He had discussed theology with Barth in Basel, walked the streets of Zurich with Emil Brunner, spent an hour in a Wiesbaden wine house with an ailing Rudolf Bultmann, met with Wolfhart Pannenberg in Mainz, and spoken to G. C. Berkouwer in Amsterdam. These interviews and several others formed the basis of a series of articles in *Christianity Today* that showed Henry's keen awareness of current debates among Barthians, Bultmannians, post-Bultmannians, and other theologians.

The series, published in 1964 as a book, *Frontiers in Modern Theology,* sparkled with revealing quotes from normally guarded religious thinkers. Brunner told Henry that he was a Barthian and had never claimed otherwise. He noted that "Bultmann's shaky throne gets more shaky day by day" and added that "the Germans are monists—they want one leader at a time."[8] Werner Georg Kummel dismissed Bultmann's existentialism because "the facts, not the kerygma, evoke my response."[9] Pannenberg criticized Barth and Bultmann for refusing "to bring Christian tradition in relation to the realm of objective knowledge." Despite his apparent later objectivism, Pannenberg judged, Barth remained a disciple of Wilhelm Herrmann, and so was Bultmann.[10] Otto Weber remarked that Bultmann emphasized the existence of the Word without having any concept of what it might be. "Bultmann's students all speak about 'the Word,'" he observed. "But now we are already seeing a movement away from the certainty *that there is* such a Word."[11]

Modern Protestant theology up to this time had been dominated by a series of giant theological figures, but Henry presented a picture of disarray in which no position was attracting a large following. He skillfully played quotes from competing theologians against one another to show that all of the century's dominant theological idols were tottering. Those who had relinquished any appeal to revelation were left with empty religious relativism; those who appealed to a nonobjective Word had no defense against post-Bultmannians, who demythologized "the Word" down to nothing. Henry proclaimed that the current twilight of theological idols marked a precious opportunity for evangelical orthodoxy. "If Christianity is to win intellectual respectability in the modern world, the reality of the transcendent God must indeed be proclaimed by the theologians—and proclaimed on the basis of man's rational competence to know the transempirical realm," he urged. "Apart from recognition of the rational Creator of men made in his image and of the self-revealed Redeemer of a fallen humanity, who vouchsafes valid knowledge of the transempirical world, the modern Athenians are left to munch the husks of the religious vagabonds."[12] If God's mind and will cannot be known objectively, he insisted, precious little is to be gained by preaching that God exists at all. The case for evangelical orthodoxy that was needed, therefore, had to focus on the problem of religious epistemology.

CARL HENRY AND EVANGELICAL EPISTEMOLOGY

Henry pursued this considerable project in his six-volume apologetics, *God, Revelation and Authority,* which paid tribute at the outset to the singular influence of Gordon Clark over his theology and apologetic approach.[13] Like Clark, he cleared the field of alternatives before making his case for evangelical orthodoxy. With Clarkian arguments, he taught that mysticism hopelessly shrouds the divine revealer in incomprehensible ineffability, that empiricism is incapable of finding the truth because it is committed to an unending search on secular presuppositions, and that non-Christian rationalism subordinates the truth of revelation to its own master concepts. The basic premise of the Christian revelationist alternative is that "the living God should be allowed to speak for himself and to define the abiding role of reason and the meaning of revelation."[14] The fact that Barthian neoorthodoxy also affirmed the primacy of a self-authenticating revelation moved Henry to maintain a running debate with Barth and Brunner throughout his apologetic. He repeatedly cautioned that while neoorthodoxy asserted the primacy of revelation for theology and Christian life, the conception of revelation that it promoted was too subjective and sporadic to provide a secure basis for Christian knowledge.

Henry argued that evangelical orthodoxy is crucially distinguished by its insistence on the objective, rational character of divine revelation: "Divine revelation is the source of all truth, the truth of Christianity included; reason is the instrument for recognizing it; Scripture is its verifying principle; logical consistency is a negative test for truth and coherence a subordinate test." It followed for him that the task of theology is to explicate the content of biblical revelation "as an orderly whole."[15] For Henry, as for Clark and Carnell, the foundational premise of Christianity was not the resurrection of Christ but the comprehensive structure of biblical revelation, of which the resurrection is a part. Though the resurrection bears an important evidential value for Christian truth, he explained, scripture does not isolate the resurrection from its own larger structure of testimony to God's saving acts in history. Scripture always speaks of Christ's resurrection within the narrative frame of biblical history. "To prefer divine revelation rather than Christ's resurrection as the foundational premise implies no denial whatever, of course, that the God of the Bible reveals himself in the empirical world of factuality and that man is inescapably confronted there by revelation," Henry observed. "Nor does such preference deny that the resurrection is of universal apologetic importance, or that sinful man's contemplation of the cosmos and of history may not be an occasion when the Spirit of God imparts new life to delinquent evangelistic prospects."[16]

What it does imply is that the fundamental premise of Christianity is not a single verifiable event but a comprehensive structure of revealed knowledge that has no basis outside itself. By definition, a *basic* axiom is undemonstrable; a basic, or fundamental, axiom cannot be deduced from any piece of external or higher or prior knowledge. This truism has particular force for Christian theology, Henry argued, because "the axioms of the Christian system of truth are not presuppositions shared in common with secular thought." Christian doctrines derive from an objective divine revelation, not from rationalistic deduction or experimental observation. Everything is at stake in the evangelical assertion of the primary axiomatic importance of divine revelation.[17]

Henry thus sided with the presuppositionalist side of the evangelical debate between presuppositionalists and evidentialists.[18] Though he conceded that some presuppositionalists, notably Van Til, made extreme or misguided claims on behalf of this position, he denied that presuppositionalist theology necessarily exaggerates the noetic (intellectual) consequences of original sin, denies the existence of any common ground between Christians and non-Christians, or submits to the demands of a coherence theory of truth. The biblical doctrine of the Fall depicts human beings as depraved in the entirety of their being, he allowed, "but this hardly means that man cannot comprehend God's revelation, or that he cannot do so prior to the regenerative or illuminative work of the Holy Spirit; far less does it mean that man's rational abilities are wholly nullified." Total depravity means that human beings are depraved in each aspect of their being. It does not mean that human intellection is totally corrupt or even that human volition and affection are totally corrupt. Total corruption would be nothingness. Moreover, Henry argued, scripture clearly regards the human will as being more pervasively depraved than human reason: "Man wills not to know God in truth, and makes religious reflection serviceable to moral revolt. But he is still capable of intellectually analyzing rational evidence for the truth-value of assertions about God."[19]

To Henry, it was the human will, not human reason, that stands utterly in need of divine regeneration. He explained that while there are two kinds of human will—regenerate and unregenerate—it is misguided to speak of human reason as either regenerate or unregenerate. The appropriate distinction with regard to reason is between valid thinking and invalid thinking. If the Fall had affected human reasoning as much as it corrupted the human will, no rationally compelling case could be made for or against anything. With Machen and Carnell, Henry thus contended that theology must judge "the sufficiency of the evidences." Theologians must apply the same tests of rationality to Christian claims that educated, rational people apply to a newspaper story or a political speech. Reason is a divine gift that allows human beings to recognize the truth of revelation. It is the possession of both Christians and non-Christians. "If a person must first be a Christian believer in order to grasp the truth of revelation, then meaning is subjective and incommunicable," Henry warned. He pressed the point against Barth and Van Til, allowing that although it is not incorrect to claim that regeneration creates new attitudes toward revelation and even facilitates our comprehension of it, "the new birth is not prerequisite to a knowledge of the truth of God."[20] Barth's definition of dogmatics as a work of the Christ-following church offered a perfect example of the modern existentialism-influenced tendency to distinguish theology from other disciplines. This appeal to an "inner history" or privileged standpoint is disastrous for theology, Henry charged. The truth claims of Christianity are as open to rational inquiry as are the claims of chemistry or sociology.[21] To make theological inquiry dependent on belief is to consign theology to a ghetto of religious feeling.

Henry countered that there is nothing wrong with subjecting revelation to rational tests. Logical consistency is a negative test of truth in all disciplines, including theology, and coherence is a subordinate test. Though many theologians joined Barth or Van Til in claiming that God is not bound by the canons of logic, Henry insisted that theology has no basis for distinguishing religious truth from nonsense apart from its appeal to sufficient reason. "When Barth tells us that the truth of theology consists necessarily in a logically irreconcilable 'yes' and 'no,' he espouses a brand of religious irrationalism that cannot commend itself to a devotee of religious truth," he charged. "The intellectual absurdities of dialectical theology do nothing at all to commend it as credible Christianity."[22]

Van Til's presuppositionalism was closer to Henry's position, and his polemics against Barth were more extreme than Henry's, but Henry found Van Til exasperatingly similar to Barth on this point. As a philosophical idealist, Van Til advocated a coherence theory of knowledge that identified truth with logical consistency, but he exempted Christian revelation from the test of logical consistency. While showing that all the alternatives to Christianity fail the tests of rationality, he then refused to submit Christianity to the same tests. As he persistently asserted, "No proof for this God and for the truth of his revelation in Scripture can be offered by an appeal to anything in human experience that has not itself received its light from the God whose existence and whose revelation it is supposed to prove."[23] To Henry, this strategy was plainly disastrous, relying on a double standard of argument which implied that Christians think with a separate system of logic and that biblical revelation may not be logically consistent.

At the same time, Henry rejected the evidentialist approach advocated by Clark Pinnock, John Warwick Montgomery, and John Gerstner.[24] Pinnock urged that evangelical theology should subscribe to a correspondence theory of truth, in which truth is found in conformity with external facts. He claimed that scripture assumes this view of knowledge, "namely, that there exists a form of correspondence between belief and facts." Pinnock conceded Van Til's objection that because evidentialist arguments are synthetic and empirical, the evidentialist approach makes Christian truth a matter of probability. He replied that a probable argument is superior to an improbable one.[25] He further conceded that most of the Reformed tradition was against him on this issue, countering that this was the great tragedy of the Reformed tradition.

In fact, genuine Calvinism gave little comfort to modern evangelicals who sought to prove the truth of Christianity on rational or historical grounds. Calvin asserted that scripture "deigns not to submit to proofs and arguments, but owes the full conviction with which we ought to receive it to the testimony of the Spirit."[26] According to the Westminster Confession, the authority of scripture "dependeth not upon the testimony of any man or Church, but wholly upon God (who is truth itself), the author thereof; and therefore it is to be received, because it is the Word of God."[27] Modern evangelicals such as Abraham Kuyper, Herman Bavinck, John Murray, E. J. Young, Clark, and Van Til were good Calvinists on this point, if not always on other subjects. Kuyper insisted that "at no single point of the way is there place, therefore, for a support derived from demonstration or reasoning." Bavinck advised that if someone inquires *why* the Christian believes that scripture is God's Word, "the Christian has no further answer." Murray taught that rational demonstration cannot be the ground of faith without usurping the authority of God's Word, for "there is one sphere where self-testimony must be accepted as absolute and final." Young asserted that "we hold to a high view of inspiration for the simple reason that the Bible teaches a high view." Clark argued that orthodox Calvinism was no more circular on this point than geometry. In 1961 the Christian Reformed Church officially committed itself to the doctrine that the self-testimony of scripture is sufficient to establish its divine inspiration and infallibility.[28]

This was the daunting evangelical tradition that evangelical verificationists stood against. Pinnock opposed it outright. Evangelical criticism of Barth's fideism often became entangled in sticky debates over the fideism of much of the evangelical Calvinist and Pietist traditions, but Pinnock forthrightly asserted that fideism of any kind betrays the apologetic mission of theology. His commitment to Arminianism became more explicit in the 1970s as he struggled to defend a verificationist alternative to classical Calvinist teaching. Pinnock observed that Reformed fideism appealed to a bare authority claim (the self-attestation of scripture) and a bare religious experience claim (the subjective accreditation of scripture as God's Word by the Holy Spirit). Both of these claims are "hopelessly vulnerable to criticism," he protested. Religious claims to authority are plainly not *self*-validating, since the world abounds with contradictary claims to religious authority. Pinnock argued that scripture should be trusted over the Koran or the ravings of Father Divine only if its credentials are superior to these rival claims. "The credentials of the gospel, its open-to-investigation form, is its beauty," he urged.[29] Scripture invites us to begin with particulars, not universals. To treat the gospel as a grand assumption that ordinary historical reason cannot verify is to "nullify" God's revelation in scripture. This revelation is objectively valid and accessible to all inquirers. "We are not asked to assume the theistic clue to ultimate reality in order to arrive at it," Pinnock urged. "Rather we are challenged to see that reality and revelation being what they are establish the validity of the Christian faith."[30]

Henry was distinctly suited to mediate this debate. As a Baptist, he belonged to a religious tradition that derives from Puritanism but is not bound to the Reformed confessions. As a Baptist presuppositionalist, he was chiefly influenced by Reformed thinkers while claiming independence from the fideistic mainstream of the Reformed tradition. The key to his mediating alternative was his consistent rationalism. Henry noted a crucial similarity between Van Til's failure to consistently uphold coherence theory and the verificationist commitment to correspondence theory. He asserted that both strategies ultimately committed different versions of the same mistake. By giving up the view that truth consists in internally consistent propositions, the evidentialists abdicated the crucial test of coherence. This was a fatal mistake, Henry charged. If the human mind cannot know reality as it is in itself, but only something that corresponds to it, even the most faithful evidentialist theologian is ultimately driven to skepticism. The language of correspondence and analogy is a house of mirrors. If we cannot know reality as it is in itself, he warned, nothing that is said to be "like" it will give us any sure knowledge. Hodge and Carnell had been right to teach evangelicalism this lesson. Reality is unknowable if we cannot know reality itself.

Evidentialist apologetics reduced Christian truth to a mere probability about something that is more or less "like" what is said to be true. Henry countered that nothing is gained if evangelicals give up the orthodox identification of truth with internally consistent propositions. "Pinnock emphasizes that scripture includes doctrinal and historical gaps which preclude the infallible elaboration of a total theological system," he observed. "But if this totally precludes the elaboration of a consistent exposition of the content of revelation, then Christianity is at great disadvantage and revelation does not count for much in the intellectual conflict of ideas." In the conflict of ideas, theologians must not appear to exempt Christian doctrine from rational criticism in any way. Whenever theologians seek or claim such an exemption, they deserve not to be taken seriously, because they betray their subject.

Henry flatly declared that no Christian doctrine that contained a logical contradiction would be worthy of being believed: "Were the doctrines of the Trinity, of divine election and human responsibility, of the two natures of Christ logically contradictory doctrines, no evangelical Christian could or should accept and believe them."[31] It followed for him that the work of theology is precisely to explicate, in as logical and comprehensive a manner as possible, the entire revelational content of the Bible. Henry conceded that no theologian has ever successfully systematized the entire content of revelation in the form of axioms and theorems. But he did not believe that this theological failing constituted a reason to abandon the project, for axiomatization is the ideal of every serious intellectual endeavor: "If rationality and system are intrinsic to theology, then the arrangement of theological teaching in axioms and theorems remains a legitimate and ideal goal."[32]

To Henry, Carnell's concession to the holistic character of scripture was not a satisfactory resting place. The Bible may fail to define its major and minor premises, and it certainly makes no effort to develop a coherent system of axioms and theorems, but he felt this was no reason not to develop a philosophical system out of scripture. He lamented that Christians often took the wrong meaning from the biblical assurance that "my ways are not your ways, nor your thoughts my thoughts." The biblical prohibition against idolatry applies only to foreign gods, he argued, not to all mental images and concepts. "One cannot permanently defer the cognitive question without either imperiling or obscuring man's relationship to God," he warned. "The existential vacuum cannot really be filled until one knows oneself to be in touch with the truth."[33] Moreover, if revelation is to be regarded as a genuine communication of communicable truth, it must emphasize divine speaking as crucial to divine action. Henry explained that it is through God's verbal revelation that the meaning of God's historical activity becomes known to us. He thus defined revelation as "that activity of the supernatural God whereby he communicates information essential for man's present and future destiny."[34]

Essential to this emphasis on revelation as divine speaking was Henry's insistence that revelation consists not merely of isolated concepts, names, and words but of propositions and judgments. He cautioned that it is not merely the words and concepts of scripture that are divinely inspired. Though words and concepts are instrumentalities of divine disclosure, it is not enough to identify inspiration with them. To say that revelation is verbal and conceptual must mean more than this, since words and concepts by themselves are neither true nor false. Only propositions bear the quality of truth. Because scripture brings readers and hearers of the Word to truth through its discursive sentences, biblical revelation consists not only of its verbal and conceptual elements but also of its units of thought. "God does not communicate in disparate concepts and disjointed words; he does not utter illogicalities," Henry assured. "Nor does he suspend his revelation on 'tongues' and ecstatic utterances, or address man in paradoxes and absurdities. Meaningful divine revelation involves communication in intelligible sentences."[35]

Henry did not deny that legitimate disputes exist within orthodox Protestantism about how particular biblical texts should be understood. Scripture raises hermeneutical problems even for those who read it entirely as God's Word. However, he insisted, what is never legitimate in orthodoxy is watering down the orthodox understanding of revelation as rationally comprehensible information given by God. Clark contended that the verbal-propositional view of revelation as "fixed truth from God" is fundamental to orthodoxy.[36] Henry agreed that this view of revelation as rational-verbal disclosure is the single necessary foundation of orthodox doctrine. Though neoorthodox theologians prattle endlessly about God as personal subject, he observed, the divine subject disclosed in revelation is also an object of human knowledge.[37] The God revealed in scripture is disclosed to readers and hearers of the Word "in the form of objectively valid truth." The only serious choices are propositional revelation and skepticism. If God is not objectively intelligible, the confessional statement that God is personal subject is meaningless.

Modern theology has been weak, unconvincing, and vulnerable to every cultural fad precisely because of its failure to defend the objective, propositional character of biblical revelation, Henry argued. Under Kant's assurance that human knowledge derives from sense experience alone, theological liberalism tried to find a home for Christian faith in religious feeling or experiences of value. Liberal theology defended its cognitive bankruptcy by subjectivizing its religious claims.

The Barthian movement blasted theological liberalism for its anthropocentrism and its accommodation of the gospel to modern culture, but from Henry's standpoint, theological neoorthodoxy produced merely a more biblical-sounding version of the same compromised culture-faith. It embraced the liberal dichotomy between faith and science, denied the propositional nature of revelation, and forfeited the objective truth character of the gospel. In Barth's case, it also denied the existence of general revelation behind special revelation. Barth made theology depend entirely on the unilateral self-disclosure of God, while insisting that the Word is never to be identified with anything, including the words of scripture. In Barth's words, it is "quite impossible that there should be a direct identity between the human word of Holy Scripture and the Word of God."[38]

The "colossal inconsistency" of this position was appalling to Henry. How could "the Word" be the basis of theology when "it" is not anything at all? By driving a wedge between the truth of revelation and the truth of biblical propositions, he objected, Barth made cognitive skepticism inevitable. He denied to seekers of the Word "any true knowledge of God." Barth's doctrine of the Word turned God's sure and intelligible revelation into something unsure, sporadic, and unknowable. To claim that scripture becomes God's Word in the form of personal truth only as the Holy Spirit moves one's reading or hearing of scripture is to nullify the basis for declaring that any creedal statement is true. Clark put the matter plainly: "A non-propositional inner meaning has no meaning at all." Real knowledge is propositional; it consists of predicates related to subjects. The object of genuine knowledge is the meaning that given words designate. "To talk of a different inner meaning, not itself a proposition, never proclaimed or thought, is a trait of irrationalism," Clark charged.[39]

Further, Henry argued, the Word is neither heard nor glorified when theology wraps it in paradox, shrouds it in mystery, or turns it into poetic imagery. Henry noted that modern Anglican theology was especially inclined to emphasize the liturgical and communal contexts of scripture in ways that played up the interpretive faculty of imagination. Emphasizing the liturgical origins of scripture, Anglicans Austin Farrer and Lionel Thornton argued that scripture presents us with poetic and symbolic images that are grasped not so much with intellectual propositions as through imagination. Farrer explained that while prose "abstracts from reality, symbol represents it."[40] Henry gave short shrift to this Anglican emphasis on imagination and countered that liturgical and symbolic interpretations of scripture have no logical support at all. They are not true to scripture and they make no sense. If Farrer's approach to Christianity were true, he explained, Farrer would not be able to express it in propositional sentences. He would have to write his theology as poetry. And if poetry were the only form that theology could take, Christianity would have no genuine theology at all. If God is only metaphorically real, personal, and transcendent, Henry declared, then Christians are "merely chasing the wind."[41]

His stronger charge against metaphorical and existential understandings of the Word was that they are untrue to scripture. "There is no basis in the Scriptures for Barth's theory that divine revelation is nonpropositional, personal truth," he insisted, invoking Clark's observation that scripture consists almost entirely of propositional assertions.[42] Clark had noted that the only exceptions were imperative sentences (mostly divine commands), the revelation of God's name, and a few exclamations.[43] Henry added the idea that even the imperative statements, though not asserting a truth, take the form of propositions, because isolated concepts do not convey truth. Even the revelation of God's name requires a propositional context in order to be intelligible. Though it is true that not all of God's Word is propositional, Henry allowed, most of the biblical text is emphatically propositional, asserting truths in the form of propositional sentences. For this reason, he declared, "evangelicals need not tremble and take to the hills whenever others charge us with rationalism."[44] Evangelical rationalism is merely a function of the distinctively evangelical willingness to submit to the whole of scripture as it exists.

UPHOLDING
INERRANCY EVANGELICALISM

And what truth claim does scripture make about its own authority? What should evangelical orthodoxy teach in regard to the doctrine of biblical inerrancy? In answer, Henry acknowledged that a strong current in contemporary evangelicalism was moving away from inerrancy doctrine. He repeatedly criticized evangelical theologians such as Bernard Ramm, Daniel Fuller, George Eldon Ladd, Paul Jewett, Donald Bloesch, Dewey Beegle, G. C. Berkouwer, F. F. Bruce, Arthur Holmes, and the later Clark Pinnock for relinquishing or failing to defend inerrancy doctrine. With particular straightforwardness, Beegle contended that the evangelical preoccupation with inerrancy reflected a disturbing lack of intellectual and religious security among evangelical thinkers.[45]

Henry countered adamantly that scripture cannot be considered truly reliable if any part of its teaching "would commit us to error." The doctrine of biblical inerrancy is a logical and necessary deduction from the scriptural assertion that scripture is inspired by God. To the neoevangelical tendency to claim that scripture can be divinely inspired and yet subject to various kinds of defects, Henry replied that "only logical imprecision can begin with errancy and conclude with divine authority." Like Gleason Archer, who emphasized the impossibility that God would ever inspire error, Henry thus contended that the doctrines of biblical inspiration and inerrancy are linked inseparably.[46] "What is errant cannot be divinely authoritative nor can God have inspired it."[47]

Inerrancy doctrine was, to Henry, an inescapable logical deduction. Because scripture is inspired by God, it must be inerrant, for God would never inspire error. This deduction shaped not only Henry's case against "errancy-claiming" evangelicalism but also his critique of accommodationist forms of inerrancy doctrine, of which Carnell's dictum that "Scripture contains errors, but teaches none" was a prominent example. In 1979, Henry noted that this formulation was routinely invoked, even by certain evangelicals who were anxious to preserve some form of inerrancy claim. The early Pinnock criticized Carnell's strategy as hazardous to the faith, but in the late 1970s, even Pinnock began to distinguish between the intended and unintended teachings of scripture.[48] Like Carnell, he began to associate inerrancy only with scripture's intended teachings. Carnell's appeal to authorial intention and the limitations of biblical sources seemed to provide a way out for evangelicals who wanted to uphold inerrancy while recognizing that, for example, Chronicles contains exaggerated figures from the public archives and Stephen's figures in Acts 7:6–16 are wrong.

But is it credible to claim inerrancy for scripture if the Bible contains numerous errors of this kind? Does the slippery notion of authorial intention really provide a better refuge for evangelicalism than the more straightforward and traditional method of harmonization? Henry pressed for a negative verdict without absolutely ruling out Carnell's approach as hopeless or impossible. Though he commended Carnell and Pinnock for struggling to affirm biblical inerrancy, he judged that they overly accommodated the doctrine to its inductive difficulties. If inspiration guarantees only scribal accuracy and not historical errorlessness, he objected, "must not every historical assertion be considered unsure unless and until it is independently verified?" With or without any appeal to authorial intention, he judged, the accommodating versions of inerrancy doctrine left evangelicalism without a secure basis for discerning where scripture inerrantly reproduces faulty information and where it inerrantly reports the truth.[49]

Henry warned that these problems multiply as soon as one takes refuge in an ultimately unknowable authorial intention. The distinction between intended and unintended biblical teaching is a nonbiblical device, he observed; scripture never distinguishes between its teaching and its incidental components. "How can the writer's internal intention be translated into external affirmation except by the very records that we possess?" Using Ernst Troeltsch's observation that as soon as historical criticism is given an inch, it takes a mile, Henry pressed this truism on evangelical theologians who sought only to accommodate small inductive problems. "Once errancy of the texts is accommodated, the universe of controversy quickly enlarges," he warned. Evangelical theologians might apply the principle of authorial intention mainly to small details, but on what basis were they to determine that the biblical writers sought to tell the truth factually in other respects? "If geographical and historical details are untrue, why should the events or doctrines correlated with them be true?" he protested.[50]

The history of liberal biblical scholarship was chastening to Henry. He warned that it needed to be more chastening to evangelicals who sought to make small concessions to biblical criticism. If evangelicals ever were to agree to discard inerrancy doctrine or redefine it to the point of meaninglessness, he predicted, they would not be able to hold the line at that point of defense. At that point, having given up the principle that divine inspiration produces real inerrancy, evangelicalism would have no principled basis on which to resist aggressive forms of biblical criticism. Just as the conservatives at Fuller Seminary warned that evangelicalism would not be able to withstand the loss of its claim to a completely inerrant scripture, Henry warned that evangelicalism would quickly degenerate into religious liberalism if its theological and pastoral leaders were to give up on real inerrancy.

The history of American Protestantism gave ample fuel to this fear. Most of America's elite universities were founded by conservative, Bible-believing Protestants. In the eighteenth and nineteenth centuries, most of them made concessions on small points of doctrine, which led to larger concessions, which led to theological liberalism, which led eventually to outright secularism.[51] In different generations, Harvard, Yale, Princeton, the University of Chicago, and many other institutions had followed this trajectory. The vast academic empire that early American Protestantism had created was lost to its modernizing and ultimately secularizing opponents. One case was especially instructive to the fundamentalists who founded Fuller Seminary. In the early nineteenth century, Andover Seminary was founded as an orthodox antidote to Harvard, which had already turned Unitarian. The founders of Andover Seminary vowed to hold fast to orthodoxy. Faculty were compelled to sign a strict creedal statement every year, but this requirement made them no more immune to the pressures of modern science, culture, and historical criticism than their colleagues at Harvard or Yale had been. By the end of the century, Andover Seminary was teaching theological liberalism, and in 1922 it merged with Harvard Divinity School.

The founders of Fuller Seminary often told this story as a warning to themselves. Carnell described the new seminary as a "new Andover" that needed to guard its orthodoxy more vigilantly than the first Andover. Eleven years later, in his resignation from the seminary, Wilbur Smith charged that Fuller Seminary was following the Andover road to heterodoxy.[52] The Fuller conservatives rarely paused to consider that before 1870, inerrancy was rarely used as a test of orthodoxy. The defining controversy at Fuller was fought over an issue that played no role in early-nineteenth-century debates over orthodoxy. It was only after Warfield, in his debates with Charles Briggs, insisted on the necessity of perfect autographs that conservatives came to view the idea of perfect pre-Bible manuscripts as a crucial test of orthodoxy.[53] It was only a generation later that biblical inerrancy came to be viewed as the bedrock test of orthodoxy.

In this respect, Henry was a follower of Warfield. He believed that biblical inspiration necessarily implied inerrancy, and that orthodoxy could be sustained only by refusing to retreat from strict inerrancy. The fact that inerrancy is a controversial concept is no reason to abandon it, he urged. If evangelicals give up on inerrancy, infallibility will be next: "Polemicists will always find their slogans, and the term *infallibility* can serve their controversial interests no less than can inerrancy."[54]

Henry gave just enough attention to problem passages to indicate how his approach to them differed from the weaker defense of inerrancy that Carnell and Pinnock proposed. Rather than concede that scripture contains errors, he exhorted, evangelical scholarship needs to search for solutions to all the Bible's problem passages. In some cases, this approach could hold several possible solutions in view without making a commitment to any particular one. In some cases, the only apparent explanation for a problem would be textual corruption; in others, it must be admitted that not enough is known to venture a solution. What all these responses hold in common, however, is the refusal to presume that the original autographs of scripture contained any kind of error. Responding to James Barr's list of problematic passages, Henry allowed that the long day of Joshua 10:12–13 (when God made the sun "stand still") remains particularly troubling.[55] Less disturbing to him was the Genesis story of a patriarch, residing outside Israel, who saves his life by persuading his attractive wife to say that she is his sister. Genesis tells this story three times, twice with Abraham as the patriarch and once with Isaac (Gen. 12:10–21; 20:1–18; and 26:6–16). Did the same rather odd episode happen three times? Henry's response typified his approach to all problems of this kind. We must not rule out the possibility that the scriptural narrative is true, he argued: "We must ask whether a leader might perhaps more than once have lusted after the attractive wife of a foreigner, and also whether a son may perhaps have learned from his father how to cope with such a situation."[56]

Elsewhere, he suggested that an alternative meaning of the Greek word *prenes* might be the answer to the problem of the differing accounts of the death of Judas Iscariot. Though Matthew 27:5 says that Judas hanged himself and Acts 1:18 says that he fell headlong (*prenes*) and burst asunder, Henry noted that "swelling up" has some textual support as a possible meaning of *prenes*. He proposed that this rendering could provide the basis for a better harmonization than the kind offered in traditional apologetic works. In his classic work *An Examination of the Alleged Discrepancies of the Bible,* biblical apologist John Haley reasoned that Judas hanged himself on a tree overlooking a precipice and then was mutilated when the rope or limb broke.[57] Henry observed that contemporary evangelical scholarship is sometimes able to provide better harmonizations than this, by virtue of its superior knowledge about biblical words and cultural customs.

But as a rule, Henry was less inclined than many evangelicals to harmonize conflicting passages or appeal to textual corruption. Lindsell, for example, solved the problem of the conflicting accounts of Peter's denial of Jesus by producing a four-Gospel harmonized account in which the rooster had to crow six times rather than twice.[58] Henry was inclined to look for other kinds of solutions. He argued that in some cases it is better to wait for further light on a passage. The problem of the slaying of Goliath is a notable example. The story that David killed the Philistine giant is told in 1 Samuel 17, but 2 Samuel 21:19 says that Elhanan killed Goliath. Moreover, 1 Chronicles 20:5 states that Elhanan killed Goliath's brother Lahmi. Many Bible-believers have harmonized the Samuel texts, notwithstanding the fact that this method creates another "biblical" account that the Bible does not contain and that also does obvious violence to the David story. Other evangelicals have treated 2 Samuel 21:19 as corrupt, though the extant texts provide no support for this conclusion. Still others have proposed that David might be another name for Elhanan, in which case David would be the slayer of both Goliath and Lahmi. Henry ruled the last solution out, arguing that it was "a staggering thought" to harmonize the text by gratuitously attributing another death to David.[59]

In this case, Henry judged that some vital piece of information needed to solve the problem is missing. Such problems should be expected. Evangelical scholarship cannot be expected to solve all the problem passages in scripture. But, he cautioned, the one thing that evangelicals must not do in searching for solutions is to solve any problem in a way that compromises the divine character and authority of scripture. Any doctrine taught by scripture is authoritative, and the Bible teaches the doctrine of its own inspiration. While the logically related doctrine of scriptural inerrancy does not require modern technical precision in reporting statistics and measurements or conformity to modern science in reporting on cosmology, it does presume that the words of scripture are the very words of God, expressed in each biblical writer's particular style.

This is what it means to affirm the doctrine of verbal inspiration, Henry maintained. Evangelical orthodoxy does not teach the dictation theory, the "intuition" theory that the writers of scripture were religious geniuses, the "illumination" theory that the Holy Spirit heightened the creative powers of the writers, or the "conceptual" theory that scripture contains inspired ideas in forms of expression freely chosen by the writers. Dictation theory turns the writers into automatons, while the other theories turn scripture into something less than God's objective Word. Evangelicalism must teach nothing less than the doctrine that God inspired the biblical writers to find the appropriate words and forms of expression to communicate God's thoughts. Verbal inerrancy implies that God's truth inheres in the very words of scripture, "that is, in the propositions or sentences of the Bible, and not merely in the concepts and thoughts of the writers."[60]

Despite his insistence that the doctrine of perfect errorlessness is a necessary deduction from inspiration and fundamental to orthodoxy, however, Henry resisted the militant evangelical claim that inerrancy is the litmus test of orthodox belief. Most of the evangelical theological establishment traditionally defined itself by its unequivocal commitment to inerrancy. (The sole formal requirement for membership in the Evangelical Theological Society [ETS], for example, is belief in biblical inerrancy. Established in 1949 as a transdenominational forum for evangelical scholarship, the society bases its existence on the single affirmation that "the Bible alone, and the Bible in its entirety, is the Word of God written and is therefore inerrant in the autographs."[61] Henry embraced this position without accepting the judgment of many ETS members that only believers in strict inerrancy qualified as evangelicals.) In the 1960s, in the wake of the turnabout at Fuller Seminary, evangelicals hotly debated the necessity of inerrancy doctrine. Francis Schaeffer became a prominent figure in American evangelicalism on the strength of his militant defense of biblical inerrancy, and in 1966 a gathering of prominent evangelicals at Wenham, Massachusetts, tried and failed to secure a statement of agreement over the issue of inerrancy. Various Fuller evangelicals were harshly castigated at Wenham for abandoning evangelicalism. American evangelicals debated the necessity of inerrancy doctrine into the mid-1970s, when a tumultuous fight for control of the Southern Baptist Convention and the publication of Harold Lindsell's *The Battle for the Bible* (1976) set off a long-building explosion over the creedal necessity of inerrancy belief.[62] Lindsell denied outright that any person could rightfully "claim the evangelical badge once he has abandoned inerrancy."[63] Evangelicals must either stand up for inerrancy or betray the cause of Christ, he lectured, and the time had passed when evangelicals could afford not to censure nonbelievers in inerrancy or press one another for their position on this issue.

For Lindsell, the time had come to draw lines and name names. His bitterness over the fate of Fuller Seminary bolstered his polemical finger-pointing. Much of the rhetorical warfare that followed amounted to a proxy fight between Fuller-oriented neoevangelicals and proponents of the upstart Trinity Evangelical Divinity School. Some evangelical fundamentalists—notably J. I. Packer—sought to keep the evangelical war over inerrancy from escalating out of control. As a British outsider to the American evangelical power struggle, Packer pleaded for a spirit of greater Christian charity among American evangelicals. He defended inerrancy doctrine while resisting some of the more extreme interpretations of inerrancy as precise, literal facticity. He affirmed that biblical inerrancy was crucial to evangelicalism while taking an essentially diplomatic approach to the American evangelical war for position and power. This posture contained considerable inner tensions in its own right, but Packer's diplomatic tack was modest by comparison to Henry's intervention.

Packer's quiet diplomacy among evangelicals implied that there was a difference between evangelicalism as a coherent theological perspective and evangelicalism as a theological movement. Henry pressed the same distinction in public, with considerably greater force. In effect, he argued that evangelicalism made no sense without the doctrine of biblical inerrancy, but evangelicalism as a movement was wrong to draw lines and exclude fellow Christians over inerrancy. Though he also justified his position on theological grounds, Henry emphasized that the ongoing campaign to make inerrancy the watershed of true evangelicalism was bad politics. He denounced "the somewhat reactionary elevation of inerrancy as the superbadge of evangelical orthodoxy."[64] He warned that the inerrancy war in the churches and seminaries was threatening not only to excommunicate a host of promising young scholars from the ranks of evangelicalism but also to exclude and demean such eminent figures as G. C. Berkouwer, F. F. Bruce, George Ladd, and Bruce Metzger. "I think it highly unfortunate that the *primary* thing that should now be said about men like F. F. Bruce and Berkouwer, men who have made significant contributions to the conservative position—even though we might have hoped for somewhat more from them—is that they are not evangelicals because of their position at this one point."[65]

Although in other contexts Henry often made the slippery-slope argument, in this context he questioned its historical validity, noting that much of the best evangelical theology was being written by nonbelievers in inerrancy. In his reading, this fact had to be counted as evidence against the repeatedly invoked slippery-slope argument. That there was now a century-long tradition of noninerrancy evangelicalism stretching back to Orr, James Denney, and Augustus Strong had to count as disconfirming evidence. Henry cautioned that the Orr tradition was wrong on account of its intellectual inconsistency. It maintained a faithful relation to evangelicalism "by an act of will rather than by persuasive epistemological credentials."[66] But this mistake about the epistemological basis of faith did not appear to be fatal to evangelicalism.

Henry worried that the more deadly mistake was the one that Lindsell and other fundamentalists were making. A precious historical moment was being squandered:

At the very moment when American evangelicalism was beginning to receive unprecedented mass media attention, leading evangelical militants were demanding heresy trials and heightened loyalty tests. They were making the movement look like "a cult squabbling over inerrancy" rather than a "dynamic life-growing force."[67] Henry warned that this was bad strategy and bad ecclesiology. Just as American evangelicalism was finally positioned to overcome its inherited know-nothing cultural image, its right flank was publicizing an in-house creedal debate and casting aspersions on some of the movement's most faithful, notable, and valuable brethren. But the debate continued as the militants replied that it was not only the Orr-type evangelicals who were being inconsistent.

Lindsell reported that he was not unhappy with the fallout from his book; American evangelicalism needed a good debate over its defining beliefs. What did make him unhappy was that Henry and Pinnock were failing the crucial test of evangelical leadership in claiming that inerrancy was essential to evangelicalism but not worth fighting over.[68] Lindsell countered that this was the one position in the debate over inerrancy that made no sense at all. If inerrancy was really all the things Henry claimed for it, he observed, how could it not be something worth fighting for? And if the doctrine of inerrancy was not worth "squabbling" about, which doctrine *was* worth fighting about? "Is the bodily resurrection worth squabbling about? Is the vicarious atonement worth it? Is the deity of Christ worth it?" he asked. Lindsell presumed that Henry regarded all these doctrines as too precious *not* to fight over. But all are derived from scripture, Lindsell cautioned, and if the Bible cannot be trusted on everything that it affirms about smaller matters, "then we cannot be sure concerning these doctrines either."[69]

Henry's posture gave comfort and legitimacy to a theological perspective that he otherwise described as mistaken, contrary to historical orthodoxy, and harmful to evangelicalism. Though he affirmed inerrancy doctrine, the effect of his strategic position was to drive a wedge between inerrancy pertaining to matters of faith and practice (the doctrines he presumably felt were worth fighting over) and inerrancy pertaining to everything else that scripture affirms. Lindsell protested that this was exactly the distinction that had jeopardized evangelical identity in the past and led to its degeneration into religious liberalism and outright secularism. Fuller Seminary was lost precisely over this point. How could Henry repeatedly denounce the reductionist "faith and practice" understanding of inerrancy in his writings and then implicitly endorse it for the evangelical movement? If inerrancy is true and fundamental, fundamentalist leaders objected, it cannot be something that is not worth fighting about. By contrast, if it is not true, then all the doctrines that evangelicals of all kinds defend have no ground of certainty. One of these positions must be true, but the one position that could not be right was the one that Henry rationalized.

This debate was marred by Lindsell's failure to grasp that Henry did not use inerrancy doctrine in quite the same reductionist manner as did most fundamentalists. Fundamentalism in the generation after Warfield typically appealed to inerrancy as a kind of magic wand or all-purpose trump card. In most fundamentalist preaching and theology, including much of the literature of the Evangelical Theological Society, verbal inerrancy effectively replaced the resurrection of

Christ as the basis of Christianity. Inerrancy was the ultimate warrant for all Christian affirmations and the answer to all critical challenges to Christian belief. Henry's appeal to inerrancy doctrine, in contrast, was closer to the spirit of old Princeton. He observed that for all their commitment to biblical inerrancy, Warfield and the Hodges never rested their theology entirely upon it.[70] Warfield's doctrine of scripture began with the assertion of its divine authority, then moved to the doctrine of biblical inspiration, and then deduced inerrancy from the Bible's testimony to its own inspiration.[71]

Henry's apologetic followed this pattern while acknowledging more clearly and emphatically than Warfield that scripture does not teach its own inerrancy. This recognition moved Henry to acknowledge that neoevangelicals such as Berkouwer and Beegle had a plausible biblical reason for not affirming inerrancy. They sought to avoid that problem of overbelief in which creedal statements not affirmed by scripture itself are made essential to orthodoxy.[72] Henry denied that inerrancy actually belongs to this category, since he regarded inerrancy as a logically unavoidable implication of biblical inspiration. But he vigorously opposed the fundamentalist campaign to deny evangelical credentials to those evangelicals who refused to draw this inference.

Henry further opposed the categorical fundamentalist denunciation of historical criticism. Lindsell used inerrancy doctrine as a trump against the consideration of any form of higher criticism.[73] Henry countered that it would be absurd to commit evangelical orthodoxy to the a priori position that historical criticism is inherently illegitimate and therefore must always be wrong. "Dr. Lindsell regards the historical-critical method as in itself an enemy of orthodox Christian faith," he observed. "He seems totally unaware that even Evangelical seminaries of which he approves are committed to historical criticism, while repudiating the arbitrary, destructive presuppositions upon which the liberal use of the method is based. Surely Dr. Lindsell does not want the seminaries to take an uncritical, unhistorical approach to the Bible!"[74]

But this was exactly what Lindsell and many other fundamentalist evangelicals were seeking. They were well aware that numerous evangelical seminaries were teaching historical criticism. This was the provocation that fired their movement. Lindsell and his comrades were determined to remove nonfundamentalist academics and clergy from positions of authority in evangelical institutions. For decades they had repeated E. J. Young's verdict that a student of the Bible "may practice the principles of criticism or he may be a believer in evangelical Christianity. One thing, however, is clear: if he is consistent, he cannot possibly espouse both." Lindsell reaffirmed that "the evangelical faith itself is mistaken if the historical-critical methodology is correct." To impose any kind of critical apparatus on the Bible is to subject God's Word to human control. It is to create a different scripture than the sacred text that God has bequeathed to us. "The historical-critical method humanizes the Bible while it downgrades the divine authorship," Lindsell explained. "It establishes hermeneutical principles foreign to the Christian faith. It radically changes the traditional understanding of the Bible so that until two hundred years ago no one really comprehended the Bible."[75]

To the militant fundamentalists, "critical orthodoxy" was a contradiction in terms. Lindsell inveighed against every critical technique that failed to operate under fundamentalist presuppositions: "To say the Book of Jonah is fiction when Jesus Christ clearly regarded it as factual, the hermeneutical principle that what Jesus said is to be regarded as truth is abandoned. When the Pauline authorship of Ephesians, 1 and 2 Timothy, and Titus is abandoned, a basic hermeneutical principle has been sacrificed." Historical criticism refuses to take biblical statements at face value, he explained. The whole point of historical criticism is to correct biblical testimony on the basis of some putatively higher knowledge. Moreover, he insisted, it makes no sense whatsoever "to regard those parts of the Bible which are untrue as the Word of God." For these reasons, Lindsell conceded nothing to Henry, Berkouwer, and the host of young neoevangelicals who were seeking to accommodate evangelical orthodoxy to some form of historical criticism. "The historical-critical method is indeed the great enemy of evangelical faith," he declared. "It is a crucial issue and will not go away. How one accepts or rejects it makes a world of difference now and forever."[76]

This debate fueled a prolonged and bitter controversy in American evangelicalism, especially in the Southern Baptist Convention and the Lutheran Church–Missouri Synod, where for the first time, in the mid-1970s, the fundamentalist sides prevailed in battles for control over major denominations.[77] It also proved deeply unsettling to major evangelical theologians whose writings were repeatedly cited as symbols of the crisis of belief in evangelicalism. Henry, Pinnock, and Bernard Ramm were prominent among these. Though many journalists and theologians praised Henry for his carefully nuanced, mediating role in the controversy, Pinnock, Ramm, and numerous other evangelicals were disturbed by the hyperrationalism and the mixed messages that his position contained. Was his emphasis on revelation as discursive mental communication true to the emphasis of scripture? Was biblical truth always reducible to propositional doctrine? If the goal of theology is to systematize all scriptural content into the form of axioms and theorems, wouldn't the achievement of this goal eliminate any further need for the Bible itself? If Henry was right that inerrancy doctrine was crucially important, how could it not be important enough for evangelicals to "squabble" over? But if he was right that evangelical orthodoxy must not close the door to historical-critical scholarship, how was evangelicalism to protect all its doctrines and every statement in scripture from criticism?

The problem of the long day in Joshua 10:12–13 became a flashpoint issue in this debate, reviving unpleasant memories of the famous "Monkey Trial" of 1925. The climactic moment of the Scopes evolution trial in Dayton occurred when Clarence Darrow subjected William Jennings Bryan to a crushing cross-examination. Bryan falteringly conceded to Darrow that he did not know how Eve could have been created from Adam's rib, he did not know how Cain attained his wife, and he had never thought about what would happen if the earth stopped its rotation to allow the sun to "stand still." A half century later, when Ramm confessed that the cosmic consequences of the last event were too mind-boggling for him to swallow, Lindsell attacked him for abandoning biblical truth. "He denies the factuality of the biblical account," Lindsell protested. "Dr. Ramm lets science stand over scripture and God. So the Bible is not normative."[78]

Henry consigned problems of this kind to a Carnellian file marked "unsolved problems." Lindsell, however, pressed hard on evangelical theologians for a verdict on the fundamental "either-or," arguing that one's response to such problem cases proved whether one was truly committed to the authority of scripture. If scripture asserts something that seems unbelievable, he argued, one must either accept the assertion on biblical authority or reject it on the basis of a rival authority, such as science. His aggressive assertion of this either-or and the institutional furor over inerrancy that embroiled American evangelicalism in the 1970s and early 1980s drove many evangelicals to rethink their position. Many were repelled by the fundamentalist campaign to drive modernizers out of denominational seminaries and pulpits. Lindsell's attack on Ramm as a symbol of the backsliding trend in evangelicalism troubled many evangelicals who admired Ramm's contributions to evangelical theology. The prospect of an evangelical movement that purged thinkers such as Bernard Ramm from its ranks was disturbing and unacceptable to them.

REFIGURING WORD AND SPIRIT: BERNARD RAMM

At the same time, it was not surprising that Bernard Ramm became a symbol of controversy in his generation's defining struggle over the nature of evangelicalism. Having begun his teaching career at the fundamentalist-dispensationalist Bible Institute of Los Angeles, he became accustomed early to theological controversy. Ramm's early work sought to defend fundamentalism from outside criticism, but this apologetic commitment also drove him to try to make fundamentalism rethink the religion-science problem.

In his early work *The Christian View of Science and Scripture* (1954), he argued that fundamentalists were creating unneccessary problems for their movement by reading scripture wrongly. The fundamentalist tendency was to treat biblical statements about nature as a kind of alternative science. Ramm's alternative to "biblical" bad science turned on his distinction between the language of science and the Bible's popular nontheoretical speech about nature. He argued that biblical language about nature is popular and phenomenal (restricted to appearances) rather than scientific. Scripture does not theorize about the actual nature of things, he noted. It does not present a theory of matter or offer any definite theorizing about any matter of science. The language of scripture about nature is, rather, nonpostulational discourse from the standpoint of untrained observers that serves as a culturally conditioned literary vehicle for the expression of God's revelation.[79] For example, the truth of Genesis is not to be identified with any scientific worldview that it may imply or contain, for the purpose of Genesis is not to theorize about scientific matters. The purpose of Genesis is to renounce idolatrous views of the universe and bring readers to faith in the Lord of the universe, who created the natural world.

This characterization of biblical language and, especially, Ramm's openness to biological evolution were strongly disputed by fundamentalists in the late 1940s and early 1950s, who tagged him from the outset as a modernizer. At the same time, the founders of mid-century neoevangelicalism for the most part welcomed his early work. Billy Graham told Lindsell that he preferred Ramm's interpretation of the scripture-science debate over Henry's overrationalistic fundamentalism.[80] Ramm's early work maintained a high view of biblical inspiration and special revelation while minimizing the conflicts between science and biblical revelation.[81] He advocated the evidentialist side of the debate between evangelical evidentialists and presuppositionalists but defended this position in a distinctively irenic voice.[82] He did not claim that his evidentialist apologetic was the only position that made sense or that it was the only view compatible with orthodoxy.

In the mid-1950s, however, Ramm's open temperament and capacity for self-criticism led him to question seriously the coherence of his theological position. Though his early writings were already landmark works in evangelical apologetics, he began to doubt that his theology made sense as a whole. An incident in a postlecture discussion made him realize how serious this inner doubt was becoming. When a student merely asked him to define the basis of his theology more precisely, he later recalled, he saw the pieces of his theology pass before him in the way a drowning victim sees parts of his life: "I saw my theology as a series of doctrines picked up here and there, like a rag-bag collection. To stutter out a reply to that question was one of the most difficult things I have ever had to do on a public platform."[83] The experience confirmed his doubts that his theology made sense. He acknowledged that his theological outlook was a grab bag of positions picked up from the wars between modernism and fundamentalism. He recognized that he had no method for dealing with scripture, science, or the relations between them. Moreover, his thinking had no sense or conception of the whole but consisted of various positions that he had adopted to defend conservative Christianity from modernist criticism.

Ramm therefore resolved to start over under the guidance of the best theological mentor he could find, and he quickly realized who that would have to be. In the academic year 1957/58, he took a sabbatical leave to study with Barth, who quickly broke apart Ramm's fundamentalist-evidentialist patchwork. Ramm was exhilarated by Barth's brilliance, his vast learning, and his deep faith. He later recalled that it was Barth who liberated him from his fearful need to defend and protect the gospel. As a typical evangelical fundamentalist, Ramm was predisposed to think and live "within the confines of a small fort with very high walls." But Barth convinced him that true belief should make a theologian free and fearless. He told his students that if they truly believed in the reality and power of God's Word, their theological pursuits "should be fearless in opening any door or any window." This bold message from the theologian he admired most was emancipating to Ramm. "A whole new strategy for my theological work came to birth," he later recalled. "I saw in rapid succession on the parade ground in my mind the futility and intellectual bankruptcy of my former strategy and the wonderful freeing strategy of Barth's theological method."[84]

Ramm had defended inerrancy doctrine not because he believed it but because he was afraid not to believe it. His earlier works had claimed too much for fear of having nothing to claim. It was Barth who made him realize that this was not a faithful or a healthy way to do theology. Like Barth, Ramm soon began to emphasize the illuminative work of the Holy Spirit in making scripture God's Word. He turned away from apologetics and produced an influential trilogy on the nature and structure of divine revelation.[85] These books explored the pattern of biblical authority, the witness of the Holy Spirit, and the nature of special revelation, seeking to explicate the central principle and pattern at work in each doctrine pertaining to revelation. Ramm argued that revelation always occurs in the double structure of objective truth (Word) and subjective illumination (Spirit). He embraced Calvin's dictum that the Word without the Spirit may "strike our ears and appear before our eyes, but not at all affect us within."[86] Affirming Barth's trinitarian understanding of the structure of revelation, in which God gives his Word and sends his Spirit to witness to and minister his Word,[87] Ramm emphasized that the witness of the Spirit produces not only knowledge of God but spiritual regeneration. To isolate scripture from the Spirit "is theologically mischievous," he warned, for true knowledge of God "is gained with a teacher and a grammar, the Holy Spirit and the Sacred Writings."[88]

Ramm judged that for most of the past century, the orthodox doctrine of the union of Word and Spirit had been obscured, if not obliterated, by an obsessive evangelical preoccupation with objectivity. Under the pressure of their desire for scientific respectability, he explained, fundamentalists adopted a strange apologetic that embraced the spirit of science and eliminated the need for the *testimonium* of the Spirit. In the hope of enlisting "the mighty voice of science" on the side of orthodoxy, fundamentalist evangelicals sought to prove that Christianity is founded on rationally verifiable truths, especially the divine inspiration of scripture. Fundamentalist apologetics abounded in "proofs" that God exists, that Christ rose from the grave, and that scripture is inspired by God. It specialized in the art of finding Einsteinian space in Genesis 1 or a theory of matter in Hebrews 11:3 or anticipations of modern chemistry in Leviticus. This strategy created more than its share of problems, Ramm suggested, but one of them was especially disastrous: This fundamentalist drive to prove that Christianity is objectively true eliminated the *testimonium* from the "orthodox" doctrine of scripture. "If inspiration could be pinned down with a sort of mathematical proof, then inspiration was really demonstrated," he explained. "Nothing was more up to date than fundamentalism, for it had Heisenberg and Einstein on its side." If unbelievers could be disarmed by a verse that anticipates Einstein, the testimony of the Spirit was not needed.[89]

Ramm conceded that his early writings contributed significantly to this tradition of evangelical obscurantism. He acknowledged with deep appreciation that it was Barth who turned his thinking away from evidentialist fundamentalism. Barth convinced him that his apologetic negated the necessary union of Word and Spirit, and that it imposed presumptuous philosophical preconditions on the reality of the Word. For all Barth's decisive and weighty influence on him, however, Ramm did not convert to Barthianism. For nearly twenty-five years after his sabbatical, he poured out a stream of neoevangelical works that sought to join Barth's doctrine of the freedom of the Word to a traditional evangelical emphasis on the objectivity and infallibility of biblical revelation. He mixed a traditional evangelical doctrine of special revelation with a Barthian understanding of the freedom and sovereignty of the Spirit. In the early 1970s, he was still defending the plausibility of inerrancy doctrine and contending that the evangelical doctrines of biblical inspiration and inerrancy provided the objectivizing elements that Barthian neo-orthodoxy sorely lacked. The third revised edition of his textbook on hermeneutics, *Protestant Biblical Interpretation* (1970), vigorously defended inerrancy doctrine from various objections, including the claim that scripture contains contradictions. Ramm leaned heavily on appeals to textual corruption, the phenomenal character of biblical language about nature, and the relativity of authorial intention in claiming that inerrancy remains a defensible feature of evangelical doctrine.[90]

His writings maintained a careful distance from Barth's theological position while defending it from overheated evangelical criticism, epitomized by Van Til's slashing attacks on Barth. Van Til and his followers charged repeatedly that Barthianism was the most destructive heresy in Christian history. They claimed that Barthian theology was not really Christian at all, and that Barth's Christian rhetoric was slippery and made his theology uniquely subversive to the faith. The heresy-hunting intemperance of these attacks deeply offended Barth. After the Dutch Calvinists began to disparage even his beloved Mozart, he called them "men of stupid, cold and stony hearts to whom we need not listen." Later, he likened them to butchers and cannibals "beyond the pale." Barth was subsequently cheered by G. C. Berkouwer's more respectful and discerning work, *The Triumph of Grace in the Theology of Karl Barth* (1956), which proved to him that not all conservative Dutch Calvinists were beyond the pale. In the preface to *Church Dogmatics* III:4 he exulted that "there are obviously 'Fundamentalists' with whom one can discuss." But the existence of appreciative evangelicals such as Berkouwer and G. W. Bromiley, Barth's English translator, never quite compensated for the bitter criticism that he took from *Christianity Today,* the Dutch Calvinists, and other evangelicals. One of the ironies of Barth's career was that for all his strident opposition to Catholicism, he generally maintained better relations with Catholic scholars than with Protestant evangelicals. Catholics such as Hans Urs von Balthasar, Henri Bouillard, and Hans Küng treated him virtually as a church father, whereas evangelicals repeatedly painted him as a disingenuous heretic.[91]

Ramm was keenly attuned to the sense of embattlement that characterized Barth's relations with evangelicals. He sought to change the evangelical perspective on Barth while taking care not to identify himself with Barth's position. Like Berkouwer and Donald Bloesch, he defended the greatness and evangelical character of Barth's dogmatic achievement, but he also judged that Barth's doctrine of scripture was seriously deficient. He urged that Barth had much to teach evangelical theology, but not about the objective authority of scripture. The crucial issue was whether scripture is directly or indirectly God's Word. "Evangelicals believe that scripture is directly revelation, not merely a witness to revelation," Ramm explained. "To Barth, inspiration is the willingness of the writers of scripture to be witnesses of revelation. To evangelicals, inspiration is the process whereby the revelation or Word of God is cast into written form."[92]

This was the key to the genuine evangelical dispute with neoorthodoxy. Like most evangelicals, Ramm also had problems with Barth's monist-like Christology, his caustic remarks about fundamentalists, and his implicit universalism, but these were secondary issues. The fundamental problem with Barth was that his doctrine of biblical inspiration was seriously inadequate. Barth rejected the concept of verbal inspiration; indeed, he gave little attention to the doctrine of inspiration at all. In Ramm's reading, Barth's understanding of inspiration was purely subjective: "It expresses the psychological state of the writers of the Scripture." Ramm failed to grasp that Barth employed a conception of inspiration as an inclusive, circular process. Barth regarded scripture as the means by which the Holy Spirit completes a circle of inspiration that began with the biblical writers. Scripture is the Word of God because "God himself now says what the text says." Barth explained, "The work of God is done through this text. The miracle of God takes place in this text formed of human words. This text in all of its humanity, including all the fallibility which belongs to it, is the object of this work and miracle." Barth taught that, in this sense, it is appropriate to speak of verbal inspiration. Verbal inspiration does not imply infallibility of the biblical Word in any of its linguistic, historical, or even theological characteristics as a human word. Rather, it means "that the fallible and faulty human word is as such used by God and has to be received and heard in spite of its human fallibility."[93]

For Barth, biblical inspiration was a circular union of Spirit and Word that included both biblical writers and scripture's readers and hearers. This conception of the meaning of inspiration was more developed than Ramm or other evangelicals recognized, but it still fell short of the evangelical test for scriptural authority that Ramm accepted. From an evangelical standpoint, the fact that Barth gave so little emphasis to inspiration as the source of revealed content in scripture made his understanding of inspiration deficient. It failed to secure objective revealed knowledge. In Ramm's judgment, that Barth gave so little importance to inspiration also contributed mightily to the disappearance of inspiration as a topic in modern theology. Among contemporary theologians, he observed, only evangelicals and a few Roman Catholics even bothered to discuss inspiration. On this issue, the evangelicals spoke with one voice: They regarded the modern neglect of biblical inspiration as a colossal and unnecessary surrender to secularism. "I am unhappy with the imbalance in neoorthodoxy in terms of the amount of space given to revelation as over against the very little space given to inspiration," Ramm remarked. He called for an evangelical dogmatics that gave as much intellectual energy to the development of inspiration as Barth gave to revelation.[94]

This was a plausible project for Ramm's later career. Having claimed for many years that evangelicalism provided a sounder structure for Barth's theological program, Ramm entered the mid-1970s with the apparent intention of refortifying the dogmatic teaching of inerrancy-claiming evangelical theology. "To the evangelical, theology is a matter of life and death, vindication or judgment," he observed.

"Theology must then be built on the most absolute foundation possible—the revelation of God in Scripture." He called for a new literature that reaffirmed the traditional evangelical doctrine of biblical inspiration in conversation with current
developments in linguistics and philosophy of language. One important issue that
this project needed to address, he proposed, was the rethinking of the traditional
evangelical prejudice against myth. He allowed that the word was loaded with apparently unredeemable connotations for most evangelicals. *Myth* was a scare
word, a term of denigration or accusation. "But what if further studies in communications show that myth is one of the valid methods of representing truth and particularly religious truth?" he asked. Was evangelicalism obliged to cling to an
outmoded prejudicial approach to myth, "or will we have the flexibility to see
myth in the new light in which modern linguistics, communications, and the study
of comparative religion see it and find a place for it in evangelical theology?"[95]

But this was hardly the question that gripped evangelical theology in the late
1970s. The controversy over inerrancy reduced evangelical discourse to questions
that Ramm thought evangelicalism had outgrown. It created a climate of suspicion
and hostility that he greatly disliked. The militancy of the strict-inerrancy back-
lash forced him to rethink his own relation to evangelicalism. Shortly after Lindsell, in *The Battle for the Bible,* condemned the rise of a noninerrancy trend in
evangelical scholarship, Ramm countered that Lindsell's understanding of Christianity was reductive, narrow, and historically peculiar. It reduced the problem of
faith to a principle that was "all too neat, all too simple, all too precise." It committed evangelicalism to a make-believe, all-controlling doctrine of scripture.
"Anyone who has lived with biblical criticism through the years knows the cluster of problems we face on every page of Scripture," Ramm observed. "If we told
a logician that there are no errors in scripture but a thousand problems (not an exaggeration in view of the huge books on Old and New Testament introduction) he
would die laughing."[96]

Evangelicalism must not commit itself to a view of scripture that would not
pass the laugh test, he implied. It must not saddle itself with a doctrine of scriptural authority that would die the death of a thousand qualifications. Ramm observed that the strict-inerrancy movement was the product of a "Bible-only"
mentality that made the scriptural *record* of revelation primordial, rather than revelation itself.[97] *The Battle for the Bible* was a showcase example of this mentality.
Like most fundamentalists, Lindsell lifted the inspired record of revelation above
the revelation to which scripture testifies. He therefore turned an unbelievable doctrine of scripture into the essence of Christianity. This mentality has disastrous implications for the evangelical doctrine of the church, Ramm noted. It turns cultists
into evangelicals while making evangelicalism incapable of recognizing Eastern
Orthodox churches or other Christian traditions as genuinely Christian. If inerrancy doctrine defines the essence of Christianity, then true Christianity is followed only by a tiny fraction of the world's Christians, many of whom are cultists.
Lindsell charged that Ramm was "infected by those who hold an aberrant view of
the Bible," but Ramm countered that fundamentalism was the aberration in Christian history.[98] "I strongly believe that the current effort to make a certain

doctrine of scripture the *Wesen* [essential nature or essence] of Christianity represents a Bible-only mentality which cannot be supported because it is so narrow
that it becomes self-defeating," he declared.[99] In common cause with Beegle,
Fuller, Jack Rogers, Donald McKim, Stephen Davis, and I. Howard Marshall,
Ramm defended the recent evangelical turn from inerrancy doctrine.

The crucial contribution to the inerrancy debate came from a more surprising
source, however. Though Ramm had defended inerrancy in the past, he had always
qualified its meaning too much for most fundamentalists. Many viewed him as a
modernizing trimmer long before he came out explicitly against inerrancy doctrine. And while Henry was a firm advocate of inerrancy, even his opposition to
the militant inerrancy movement was not altogether surprising. Henry's ambitions
for evangelicalism as a social movement had always tempered his doctrinal militancy. During his term as editor of *Christianity Today,* he gave much less emphasis to inerrancy than the magazine gave to the issue afterward, under Lindsell's
editorial guidance. Though it stunned Lindsell in the late 1970s to find Henry
among his critics, Henry's reasons for refusing to make inerrancy the "superbadge" of evangelical orthodoxy were neither new nor surprising.

FUNDAMENTALISM RECONSIDERED: CLARK PINNOCK

The shocker came from Clark Pinnock. For ten years, right up to the moment
of Lindsell's 1976 blast against backsliding evangelicalism, Pinnock had produced one aggressive book after another that made the case for inerrancy doctrine
and evidentalist apologetics.[100] In 1968 he had railed against the cowardly "con-
spiracy of silence" in the Southern Baptist Convention that was purportedly allowing false doctrine to erode the church's orthodoxy. "To affirm Christ and reject
infallibility is an act of intellectual impenitence and schizophrenia," he had
charged. "In the past a professor trembled to contradict God's Word; now he trem-
bles to go against the current liberal consensus." He had warned that the church
would disintegrate if it failed to purge its colleges and seminaries of modernizing
academics, saying, "We have tried resolutions and they have not worked. It is time
for action, before it comes too late to act. It takes but a few rebels to overthrow a
government, and a few rioters to burn a city. Our Church could be destroyed if we
do not take steps to ensure that the integrity of the gospel is preserved."[101]

With fervent assurance, the early Pinnock reasoned that the authority of scripture rests on the datum of the incarnation. "As soon as a person comes to faith in
the divine Son of God, the question of authority is settled," he asserted. "The Bible
is not infallible because *it* says so—but because *He* says so."[102] He maintained that
Christians know that scripture is God's infallible Word because Christ assumed
and claimed that it is. With equal assurance, he maintained that because scripture
is God's Word, it is inconceivable that scripture would ever employ such literary
forms as myth, midrash, legend, etiological (origin) tale, or saga. Since all these
forms practice and involve the reader in deceit, he explained, all are inherently unworthy. The notion that any of them might be a vehicle for God's Word must be

ruled out. For the same reason, Pinnock ruled out the notion that some biblical writers might have used pseudonyms.[103] Following the Lutheran dogmatician Robert D. Preus, Pinnock reasoned that God would never have inspired anyone to practice fraud or forgery. The claim that scripture is verbally inspired by God is incompatible with the judgment that scripture contains deceitful forms of literature or deceitful authorship claims.[104] It does little good to affirm biblical inerrancy, Pinnock warned, if one does not guard against hermeneutical relativism.

In Pinnock's early reading, this was the key problem (aside from its denial of inerrancy) with the tradition of evangelicalism that Orr and James Denney pioneered. For all his devotion to biblical inspiration, Orr established a form of evangelical theology that implicitly undercut the divine authority of scripture on hermeneutical grounds. He argued that evangelicals should not prejudge or resist whatever literary forms scripture actually contains. The notion that certain literary forms are illegitimate for divine purposes is not a biblical principle, Orr observed. This notion is rather an extrabiblical assumption that misguided "defenders" of scripture bring to the biblical text.[105] Ramm pressed the same argument a step further. He noted that the ancient Hebrew and early Christian cultures that produced the Bible saw no reason not to employ saga, legend, and pseudonymity in expressing God's Word. Since they clearly did employ these literary forms in writing Holy Scripture, he argued, Christians today are obliged to accept these forms as vehicles of the Word. Revelation is no less divine when it accommodates our natures and worldly conditions in literary forms that were current during biblical times. If the Bible is literature, he asked, "why should it be subjected to criteria . . . beyond the boundaries of literature?"[106]

The early Pinnock's declaration of why it should not was categorical and withering. Ramm's entire hermeneutical departure was destructive for evangelicalism, he judged. It subverted the absolute character of biblical truth. "Ramm measures veracity by a relative cultural standard, rather than by an absolute truth standard," he objected. To affirm that God's Word might be expressed in scripture through legend or saga is to subject evangelical truth claims to a hermeneutical abyss. It is to break the link between biblical affirmation and reality. "Simple honesty cannot be excluded from any truth criterion," Pinnock urged. "Where statements of fact are intentional, we must suppose they do correspond to what is indeed the case."[107] The answer to Ramm's proposal was that evangelical theology could not endorse hermeneutical relativism and survive.

Pinnock cautioned that this was not to admit that evangelical theology rejects any literary form that scripture actually employs. The question of whether scripture actually uses saga or myth, he explained, "can only be answered at an earlier point"—the point at which controlling presuppositions about scripture are established. Because evangelicalism assumes that scripture is God's inspired Word, he explained, evangelicals are required to accept as historical fact every event that scripture presents as historical. As a strong opponent of fideism, however, Pinnock did not appeal merely to the necessity of beginning with correct presuppositions; he argued that scripture everywhere "is jealous of historical reality." In his reading, the evidence did not compel any judgment that Genesis uses myth or that

Matthew and Luke employ nativity saga and midrash in their accounts of the birth of Jesus. Modern biblical scholarship often claims to find myth or saga in scripture, he noted, but this is not because scripture obviously employs these literary forms. The modernist claim that scripture contains saga is rather a function of the modernist *judgment* that some biblical material is legendary. Biblical scholars label Genesis as myth and the infancy narratives as saga simply because they disbelieve the plain assertions of scripture in these accounts.

To Pinnock, it was therefore repugnant to claim, as Ramm was already suggesting, that evangelical theology needed to be prepared to hear God's Word through myth or saga. It is axiomatic that God would never speak through such unworthy forms, and there is no incontrovertible evidence that scripture contains them, he insisted: "Evangelicals reject the neoorthodox tendency to mythologize scriptural narratives because (1) it is a denial of what scripture teaches, and (2) it represents a docetic dehistoricizing of redemption."[108] Though Pinnock often appropriated Ramm's arguments on other subjects, his rejection of Ramm's openness to biblical saga contained a weightier negative judgment: He implied that Ramm's method was not orthodox but neoorthodox. Long before Ramm concluded that this was indeed his theological perspective, Pinnock denounced the neoorthodox spirit of Ramm's approach to scripture.

All of Pinnock's early books focused their critical fire on the "disastrous" mistakes of neoorthodoxy. *Set Forth Your Case* (1967) repudiated the neoorthodox wedge between God's Word and the words of scripture: "The bane of modern theology has been the insistence that the acts of God are visible only to the eyes of faith, and the Word of God is never to be identified with any given text."[109] Hence, in the mid-1970s, no evangelical theologian appeared more determined or equipped than Pinnock to press the case for a credible fundamentalist alternative to neoorthodoxy. He had earned his doctorate in New Testament under F. F. Bruce at Manchester University and also had worked for a time with Francis Schaeffer, whose writings modeled for Pinnock the kind of aggressive, opinionated apologetics that he sought to write. With greater intellectual sophistication than either Lindsell or Schaeffer, Pinnock's early writings exhorted the evangelical community to defend inerrancy doctrine without equivocation. With an even more extreme militancy than Lindsell, he insisted that evangelical institutions needed to face up to the necessity of purging all modernizers from leadership positions.

But in the mid-1970s, Pinnock began to question whether the cause of inerrancy was worth all the turmoil and hostility it was causing in the evangelical movement. Though he never doubted that the evangelical struggle against theological liberalism in the Southern Baptist Convention had been necessary, he became less sure that this struggle had to make inerrancy the litmus test of orthodox belief. Was it really necessary for inerrancy believers to keep the evangelical movement in a state of perpetual acrimony? Was the doctrine of perfect errorlessness worth the suspicion and divisiveness of the past decade? Pinnock had relentlessly defended his acquired version of the evangelical gospel, but he began to feel that something was spiritually lacking in it. He felt unsettled not only about the state of American evangelicalism but about his own faith. It is hardly enough to defend Christian belief if we lack a vibrant, compassionate, outward-reaching spirituality, he re-flected. Christ is neither served nor honored by a brittle orthodoxy.

This was not the first time that Pinnock had made a critical reassessment of his relationship to evangelicalism. He had grown up in a liberal Baptist family and church in Toronto "where the gospel was not clearly explained or confidently con-fessed." Under the influence of his grandmother and a devoted Sunday school teacher, he had converted as a teenager to Youth for Christ–style evangelicalism. Years later, he recalled that he could never fathom why so many pastors watered down the gospel message of Christ's redeeming death and resurrection. "It has been about thirty years since I was saved, and I have never been able to shake off the feeling of outrage at the arrogance of the liberal decision to revise the New Testament message to make it acceptable to modern men," he recounted in 1985. "I suppose that my deepest concern as a theologian today is to expose and refute this deadly error."[110] As a student and later as a young academic, Pinnock em-braced the Reformed evangelicalism of Henry, Van Til, and John Murray, believ-ing "that Calvinism was just scriptural evangelicalism in its purest expression."[111] His early writings reflected this assumption. With a characteristic Reformed in-sistence that biblical Christianity is "rooted in rational truth," he criticized the charismatic movement for its emotionalism and irrationality, describing the gift of tongues as a mindless release from anxiety accompanied by "soft babblings from the throat."[112]

Then, in 1967, Pinnock attended a home prayer meeting in which he witnessed the energy and healing power of the Spirit. He met people who were "alive unto God." They were eager to pray and expressed great joy in God's palpable pres-ence. The evening passed quickly. "I was touched by God that night," Pinnock later recalled. The experience of praying with people who knew and celebrated God's loving Spirit opened his eyes to a "dimension of the Spirit which the New Testament describes but is so often absent in churches today." Scripture came alive for him again, and the prospect of living a Christian life regained its earlier ex-citement. His new openness to the charismatic gifts of the Spirit brought him into contact with charismatics and Pentecostals and deepened his interest in the theol-ogy of spiritual experience. Though he avoided Pentecostal language about the "baptism of the Spirit," he boldly proclaimed that what the church needed above all was the kind of "infilling of the Spirit" that he experienced among Pente-costals.[113]

In the early 1970s, while teaching at Trinity Evangelical Divinity School, Pin-nock also moved away from the deterministic absolute-sovereignty thinking of Reformed theology. His study of the book of Hebrews raised the question that turned him against his acquired Calvinism. If it is true that Christians cannot fall away from Christ, as Calvinism teaches, he reflected, why does the New Testa-ment repeatedly warn against the danger of falling away? If Christians actually en-joy absolute security from the possibility of losing their faith, why does Hebrews exhort its Christian readers and hearers to persevere in the faith (Heb. 3:12) and not fall away from Christ (Heb. 10:26)? "It began to dawn on me that my security in God was linked to my faith-union with Christ and that God is teaching us here the extreme importance of maintaining and not forsaking this relationship," Pinnock later recalled.[114] To his surprise, his thinking began to move in an explicitly Arminian direction.

During the same period, Pinnock was also influenced by a group of radical evangelical students at Trinity, led by Jim Wallis and Joe Roos, who strongly criticized the political conservatism of established evangelical Christianity. These students reclaimed the anarchist-pacifist witness of the Anabaptist peace tradition and, reflecting the postnationalist and antiwar character of their politics, founded a magazine called *The Post-American*. Pinnock became their key faculty advocate at an institution that barely tolerated their existence. He later served as a contributing editor to the renamed *Sojourners* magazine and sought to maintain the commitment of the *Sojourners* community to a firmly evangelical theology.[115]

All these influences moved Pinnock to reconsider his conception of evangelical orthodoxy and his relationship to establishment evangelicalism. In 1974 he left Trinity to teach at Regent College in Vancouver; three years later, he returned home to Hamilton, Ontario, to teach at the more liberal McMaster Divinity College. Though his attraction to radical politics faded in the early 1980s, Pinnock sustained a deep interest in charismatic experience and also wrote extensively on the implications of Arminian evangelicalism for the doctrines of election, total depravity, and atonement.[116] This Arminian turn eventually produced some of his most daring and provocative theological work. Pinnock's commitment to rethink what it means to be evangelical but not Reformed moved him to reconsider basic doctrines about the nature of God that had gone largely unquestioned in traditional evangelicalism.

But it was the battle for the Bible that gripped his attention in the mid-1970s and drove him to rethink his fundamental position. He was already lamenting the spiritual cost of inerrancy politics when Lindsell published *The Battle for the Bible*. The book's inflammatory impact confirmed Pinnock's growing belief that the price of inerrancy conformity was too high. He publicly chastised Lindsell for fomenting "a new wave of bitterness and controversy" and dissociated himself from Lindsell's "militant tone and sweeping tactics." Recalling Orr's warnings on this theme, Pinnock argued that it was foolish, if not suicidal, for the evangelical movement to become obsessed with the accuracy of minor details in the Bible. Though evangelicalism should not give up the doctrine of biblical inerrancy, he reasoned, it needed to distinguish between the containment of error and the teaching of error when it explained what inerrancy was about. "Inerrancy refers to the *subjects* rather than to all the *terms* of Scripture," he proposed. Inerrancy was not about perfect errorlessness but about the protection of biblical teaching from error. Carnell's earlier distinction was apt: The best solution to the inerrancy problem was to distinguish between inerrant biblical teachings and the possibly errant materials that scripture utilizes in formulating its teachings.[117]

Against his own, earlier work, Pinnock urged that it was "divisive sectarianism" to claim that the doctrine of perfect errorlessness was the only orthodox view of biblical authority or the only serious alternative to theological liberalism.[118] Without noting that he previously had repudiated this solution for "severely undercut[ing] the truth value of the Bible," he now embraced Carnell's distinction between intended meaning and incidental detail.[119] He redefined inerrancy "in a *qualified* sense, relative to the intended assertions of the text."[120] Pinnock judged that the theory of perfectly errorless autographs was an abstraction that had died the death of a thousand qualifications. Rather than obscure or impede the dynamic authority of scripture with an unbelievable overarching dogma about it, he urged, it was better simply to admit the existence of problem passages in God's Word. Rather than judge a text by a criterion of meaning and truth that did not derive from scripture, it was better to judge the meaning and truth of biblical texts by their specific purposes. In virtually the same words that Carnell had used a generation earlier, Pinnock thus asserted that "the Bible *contains* errors but *teaches* none."[121]

The problem was that neither Carnell nor any other evangelical had done much more than assert this distinction over the past two decades. Having finally embraced Carnell's approach, Pinnock had to face his own past criticism of the dangers and weaknesses of this solution. Carnell had invoked the distinction between intentional teaching and incidental detail to salvage a substantive notion of biblical infallibility that accommodated some of the inductive problems with perfect errorlessness, but his work did little more than redefine the scope of inerrancy. He did not develop the doctrinal implications of infallible-teaching inerrancy or show how it worked in practice or defend it from outside criticism. To this arduous task Pinnock committed his considerable intellectual energy.

"His pilgrimage has been inexplicable," Lindsell bitterly remarked of him, but in fact, Pinnock carefully explicated the doubts and reasons that drove him to rethink his position.[122] He noted that even Warfield had conceptualized inerrancy relative to the intention of the text rather than to every detail of scripture. Warfield had taught that the primary question to be asked whenever scripture is interpreted or subjected to criticism is "What was the professed or implied purpose of the writer in making this statement?"[123] Pinnock urged that this question held the key to the revision of inerrancy doctrine that evangelicalism needed. By pressing the question of authorial intention, he explained, evangelicalism could acknowledge the existence of errors in scripture (as Warfield did not) while retaining its claim that biblical teaching is infallible. The errors that scripture contains belong not to its intended teachings but only to its incidental, unintended teachings.

The doctrine of inerrancy is a possible inference from the biblical doctrine of inspiration, Pinnock allowed, but it is not the only possible conclusion that can be drawn from this doctrine. The notion that inspiration *must* have produced an errorless text is unwarranted. The vehicles of God's inspiration, after all, were fallible human agents, and there is no infallible teaching about the degree to which God's inspiring influence overcame their limitations. "We are simply not in a position by sheer logic to judge how God ought to have given his Word," Pinnock cautioned. "The logic of the case for inerrancy has been confused by a mistaken piety and the errorlessness of the Bible defended, not so much out of the conviction that it *is* inerrant as from the belief that it *must* be."[124] Behind this mistaken evangelical piety lies an oversold fear, he suggested, for only a frightened orthodoxy thinks it must have a perfect revelation in hand if its faith is not to be destroyed.

This was the crucial point for Pinnock. The battle for biblical inerrancy was not making the evangelical movement stronger, healthier, more faithful, or more compelling. Instead, it was heightening the movement's climate of fearfulness and hostility. A vibrant evangelical movement that heard God speaking through the Word would not be so preoccupied with Bible trivia and so terrified of losing its faith. "To say that unless every point can be established, the entire edifice will come crashing down seems to indicate the fortress mentality of an orthodoxy in decline," Pinnock judged. "When the awareness of God speaking powerfully through scripture begins to subside, it is necessary to cling to rationalistic arguments in order to defend the Bible, and scholastic orthodoxy is born."[125]

Instead of protecting the faith of new believers, the fundamentalist evangelical insistence on strict inerrancy absurdly jeopardized the faith by setting up a domino effect to destroy it. "Imagine a student, convinced that a single flaw in scripture invalidates the whole Bible, confronting what he sincerely believes to be a surd inconsistency in the text," Pinnock wrote. "Is he not likely to abandon all his convictions forthwith, and would he not be less likely to do so had he not been persuaded to equate inspiration and inerrancy?" The crucial distinction, then, should be between a doctrine of inspiration that supports infallible teaching and a doctrine that insists on the necessity of an errorless text. Inspiration that inspires infallible teaching is credible and biblical, Pinnock argued; but the claim that inspiration must produce an errorless text is not credible, is not required by scripture, and is disastrous for the church. "What right have we to argue that a view of inspiration cannot be high and strong unless inerrancy is implied in it?" he asked. "It is a gross overstatement which can only have bad effects itself; indeed, it may well be a self-fulfilling prophecy."[126]

Instead of emphasizing the saving truth of the biblical testimony to Christ, American evangelicalism increasingly emphasized "the precise accuracy of minor details." Pinnock noted that this mentality distorted the nature of scripture: "Minute inerrancy may be a central issue for the telephone book but not for psalms, proverbs, apocalyptic, and parables," he observed. "Inerrancy just does not focus attention correctly where the Bible is concerned." In his judgment, what it did replicate was the spirit of Pharisaic legalism that Jesus condemned. The Pharisees fretted over biblical details, but they were closed to the saving Word that Jesus embodied and proclaimed: "Their 'high view' of biblical inerrancy served to conceal their unbelief." Though evangelicals routinely claimed that Jesus embraced the Jewish view of scripture that prevailed in his time, Pinnock countered that this claim was plainly mistaken: "He did not teach us to concern ourselves chiefly with niceties of detail, but to hear God's Word issue forth afresh from the text."[127]

The parallels between his perceptions of ancient Pharisaism and modern evangelicalism were chilling enough to Pinnock to make him call for a halt to the battle over inerrancy. He observed that numerous academic and clerical leaders had already been excommunicated from the evangelical community because they could not accept Warfield-style inerrancy doctrine. He urged evangelicals to stop this self-destructive process before it went any further: "I urge charity toward those whose hesitation over inerrancy is due to their honest judgment and not to any weakness of their evangelical convictions." Having provided the fundamentalist reaction with much of its intellectual firepower, Pinnock now pleaded with conservatives to stop wielding inerrancy "like a sledge hammer to destroy the work of God."[128] Having argued for years that evangelicals should not shield themselves from unwelcome evidence, he now judged that strict inerrancy doctrine could be upheld only by ignoring considerable evidence.

It was telling to Pinnock that leading evangelical theologians were defending inerrancy with a century-old list of problem passages and stock harmonizations, and he called this a tragic spectacle. He noted that the best evangelical scholars tried to avoid the inerrancy debate, but even this tactic gave them little freedom from it. The commitment of the evangelical establishment to a very restrictive conception of biblical inerrancy had a chilling effect on virtually all evangelical scripture scholarship. For example, Pinnock observed, "no one is giving us much help with handling the newer issues such as 'canonical shape,' redaction criticism, the history of transmission within the Bible, and so forth."[129] Even the best evangelical scholars were deterred from pushing evangelical scholarship forward because of the political force of inerrancy doctrine. The result was that theologians like himself had to consult nonevangelicals to learn what the problems or issues in biblical scholarship were.

At the same time, Pinnock exhorted outsiders that the inerrancy debate deserved to be taken seriously on its own terms. The evangelical conflict over inerrancy was not "just a scholastic interchange on trivial questions stemming from overbelief," he cautioned. It was rather a serious and defining struggle within conservative Protestantism "to discover how best to respond to the challenge of modernity, and in particular its skeptical attitude toward the unique authority and relevance of Holy Scripture."[130] In the late 1970s he conceded that the prospects for the kind of inerrancy doctrine that he supported were not promising. Evangelicals such as himself were being attacked from both sides. Fundamentalist evangelical leaders were accusing them of betraying the faith, while liberal Protestants such as James Barr ridiculed their attempts to salvage inerrancy doctrine in some form.[131] "From both sides it seems that this moderate position is unstably tottering between inerrancy and non-inerrancy and likely to come down eventually on the non-inerrancy side," Pinnock judged. He feared that the best evangelical scholars were moving toward neoorthodoxy, and that the most militant sector of the evangelical establishment was on the verge of gaining complete control over evangelical institutions.[132]

Pinnock drew some encouragement from the fact that official Roman Catholic doctrine on biblical authority embraced an infallible-teaching model much like his own. The use of historical-critical methodologies in Catholic biblical scholarship was legitimized in 1943 by Pope Pius XII's encyclical *Divino Afflante Spiritu,* but in 1962, at Vatican Council II, the first draft of the Constitution on Divine Revelation (*Verbum Dei*) contained a strict-inerrancy statement on biblical authority. The legitimacy of biblical criticism of any kind within Roman Catholicism was thrown into question. The precise teaching of the church on this enormously significant question was vigorously debated at Vatican II before a substantially revised statement was approved. The final version of *Verbum Dei* repeated the assertion of *Divino Afflante Spiritu* that God made full use of the "powers and faculties" of the biblical writers in inspiring scripture. It added that "though he acted in them and by them, it was as true authors that they consigned to writing whatever he wanted written." The next sentence carefully described the kind of infallibility that inspiration implies: "We must acknowledge that the books of Scripture, firmly, faithfully and without error, teach that truth which God, for the sake of salvation, wished to see confided to the sacred Scriptures."[133] Vatican II thus discarded the language of perfect errorlessness in favor of a salvation-oriented infallible-teaching model of inerrancy.

The fact that official Catholic teaching on biblical authority was so close to his own position was encouraging to Pinnock, but he also recognized that the strongest theological trend in Catholicism after Vatican II was against inerrancy doctrine altogether. For the same reasons, he noted, the most accomplished and technically proficient scholars in Protestant evangelicalism were likewise turning against inerrancy doctrine. On various occasions he mentioned Ramm, Bruce, Berkouwer, Ladd, Beegle, Jack Rogers, Donald McKim, I. Howard Marshall, Harry Boer, and H. N. Ridderbos as examples of this trend. Though it was telling to Pinnock that none of these thinkers had developed an alternative theology of inspiration, he observed that they were quite clear in explaining why evangelicalism was wrong to commit itself to inerrancy language. They judged that the assumption of scientific accuracy that the theory of perfect errorlessness presumed was neither credible nor biblical. They noted that scripture itself plainly subordinates the value of precision to other ends in many of its accounts. Moreover, they observed that the character of biblical inspiration as attested by scripture is more practical and much less formal than traditional Catholic and Protestant orthodoxies presumed.[134]

Pinnock agreed on all counts. The idea of inspiration is related not to an abstract perfection, he affirmed, but to "the sufficiency of scripture through the Spirit of God to nourish and instruct the church for its faith and life."[135] What Pinnock questioned was whether this school of evangelicals could develop a strong enough alternative to forge a new consensus on what evangelicalism should teach about biblical authority. In his judgment, the kind of revisionist evangelical history that Rogers and McKim promoted, which emphasized the differences between Reformationist and Scholasticist Protestantism, had little or nothing to contribute to this project of reinterpretation. Pinnock put no stock in revisionist attempts to prove that premodern orthodoxy was less rigorous than old Princeton in its view of biblical accuracy.[136] He warned that modern inerrancy proponents had not been wrong in claiming that premodern orthodoxy assumed scripture contains no errors; it was futile to obscure this heritage. Rogers and McKim emphasized that modern inerrancy doctrine was a product of seventeenth-century Protestant scholasticism, but Pinnock took no comfort from Luther's freewheeling approach to scripture. He cautioned that every Christian orthodoxy in Christian history has been constructed within a biblical house of authority, and the new evangelicalism must not justify its revisionism by obscuring this historical record. What was needed, rather, was to explain why a perfectly orthodox revision of traditional teaching was needed. Virtually every orthodox theological tradition, from the Greek Fathers to the Latin scholasticists to the Reformers to old Princeton, exaggerated the inspired perfection of scripture and underemphasized its humanity, he judged. The task for a new evangelicalism was to improve on this record, acknowledging straightforwardly that "the old view of the Bible that we treasure is not biblical and serviceable in every detail today."[137]

RETHINKING INFALLIBILITY

The challenge facing the new evangelicalism was to become the first orthodoxy to overcome the conventional orthodox neglect of the humanity of scripture. Pinnock urged that evangelicalism did not need a scripture that was incapable of error or a church tradition that smothered the scriptural voice of the Word. The evangelicalism that was needed would liberate scripture from orthodox overbelief and from the suffocating traditionalism of church-centered Christianity. It would offer "a systematic treatment of the scripture principle that faces all the questions squarely and supplies a model for understanding that will help us transcend the current impasse."[138]

During his fundamentalist period, Pinnock always founded his scripture principle on 2 Timothy 3:16–17, the only place in scripture where the term *inspired* (*theopneustos*) occurs. He continued this practice as a neoevangelical, but now he paid attention to Paul's emphasis on practical spirituality. In 2 Timothy 3:16–17, Paul describes all scripture as inspired by God "and useful for teaching, for reproof, for correction, and for training in righteousness, so that everyone who belongs to God may be proficient, equipped for every good work." Pinnock noted this time what Paul did not say: "He does not present a theory about a perfect Bible given long ago but now lost, but declares the Bible in Timothy's possession to be alive with the breath of God and full of the transforming information the young disciple would need in the life of faith and obedience." This was the message that evangelicalism needed to absorb and proclaim, he urged. It is the practical effectiveness of scripture in bringing about a transforming relation to Christ that matters utmost. "We must not shift the emphasis to the unavailable Bible of the past, about which one can speculate, or to the inaccessible Bible of the future, after the experts will (supposedly) have cleared away every perplexing feature of the text, removing all possibility of doubt."[139]

The scripture that we need to be able to trust is the one we already have. Moreover, Pinnock urged, the practical focus of scripture on the communication of God's saving work in Christ is the focus that evangelicalism needs to adopt: "This is the doctrine of Scripture I am concerned to discuss and defend: Not the Bible of academic debate, but the Bible given and handed down to be the medium of the gospel message and the primary sacrament of the knowledge of God, his own communication, which is able to reconcile us to God so that we might come to love and obey him." Christians typically believe that scripture is God's Word not because they have studied up on apologetics but because scripture has introduced them to a saving knowledge of Christ, just as Paul promised it would. Pinnock still believed that apologetics should play a supportive role in reinforcing one's faith in Christ, but he emphasized that faith rests ultimately on the movement of God's Spirit, not on rational argument. "Therefore let us not quench the Spirit in our theology of inspiration, whether by rationalist liberal doubts or by rationalist conservative proofs, because both shift the focus away from the power of God in the Scriptures and onto our ability to rationally comprehend these matters."[140]

He cautioned that this did not mean that evangelical theology should retreat from a substantive understanding of revelation. Neoorthodoxy goes too far in playing up the metaphorical character of revelational God-language, Pinnock judged. "Though I appreciate the emphasis upon God-given metaphors and agree that they are richer than propositions, I am nervous when I see a theologian seem to back away from the factual and cognitive content of them, given the widespread retreat from content in the liberal movement," he explained. It would not suffice for evangelicalism to appeal to revelation if, like neoorthodoxy, it stripped revelation of any substantive content: "What has gone wrong in nonconservative modern theology across the board is the retreat from contentful revelation, with devastating results for dogmatic theology."[141]

Pinnock recognized that liberal and neoorthodox theologians had serious reasons for moving away from the notion of revelation as propositional information. "The Bible teaches some awkward things that modern people have difficulty receiving, and some think the only way to deal with that is to qualify its authority and deny its infallibility." How can we accept the biblical creation accounts after Darwin? How can we claim that scriptural teaching regarding women or homosexuality is infallible? How can we take seriously the biblical doctrine of salvation through the blood of Christ alone? Pinnock observed that modern theology deals with these problems by retreating from the notion that divine revelation bears any necessary content: "Though the cost is awfully high (the entire basis of doctrinal and ethical theology in any traditional sense disappears) it is considered worth paying by the liberal theologians. It leaves them free to pursue enticing doctrines of their own making and preference."[142]

The latter claim informed his dismissal of a deeper neoorthodox objection to his position. Barth rejected the concept of revelation as information primarily because this idea turns revelation into an object that is subject to human control. The Word of God is not a thing but pure event, Barth contended; it does not disclose propositional information about God but reveals God himself. To confess that the Bible is God's Word is to make a confession of faith, "a statement made by the faith that hears God Himself speak in the human word of the Bible." Barth cautioned that the Bible is God's Word, however, only "so far as God lets it be His Word, so far as God speaks through it." Otherwise it would be some "thing" that human beings have power over. It would not be revelation (which is its own basis) but an object that human beings possess, use, and base arguments on. Barth warned that it is not even accurate to say that scripture becomes God's Word when we accord it faith, for this understanding also turns revelation over to human control. Scripture becomes God's Word not because we accord it faith but because by an act of divine freedom "it becomes revelation for us."[143]

Pinnock gave this position remarkably short shrift. He dismissed the Barthian critique of the orthodox objectivization of the Word as a pious evasion. "Piously declaring that revelation is not something human beings can possess or control, this view has delivered it over to autonomous human beings to do precisely that," he charged.[144] Without the constraining force of revealed propositions, theologians make up whatever they want to believe. Rather than acknowledge the seriousness of Barth's claim that orthodox objectivism domesticates the transcendence of the Word, Pinnock simply repeated that orthodoxy must be both objective and subjective. He treated Barth's fundamental challenge to evangelicalism as a kind of trick.

Pinnock later recalled that his early writings defended strict inerrancy "because I desperately wanted it to be true. I wanted it to be true so badly that I passed over the obvious problems."[145] In mid-career he resolved to face up to the problems. Realizing that "the case for total inerrancy just isn't there" and that American evangelicalism was needlessly tearing itself apart over the issue, he redrew the line at infallible-teaching inerrancy and invested the same passion he had earlier shown for strict inerrancy in defending this fallback position against theological relativism. He observed that liberal biblical scholars cared most about reading scripture critically, but "what we ought to care most about is what God is teaching us in and through the text," which includes a great deal of propositional information. This is the battle line that a renewed evangelicalism must defend, he exhorted: "Inerrancy simply means that the Bible can be trusted in what it teaches and affirms."[146]

This redefinition opened up the problem of literary forms. Pinnock reconsidered his earlier judgment that various literary forms must be ruled out as possible vehicles of God's Word. Evangelicalism can still assert the inerrant truth of scriptural teaching while accepting Ramm's judgments about the multiplicity of scriptural literary forms, he reasoned. By this reading, the inerrant truth of a parable is parabolic, just as the inerrant truth of poetry is poetic and the inerrant truth of fable is fabulous. "If Matthew gives us some fictional midrash, then it is inerrant according to the demands of this genre," Pinnock explained. "All this means is that inerrancy is relative to the intention of the text." By the mid-1980s, Pinnock began to sense that the prospects for a revised evangelicalism of this kind were brighter than he had thought when he first moved in this direction, for a critical mass of evangelical theologians and pastors seemed to be moving in the same direction. If a renewed evangelical movement should come to embrace an infallible-teaching model of inerrancy, he predicted, the turnabout would force "the strict conservatives to give up the term themselves, just as they have given up the term *evangelical,* for much the same reason."[147] A new evangelical movement that was truly evangelical but also truly postfundamentalist was within reach.

Pinnock's discussion of the myth problem disclosed how far the new evangelicalism was capable of going in refiguring the nature and forms of revelation. With Ramm, he noted that the traditional evangelical impulse was derisive toward myth;

evangelicals typically thought of myth as a primitive mode of discourse, "practically devoid of value for teaching truth." The very notion of "Christian myth" was therefore excluded or dismissed in most evangelical theologies. Pinnock offered no theory or definition of *myth,* but assuming a conventional sense of the term, he judged that the New Testament contains occasional fragments of genuine myth and that the Old Testament contains a good deal of mythical material. The allusion to the bodies of the saints being raised on Good Friday was a notable New Testament example (Matthew 27:52), as was the reference to healings of the sick made possible by contact with pieces of cloth that had touched Paul's body (Acts 19:11–12). For the most part, however, the New Testament is emphatically antimythical, he judged. It grounds the message of salvation in factual occurrence (1 Cor. 15:14; Acts 26:26) and denounces even the category of myth (1 Tim. 1:4; 4:6; 2 Tim. 4:4; Titus 1:14). Second Peter 1:16 declares that "we did not follow cleverly devised myths when we made known to you the power and coming of our Lord Jesus Christ, but we had been eyewitnesses of his majesty."

Evangelical Christianity must stand with this gospel insistence that the gospel is factually grounded, Pinnock assured. At the same time, he urged, evangelicalism has been grievously wrong to commit itself to the indefensible claim that scripture contains no myths or legends. Besides the occasional mythical element in the New Testament, the Old Testament contains ample mythical or legendary material. For example, the biblical stories of the Flood and the Tower of Babel are worked over from mythical pagan texts (Gen. 6:1–11:9). Psalm 74:13–14 recounts that Yahweh smashed the sea monster in two "and broke the heads of the dragons in the waters." Psalm 95:3 calls the Lord "a great King above all gods." According to Genesis 5:1–32, the antediluvian patriarchs lived an average of 857 years, and in Judges 9:7–15 the prophet Jotham speaks of the trees going forth to anoint a king over them. Elsewhere the Bible mentions night hags (Isa. 34:14), a rock that followed Moses in the wilderness (1 Cor. 10:4), and a coin turning up in a fish's mouth (Matt. 17:24–27). It describes a day when the sun went backward (Isa. 38:8) and a day when the sun stood still (Josh. 10:13), and it contains the wild and crudely legendary exploits of Samson and Elisha.[148]

Pinnock observed that no one who read these accounts anywhere else would have any difficulty assigning them to the categories of myth and legend. He judged that evangelicalism had pretended for too long that because these accounts are contained in scripture, they must be something else. Evangelicals have routinely assumed that God would never speak through such an unworthy literary form as myth. "We worry that if we were to allow it in Christianity we would introduce fiction and error into our religion," Pinnock observed. But this mentality imposes alien conditions on how God's Word may be expressed. It presumes to judge in advance what the Word of God should be, before it is encountered. In this way, Pinnock cautioned, "we not only narrow down the scope of revelation but close our minds to aspects of the Bible itself."[149]

It is not biblical to insist that myth is incompatible with God's Word, or that legends are unworthy vehicles of God's truth, or that historical accounts in scripture must conform to the standards of modern historiography if they are to be regarded as truthful. Scripture is loaded with contrary evidence. Genesis 10:1–32, for example, refers to the ancestors of Egypt and Canaan and Sidon as individual persons named Egypt, Canaan, and Sidon. Pinnock likened this scriptural technique to reading about Mr. Canada and Miss France. He noted that the period between Levi and Moses was 430 years, but Exodus 6:14–25 allows for only four generations. The census figures in Numbers 1:45–46 are exaggerated, as are most of the accounts in which Chronicles differs with the books of Samuel and of Kings. The Gospel accounts often disagree as well, he acknowledged. How often did Jesus go up to Jerusalem? On what day was he crucified? What was written on the sign above his head? How often did the rooster crow? The fact that scripture gives different answers to these and many other questions does not mean that scripture fails to fulfill its purpose, he urged, and this is the crucial matter. The Bible was written to lead people to Christ, on historiographical principles that were accepted by the ancient world. "We ought neither to charge the Bible with error nor to knock our own heads against a wall trying to eliminate what we should just accept," he counseled. "If we would just stop objecting to the form of the Bible for our own apologetic reasons and let the phenomena be what they are, we could be more relaxed with the Bible and do less violence to the text and to ourselves. So many of our difficulties are not in the Bible at all, but in our own heads."[150]

Warfield-style inerrancy theory assumed that because scripture is divinely inspired, it cannot contain anything that is wrong or legendary. Pinnock countered that this control belief made an unwarranted a priori presumption about the kind of text that God must have inspired human writers to produce. Though Warfield claimed to follow the inductive approach by deriving his doctrine of biblical inspiration from biblical exegesis, his defense of inerrancy was strongly deductive. Scripture had to be errorless if it was inspired.[151] Pinnock urged that this is exactly what evangelicalism must not do to scripture. It must not impose outside assumptions about biblical revelation on the Bible. It must not presume to know from the doctrine of inspiration what biblical revelation must be like in detail. Since scripture says nothing about its own inerrancy, Pinnock explained, defenders of the strict-inerrancy position must get it from somewhere else.

With knowing recollection from his own case, he pointed to the high Calvinism of the post-Reformation Reformed tradition, especially as encoded in the Westminster Confession. "Inerrancy thinking is deductive thinking rooted in the assumption of total divine control," he explained. The Westminster Confession asserts that "God from all eternity did, by the most wise and holy counsel of his own will, freely and unchangeably ordain *whatsoever* comes to pass."[152] Pinnock recounted that it was out of this theological presupposition of total divine control that strict-inerrancy doctrine entered the language of Christianity. To orthodox Calvinism, it is not only the words of scripture that are predestined in God's immutable decrees but also everything else that exists. Even the words of *Time* and *Newsweek* cannot be other than they are. Warfield compared God's inspiration of scripture to a church builder who, desiring a rose-colored light in his church, installed rose-colored panes of glass. In the monergistic view of God's pervasive control over the world that Warfield assumed, the only actions in the world that count are God's.

Pinnock judged that this explained the tendency of strict-inerrancy advocates to disavow the theory of mechanical dictation while speaking about scripture as though it were dictated. Warfield's followers routinely claimed not to believe in dictation, he observed, but this disavowal was merely formal. Materially, they believed in dictation. That is, materially, the human component of scripture counted for nothing in the theologies of strict-inerrancy proponents. Since they believed that God predestined every detail of the autographs, they could not explain any difficulty in the text apart from scribal error as the consequence of human error. The strict-inerrancy position thus "makes nonsense of human authorship and is tantamount to saying God dictated the text," Pinnock argued. "It is quibbling over words to deny it so vigorously."[153]

He was careful not to overemphasize the logical and historical connections between Calvinism and fundamentalism. Many Calvinists are not fundamentalists; many Calvinists do not believe in absolute double predestination; and many strict-inerrancy advocates are neither members of the Reformed tradition nor especially influenced by Calvinist theology. Pinnock did not reduce the problem of inerrancy to the problem of Calvinism, nor did he want the current evangelical debate over inerrancy to become a debate over his own commitment to Arminianism.[154] He recognized that many Arminians are fundamentalist in their thinking about scripture, especially those from the Baptist and Pentecostal traditions. At the same time, he emphasized that it was only with the emergence of a high-pitched conflict between high Calvinism and modernist theology that strict inerrancy became an important feature of evangelical orthodoxy. Though he cautioned that all premodern orthodoxies took biblical inerrancy for granted, and though he generally sought to keep the evangelical debate over predestination out of the evangelical discussion of scriptural authority, Pinnock nonetheless felt compelled to point to the historical and logical connections between Calvinism and strict-inerrancy thinking. "If God really is in total control of all things, then he must have willed all the tragedies and atrocities that have happened throughout history," he observed. Calvinism teaches that God wills even the most horrible tragedies that occur in order to bring about some higher purpose of God's own. To claim that this teaching does not make God the author of evil "cannot change the fact that it surely does so," Pinnock warned. "God is the one responsible for everything that happens if he willed it so completely, and he must take the blame."[155]

Pinnock worried that the moral insensitivity of Calvinism turned many potential evangelicals into atheists. He cautioned that the Reformed tradition had overinfluenced, if not overpowered, evangelical theology as a whole. A better evangelical alternative would give due weight to the reality of human freedom, including the creative human contribution to scripture. "It makes nonsense of genuine human authorship to say that God is in total control of the Bible's composition," he asserted. "It leads directly to Docetism, which reduces the human aspect to merely nominal." In the name of a need for secure religious knowledge, he explained, evangelical fundamentalists prescribed a doctrine of biblical inerrancy that is not believable, is not in the Bible, and does not take account of the obvious human dimension of scripture. The evangelical theology that is needed "will allow for a human element in the composition of Scripture, but also a strong role for the Spirit to ensure that the truth is not distorted by the human receptors."[156]

God's dynamic Spirit incites and superintends the writing and hearing of scripture as God's Word. The Spirit is present in scripture not in the mode of all-determining control but in the modes of stimulation and guidance. Pinnock urged that scripture does not aspire to a higher degree of perfection than the assurance that its teaching regarding faith and practice is reliable. "Though expecting only truth, we can be open to diversity, to various genres, to perplexing features, to intents of different kinds, all the while keeping our eyes on the basic thrust the Scriptures were given to deliver," he proposed. The upshot was that evangelical orthodoxy could be more open to both the human components of scripture and the revelation that scripture actually contains. "In the end this is what the mass of evangelical believers need—not the rationalistic ideal of a perfect Book that is no more, but the trustworthiness of a Bible with truth where it counts, truth that is not so easily threatened by scholarly problems," Pinnock argued.[157] In the end, he was siding with Orr in the epochal struggle to define evangelical orthodoxy.

But is it credible to concede as much as Pinnock did to biblical criticism and still hold on to inerrancy as infallible teaching? Does inerrancy doctrine, even in the form Orr and his followers championed, stand up to the inductive scrutiny that Pinnock prescribed? What about the biblical teaching that God commanded the genocidal extermination of the Canaanites (Deut. 2:31–35; 3:1–8; 7:2; Josh. 6:15–21; 8:25–26; 10:40; 11:12; 11:20)? What about the imprecatory psalms, which celebrate such things as the beating to death of babies? What about the Bible's patriarchal teaching regarding women's place and its severe strictures against homosexuality? Pinnock acknowledged that his redefinition of biblical infallibility opened evangelicalism to greater pressure from questions of this kind. He counseled that evangelicals must try to cope with these kinds of problems without relinquishing any part of the infallible-teaching principle. He observed that the Canaanites were an especially wicked people who practiced child sacrifice and religious prostitution, and that curses on Israel's enemies were a constitutive part of God's covenant with Israel. He argued that modern acceptance of homosexuality as morally legitimate simply replaces the biblical ethic with a humanist ethic.[158]

He pointedly criticized Paul Jewett for relinquishing the scripture principle in seeking to accommodate feminist criticism of Pauline theology. In his controversial book *Man as Male and Female,* Jewett argued that some of Paul's statements about women's roles contradict the spirit of his declaration in Galatians 3:28 that in Christ there is neither male nor female. In particular, he pointed to the lingering influence of a rabbinical interpretation of the second creation story as a key source behind such statements as 1 Corinthians 14:34–35, Ephesians 5:22–24, and especially (whether Pauline or not) 1 Timothy 2:11–15. Having judged that these culturally conditioned biblical statements are unworthy by comparison to Paul's breakthrough statement in Galatians 3:28, Jewett reasoned that they were not divinely intended and are not binding today.[159] Pinnock countered that the logic of this approach to scripture negated the basis of appealing to scripture on behalf of any conviction, including feminism. Instead of claiming that some biblical texts are not inspired, he contended, an evangelical approach must always respect the divine authority of the Word while also recognizing that some texts are too contextually embedded to remain authoritative for us.

This interpretive principle kept Pinnock's approach open to the problem of cultural relativism. He reasoned that because biblical revelation is progressive in character, "moving from premessianic to messianic revelation," it is always crucial for the interpreter to be attentive to the place and role of a given text in the organism of scripture. Though everything in scripture is inspired by God, not everything in scripture remains authoritative for us. Many biblical texts speak only to the cultural or religious situation in which they were written. "An Old Testament text may have been the Word of God to ancient Israel and not be God's Word to us now," he explained. "We run the risk of Judaizing the church if we forget this."[160]

Other kinds of interpretive complexity inhere in the diversity of literary forms and purposes that scripture contains. In forms ranging from legend to poetry, history, wisdom, parable, and apocalyptic, some passages seek to inspire our hope, some challenge our will, some instruct us in doctrine, and so on. Scripture communicates truth in every case, Pinnock observed, "but not the same kind of truth." The work of biblical theology is to pick out the kind of truth claim that each biblical text makes on us. Evangelical theology must assume that biblical teaching is always divinely inspired and infallible, he explained, but this does not mean that all biblical teaching applies authoritatively to us. As a critical mass of evangelical theologians and pastors was moving toward an understanding of biblical inerrancy as infallible teaching, the evangelical movement needed to become capable of discussing cultural relativity in scripture without raising a storm of anathemas.

Pinnock cautioned that he was serious about holding on to inerrancy. His revisionist position still preserved the heart of traditional evangelical teaching about inerrancy. He exhorted evangelicals never to concede that scripture contains any outright contradictions. "If contradiction exists our doctrine of Scripture is overthrown," he warned. His book *The Scripture Principle* ended with a plea to evangelicals that "it would be wise for us to continue to speak of biblical inerrancy." If inerrancy means that scripture can be trusted to be truthful in all that its teaching affirms, he exhorted, "then inerrancy is what we must hold to."[161] But he also realized that a sizable segment of the new evangelical movement was moving beyond his mediating position. Figures such as Ramm, Beegle, Rogers, and McKim were casting off much of the presuppositional structure of traditional evangelicalism that Pinnock was struggling to preserve.

In the succeeding decade, with the rise of a new generation of postmodernist-oriented evangelical theologians, Pinnock joined their effort to rethink the epistemological assumptions of evangelical orthodoxy. His later writings contributed significantly to the evangelical appropriation of antifoundationalist postmodern philosophy. As a respected elder figure in a movement of mostly young theologians, he supported the "postmodern" evangelical claim that it was time for evangelicals to move beyond the categories and defensive positions established by the modernist-fundamentalist conflict. While insisting that he still held out for an "authorial intention" attribution of inerrancy, with each book he inched further away from evangelical fundamentalism. One century of overdetermining evangelical debate with modernism was enough.

TAKING THE BARTHIAN OPTION

At the critical turn in the broader evangelical reassessment of evangelical antimodernism, however, it was Ramm who made the strongest statement about the direction in which evangelical theology needed to go. It was also Ramm who decisively influenced and inspired a new generation of evangelical theologians to rethink evangelicalism.

His basic proposal was that evangelicals needed to adopt Barth's method of dealing with modernist criticism. Ramm declared that the burden of antimodernism had warped evangelical theology for long enough. It had made evangelicals give major significance to minor issues and impeded them from carrying out any constructive engagement with modernity. Because evangelical theology had been defensive and reactionary, he argued, it had made little contribution to modern thinking about theological method. Ramm believed that there was no reason evangelicalism could not deal constructively with historical criticism and modern science, but he warned that evangelical theology would never fulfill this ambition as long as it remained the prisoner of modernism. "Evangelicals have not come to a systematic method of interacting with modern knowledge," he observed.[162] What was needed in evangelical theology was a faithful and sophisticated explication of the gospel faith that did not assume a posture of defensive hostility toward the various modes of criticism engendered by the Enlightenment.

For all the criticism that evangelicals heaped on Barth, this was precisely what his theology offered to the evangelical movement. Evangelicals routinely condemned Barth's wedge between God's Word and the words of scripture, but Ramm countered that it was this methodological move that allowed Barth to grant biblical criticism its rightful place without surrendering the evangelical view of scripture as God's inspired Word. Old School orthodoxy pinned its doctrine of the Word on the existence of hypothetical errorless autographs, but Barth rightly pushed this infallible point of reference to God himself. It is God who is utterly infallible, rational, and free from all contradiction or paradox. In its primal sense, the Word of God is this infallible God himself, in his self-disclosing act of revelation. But revelation can take place only under the veil of historical forms, Barth taught. The key to Ramm's prescription for a revised evangelicalism was this two-sided Barthian emphasis on the divinity of the Word and the necessarily human character of the Word revealed.

Barth persistently cautioned that God's infallible Word undergoes a diffraction as soon as it enters the human sphere. The Word came to the biblical writers in their own language, he explained, but no writer or language is nearly perfect enough to perfectly reflect God's Word. The wedge between the pure Word in itself and the inspired witness to it was established first by the limitations of language. Barth noted wryly that numerous modern philosophers (especially Hegel) have dreamed of bridging the gap.[163] Much of modern philosophy, from Hegel to Heidegger and beyond, has been haunted by the dream of a pure conceptual language that would be the perfect language of truth. Ramm noted that fundamentalist evangelicals have been especially stubborn keepers of this dream. "It is amazing how the current evangelical stress on propositional revelation is but an alternate version of this Hegelian theory of a pure conceptual language," he observed.[164] Like Hegel, evangelicals were consumed by their yearning for a language of truth that negated the *diastasis* (separation) between a person's words and mental concepts.

Ramm recognized that Barth had no interest in promoting a skeptical view of language. As a dogmatic theologian, Barth did not claim that language cannot effectively bear the Word of God. He repeatedly affirmed that as a witness to revelation, biblical language is adequate for the purposes of revelation. The Word exists "in, with, and under" the culturally conditioned biblical text. Thus, through the movement of the Spirit, the Word is effectively expressed through the text.[165] Ramm noted that all Barth's expressions about scripture as the Word of God were emphatic on this point. Barth spoke of the "indirect identity" of God's Word and Holy Scripture and of the "brokenness" or "diffraction" of revelation, and especially of scripture as a witness to revelation. Ramm cautioned, however, "If there is no interval between the Word of God and the words of Scripture, then not one trace of an old world view can be allowed to stand in the text, for that would be approving an error." The price that fundamentalist evangelicalism paid for refusing to distinguish between scriptural words and God's Word was that "the accuracy of every biblical statement must be defended down to the last decimal point."[166]

Ramm argued that evangelical theology at its best has resisted this indefensible conclusion. At its best, he explained, the evangelical tradition has at least acknowledged the *diastasis* between Word and biblical words and accepted that this distinction is more than a formal one. Whenever evangelicalism has affirmed that scripture bears a material human dimension or recognized that the problematic passages in scripture reflect this human dimension, it has at least minimally acknowledged the diffraction between God's Word and the words of scripture. The crucial difference between Barth's theology of the Word and traditional evangelicalism was that Barth explicitly built the *diastasis* between Word and biblical words into his theology of revelation. Barth conceived the diffraction between Word and biblical words as a material qualitative distinction. The upshot of this difference, Ramm explained, is that Barth was able to take the humanity of scripture in stride, while evangelicalism tied itself in knots trying to cope with "problem passages." On Barthian terms, there is no reason to deny that scripture contains errors or that it often expresses God's Word through saga and legend (though Barth consigned the Bible's mythical elements to the category of saga).[167] To take the human character of scripture seriously along Barthian lines is to be released from hyperorthodox anxieties that scripture cannot be inspired if it contains errors or legendary elements.

Evangelical theology typically resisted any acknowledgment of scriptural error that gave a material meaning to its formal acknowledgment of the humanity of scripture. It also routinely lambasted Barth for subjectivizing the divine character of scripture. In virtually the same words, the objection that Barth treated scripture as a "mere witness" to revelation, rather than as revelation itself, had been repeated by Henry, Van Til, Clark, Klaus Runia, the early Pinnock, and a host of others.[168] Ramm countered that this literature of complaint revealed more about the evangelical desire to possess revelation than about Barth's purported failure to uphold the objective character of scripture as God's Word. As much as Barth may have spoken about the break between the Word in itself and the biblical text, Ramm observed, he unfailingly emphasized that the Word *is* disclosed "in, with, and under" the text. Barth repeatedly characterized the biblical writers as objective, reliable witnesses of divine revelation.[169] Though he emphasized the deflection of the Word by limited human experience and language, he insisted nonetheless that the Word itself is disclosed through the movement of the Spirit to faithful readers and hearers of scripture.

This view of revelation is neither totally subjective nor totally lacking in content, Ramm noted: "Those who deny that Barth teaches propositional revelation have not consistently followed Barth's understanding of Holy Scripture." In Barthian terms, the objective revelation of the Word in scripture is expressed conceptually as a "picture" (*Bild*) or as the "substance" (*Sache*) or "Word" (*Wort*) that good exegesis seeks to uncover. Though the words of scripture are not immediately God's Word, the Word is *in* scripture on account of the inspiration of scripture. Moreover, the "Barthian" notion that the Word cannot be known or recognized apart from the internal witness of the Spirit is hardly a novel claim, Ramm observed, since Calvin was no less insistent on this point.

Barth's novel move was to extend this concept into his doctrine of scripture. He spoke of scripture unfailingly as a witness to revelation. Ramm cautioned that evangelicals routinely misrepresented the purpose and import of this move, since Barth did not completely subjectivize the meaning of the Word in scripture. In keeping with biblical usage, Barth regarded a "witness" not as a detached observer but as one who participates in an event. In the biblical context, the event in which the witness participates is the *content* of the witness. In Barth's understanding, scripture was thus a witness to revelation because the writers of scripture were participants in the experience of revelation. "Barth does not have the purely subjective, purely existential view of Scripture of which he is so frequently accused," Ramm remarked.[170] The point of calling scripture a witness to revelation is not to deny that there is an objective sense in which scripture bears the Word but only to highlight the role of the biblical writers as active participants in the revelatory task of bearing witness to the Word.

Barth's distinction between ordinary history (*Historie*) and salvation history (*Geschichte*) gave further fuel to the charge that his theology completely subjectivized biblical revelation. Van Til and Clark were especially vocal proponents of the view that Barth's appeal to "salvation history" was an evasive semantic trick. They argued that his purpose in appealing to this concept was to establish a basis on which dogmatic claims about God's revelatory acts could be made without having to affirm the historicity of these events. On this reading, *Geschichte* referred to a different plane or kind of history than ordinary history; its supposed referent was a realm of divine events. Barth's evangelical critics claimed that because he did not believe in the actual historicity of the resurrection or the virgin birth of Christ, he appealed to the obscurantist idea of salvation history as a way of justifying his dogmatic claims on these themes. Van Til explained that "Barth cannot tolerate the idea that this resurrection should be directly identified with any fact of ordinary history." His often-quoted conclusion was that Barth's subjectivism and his emphasis on indirect communication made it impossible to find Jesus Christ at all in his theology.[171]

Here again, Ramm attacked the heart of the evangelical case against Barth's theology. He countered that it was ridiculous to foist on Barth's theology the notion that *Geschichte* is analogous to Kant's noumenal space and time as distinguished from empirical space and time: "Barth would be out of his mind to postulate two geographies, two spaces, two times, and two historical series, one of which was that of ordinary human history and the other of divine events." Barth believed that the crucified Christ was raised from the dead in historical space and time, not in some noumenal realm of divine extrahistory, Ramm declared. This belief is plainly affirmed throughout *Church Dogmatics*. Barth described the resurrection as an event that "actually happened among men like other events, and was experienced and later attested by them."[172] The resurrection appearances were seen with human eyes and heard with human ears, he affirmed, "in space and time, by the lake and in the cities of Galilee, in Jerusalem, and on the way to it, in the circumstances of specific individuals."[173] With emphatic specificity, Barth asserted elsewhere that Christ's resurrection "did not take place in a heavenly or supra-heavenly realm, or as part of an intra-divine movement or a divine conversation, but before the gates of Jerusalem in the days of Tiberius Caesar and therefore in the place and time which are also ours, in our sphere."[174] Salvation history took place in our sphere, not in some Kantian noumenal world or Platonic heaven beyond the world of ordinary historical experience. Barth's distinction between ordinary history and salvation history thus had nothing to do with different kinds or levels of history, Ramm explained, but referred only to different kinds of historical knowledge.

Though he curiously failed to explain what this meant, and though he also failed to acknowledge that Barth sometimes did appeal to *Geschichte* as a way of evading historical questions, Ramm was right to insist that the crucial point at issue was the question of what constitutes historical knowledge.[175] During his "crisis theology" period, Barth did claim that "time and place are a matter of perfect indifference" to Easter faith, but in *Church Dogmatics* he described the resurrection of Jesus as objective and historical.[176] Jesus was raised from the dead in the same empirical history in which we live, he affirmed. But as a datum of knowledge, he cautioned, echoing Martin Kähler, the resurrection was not a public event, open to anyone regardless of faith.[177] Jesus never appeared to Pilate or to his Jewish opponents or to the Roman Senate or to anyone else who might impress a secular historian. Barth affirmed the historiographical principle that an event can be deemed to be historical (factual *Historie*) only if the "how" of its outline can be known independently of the standpoint of the observer and within its general and specific contexts.[178] Moreover, the event in question must have such a character as to be comparable to other historical events. But in the case of the resurrection, there is no such thing as an outside or impartial witness, and the "what" that is claimed is not analogous to any known historical event.[179] In the modern critical sense of the term, therefore, the resurrection narratives contain only a "tiny margin" of *Historie,* Barth contended—and Christian theology must not pretend otherwise.[180]

This is precisely the kind of argument that made many evangelicals hostile to Barth. Ramm undoubtedly worried that his case would be undermined if he explained Barth's understanding of the relation of kerygmatic *Geschichte* to factual *Historie*. He was trying to persuade evangelicals that Barth was their friend, if not the exemplar of a better evangelicalism. His lawyerly argument therefore made a case for Barth's approach to theology that emphasized his kinship with evangelicalism. Ramm acknowledged in an afterword that certain aspects of Barth's theology continued to trouble him. He still harbored reservations about Barth's nearly explicit universalism, his Christomonist tendency, and his apparent supralapsarianism (the view that God decreed the election or nonelection of all individuals before the Fall). Nor was he sure that Barth kept his theology as free from metaphysical dependence as he claimed.[181]

Ramm agreed with Barth, however, that a genuinely evangelical theology must assiduously safeguard its independence from philosophical control. Against the Bultmannians, Whiteheadians, and various other proponents of theological demythologizing who argued that modern theology must replace an outmoded supernaturalist worldview with a credible modern worldview, Barth insisted that Christian theology should not be in the business of endorsing worldviews at all.[182] He taught that the work of theology is to explicate the meaning of the Word that is expressed through, but which also transcends, the ancient worldviews presupposed by the biblical writers. The theologian should be free to make use of various worldviews or philosophical systems as they facilitate the task of explicating the meaning of the Word, he allowed, but theology must never sacralize any particular worldview or commit Christianity to any particular ideology or philosophical system.

This was the key to Barth's superiority as a guide for evangelical theology, Ramm asserted. Though he curiously failed to connect Barth's exaltation of the open Word to his critique of demythologizing, Ramm called for a Barthian rethinking of evangelicalism precisely on the basis of Barth's affirmation of the primacy of the open revelatory Word against all forms of theological accommodationism and authoritarianism. In an evangelical context, the implications of this argument played out most pertinently as a critique of evidentialist apologetics. Barth straightforwardly opposed all apologetic strategies that would seek to establish an epistemological basis for faith outside revelation. As Ramm observed, "One of Barth's basic presuppositions with reference to the truth of the Christian faith is that if something external to the Word of God is necessary to establish the Word of God as true, then it is greater than the Word of God."[183] Barth repeatedly reminded his students, especially those from an evangelical background, that that which establishes is always greater than what is established. If faith requires some basis outside the Spirit-illuminated Word for its credibility or coherence, then some product of human cognition and control is given priority over God's Word.[184] This delegation of authority to something other than the Word is precisely what theology must never do, he insisted, even in the name of religious "certainty" or orthodoxy.

Barth's alternative began with the principle that revelation establishes itself. In accord with this principle, he conceived the work of theology as faith seeking understanding. In Ramm's assessment, this was the only approach to theology that consistently explicated the purported evangelical conviction that "there can be nothing greater than the Word of God." To subject the gospel faith to rational tests outside Christianity is to grant highest authority to reason, not to the Word. "It is a very odd maneuver to think that one first establishes Christianity as true in terms of some philosophical or rational or empirical test and then transfers that conviction to the truths of the Gospel," Ramm remarked. "Oranges cannot verify apples. The philosophical calculus cannot verify the Gospel calculus!"[185] If evangelical theology could finally learn this lesson from Barth and Calvin, he suggested, it would spare itself much confusion and anguish over misguided causes it had adopted.

Ramm's manifesto for a new evangelicalism marked a turning point in the debate over the parameters of modern evangelicalism. One of the two major American evangelical theologians of his generation, his conversion to neoorthodoxy provoked intense controversy. His stature in the field made this inevitable; but Ramm's argument took on a significance that transcended the impact of its conversion story. Though many of his conservative critics tried to dismiss his later position as an outright abandonment of evangelical Christianity, Ramm's influence heightened among a younger generation of evangelicals who found his arguments compelling, if not altogether convincing.[186] Neoorthodox theologians such as Thomas Torrance, Otto Weber, and Helmut Thielicke had long received a respectful hearing among many evangelicals.[187] Moreover, evangelical theologians such as Berkouwer, Geoffrey Bromiley, and Donald Bloesch had long argued that Barth deserved to be taken seriously as a contributor to the evangelical theology that was needed.[188]

By 1980 the evangelical movement contained a critical mass of younger theologians who were predisposed to move in this direction. Ramm's endorsement of Barthian theology as the model for the next phase of evangelicalism conferred a new sense of legitimacy on this option. Many evangelical theologians joined the North American Karl Barth Society and accepted Ramm's challenge to rethink evangelicalism along Barthian lines. Some of them soon surpassed Ramm in appropriating the postmodern aspects of Barth's theology. Ramm proposed that Barth could show evangelicals how to cope with modernity, but some evangelicals were concerned with moving beyond modernity. For the past half century,

evangelical criticism of Barth had focused on three major issues: Barth was an irrationalist, he did not believe in the objective divinity of scripture, and he strongly
implied that he did believe in universal salvation. With the rise of a generation of
evangelical theologians who viewed evangelical objectivism as a stumbling block
to vital Christian faith and thinking, however, the stock objections to neoorthodoxy lost their force. Ramm convinced many evangelicals that the old objections
sold short the sovereign freedom of the Word.

Like many evangelicals, Ramm had more problems with Barth's near affirmation of universal salvation. Barthian neoorthodoxy was clearly disinclined to speak
about eternal damnation even as a possibility. Barth and his followers rarely managed to assert that anyone *needed* to repent and believe the gospel in order to be
saved. In his generally favorable assessment of Barth's theology, Donald Bloesch
complained that Barth's universalism caused him to "not take unbelief with the utmost seriousness."[189] Bloesch and Ramm both objected that the reality of damnation is part of the gospel message. Without the doctrine of final judgment, Ramm
explained, God is transmuted into a kind of celestial Santa Claus who gives toys
and happiness to everyone. Evangelicalism is nothing without the certainty that repentance and personal acceptance of Christ are necessary for salvation—or so it
seemed, even to Ramm. In the succeeding decade, however, Pinnock and a host of
younger evangelicals reopened even this staple of evangelical faith and thus
opened up a serious debate about the kind of God that evangelicalism worships.
This time "the fundamentals" really were the points of dispute.

Arminian and Catholic Options: Opening Up Evangelicalism

Evangelicalism has always been more diverse than its image. Despite the steady stream of books from Grand Rapids, Michigan, that have portrayed evangelicalism as monolithically middle-class, Reformed, white, Republican, and preoccupied with correct doctrine, American evangelicalism has always included sizable groups who do not admire the Westminster Confession or vote conservative. In sheer numbers, the various offshoots of Anabaptist radicalism, conservative Lutheranism, German Pietism, Wesleyan Holiness teaching, dispensationalist separatism, community church evangelicalism, and Pentecostalism have long rivaled the following of the semiofficial evangelical establishment. For many years, most of these groups implicitly ceded the right of intellectual leadership to a more cultured and credentialed Reformed establishment. The right to speak for evangelicalism was presumed to belong to Puritan-rooted Baptists such as Henry, Carnell, and Billy Graham and to Calvinists such as Clark, Van Til, and Berkouwer. The existence of other evangelical groups was generally acknowledged, but so was the leadership role of the evangelical establishment. Some groups disqualified themselves from leadership roles because of their secluded confessionalism or separatism, but even among Methodists and others who regarded themselves as participants in a transdenominational evangelical movement, Reformed hegemony was generally taken for granted. Only the Calvinists were assumed to be qualified to make evangelicalism respectable in American society or to play a culture-forming role within it.

The most significant early wave of dissent from this arrangement arose in the 1970s with the coming-of-age of the 1960s generation. To young evangelicals who supported the Civil Rights movement and opposed America's war in Vietnam, the nearly monolithic political conservatism of the evangelical establishment was deeply disturbing. People such as Jim Wallis, Donald Dayton, John Alexander, and (for a few years) Clark Pinnock strongly criticized the right-wing politics of the evangelical establishment, arguing that evangelical theology should not lead to political conservatism but rather to forms of political engagement that oppose war and promote equality. These views were promoted in new magazines such as

The Post-American (later *Sojourners*) and *The Other Side* and gave rise to new so-cial activist organizations. Antipoverty activist Ron Sider became a leading evan-gelical voice for economic justice and antimilitarism, while Virginia Ramey Mollenkott and Nancy Hardesty sought to reinterpret evangelicalism in the light of feminist criticism.[1] In its early years, *The Post-American* featured very conser-vative theological articles next to articles that stridently condemned American militarism and social injustice. For several years the magazine made the case for Christian anarchist-pacifism in nearly every issue, while carefully avoiding in-house debates over biblical inerrancy.

The success of *Sojourners* in particular made it clear that something new was happening in American evangelicalism. A critical mass of evangelical churchgo-ers and activists found the magazine's political radicalism more compatible with the gospel ethic than the cold war conservatism of the evangelical establishment. Many were especially galled by the negative treatment that *Christianity Today* gave to the Civil Rights movement. Under Carl Henry's leadership, the magazine defended "voluntary segregation" and claimed that Martin Luther King Jr.'s inte-grationist ideology was implicitly Communist. It condemned the demonstrations and campaigns of civil disobedience that King and his associates organized, in-cluding the massive 1963 March on Washington at which King gave his "I Have a Dream" speech. *Christianity Today* denounced the March on Washington as a "mob spectacle." The magazine's editors made it clear that they regarded interra-cial marriage as repugnant, and when James Meredith sought to enter the Univer-sity of Mississippi as a student, *Christianity Today* applauded the State of Mississippi for refusing to admit him. It also stoutly supported America's inter-vention in Vietnam, rebuking war protesters and calling for harsh sanctions against draft resisters.[2]

The spectacle of an evangelical establishment that routinely defended Ameri-can segregation and foreign military intervention drove Dayton, David Moberg, and others to figure out what had, to them, gone wrong in evangelicalism. Much of nineteenth-century evangelicalism was abolitionist, antimilitarist, and anti-capitalist, but now Moberg wrote, *evangelicalism* had become synonymous with the defense of racial privilege and American power: "A century ago evangelicals were in the forefront of social concern, but now we have become so identified with 'the successful,' in terms of the world's ideologies, that we put brakes on nearly every proposal for dealing with social problems in a manner consistent with the realities of our complex urban-industrial world." Evangelicals were turn-ing scripture on its head, he observed, ignoring the biblical warnings about those who "grind the faces of the poor" (Isa. 3:15) and those who refuse to help the af-flicted (Matt. 25:41–46): "Instead of helping to alleviate the ills of the poor and underprivileged, we react against those who try to do so." In their drive for eco-nomic gain and cultural prestige, modern evangelicals stood in danger of hearing the judgment curse of the Lord "as well as the curses of earthly protest move-ments."[3]

How did it happen that evangelical leaders could be counted on to defend some of the worst aspects of American society? Why was it impossible to criticize the

Vietnam War at any evangelical college or seminary without being condemned as a Communist? These were existential questions for Wallis and Dayton in the 1960s. They were vaguely aware that their religious tradition had not always automatically opposed popular movements for peace, racial equality, and women's rights. The father of modern revivalism, Charles Finney, had been an abolitionist and antimilitarist; the Holiness movements had been the first to ordain women to the preaching ministry; William Jennings Bryan had made his early fame as a fiery populist. Why was modern evangelicalism so repressive by comparison? Moberg's emphasis on the status-seeking opportunism of evangelical leaders provided part of the answer, but it was mainly a sociological answer. He focused on the worldly ambitions of evangelical leaders, using sociological categories, and then criticized these ambitions with quotes from scripture. For Dayton, however, this was not enough. In search of further clues about the reactionary turn in his tradition, he plunged into its nineteenth-century history — and found that early American evangelicalism was richer in egalitarian sentiment and more pluralistic in its theological expressions than he had anticipated.

His findings were published in a ten-part *Sojourners* series titled "Recovering a Heritage." Dayton traced the connections between Finney-style revivalism and the establishment of Oberlin College, Wheaton College, and other evangelical institutions. He described the kingdom-oriented reformism of Wheaton's first president, Jonathan Blanchard; the contributions of Theodore Weld and other evangelicals to the antislavery underground railroad; the campaigns for racial integration that Methodist and other Wesleyan groups waged; the explicit feminism of various Holiness movements; the antipoverty idealism of the Salvation Army and other, lesser-known groups; and the remarkable blend of Christian radicalisms that Oberlin College embodied. Most of these evangelical currents were postmillennialist, he noted; they believed that Christ's kingdom was not merely to be waited for but to be worked upon, spreading righteousness throughout the world.[4]

Moreover, the spirit of antimilitarism and democratic egalitarianism that much of the early revivalist movement engendered was still alive among some of the founders of modern fundamentalism in the 1880s and 1890s. The founder of Gordon College and Gordon-Conwell Seminary, A. J. Gordon, was not only a militant fundamentalist but also an abolitionist and a feminist. Dwight Moody's conversion to dispensational premillennialism contributed greatly to what Moberg called "the great reversal" in evangelical social concern, but even Moody clung to a way-of-Christ pacifism throughout his preaching career. Dayton pointedly observed that these aspects of nineteenth-century American evangelicalism were censored by the movement's fundamentalist successors. The social and political radicalism of the Wesleyan movements in particular became an embarrassment to later fundamentalists. Finney's writings were aggressively bowdlerized by fundamentalist editors who sought to claim a sanitized version of his legacy for their own ministries.[5]

Why did evangelicalism lose its concern for the poor and afflicted? Dayton endorsed Moberg's sociological explanations. Radical movements of any kind are difficult to sustain for more than a generation. Finney-style revivalism thrived on high levels of spiritual intensity and moral fervor, but even Finney found it very difficult to reproduce these qualities over time. Some of the Wesleyan movements formed new sects, others were absorbed by the mainline denominations, but in both cases, the children of the revivalists were less inclined than their parents to prize their alienation from the dominant culture. They did not regard strangeness or countercultural purity as a sign of their salvation but wanted rather to belong to America. A poignant example in Dayton's experience was that many of his friends hid the fact that their mothers or grandmothers had served as ministers in an earlier phase of American evangelical history, as if it were too shameful or abnormal to acknowledge.

Dayton rehearsed other explanations for the eclipse of evangelical social concern in the late nineteenth century. The sheer horror of the Civil War dispelled the sense of optimism and hope that had fueled much of Oberlin-style revivalism. Moreover, with the abolition of slavery, the kind of social issues that came to the fore in American politics became more personal in nature. Evangelical social energies were channeled into the temperance movement, the "purity crusade," and other concerns pertaining to godly living and personal morality. Dayton's account of the great reversal gave equal weight to specific theological factors, however. Following Ernest Sandeen, he emphasized the reactionary effects of the premillennialist upsurge and the influence of Princeton theology conservatism. Like Sandeen, he argued that a hyperconservative biblical literalism was the bridge that linked these otherwise disparate forms of conservative Christianity.[6]

Premillennialist eschatology negated even the idea of a Christian mission to reform social conditions. Armed with Darby's apocalyptic reading of scripture, premillennialist leaders insisted that the church had no social mission to promote social justice. Their preaching redirected American evangelicalism away from its earlier social commitments. This reorientation made popular fundamentalism more congenial to the guardians of Princeton orthodoxy, who had never supported abolition, racial integration, feminism, or any other egalitarian reforms. In the 1850s and 1860s, Charles Hodge had denounced Finney's abolitionism and condemned his call for civil disobedience against the fugitive slave laws. Though he also criticized Southern Presbyterians (such as James Henley Thornwell) who supported slavery, Hodge pronounced that the abolitionists were removed from the "controlling intellect or moral feeling" of Northern intellectual culture. The notion that slavery is morally evil is the product of a sectarian mentality, he contended: "It has no power over those who reject that principle, and therefore it has not gained ascendancy over those whose faith is governed by the word of God." Hodge taught that the moral issue of slavery, like that of political despotism, belongs to the category of *adiaphora,* things to which biblical faith is indifferent. Yet he was equally certain that biblical faith is not indifferent about the rights of women. "There is no deformity of human character from which we turn with a deeper loathing than from a woman forgetful of her nature and clamorous for the vocations and rights of men," he declared. With a sharp and often caustic edge, he warned repeatedly that the prospect of two autonomous votes in the same household was incompatible with the biblical doctrine of male headship.[7]

Dayton's retelling of the triumph of Northern fundamentalism in the evangelical movement was more than a plea for a recovery of evangelical social conscience, however. At least implicitly, it was also a call for the recognition of a genuine theological pluralism in American evangelicalism. The conflict between Hodge and Finney was rooted in rival theologies. Princeton theology taught that all social structures and historical events are the products of God's all-determining decrees, but Finney countered that orthodox Calvinism distorts the actual witness of scripture. Every page of scripture assumes that people are free to choose against evil, he insisted. The Bible does not prescribe any kind of pious resignation toward personal or social evil but rather commands the faithful to spread Christ's regenerating gospel across the earth.

Finney taught that the differences between Hodge's Calvinism and his own Arminian revivalism were rooted in a deeper conflict of perceptions about the moral nature of God. Scripture does not picture God as living above moral law, he insisted; in the witness of scripture, God is pictured as *being* the highest moral law unto himself. He rejected the orthodox Calvinist and Lutheran representation of divine sovereignty "as consisting in a perfectly arbitrary disposal of events." The true sovereignty of God consists in the independence of God's will in consulting his own mind, making his own selections, and using his own means to accomplish his ends, Finney argued: "In other words, the sovereignty of God is nothing else than infinite benevolence directed by infinite knowledge." God's rule of action is made by God's reason alone; God knows no law that is not given to him by his own reason. The sovereignty of God consists in the disposal of all things and events in such a way as to meet the ideas of God's reason.[8]

To Finney, this was what it meant to affirm that God "accomplishes all things according to his counsel and will" (Eph. 1:11). He denied that Ephesians excluded the moral freedom of human agents. The sense of scripture is rather that God's infinite knowledge enables God to select a means and end "that should consist with and include the perfect freedom of moral agents." The moral commands of scripture made no sense at all if moral agents possessed no power in Christ to obey them.[9] Moreover, he urged, the entire Pauline doctrine of the "new creation in Christ," brought about by the regenerative power of the Holy Spirit, is mere rhetoric if sanctification in its entirety is not attainable in this life (2 Cor. 5:17). Scripture never intimates that the death of a saint in Christ is the terminating point of a saint's service to the devil, Finney observed; that is, scripture never pictures death as an indispensable means to sanctification. To claim that sanctification can be actualized only after death is to give death a spiritual power or influence that is equal to the Holy Spirit.

Finney protested such belief as perverse. In scripture, death is always the enemy. Death is always linked with sin as the prime symptom of the Fall. The gospel preaches regeneration in this life over the power of sin and death, Finney observed, but most of the churches reduced this promise to pitiful otherworldliness. In effect, they reduced the gospel promise of new life in Christ to a mere hope for some kind of life beyond death. "How striking is the contrast between the language of the church and that of inspiration on this subject!" he scolded. The church consoles people that death will deliver them from the devil, but scripture teaches that death is the enemy and that Christ's Spirit can make a Christian sanctified in this life.[10]

The intense moral perfectionism of Finney's revival preaching was virtually a recipe for spiritual burnout, but it was also emancipating in crucial respects. It proposed to take the gospel message seriously, not only as a promise of eternal life beyond the grave but also as a promise of deliverance from the bondage of personal and social evil in this life. If Paul's declaration that the regenerate believer is a new creature means anything, Finney reasoned following John Wesley, it must mean that the Christian is a new creature in this life. And if the body of Christ is not meant to recognize distinctions on the basis of race or gender (Gal. 3:28), this cannot be a norm that applies only to a heavenly afterlife. The presence of the kingdom should be and is subversive to this world.

Dayton played up the differences between the emancipatory aspects of this kind of evangelicalism and the mutated evangelicalism that succeeded it. The contrasts were heightened for him personally by the fact that he was raised in the Wesleyan tradition that created Wheaton College and supported Finney's revival campaigns. The Wesleyan Church of his experience was hardly prophetic. His teachers were the kind of Wesleyans who censored Finney's writings and denounced Martin Luther King Jr. as a Communist. By most appearances, he acknowledged, his church confirmed the prejudices of the dominant paradigm of American Christianity. On this account, the conservative churches were sectarian, socially regressive, and politically reactionary or apolitical, whereas the "mainline" churches were liberal, progressive, intellectual, and ecumenical. Dayton did not dispute that much of his tradition seemed to aspire to exactly this schematism. His teachers routinely condemned current movements for social justice and ecumenism.

But this picture was both recent and misleading, he noted. Historically, the mainline churches had been allied with the dominant culture; they had blessed the status quo and maintained their privileges within it. It was the nonconforming evangelicals who produced significant movements for racial integration, feminism, and social justice. In the seventeenth and eighteenth centuries, when the mainline state churches turned to an arid intellectualism, it was the Pietist movement that took up a great concern for the poor and oppressed. In the nineteenth century, while the mainline churches prided themselves on their enlightened attitudes toward women and racial minorities, it was the evangelical Wesleyan and Holiness movements that actually ordained women to the ministry and organized serious antislavery campaigns. A century later, these churches were still ordaining women in higher proportions than the "progressive, mainline" churches, despite their purported antifeminism. "In pursuing some of the ironies of this fact, I have learned a great deal about how ideology determines the way we see and understand the world, how scholarship serves ideology, and how evenly bigotry is distributed throughout the culture," Dayton remarked.[11]

Most of the mid-century fundamentalist evangelicals who had created the modern evangelical establishment shuddered at the offshoots of German and English and American Pietism. Many drew a sharp line between denominationally tamed Methodists (who made good evangelicals if they were not already lost to modernism) and all of the less-cultured Holiness and Pentecostal movements. The evangelical establishment was led and controlled by Reformed-oriented conservatives who gave little consideration to the notion that modern evangelicalism had much to learn from the spiritual descendants of Finney, Moody, or even John Wesley. Evangelicalism, they believed, needed intellectual prestige, not the sloppy emotionalism of Arminian revivalists. Billy Graham's revival preaching called unbelievers to "make a decision for Christ," but Graham was careful not to cross the border into wilder Arminian territory. Through Graham's ministry and such institutions as Wheaton College, Inter-Varsity Christian Fellowship, and *Christianity Today,* the evangelical movement succeeded in creating a significantly transdenominational image and ethos, but Reformed evangelicals either dominated or controlled most of these institutions. Their conception of ecumenical evangelicalism assumed a Reformed center.[12]

UPHOLDING THE WESLEYAN DIFFERENCE

Today, the evangelical establishment is still dominated by Calvinists, but evangelical theology is no longer as dominated by Calvinism as it was for much of the past century. Some of the same evangelical thinkers who are calling for a shift away from inerrancy authoritarianism are also claiming that there are other traditions within existing evangelicalism that are more faithful to the spirit of biblical faith than the creedal intellectualism engendered by a Reformed establishment. Some urge that certain Arminian currents in evangelicalism have much to contribute to the creation of a truly postfundamentalist evangelical movement. Methodist evangelical William J. Abraham presents a sharp and influential version of this proposal, arguing for a Wesleyan-style evangelicalism that is not fundamentalist precisely on account of its Wesleyan elements.

"I am convinced that there are versions of the [evangelical] heritage that can be distinguished from modern fundamentalism and its recent offspring, conservative evangelicalism," Abraham declares.[13] In his reading, nothing has characterized or limited modern evangelical theology more than its driving desire to become respectable. Though evangelical thinkers routinely criticize liberal theologians for accommodating the gospel to modernity, he observes, they have devoted themselves no less exclusively to developing antimodernist apologetic systems. That is, evangelical theology has been no less preoccupied than theological liberalism with defending itself from modernist criticism. The very term *evangelicalism* has become associated predominantly with the legacy of mid-century Reformed neoevangelicalism, which sought to rescue the doctrinal content of early twentieth-century fundamentalism. Abraham allows that this project produced some interesting work, but he judges that its useful phase has long past.

Carl Henry's massive apologetic enterprise epitomizes for Abraham the spiritual bankruptcy of conservative evangelicalism. "One looks in vain here for a fresh, invigorating expression of the Christian gospel," Abraham observes. "There is nothing here that humbles the soul before God, drives one to Christ in fresh love and adoration, inspires one to love one's neighbor as oneself, or encourages one to preach more faithfully." Henry defends traditional Christology from various critiques, but Christ's enlivening Spirit itself is missing from his theology. Several thousand pages of "turgid scholasticism" reduce the Spirit to the end of an argument, Abraham laments: "Readers swirl around in a sea of names who are either called in defense as witnesses to the truth or carefully worked over as inconsistent heretics. A dead and barren orthodoxy decked out in a magnificent display of learning is presented as the riches of Christian faith."[14]

Abraham counters that the gospel spoken in the voice of scripture is far more compelling than Henry's scholasticism. Even educated readers of Henry's lifeless prose "will soon find themselves suffering from either boredom or indigestion," he judges. Like much of his intellectual tradition, Abraham argues, Henry's apologetic is spiritually deflated and intellectually unbalanced. His idea of upholding the faith is modeled on a shooting gallery: "There is no compelling account of Christ; there is next to nothing on the doctrine of Christian life or the work of the Holy Spirit in renewal; there is very little on the nature and demands of Christian community." Henry defends conservative evangelicalism mostly by criticizing its rival worldviews, especially on the level of epistemology. Four massive volumes on epistemological issues crowd out any presumed interest in the inward testimony of Christ's Spirit. The effect is "strange in the extreme," Abraham charges. In its preoccupation with warding off modernist criticism, Henry-style evangelicalism makes epistemology the battleground of rival truth claims. It stakes the truth of the gospel on its success in building a convincing epistemological foundation. But this defense of the gospel heightens the jeopardy modern criticism places on Christianity, Abraham observes. It makes the truth of the gospel dependent on the credibility of a highly dubious philosophical structure. Henry's apologetic buries the living reality of Christ's Spirit under the claims of an ideological system that is neither compelling nor convincing. [15]

In his early work Abraham urged that evangelicals are bound together by a stronger "continuity in depth" than the mere "surface-continuity" of old doctrines that evangelical theologians are inclined to emphasize. He sought to refurbish a moderate form of the evangelical doctrine of biblical inspiration by appealing to "the wider insights of reason and experience," but the experience of pressing this argument convinced him that the project itself was the problem. He judged that it is precisely their obsession with epistemology that drives evangelicals to invest ultimate significance in extreme versions of inspiration doctrine. This obsession is self-reinforcing: The evangelical fixation with inspiration as the solution to an epistemological problem heightens the evangelical preoccupation with epistemology. An extreme view of inspiration is offered as the answer to an epistemological problem, but this answer creates impossible problems of its own that intensify the evangelical preoccupation with epistemology.

Abraham emphasizes that the evangelical commitment to inerrancy doctrine grew out of the evangelical commitment to a dictation theory of inspiration. His early work *The Divine Inspiration of Holy Scripture* urged that evangelicals needed to stop evading the implications of this historical truism. "The fact is that prior to modern times many Christians really did believe that the Bible was dictated by God," he observed. In earlier periods, this identification of inspiration with dictation was relatively harmless: "It was simply part of the mental furniture of many of our forefathers." The Protestant scholastics reasoned that scripture could not contain any errors if God verbally inspired the very words that scripture contains. The problem for contemporary evangelicalism is not the fact that the old Protestant churchmen didn't know any better, Abraham argued, but rather that their modern successors have insisted on upholding a claim that dictation theory requires, even while claiming that dictation is not and never was an orthodox doctrine.[16] Hodge and Warfield realized that the dictation theory is indefensible, but their conception of the human dimension of scripture was as empty of material meaning as that of their orthodox forebears.

Abraham notes that the same mentality is vividly reproduced in the writings of contemporary conservative evangelicals. His judgment of their legacy is unsparing. The evangelical doctrine of biblical inerrancy creates enormous problems for Christian preaching and apologetics that no evangelical has come close to solving, he observes: "It inhibits an honest reading of the text, as it is, blemishes and all. It fosters an obsession with epistemological questions that overshadows the substance of the gospel. It creates expectations in young converts that can never be fulfilled and then proceeds to provide circuitous harmonizations and theories to relieve the ensuing disappointment. It is not based on scripture itself, it is ultimately irreconcilable with the actual phenomena of the Bible, and it is not required for construing scripture as normative for Christian faith and practice."[17]

Evangelicalism has been distorted by its fixation on false choices, he argues. It was never the case that the truth or falsity of Christian faith hung entirely on its capacity to provide an airtight epistemological answer. By claiming that the epistemological problem bears this kind and degree of importance, modern evangelicalism has ironically become a form of theology that looks past the substance of the gospel. In the name of preserving the authority of scripture, conservative evangelicalism has obsessed over issues and positions that are extraneous to scripture. It commits the gospel to positions that are not in the gospel and thereby distorts the sense and meaning of gospel faith. This model has ruled the evangelical world for too long already, Abraham urges. What is needed today is not a refinement of the traditional, epistemologically fixated model but a different kind of evangelicalism: "The obsession with epistemology has to be completely abandoned, while the weight given to the place of doctrine needs to be reevaluated." This rethinking must include a greater openness to the insights of modern biblical scholarship and other forms of modernist criticism, he argues. It is not enough to renew the Carnell-Henry apologetic project, for "that tradition is now exhausted; not even a good dose of classical Christian doctrine will save it."[18]

The central evangelical debate of the 1980s pitted those who held a high doctrine of biblical inspiration against those who held a near-dictation view. Both sides claimed that their position was the central church tradition on inspiration.[19] Abraham's early work set out to strengthen the more moderate position, but his research ultimately convinced him that the debate itself framed the issue wrongly.

In his judgment, Christian theological history is too complicated and diverse to yield a single dominant view of the meaning of inspiration. To claim that any particular doctrine of biblical inspiration is the "central" orthodox view is to distort a complex historical inheritance. No single theory can do justice to the different ways of conceiving biblical inspiration and authority that distinguish the church's great theologians from one another. Moreover, the premodern thinkers whom evangelical theologians cite to support their position believed in divine dictation. Conservative evangelicals scrutinize the writings of Francis Turretin, John Gerhard, and John Owen for statements that support inerrancy, but they routinely ignore statements that support dictation. This procedure exposes the bankruptcy of modern conservative evangelicalism, Abraham argues. Conservative evangelicalism is deeply committed to a doctrine of inerrancy that is inseparable from a discarded view of inspiration. "The modern doctrine of plenary inspiration is in the end nothing more than an ingenious way of holding to inerrancy when its roots have been repudiated," he explains. "All the historical scholasticism one can muster, all the technical theological dexterity one can develop, all the highbrow hermeneutical skill one can deploy—none of these can undo this fact."[20]

He urges that evangelicals should therefore stop defending the Mosaic authorship of the Pentateuch, the single authorship of Isaiah, and an early date for Daniel. Evangelical scholarship has held out for too long against the evidence on these matters because it has been tied to the vestige of a mistaken view of inspiration. Instead of fighting the evidence in biblical scholarship, Abraham argues, evangelical scripture scholars should invest their energies in exploring how scripture functions as canon in the life of faith. Instead of making the life of faith subordinate to epistemology in theology, evangelical theologians should give highest priority to the Holy Spirit's work in making Christians. "We need to reorder our priorities so that the primary emphasis is placed not on right doctrine but on right relationships with God and with each other," he urges. His model of exemplary evangelicalism is John Wesley.

Wesley held doctrine in high regard, but he placed doctrine second in importance to personal acquaintance with Christ. He affirmed the primacy of scripture for theology, but he also affirmed the crucial roles of tradition, reason, and experience in interpreting scripture. He was steeped in the writings of the church fathers and warned against the Protestant tendency to give short shrift to the mediating function of Christian tradition. He emphasized the all-embracing love and goodness of God as embodied and revealed in Christ. Though Wesley assumed a dictation theory of inspiration, he never made this belief an essential element of Christian faith. His concern was always with the saving message of scripture, rather than with theories about the origins of scripture. To him, the important truth of the Bible was its truth as a book of salvation. His central themes were the new birth in Christ, justification by faith, the witness of the Spirit, and the possibility of sanctified life in the Spirit.[21]

Wesley's emphasis on God as the loving and good Father made known through Christ and the Spirit acted as a control on his understanding of God as providential ruler. Wesley embraced the biblical picture of God as all-powerful and transcendent, but his biblically grounded belief in God's loving goodness made the Calvinist theology of double predestination unacceptable to him. Moreover, though his evangelistic preaching of Christ as Lord and Savior was directed to the individual heart, it was never merely individualistic. Wesley was a pragmatic idealist in his approach to social issues. He opposed slavery, he organized relief agencies for the poor and afflicted, and he taught that all people are equal in God's sight. He emphasized the pervasive reality of sin in all human affairs but also taught that where sin abounds, grace abounds much more. For Wesley, the heart of the gospel was the good news that, through Christ's sacrifice and the outpouring of his Spirit, the triumph of grace in this life has been made possible.[22]

To Abraham and numerous others, these are the elements of a better kind of evangelicalism. Unlike the Reformed and premillennialist theologies that have dominated modern evangelicalism, the Wesleyan tradition does not subordinate spiritual renewal to doctrine, emphasize a core of "fundamental" beliefs, privilege biblical inerrancy over other doctrines, or picture God as an absolute predestining monarch. "In Wesley we have a splendid model of the evangelical tradition at its best," Abraham remarks. The key to Wesley's greatness as a model for evangelicalism is that he combined Spirit-filled personal religion with respect for tradition. Wesleyan theology holds together aspects of the Christian tradition that are usually pulled apart in evangelical theologies. It affirms the primacy of scripture but also affirms reason and experience as sources of theology. The crucial point is not that Wesley worked out the most compelling or sophisticated theological method, Abraham notes. What is crucial for evangelicalism is that Wesley's theology exuded a creative, open, and warm-hearted spirit. He lived out the joy and redemptive power of the faith without being defensive toward it. He did not isolate faith in a protected box of revelation but regarded everything in life as source material for theology.[23]

WORD AND SPIRIT
IN THE WESLEYAN TRADITIONS

This argument has an ample heritage. In the late nineteenth century, English and American Methodist theologians such as Miner Raymond, John Miley, William Burt Pope, and Amos Binney sought in the name of a Wesleyan evangelical piety to fend off the aggressive creedalism of what became the fundamentalist movement. Like Abraham, the nineteenth-century Methodist theologians viewed Methodism as a healthy, gospel-centered corrective to orthodox and reactionary Christian movements. They gave particular critical attention to the rising tide of creed-fixated premillennialist movements. The Methodist theologians defended Wesley's postmillennialist eschatology and also made a case for his Arminian doctrine of grace, his conception of scripture as a book of salvation, and his insistence on the simultaneity or close relation between the experiences of justification and sanctification.[24] Miley's influential *Systematic Theology* (1893) emphasized that just as the work of justification is incomplete without regeneration, so the Holy Spirit's work of personal regeneration is incomplete without entire sanctification. With the appearance of an afterthought, he placed his brief discussion of biblical inspiration in an appendix.[25]

The main Holiness offshoots of the Wesleyan tradition were a bit slow to produce their own systematic theologies, but when they finally began to do so, at the height of the fundamentalist upsurge, they also inveighed against the legalistic spirit of fundamentalism. In the 1920s, Holiness groups such as the Free Methodist Church, the Wesleyan Church, the Church of the Nazarene, the Salvation Army, and the Church of God were drawn into the modernist-fundamentalist controversy. As Paul Merritt Bassett observes, many Holiness people were sympathetic to fundamentalism.[26] As the conflict over fundamentalism absorbed virtually all the Protestant churches, many also grew uneasy with their tradition's theological dependence on Methodism. The problem for fundamentalist-generation Holiness people was not only that Methodism seemed increasingly foreign but also, at least implicitly, that it was suspect in its capacity to defend the fundamentals. This situation spurred Holiness followers on both sides of the conflict to call for their own theologies, produced by theologians of their own denominational traditions. Much of the popular literature that this call produced in the 1920s and 1930s made Wesleyanism speak the language of creedal literalism and epistemological certainty. In the context of a deepening split in the churches between theological modernists and fundamentalists, many Holiness followers sided with the fundamentalists.

But the major Holiness theologians spoke against the popular tendency to equate Holiness teaching with fundamentalism. The key elements of a genuinely Wesleyan evangelicalism were retained by such influential Holiness theologians as R. R. Byrum, A. M. Hills, and especially H. Orton Wiley. Byrum's *Christian Theology* (1924) defended the continuity of Church of God teaching with the Methodist theologies of Pope and Miley. A. M. Hills's *Fundamental Christian Theology* (1934) contended that authentic Nazarene teaching is not fundamentalist but rooted in the Wesleyan Pietism of Methodist theology. Hills defended an infallible-teaching model of biblical infallibility and judged that the biblical autographs contained various inconsequential errors.[27] Between 1910 and 1950, Wiley expounded this understanding of the Wesleyan Nazarene heritage with extraordinary rhetorical force.

As a college president, teacher, magazine editor, evangelist, and Nazarene theologian, Wiley exerted a singular influence over the self-understanding of American Wesleyanism between 1910 and 1950. He could match any fundamentalist in denouncing the faithlessness and antisupernaturalist bias of theological liberalism, but his critique of fundamentalism was equally sharp. Wiley regarded the fundamentalist movement as a tragic recapitulation of the scholastic mistake. He taught that while Luther and Calvin at least tried to maintain a balance between the formal and material principles of salvation, their orthodox successors divorced the written Word of scripture from the living Word of Christ. Protestant scholasticism suffocated the spiritual force of the biblical Word. In the preaching and theology of Protestant orthodoxy, he explained, scripture was no longer the fresh Word of Christ or the outflow of the Spirit's presence "but merely a recorded utterance which bound men by legal rather than spiritual bonds." [28]

Protestant orthodoxy prized formal knowledge over spiritual knowledge and thus lost its spiritual knowledge altogether. "The views of God attained were merely those of a book, not those of the Living Christ which the book was intended to reveal," Wiley argued. The results were disastrous for Protestantism. Instead of coming to know God himself, Protestants contented themselves with seeking God's will; instead of finding a personal relationship with the living Christ, Protestant creedalism turned Christ into a merely historical figure. "They gave more attention to creeds than to Christ," he recounted. "They rested in the letter, which according to Scripture itself kills, and never rose to a concept of Him whose words are spirit and life. The Bible thus divorced from its mystical connection with the Personal Word, became in some sense a usurper, a pretender to the throne."[29]

Protestant orthodoxy turned scripture into a storehouse of facts and thus killed off the life-giving Spirit that makes scripture God's living Word. It sought to protect faith by resting faith on logic. Wiley argued that modern fundamentalism had repeated exactly this wrongheaded tack. Modern fundamentalism was a reactionary phenomenon because it resorted to "a mere legalistic defense of the Scriptures," he judged. In the name of saving biblical truth, it betrayed the saving message of the written Word. Wiley countered that true evangelical faith indwells and witnesses to a deeper spiritual reality. Since genuine gospel faith does not live by the letter, he explained, it does not rest in its capacity to defend itself rationally. Since it does not rest in facts that must be defended by reason, it does not invest any importance in debates about higher criticism of scripture or biblical inerrancy. Those who are filled with the Holy Spirit "have a broader and more substantial basis for their faith," he argued. "It rests in their risen Lord, the glorified Christ. They know that the Bible is true, not primarily through the efforts of the apologists, but because they are acquainted with its Author. The Spirit which inspired the Word dwells within them and witnesses to its truth."[30]

For Wiley, as for his tradition, the guardian of orthodoxy was the Holy Spirit. Scripture has authority because the Holy Spirit inspires faith in its saving sufficiency. The movement of faith begins not with creedal assent to biblical inspiration or authority but with one's saving communion with God through Christ. Belief in the authority of scripture arises rightly as a by-product of one's coming to know Christ as living Lord and Savior. Put differently, the Holy Spirit testifies first to the sufficiency of scripture for salvation before witnessing to the authority of scripture. The order is crucial. "While we honor the Scriptures in giving them a central place as our primary source in theology, we are not unmindful that the letter killeth but the Spirit maketh alive," Wiley explained.[31] Christ, the living Word, must always take precedence over the written Word, for Christ, not scripture, is the object of faith.

Classical evangelicalism and fundamentalist evangelicalism are linked in their emphasis on the primacy of biblical authority. The major Reformed confessions all asserted the divine inspiration and authority of scripture before speaking of anything else. Statements such as the First Helvetic Confession (1536) and the Second Helvetic Confession (1566) taught implicitly that one must accept the authority of scripture before one can know Christ or find a genuine relationship with

God.[32] In its genuinely Wesleyan forms, however, the Pietist traditions have operated out of a different sense of the meaning of biblical authority. John Wesley lived and died as an Anglican priest, and his salvation-focused conception of biblical authority was rooted in his Anglicanism. Unlike the Reformed and Lutheran confessions of the sixteenth century, which began with assertions about the authority of scripture or the nature of God, the Anglican Thirty-Nine Articles of Religion spoke about scripture only after making confessional statements about faith in the Holy Trinity, the Word incarnate, Christ's descent into hell, the resurrection of Christ, and the Holy Spirit.[33] In Christianity, the Thirty-Nine Articles implied, the primary issue is one's relationship with God; a proper view of scripture comes from one's relation to God, rather than the other way around.

Moreover, Article 6 said nothing about the primacy, plenary inspiration, or inerrancy of scripture but stated simply that "Holy Scripture containeth all things necessary to salvation." To early Anglicanism, the saving purpose of scripture was more important than any proposed belief about its revealed nature; the authority of the Bible arose first and principally from its sufficiency for redemption. The Puritans claimed that scripture is "the only rule of all things," but early Anglicanism, including its preeminent theologian Richard Hooker, countered that scripture contains only all things that are necessary to be known for our salvation. The point of the Anglican doctrine of scripture was not to hold up the Bible as an object of revelation but to revere scripture as the community-shaping vehicle through which the Spirit reveals salvation.[34]

This emphasis on scripture as the church's vehicle to salvation was eclipsed in much of seventeenth-century Anglicanism by the ascendancy of orthodox scholasticism. Though some of the Caroline divines resisted the rationalistic spirit of scholasticism and developed distinctively Anglican approaches to theological authority, method, and especially moral theology, many others adopted the scholastic practice of making biblical authority the controlling category of all theology. Anglican scholasticism developed its own forms of "high and dry" orthodoxy that appealed to reason prior to faith.[35] Wesley's reform movement in the succeeding century preached against what he perceived as the spiritual ravages of this trend. Against the rationalist tendency to reduce biblical revelation to a static word, he insisted on the necessary *testimonium* of the Spirit in making scripture God's Word. Against the lukewarm piety of his time, he called the church to faithful thanksgiving for Christ's mercy and sanctifying grace. Against the sterile biblicism of his time, he called the Church of England to return to its earlier understanding of scripture as the Spirit-illuminated guide to salvation.

Though he accepted the traditional assurance that scripture is free from error on account of its divine dictation, Wesley did not make this belief serve as a foundational principle in the manner of Reformed or Lutheran orthodoxy. For him, scripture was the means to salvation, not a storehouse of proof texts for dogmatic claims. Wesley desired to be a "man of one book," as he famously put it, because scripture alone discloses the way to heaven. In God's presence, he explained, the words of the book can show us the way to heaven. The Spirit is the sole agent of the Bible's saving sufficiency. Scripture is important not because it contains information that satisfies reason, experience, or even the desire for true religious doctrine but because it is the unique means by which the Spirit leads us to salvation.[36]

For this reason, Wesley was prepared to accept that the Bible might contain incidental or historical errors. He reasoned that if the Holy Spirit has inspired scripture to show Christ as the way to salvation, the kind of infallibility that is needed is infallible sufficiency for salvation, not historical or scientific precision. It was not the purpose or obligation of the Spirit to correct any possible mistakes in the Gospel genealogies, for example, because these records, as reproduced in scripture, bear a spiritual purpose. Their function is to help bring people to salvation in Christ, not to provide a disinterested, precise historical account. Wesley speculated that in some cases historical or scribal errors in scripture might serve the Spirit's purpose in bringing unbelievers to a saving relation with Christ.[37]

Further, he was mindful of the dangers that attended any exaggerated claims about the scope of biblical authority. Wesleyanism was the first great Christian movement to arise in the wake of Enlightenment criticism. Faced with the extraordinary gains of modern science and philosophy in explaining how the world works, Wesley sought to avoid unnecessary conflicts with reason. He counseled that Christians should ask only two questions when confronted with Enlightenment claims: (1) Do they benefit humankind? (2) Do they claim to be sufficient for salvation?[38] Christianity has nothing to fear from critical disciplines that do not presume to correct the saving message of scripture, he taught. Though he believed in the verbal inspiration of scripture, Wesley usually refrained from making expansive deductions from it that jeopardized the possibility of Christian belief. By focusing his doctrine of scripture on its saving purpose, he avoided the trap that ensnared much of Protestant orthodoxy and all of the later fundamentalist movement.

Wesleyan evangelicals thus have ample warrant for claiming that their tradition contains at least the possibility of a gospel-centered evangelical alternative to the scholasticism and fundamentalism of the conservative evangelical establishment. In recent years, Wesleyan Holiness theologians such as H. Ray Dunning and J. Kenneth Grider have reaffirmed Wiley's dynamic theory of inspiration and his judgments against fundamentalist inerrancy doctrine.[39] Similar arguments for an evangelicalism that emphasizes the interaction of Spirit and Word have been advanced by Pentecostal scholars such as Gerald Sheppard, Gordon D. Fee, Scott A. Ellington, and Steven J. Land, all of whom argue for a theologically open-ended, charismatic evangelicalism that leaves behind its mistaken alliance with fundamentalism. The inerrancy purges of the 1980s convinced many evangelicals that Wiley and other early evangelical critics of fundamentalism were right to warn against its consuming legalism. Some have found the basis of what Land calls "a much fuller doctrine of the Word of God" in the Spirit-Word interactionism of the Wesleyan and charismatic traditions.[40]

The Holiness offshoots of Wesleyanism have been notable for the brutality of their polemics against one another, but they have also produced theologies that give appropriately peaceable witness to the claims of Holiness teaching about the sanctifying work of the Holy Spirit. Wesley continually exhorted his followers not to demonize their opponents. His own polemics repeatedly called his Christian opponents to recognize their spiritual fellowship under God's grace.[41] With nearly equal spiritual passion, Wiley urged that it was not only ridiculous but blasphemous to speak in a mean-spirited or conceited way about the Holy Spirit's cleansing of the heart from sin. "We tread here upon sacred ground," he cautioned. "We are through the blood of Jesus to enter the holiest *by a new and living way, which he hath consecrated for us, through the veil, that is to say, his flesh*" (see Heb. 10:19). The work of grace that Wesleyan theology describes in its teaching on the fullness of salvation from sin must be experienced before it can be understood at all, Wiley emphasized. The truth of sanctifying grace can never be demonstrated by mere argument, "for spiritual things can be known only by experience."[42]

Modern evangelicalism in its dominant voice uses the term *Arminian* only as an epithet or scare word. This comes from a long-standing tradition. In the eighteenth century, Wesley observed that many Protestants held the same feeling for Arminians that they held for mad dogs. He ruefully noted that many of them actually knew very little about the revision of Calvinist predestinarianism that Jacob Arminius proposed in the early seventeenth century, except that it was "something *very* bad, if not *all* that is bad!"[43] The Methodist-Wesleyan tradition, however, is unabashedly Arminian in its approach to the issues of general redemption, predestination, free will, and forensic justification. In the spirit of early Anglican Arminianism, Wesley emphasized the theme of "general redemption," that God's grace is sufficient for all people because Christ died for all. He reminded his Calvinist critics that no Christian ever affirmed the doctrines of original sin or justification by faith with stronger conviction than did Jacob Arminius. At the same time, he insisted, Arminius was right to reject the Calvinist doctrines of unconditional double predestination and irresistible grace.[44] For Wesley, as for his movement, the Reformed and Lutheran emphasis on predestination was disastrous. It prevented orthodox Protestants from recognizing that Christ gave his life for all people. It distorted the preaching of the churches and stunted their attempts at mission and evangelism. It cast a shadow over the spiritual lives of the elect and made God the author of all sin, "the destroyer of the greater part of mankind without mercy."[45]

By emphasizing the differences between the spirit of Wesley's evangelicalism and the inerrancy rationalism of the modern evangelical establishment, Abraham seeks to establish that gospel faith does not thrive or flourish best in a doctrinal house of authority. He presents Wesleyan Pietism as an evangelical antidote to the conservative evangelical obsession with doctrinal security. However, this argument contains a more deeply subversive theme than its pitch for Wesleyan theology or even its critique of inerrancy doctrine. The more subversive truism that Abraham drives home is that there are different kinds of evangelicalism. There is no such thing as a central orthodox tradition with regard to any of the major theological questions, he observes. Christian theology over the centuries has been too variable to justify any tightly defined claim about what "the orthodox tradition" has "always taught" about Christ or the attributes of God or the authority of scripture. Most conservative evangelical appeals to history appeal to the idea of singular orthodox tradition, but Abraham counters that this image of an orthodox "thin red line" is the defining illusion of modern evangelicalism.

Evangelicals routinely link Warfield and the Hodges to Wesley, Turretin, the Westminster divines, Calvin, Luther, Hus, Augustine, and Irenaeus, all the way back to Jesus and Paul. The historical picture is that of a core evangelical faith that was lost by a paganizing church and then recovered by a faithful Protestant remnant. But this picture is hopelessly distorted, Abraham cautions. There is no line that exclusively connects Warfield to Wesley and Augustine, nor is there even any core of doctrine that unites modern evangelicals. "The term 'evangelical' meant one thing during the Reformation; it meant another in the period of the eighteenth-century revivalists; it means something else today," he remarks. "Great figures like Luther, Calvin, and Wesley are not replicas. They represent profoundly different accounts of a complex vision of the Christian tradition."[46]

Moreover, the ample disagreements that divide modern evangelicals confirm that "evangelicalism" is an inherently contested concept. Its meaning cannot be defined precisely, because it is claimed by groups that bear fundamental differences from one another in the ways in which they define themselves. This is not a bad thing, Abraham counsels. Unlike fundamentalism, there is such a thing as a genuine *tradition* of evangelical thought, because disagreement and self-critical debate are tolerated within the family of traditions that comprise evangelicalism. Fundamentalism can be called a theological tradition only as a courtesy; it does not permit critical debate, and it treats ideas as propaganda. The separatist impulse is inherent in fundamentalism, which explains why fundamentalists are never able to stand together for long.[47]

The problem with modern evangelicalism is that evangelicals have tried to clean up the fundamentalist project while embracing its primary categories. Correct doctrine is still regarded as the salvation of the church, and inerrancy secures the foundations of correct doctrine. This is the presuppositional structure that a renewed, self-critical, and consciously pluralistic evangelicalism must give up, Abraham proposes. Evangelicalism must subordinate its concern with doctrine to spiritual renewal. The essence of the evangelical tradition must be found in faithful, Spirit-filled living rather than in any list of fundamental beliefs. Evangelicalism cannot be indifferent to doctrine, but it must repudiate the kind of doctrine that reduces theology to biblical taxonomy. The promise of a reoriented evangelicalism is that a consciously pluralistic evangelical movement may develop a richer account of the life of faith. Such a movement may begin to produce again the kind of open-ended narrative theology that Wesley pioneered, which is the kind of theology that scripture contains.

APPEALING TO THE GREAT TRADITION: CATHOLIC EVANGELICALISM

Abraham recognized in the mid-1980s that a sizable group of evangelicals already shared his critique of the literalism and spiritual bankruptcy of their tradition. His call for a "great revival" of the "full evangelical tradition" urged them to face up to the fact and implications of evangelical pluralism as well. On this point, as he knew, most evangelicals were disposed to hold out for the thin red line. A notable example was the group of evangelicals associated with the Chicago Call. In 1977, Robert E. Webber and Donald Bloesch organized a conference of evangelical leaders and scholars that issued an appeal, known as the Chicago Call, for a more catholic and historically rooted evangelicalism. The Chicago Call deplored the individualism, spiritual shallowness, and historical uprootedness that its authors judged to be pervasive in American evangelicalism. It called for a new evangelical movement that affirmed the historic creeds, sacraments, and ecclesial ethos of classical Christianity. "We believe that today evangelicals are hindered from achieving full maturity by a reduction of the historic faith," it declared. "There is, therefore, a pressing need to reflect upon the substance of the biblical and historic faith and to recover the fullness of this heritage."[48]

The Chicago Call was issued in the form of an eight-point manifesto that urged evangelicals to affirm the roots and catholic heritage of Christianity, the authority of scripture, the identity-conferring authority of the historic creeds, the holistic character of salvation, the value of sacramental practices and theology, the centrality of Christ's redemptive work to Christian spirituality, the need for church authority, and the hope of Christian unity. It noted that evangelicals tend to assume, wrongly, that their devotion to the authority of scripture and their openness to the Holy Spirit make them spiritually free from the church's past. This mentality cuts evangelicalism off from the spiritual resources of the greater Christian tradition, the Callers lamented. It also makes evangelicalism culturally provincial and blind to the work of God's Spirit in the Roman Catholic and Eastern Orthodox traditions. The Callers admonished that the evangelical impulse to proclaim the saving grace of Christ and the church-reforming Word of scripture is not a Protestant invention. The same evangelical impulse has animated the creeds and doctrines of the ecumenical councils, the piety of the early church fathers, the Augustinian theology of grace, the zeal of the monastic reformers, the spiritual devotion of many Christian mystics, and the integrity of Erasmian ecumenists. In modern times the Protestant descendants of the Puritan and Pietist traditions carried forward this impulse, but it was also carried forward, without evangelical acknowledgment, in parts of the Orthodox and Catholic traditions. The Callers thus exhorted, "We dare not move beyond the biblical limits of the Gospel; but we cannot be fully evangelical without recognizing our need to learn from other times and movements concerning the whole meaning of that Gospel."[49]

Webber put the matter plainly in his programmatic call for a "mature" evangelicalism. Modern evangelicalism has deviated from its Reformation heritage by digressing from the historical Christian orthodoxy to which the Reformers appealed, he argued: "Therefore, if evangelicalism as a movement is going to be more representative of the historic faith it must become more conscious not only of the cultural shape of its own faith, but also by way of contrast, to the aspects of the historic Christian faith which it has forgotten."[50] This call to a more sacramental and historically rooted orthodoxy was supported by numerous Reformed and Methodist evangelicals and a smattering of others, notably Dayton, Richard Lovelace, Roger Nicole, and Thomas Howard.[51] Howard spoke for many of the

Callers in noting that the strongly propositional character of the evangelical imagination tends to make evangelicals suspicious of sacramental piety. Evangelical thinking about scripture is propositionalist; evangelical theology and preaching are propositionalist; even evangelical piety is propositionalist, focusing on Bible study. "The notion that the greatest mysteries of the faith will never quite yield themselves to our efforts to articulate them, while of course affirmed by Protestant imagination, nevertheless finds itself at times crowded into a corner in the great effort to articulate Christian vision in satisfactory propositions," he observed.[52] Howard endorsed the call's observation that the Christian doctrines of creation and incarnation cannot be fathomed adequately apart from the awakening of a sacramental consciousness. Propositionalism by itself bears little capacity to evoke awareness of God's purpose in the world or the sacredness of daily living.

The Callers were careful to avoid the polemical excesses of the Oxford Movement. In the nineteenth century, John Henry Newman's Oxford Tractarians blasted the individualism and "religious anarchy" of the Reformation in making their case for a recovery of high church orthodoxy in the Anglican Church. The Tractarians took it for granted that their cause required an unsparing polemical delineation between catholic orthodoxy and the various offshoots of the Reformation.[53] Webber's group took careful distance from this mistake. They argued that Luther and Calvin belong to the great tradition of classical Christian orthodoxy, and that the hope of a genuinely catholic evangelicalism lies in the modern evangelical recovery of the catholic elements in Lutheran and Calvinist Christianity.

These assurances failed to impress evangelical critics who found the call overly warm toward Catholicism and Eastern Orthodoxy, however. Some objected that the Chicago Call obscured the reasons for the existence of Protestantism. Others disliked the very idea of catholic evangelicalism. David F. Wells granted that there was, indeed, something wrong with an evangelical culture that produced a continuous celebrity parade of gold-plated evangelists, sequined television hosts, and jocks for Jesus, "but I cannot be persuaded that we would be substantially better off venerating Catholic saints than pretty starlets, or that sober-faced genuflectors and swingers of incense are much to be preferred to the vacant worshippers some of our churches are creating."[54]

Wells countered that the Protestant tendency toward individualistic piety is not a fault but simply a function of the genuinely Protestant refusal to subject the biblical Word to creedal formulations. The creeds are often wrong, he cautioned. The Nicene Creed contains Origenist concepts; Chalcedon conferred on Mary the title "Mother of God"; the Fourth Lateran Council endorsed Cyprian's dictum that outside the church there is no salvation; the Augsburg Confession prescribes the eucharistic doctrine of consubstantiation; the Marburg Articles teach baptismal regeneration; and the Westminster Confession identifies the pope as the Antichrist. Evangelicalism will not get stronger by granting authority to any of these statements, Wells argued. Moreover, he warned, the call's language about creation, the incarnation, and human life as sacramental derives not from scripture but from Greek and Russian Orthodoxy, in which a sacrament is anything that becomes a vehicle of God's grace.

The Chicago Call was seeking to enlarge evangelicalism by appropriating Christian traditions that are both non-Western and extrabiblical. Wells observed that Christ himself instituted only two sacraments, Baptism and the Lord's Supper, but Webber's group wanted to infuse the entire created order with sacramental significance. "Forgive me for asking, then, but on what grounds do the Callers prescribe as sacramental what the church's head, our Lord Jesus Christ, declined to do?" he asked. His judgment on the catholic evangelical enterprise as a whole was withering: "This may be a time of small happenings, of Pygmy spirituality, but a mass pilgrimage into the world of Anglo-Catholicism is not, with all due respect, what we need right now. Indeed, it is not what we need at any time."[55]

Webber's programmatic defense of catholic evangelicalism was titled *Common Roots*. It presented evangelicalism as a coherent theological tradition that is divided mostly by differences in emphasis and style. Evangelicals disagree over the weight that they give to various parts of the gospel message, he allowed, but none of these disagreements is deep enough to threaten the integrity of the evangelical tradition. One of the purposes of cultivating a deeper awareness of the common historical and doctrinal roots of evangelicalism was to mitigate its current disagreements. "The recovery of both the negative and the affirmative, the transcendent and the immanent will come only as we regain a truly incarnational understanding of the faith not only in our perception of the church, in our worship, in our theology, in our mission, but also in our personal and collective spirituality," he urged. Evangelical groups tend to define themselves by their one-sidedness in a particular area, but what is needed is to regain a "balanced sense of spirituality," drawing on the entire heritage of orthodox Christianity.[56]

This appeal to a panevangelical commonality was certainly more attractive and good-spirited than the accusative rhetoric of fundamentalism, but Webber's vision of "unity through common roots" glossed over the deep disagreements within evangelicalism. He and Bloesch urged that the dream of panevangelical unity could be fulfilled by appropriating neglected aspects of the church's common catholic past, but this proposal underestimated the fundamentally contested character of evangelicalism and its conflicting claims to an "orthodox" past. The sharpness of Wells's polemic was symptomatic of the deep differences in theology and sensibility that evangelicalism contains. Even in theory, much less in practice, a catholicizing turn would unify only small segments of the array of groups that presently identify themselves as evangelical. Many evangelicals are fervently committed to the uprooted, individualistic Protestantism that Webber and Bloesch criticize. A sizable rival group maintains that only the classical Reformed and Lutheran (and sometimes Anglican) traditions are authentically evangelical. Evangelicalism is a fundamentally contested family of religious traditions, precisely because most of its leaders have prized theological identity over any kind of unity.

Evangelicals have clashed for centuries over the nature of biblical authority, the authority of the church, the nature of divine predestination, the work of the Holy Spirit, the relation between justification and sanctification, the scope of sanctification, the relation between reason and revelation, and the possibility of fellowship between evangelicals and nonevangelicals. In the mid-1980s, American evangelicals waged a ferocious battle over the meaning of biblical inspiration. Abraham aptly observed at the time that this conflict was bound to give rise to a host of related disagreements. Evangelical disagreements over matters of fundamental doctrine are increasingly public, divisive, and politicized, he noted, but Webber's proposal came "nowhere near explaining this state of affairs."[57]

Webber's catholicizing strategy sought to avert hard decisions about disputed issues. The Chicago Call proposed to redeem the evangelical present by enlarging its catholic identity, but it glossed over the question of how particular elements from the past should be affirmed or repudiated. Like the reforming fundamentalists who founded Fuller Seminary, the Callers grasped that modern evangelicalism is too thin and reductionist; but they also shared the early neoevangelical reluctance to think this critique through. Rather than acknowledge that inerrancy doctrine is indefensible or that the evangelical preoccupation with correct doctrine has been misplaced, the Callers preferred to imagine a fantasized panevangelical catholicism. Abraham responded that this was not nearly enough. He applauded Webber's call for a deeper appreciation of the church's catholic heritage and endorsed Webber's suggestion that evangelicals need to develop better forms of piety. "But as they stand, Webber's proposals are cosmetic and superficial," he judged. The call amounted to a timid replay of the mid-century attempt to reform fundamentalism. The original neoevangelicals had glimpsed part of the problem but never broke free from fundamentalism. What is needed, Abraham urged, is a "radically different model" of evangelicalism that makes the break.[58]

THE ARMINIAN TURN

Abraham's manifesto for a new evangelicalism became a key marker of what *Christianity Today* later called the beginnings of an "evangelical megashift."[59] This change in theological sensibility does not always reflect a preference for a more progressive evangelical politics. Pinnock became a major theorist of "new model" evangelicalism, for example, though his writings on politics also promote a mixture of P. T. Bauer's free-enterprise ideology and Michael Novak's neoconservatism.[60] Nor does new-model evangelicalism necessarily bear any particular confessional stamp. Some neoevangelicals join Abraham and Pinnock in extolling the Arminian spirit of the Pietist tradition, but most neoevangelical thinkers are still, like Pinnock, members of the Baptist, Presbyterian, or Reformed church traditions. In its modern history, Reformed evangelicalism has given birth to numerous "new school," "New Light," and other reform-oriented pietistic movements. Today, the theorists of a postconservative evangelical trend are coming from churches across the entire evangelical spectrum.

Considerable irony lies in the fact that many of these thinkers have been deeply influenced by the fictional and apologetic writings of C. S. Lewis. Lewis is widely regarded as the master apologist of Christian orthodoxy in this century, but his theology was explicitly Arminian and provocatively opposed to classical Protestant teaching on several points. Robert Brow observes that these elements have played a decisive role in the past generation in changing the religious sensibilities of evangelicals. Through the influence of Lewis's enormously popular writings, many evangelicals have adopted a religious worldview that stands on the far edge of Arminian revision.

His conception of eternal damnation is a key example. Lewis rejected the notion that God sends people to hell by a judicial sentence for failing to hear or comprehend the gospel message. In *The Great Divorce,* he pictured eternity as a gray city in which individuals bear the freedom to move into the light of heaven. Since heaven and hell are destinations of the heart predicated on human freedom, he reasoned, it cannot be that anyone is in hell who would rather be in heaven. Hell is self-centered and self-chosen separation from God. In *The Problem of Pain,* Lewis described hell as the appropriate end for those who choose to reject God's fellowship-creating love. Hell is the opportunity to remain in self-centered alienation from God; it is the state of being in which boring, alienated living goes on forever. Lewis was adamant that the doctrine of hell should not be understood to be about God's imposition of external penal conditions on the damned, for "the doors of hell are locked on the *inside*." The penalties of hell are limited to the intrinsic consequences of the choice to live in sin, he argued. Theologically, hell symbolizes the reality that the goal of life can be missed. The goal is missed by people who actually prefer the "freedom" of living apart from God, in darkness, to living according to the light, in communion with God. Egocentrism leads to hell and is fulfilled there.[61]

Lewis's profound sense of Christ as eternally preexistent Word and his opposition to any kind of atonement creedalism also militate against a narrowly penal-substitutionary view of salvation. In *Mere Christianity* he argued that no particular theory of atonement should be held up as important or exclusively orthodox. Moreover, Lewis's rootage in Johannine Logos Christology corrects the traditional evangelical fixation on the *moment* of Christ's saving death and the *moment* of one's saving conversion to Christ. Evangelical revivalism and fundamentalism emphasize that salvation was not purchased until the moment of Christ's death on the cross; but in the Narnia stories, as well as in his apologetic writings, Lewis portrayed the Son of God as eternally both "lion" and servant. Christ is the redeeming Shepherd and Lamb (or Lion and Servant) who saves us not only in his death but in and through his eternal life.[62] In and through Christ's life, death, and resurrection, human myth became saving fact. As Shepherd and Lamb, Christ absorbs our sin throughout human history and expresses this relation to humanity in his incarnation and sacrificial death.[63]

This account of the incarnational process of salvation and the nature of eternal life has deeply influenced millions of readers over the past half century, including many evangelicals. Though he tended to play down denominational differences in his focus on what he called "mere Christianity," Lewis's Anglicanism clearly influenced his conception of what is essential to Christianity. His apologetic and fictional writings reflect the incarnational emphasis of Anglican theology and liturgics.[64] Through Lewis's writings, this outlook has become the common possession of evangelicals across the spectrum of evangelical church traditions. Brow observes that the influence of Lewis's processive incarnationalism among evangelicals deepens every time that evangelicals read the Narnia stories or Madeleine L'Engle's time-travel fantasies to their children. "A whole generation of young people have breathed this air, making their thinking very different from that of 'old-model' evangelicalism, even where there is shared commitment to Jesus as Savior and the Bible as the authoritative Word of God," he remarks. The split between a Lewis-influenced new model and the old-model juridical theology "is dividing evangelicals on a deep level."[65]

Brow's account of the ascendancy of non-Reformed thinking in evangelical theology bears some of the limitations of advocacy. As an advocate of "new-model evangelicalism," Brow has a tendency to exaggerate the newness of the shift in consciousness that he describes. As an Anglican evangelical, he also fails, curiously, to explain the significance of Lewis's Anglicanism or its link to his own perspective. Lewis's conception of salvation as processive, incarnational, and predicated on freedom did not come from nowhere. It reflects the Anglican tendency to seek a unitive basis for its patchwork of theological traditions in its practice of a common incarnational liturgy. The unstated implication of Brow's argument is that a more compelling evangelicalism would drop its Augustinian baggage and appropriate more of the incarnationalist spirit of the Anglican tradition.

One of the chief theorists of new-model evangelicalism takes a slightly different lesson from Brow's proposal, however. Pinnock argues that "Brow's 'new' evangelical thinking is really the old Arminian or non-Augustinian thinking." The shift in theological thinking that Brow calls for has thicker rootage in evangelical history than Lewis's orthodox Anglicanism, he suggests. After all, it is not really a new thing for evangelicals to say that hell is a fate freely chosen. Nor is it new for evangelicals to dispute juridical understandings of salvation or to reject absolute-sovereignty models of divine reality. "What *is* new is that the dominance of Calvinist thinking in evangelical theology is being challenged by a wave of Arminian thinking breaking on its shores," Pinnock observes. For him, it follows that the real issue is one of control: "Will the Augustinian old guard that dominates the structure of official evangelicalism surrender some of its power to a resurgent wave of Arminian thinking? Or will it fight to retain control?"[66]

In recent years, Pinnock has led the fight to gain a higher place for Arminian thinking in evangelical theology. He calls this option "free will theism," theology of the "openness of God," and, with Brow, "creative love theism." Creative love theism is rooted in the affirmation of 1 John 4:8 that "whoever does not love does not know God, for God is love." It explicates the desire expressed in Ephesians 3:17–18 that humanity shall come to comprehend the breadth, length, height, and depth of love. Pinnock and Brow explain that this model "celebrates the grace of God that abounds for all humanity" and that it privileges family metaphors over courtroom images for God's relationship to humanity: "It embraces a wideness in God's mercy and rejects the idea that God excludes any persons arbitrarily from saving help."[67] On the strength of biblical testimony to God's loving reciprocality, it emphasizes the openness and relationality of God to humanity and sees the doctrine of God's inner-Trinitarian fellowship as an important corrective to monarchical theisms that picture God as an all-determining transcendent (male) ego.

Pinnock unfailingly emphasizes that creative love theism is more attractive and inspiring than Calvinism, but he cautions that the more important reason to embrace it is that scripture everywhere assumes it. The Bible declares that God desires to save all people (1 Tim. 2:4; 2 Peter 3:9) and that God's grace has been given for the salvation of all people (Titus 2:11). Scripture contains numerous calls to repentance (e.g., Ezek. 33:11; Matt. 3:2; Acts 2:38; Acts 17:30) and warnings against falling away (1 Cor. 10:12; Heb. 6:4–6; 2 Peter 2:20–21). Orthodox Calvinism teaches that God causes everything that happens in the world, Pinnock observes, but scripture teaches that God's dealings with humankind are reciprocal and conditional. Calvinism swallows the biblical theme of divine-human mutuality in its doctrine of the divine decrees, but scripture teaches that even the good news of God's grace will not benefit us unless it is "mixed with faith in the hearers" (Heb. 4:2). Because the Bible assumes that God has made us to be able to accept or reject his purposes for us, Pinnock explains, it also assumes that what happens between God and us "is not simply the product of a set of premundane divine decrees."[68]

As a response to the question of how divine omniscience might be compatible with human freedom, the Arminian tradition is linked to the theologies of the early Greek Fathers, Augustine, and Aquinas, who argued that because God lives in the eternal present outside time, God views past, present, and future together. Augustine taught that God sees as present future acts that will come about through free will. The fact that God foresees all future free actions does not deprive these acts of their freedom, since God stands outside time. In the early seventeenth century, Arminius reclaimed this argument as a corrective to the overdeterminism of the Calvinist and Lutheran churches. He proposed that the problem of God's possible knowledge of future contingencies is put to rest by the recognition that there are no future contingencies for God. All things are present to God and coexist with God "in the infinite Now of eternity, which embraces all time."[69]

This position marks the point of departure for Pinnock, Jack Cottrell, Richard Rice, and other new evangelical thinkers committed to what they call "the openness of God." Cottrell defends the classical Arminian position, in which God is viewed as having limited his power in relation to the world in order to give his creatures freedom to live and flourish within it.[70] Richard Rice argues that classical Arminianism still assumes an exaggerated conception of divine omniscience. If God has precise knowledge of our future actions, these acts cannot be said to be truly free, he urges. Just as God cannot *do* certain things even though God is omnipotent, God also cannot *know* certain things even though God is omniscient. These include future free choices that are not objects of knowledge on the basis of existing conditions. To affirm the reality of truly free future choices is no more a denial of omniscience than it is a denial of omnipotence to recognize limitations on God's power.[71]

Pinnock goes all the way with Rice, rejecting all attempts to reconcile human freedom with a maximalist model of divine power. "In an attempt to preserve the notion of God's power as total control, some advocate what they call biblical compatibilism, the idea that one can uphold genuine freedom and divine determinism at the same time," he observes. "This is sleight of hand and does not work."[72] Pinnock counters that "total control" thinking is refuted by the mere fact that people rebel against God's will. Scripture teaches that much that happens in the world occurs against God's will. Things happen that are not supposed to happen, he observes, and the Bible pictures God as being grieved and angered by human evil. God is also portrayed as being forced to change his mind or his course of action on account of human actions. Like the biblical witness, Pinnock explains, free-will theism pictures God as antecedently actual and involved with his creatures in give-and-take relationships. Scripture preaches against sin because it assumes that creatures have the capacity through God's Spirit not to live in sin. It calls sinners to accept Christ as Savior because it believes that Christ's sacrifice was offered to redeem the sins of all people. To make these claims unreal in order to assert God's total control is to turn the gospel message into nonsense, he insists: "To say that God hates sin while secretly willing it, to say that God warns us not to fall away though it is impossible, to say that God loves the world while excluding most people from an opportunity of salvation, to say that God warmly invites sinners to come knowing all the while that they cannot possibly do so—such things do not deserve to be called mysteries when that is just a euphemism for nonsense."[73]

In biblical faith, the all-powerful God delegates power to fallible creatures, sharing power with them and making himself vulnerable. God invites us to be covenant partners with him, Pinnock observes, opening up the possibility of loving fellowship but also the possibility of rebellion against the divine plan. Greek-influenced classical orthodoxy has traditionally denied that God is subject to external, internal, or sensational passibility, but in scripture, God says that "my heart recoils within me; my compassion grows warm and tender" (Hos. 11:8). The theme of divine pathos or suffering is prominent in scripture. "God suffers when there is a broken relationship between humanity and himself," Pinnock notes. "The idea of God's impassibility arises more from Plato than from the Bible."[74]

Classical theism pictures God as an all-determining transcendent ego; it therefore privileges the model of God as judge. Creative love theism pictures God as a mutual, interrelating Trinity of Persons and therefore privileges family images over juridical ones. "Theologians like Anselm and Calvin have led us astray when they have interpreted salvation in heavily formal and legal terms," Pinnock and Brow maintain.[75] The classical tradition thus often appears to suggest that God's wrath had to be placated before God could bring himself to love sinners. But this suggestion is plainly unbiblical, they observe. It was because God loved us "while we still were sinners" that God took on our condition and died for us (Rom. 5:8).

A WIDENESS IN GOD'S MERCY

What, then, does creative love theism do with the biblical testimony to hellfire and damnation? If God loves God's children in the manner that many of us love

our children, only more so, how can God sentence any of them to everlasting torment in hell? Scripture plainly teaches that many will not be saved. If creative love
theism is truly biblical and evangelical, what can it possibly say about biblical
teaching pertaining to damnation? Pinnock has played a leading role in urging
evangelicals to rethink their teaching on this matter. Though he has not developed
a systematic statement of his position, his various writings on the subject advance
four main lines of argument that, taken together, propose a significant revision of
evangelical teaching.

He rules out Karl Barth's nearly explicit universalism. Barth contended that
texts such as Romans 5:18–19, 1 Corinthians 15:22, and 2 Corinthians 5:18–19,
in which Paul states that Christ has reconciled all persons to God through his saving death, should be taken literally. All people have actually received the benefit
of Christ's reconciliatory sacrifice, Barth maintained, though many people are not
aware of it. The Pauline vision of the eschatological triumph of grace contains a
universalist implication that should not be dismissed, Barth urged. In Colossians
1:19, Paul remarks that God has determined through his Son, as his image and as
the firstborn of the whole creation, to "reconcile to himself all things." Barth exhorted that Christians should at least consider whether this teaching "could not
perhaps have a good meaning."[76] The Pauline image of a wholly reconciled creation in which God is "all in all" seems to exclude the notion of an everlasting hellfire or realm of eternal separation from God.[77]

The problem is that scripture abounds in images of hellfire, Pinnock cautions:
"Although I wish universalism were true, the Bible's repeated warnings of final
loss at the Great Judgment negates it."[78] If the triumph of grace means that God
intends to raise up all people to eternal life at the great judgment, why does
Matthew 25:41–46 teach that many will be condemned to damnation? Pinnock and
Brow raise similar objections to Lewis's portrayal of hell as separation: "The picture of hell in Lewis may be drab and dull, but it is no lake of fire. Does it do justice to the terrible imagery in Scripture?"[79] If hell is not really a state of wrathful
punishment, why does scripture insistently portray it as such? Moreover, they observe, for all of Lewis's efforts to make moral sense out of biblical teaching in this
area, he still portrayed hell as endless vindictive punishment. Lewis's eschatology
did not envision the whole creation as reconciled to God but suggested that pointless alienation will persist throughout eternity.

Pinnock's alternative combines four interpretive moves that are relatively
novel for evangelicalism, but which have ample precedent in Christian tradition.
The first is that general revelation is often redemptive. Because evangelicals tend
to be fixated on special revelation, he argues, they usually fail to perceive the
"wideness in God's mercy" that is implied in Christian teaching about general revelation. Neither Abraham nor Job possessed much knowledge about God, but they
gave as much of themselves as they could to as much of God as they understood.
Scripture is clear in regarding such faith as saving. If scripture is right to regard as
redemptive the faith of a pagan believer such as Job, Pinnock contends, it must be
the case that this way to salvation is still open to others who have not been evangelized. The evangelical tendency to assume otherwise is unbiblical. "This latter

hesitation needs to be confronted," he asserts. "Why would it make any difference if Job were born in A.D. 1900 in outer Mongolia? Why would God not deal with him the same way he dealt with him in the Old Testament?" There is no biblical or rational basis for claiming that general revelation was redemptive only before Christ's death on Calvary. Those who have not been evangelized in our time are in the same spiritual situation as the pagans who lived before Christ, Pinnock reasons. Thus, on the basis of scriptural teaching, there is significant reason to conclude that many people are saved through their response to the grace of general revelation, for "obviously the unevangelized can be saved by faith just like anyone else."[80]

This line of argument leads to Pinnock's second move—his most far-reaching and surprising—which is to embrace, in evangelical form, the doctrine of universal inclusivism, pioneered by Karl Rahner's theory of "anonymous Christianity" and promulgated as Catholic doctrine at Vatican II. While rejecting the imperialist connotations of Rahner's language, Pinnock accepts his suggestion that the Holy Spirit may be operative within various world religions to prepare people for the gospel of Christ. If God is present as Creator and Redeemer everywhere, Pinnock reasons, it is surely valid to infer that divine grace is prevenient everywhere. God's ever-gracious Spirit is not confined to the walls of the church. And if God's grace is at work in some way among all people, it is surely reasonable to infer that God is active within various world religions. Pinnock is more cautious than Rahner (and closer to Vatican II) in speaking of the *possible* salvific status of non-Christian religions. His "modal" inclusivism does not claim that God must or always does work salvifically through other religions. He notes that it would be strange if all religions were equally salvific. Moreover, there is no reason to assume that God works exclusively through religious forms. Even Vatican II spoke of the possible salvation of atheists. "It seems wiser to say that God *may* use religion as a way of gracing people's lives and that it is *one* of God's options for evoking faith and communicating grace," Pinnock judges. "Whether God makes use of religion is a contingent matter to be explored case by case with discernment."[81]

His third theme is the so-called doctrine of a second chance, taught by Augustine, Athanasius, and other church fathers. A cautious form of this doctrine was reaffirmed by the Catholic Church at Vatican II.[82] Several biblical texts refer to or imply an opportunity to accept the gospel after death, notably 1 Peter 3:19–20, 1 Peter 4:6, and 1 Corinthians 15:29. Augustine cited these texts as support for the early Christian belief in the possibility of after-death conversion in *limbus* for people who lived before Christ. More expansively, the church's first systematic theologian, Origen, taught that these scriptural texts, combined with 2 Corinthians 5:18–19 and Colossians 1:20, support the doctrine of universal restoration. Origen argued that the souls of all unregenerate persons will be purified after death in a punishment of limited duration.[83]

While cautioning that Origen's universalism probably goes too far, Pinnock contends that the idea of after-death conversion has enough biblical support to warrant more expansive possibilities than those Augustine mentioned. At the very least, he reasons, it makes sense that those who have not heard the gospel in this life should be "given the opportunity to plead the blood of Christ" after death. If the biblical testimony to damnation is too strong to stretch the idea of after-death conversion or purification into a hope for universal salvation, the Catholic doctrine of *limbus* at least opens the door to a more inclusive understanding of salvation than evangelicalism has typically sanctioned. The church fathers were commendably concerned about how faithful people before Christ might have been saved. "Such thinking holds promise and we need to extend it further," Pinnock urges. It is wrong to think of God as being absent from the world except under the name of Christ: "We do not need to think of the church as the ark of salvation, leaving everyone else in hell; we can rather think of it as the chosen witness to the fullness of salvation that has come into the world through Jesus."[84] Much of what seems morally objectionable in traditional evangelical teaching about salvation can be mitigated, he proposes, by a strong conception of the redemptive possibilities of God's general revelation and prevenient grace, and the assurance that (at least some) unbelievers can be brought to Christ after death.

The crucial problem remains, however. Even if the way to salvation is wider and more variable than evangelicals usually claim, evangelical teaching about damnation itself is still deeply repulsive. It asserts that the souls of unregenerate persons are subjected to everlasting torment in hell. Pinnock's fourth move calls this traditional reading of scripture into question. Evangelicals have routinely assumed that the biblical imagery of hellfire implies endless punishment, he notes; but fire is destructive and consuming. In Matthew 3:10–12, John the Baptist speaks of the damned as tree branches and chaff who will be thrown into God's "unquenchable fire" and burned up. The word for "hell" that Jesus used repeatedly — *gehenna* — is a Hebrew loanword that referred to the Valley of Hinnom, a fiery pit below the east wall of Jerusalem where garbage was thrown to be consumed. In Matthew 10:28, Jesus remarks that one should not fear those who kill the body but cannot kill the soul; "rather fear him who can destroy both soul and body in hell." These images suggest annihilation, not endless torment, Pinnock argues. The doctrine of damnation that best fits the biblical data is that unregenerate persons are annihilated at death or at some point after death. This picture is dreadful enough without reading into it the notion that the damned must be tortured endlessly in hell, he urges: "How can one imagine for a moment that the God who gave his Son to die for sinners because of his great love for them would install a torture chamber somewhere in the new creation in order to subject those who reject him to everlasting pain?"[85]

Matthew 25:46 refers to hell as "eternal punishment," and Pinnock proposes that this is precisely what hell is — eternal punishment, not the everlasting torture or punishing of immortal souls. God declares his judgment on the wicked and condemns them to the eternal punishment of extinction. Psalm 37 speaks of the wicked fading like grass and being cut off forever. Malachi 4:1–2 speaks of the damned being burned up and existing no more. In 2 Thessalonians 1:9, Paul declares that the damned "will suffer the punishment of eternal destruction, separated from the presence of the Lord and from the glory of his might." Twice in Philippians he speaks of the enemies of Christ, who are bound for destruction or who show "the evidence of their destruction" (Phil. 3:19; 1:28). In Romans 6:23 he speaks of the wages of sin as death, while Revelation 20:11–15 refers to a "second death" to which the damned are condemned at the final judgment.

Biblical teaching about damnation is harsh enough without making it sadistic, Pinnock urges. The view of hell as destruction is truer not only to the Bible's references to hell but also to the Bible's descriptions of God as just and loving. In scripture, the wrath of God is poured out to warn sinners and bring them to redemption. Pinnock and Brow propose that when God's wrath fails to bring sinners to redemption, hell must mean annihilation, "because otherwise the picture would be one of God endlessly tormenting people for no reason except retribution." No human crime or accumulation of crimes could possibly merit everlasting torture. God cannot be just if God tortures people endlessly for believing the wrong theology or for making the wrong moral choices. "How could one respect, let alone worship, a torturing God?" they ask.[86] Unending punishment produces nothing good and serves no purpose except vengeance.

The annihilationist argument has some biblical data working against it. Matthew 25:46 uses the same word *(aionion)* when it distinguishes between the two forms of "eternal" existence. The righteous will go "into eternal life" and the unrighteous "into eternal punishment," it asserts. Similar references to the eternal damnation of the unrighteous occur in 2 Thessalonians 1:9 and 2:6, Hebrews 5:9 and 6:2, Mark 3:29, Matthew 18:8, and Revelation 14:11. Pinnock proposes to get around this parallelism by distinguishing between two kinds of eternity. For the righteous, he argues, eternity means the experience of everlasting life, but for the damned, it means only the termination of existence. Salvation as eternal is experienced by the righteous, but damnation as eternal is experienced only in God's mind, since the subjects of damnation no longer exist to experience anything. John R. W. Stott adds that the main function of fire is "not to cause pain, but to secure destruction." Scripture refers to the fire itself as eternal, he allows, "but it would be very odd if what is thrown into it proves indestructible. Our expectation would be the opposite: it would be consumed for ever, not tormented for ever."[87]

Evangelicals have traditionally assumed that biblical teaching compels belief in hellfire as everlasting torment, but this presumption has lost its hold over numerous evangelical scholars. The Bible's references to damnation are scattered, unsystematic, and highly metaphorical. Because biblical teaching on this subject is open to various readings, and because the notion of unending torture is repugnant, numerous evangelical theologians have begun to dispute traditional teaching about damnation. Some, including Pinnock and Stott, contend that hell as annihilation is the only alternative to universalism that is both biblically supported and morally acceptable. Stott repudiates the "horrible sickness of mind or spirit" that leads some evangelicals to speak glibly, even gleefully, about the threat of hellfire. Speaking of hell as unending torment, he remarks, "I find the concept intolerable and do not understand how people can live with it without either cauterizing their feelings or cracking under the strain."[88] Building on earlier biblical defenses of annihilationism by Basil F. C. Atkinson, Harold E. Guillebaud, and Edward William Fudge, an influential group of evangelicals led by Stott and Pinnock has thus begun to argue vigorously for the exegetical and moral superiority of the annihilationist interpretation.[89] They argue that the endless-torment view has been dominant in evangelicalism not because it possesses an unshakable basis in scripture, but rather because evangelicals have customarily taken much of their worldview from Platonism.

Platonism teaches that, by their nature, souls must exist forever. Pinnock observes that the deep influence of this belief on evangelicalism is reflected in the standard evangelical assumption that every soul is an immaterial substance that must spend eternity somewhere. But this view is not consistent with biblical teaching, Pinnock objects. Biblical teaching on eternal life is dynamic and supernatural. It proclaims resurrection of the whole person as a gift of God, not immortality by natural possession. Scripture never claims that human beings are created with a natural capacity for eternal existence; it claims that through Christ, resurrection is made possible. It claims further that God is able to destroy both body and soul in hell (Matt. 10:28). Stott adds that, according to scripture, only God possesses immortality innately (1 Tim. 1:7; 6:16). We are immortal only by grace, not by nature. This is the orthodoxy that evangelicalism should embrace, Pinnock and Brow assert: "The idea of natural immortality seems to have skewed the Christian teaching about hell. It was a mistake and we should correct it."[90]

New-model evangelicalism would not be evangelical if it did not claim to recover a lost orthodoxy. Pinnock urges that the idea of conditional immortality not only recovers a lost biblical idea of eternal life but also offers a third option between a repugnant traditional doctrine and an unbiblical universalism. Similarly, his group of "open view" theologians proposes to correct traditional evangelical thinking about God "without overcorrecting the error."[91] At every turn, evangelical theologians are rethinking traditional notions about divine sovereignty, the nature of salvation, the role of experience in theology, the relation of Word and Spirit, and the nature of damnation.

Evangelical theology is still dominated by Calvinists; as Pinnock observes, "They pretty well control the teaching of theology in the large evangelical seminaries; they own and operate the largest book-publishing houses; and in large part they manage the inerrancy movement."[92] Though Calvinists continue to control most evangelical institutions, in recent years they have clearly lost control over the terms and boundaries of evangelical discussion. The defining debates in present-day evangelicalism are being shaped by thinkers who want to make their tradition less deterministic, less forensic, more open to pluralism and spiritual experience, and, especially, more open to the biblical picture of God as relational, vulnerable, and personally affected by the world. "The drift away from theological determinism is definitely on," Pinnock notes.[93] The discussion currently taking place in evangelical theology is first a debate about themes and positions over which Pietist evangelical movements have long dissented from the dominant Reformed tradition. This is not to suggest that Pietist evangelicalism is necessarily progressive or emancipatory. It has produced some of the most repressive and mean-spirited movements in Christian history. Some of the offshoots of American revivalism have been breeding grounds for bigotry movements, know-nothingism, and authoritarian politics.

Yet it is also in these little-esteemed religious currents that much of the present creative ferment in evangelical theology is taking place. The possibility of a progressive evangelicalism is being enhanced by the breakthrough of marginalized forms of evangelical thinking and witness. It is possible, however, that this development will ultimately produce little more than a rerun of old debates. It may be that the Arminian turn in evangelical theology will ultimately accomplish little more than a gain in status recognition for long-standing non-Reformed positions. The better possibility is that a new kind of evangelicalism will be created that moves beyond the boundaries of the classical, Pietist, and fundamentalist movements. In a postmodern cultural context, this possibility will hinge on how evangelicals rethink the antimodernism of their tradition.

Postconservative Evangelicalism: Dialogues in Search of a Generous Orthodoxy

The real-world fallout from the rift between theological liberalism and evangelicalism has prompted periodic calls over the past generation for serious theological dialogue between advocates of these positions. In 1972, evangelical pastor Richard Coleman declared that "the time has come, in fact it is long past, to take completely seriously the growing and deepening division between liberal and evangelical Protestants." Nearly every American denomination has been racked by controversies and protest movements rooted in the polarization between theological liberalism and evangelicalism, he noted, yet very little dialogue between these positions ever took place.[1]

More than a decade later, Lutheran theologian Mark Ellingsen observed that there was still very little dialogue in the churches between advocates of these theological orientations, despite the fact that the liberal-conservative chasm was deeper than ever. With a special exasperation that came from trying to be a dialogue-engaging ecumenical evangelical, Gabriel Fackre noted sharply that most nonevangelical theologians simply refused to take evangelical theology seriously. "It is time to end academic parochialism and invite evangelicals into the conversation," he urged.[2] Reflecting on these complaints, Roger Olson later judged that theological liberals and conservatives "have largely gone their separate ways," and neither side appeared to possess enough interest to pursue "the right kind of evangelical-liberal theological dialogue."[3]

But Olson still believed there could be such a thing as a "right kind" of dialogue between theological liberals and evangelicals. The right kind of dialogue would require a substantial degree of mutual interest and respect, he proposed, as well as an appropriate strategy to find areas of agreement. In the late 1980s, two pairs of dialoguers showed that at least the "mutual interest and respect" prerequisite was not beyond the boundary of possibility. In 1988, liberal Anglican David L. Edwards and evangelical Anglican John Stott conducted a wide-ranging exchange that was structured as a review and assessment of Stott's major writings.[4] Shortly afterward, Clark Pinnock and liberal process theologian Delwin Brown conducted a more systematic exchange over liberal and evangelical understandings of theological method and authority, God, human nature and sin, Christ, salvation and eschatology.[5] Both dialogues were models of civility and intellectual fairness. Each thinker clarified his position and defended it from criticism, without resorting to any kind of personal attack or misrepresentation of the other's position. Though Pinnock observed that between liberals and evangelicals "the stereotypes are awful and the divisions very deep," both pairs of dialoguers sustained a convincing tone of mutual appreciation and respect in exploring the reasons behind their religious differences.[6]

AUTHORITIES IN DISPUTE: LIBERALISM AND EVANGELICALISM

But neither exchange got very far. Both focused on a narrow range of doctrinal issues that pushed spiritual and liturgical topics to the margin. Having assumed that "theological dialogue" meant analysis of doctrinal positions, both sets of dialoguers repeatedly invoked the same underlying difference between them as the cause of substantive disagreement. Brown noted at the outset that discussions between liberals and evangelicals "usually move rather quickly to disputes about the authority and nature of the Bible."[7] He and Pinnock resolved not to let the authority question overwhelm their exchange of views, but on issue after issue they found that their very different conceptions of Christianity were driven by a difference in primary allegiance. Brown explained that when he was forced to choose between scriptural teaching and the best of modern knowledge, his criterion for deciding what constitutes a true belief was "the fallible and revisable criteria of modern knowledge."[8]

Pinnock repeatedly countered that this was the crucial difference between liberal and evangelical Christianity. Genuinely Christian theology does not "look for answers in the culture," he argued. Modern ideologies such as feminism and Marxism may raise certain questions that the faithful Christian should bring to his or her reading of scripture, he allowed, but no ideology or other kind of belief should be allowed to stand in judgment of anything in the Bible. "I approach feminism as I would approach Marxism or existentialism, listening to what people are claiming and not jumping on their bandwagon," he explained. "I compare what they claim with my Christian worldview before making up my mind on the subject. I won't be bullied. Ideologies however popular do not determine what I think, not if I can help it anyway." Even the best of modern knowledge—scientific or otherwise—cannot stand as a norm or the source of any norm above scriptural teaching, he cautioned: "I stand beneath the Word of God."[9]

Stott and Edwards were slower to press the point, but their exchange ultimately highlighted the same difference. Edwards criticized Stott's "lingering inclination toward fundamentalism," as reflected in his belief in, for example, the historicity of Adam and Eve, the Mosaic authorship of the tabernacle regulations, and the divine command to exterminate the Canaanites. Stott countered that on each point Edwards allowed modern thought to control his judgment of biblical teaching.

Much more than Pinnock and Brown, the two Anglicans achieved a good deal of genuine give-and-take about the meanings of biblical teaching, but Stott noted that they did not hold the same stake in these arguments. Edwards often tried to prove that his position was more biblical than Stott's, but the deeper difference between them, as Stott observed, was that Edwards was not bound by scriptural teaching. "I mean, if you could prove this to me, I would want to change my mind and position at once," Stott explained, referring to their conflicting interpretations of scripture. "But if I could show you that my position is more biblical than yours, would you be willing to change?"

In this case, the question answered itself. As a biblically oriented liberal, Edwards generally sought to claim scriptural support for his position, but he was not willing to change his position on the basis of a bare authority claim. He would not embrace any belief, even one taught by the Bible, that his heart and mind did not accept. Stott warned that this is the fatal presumption of theological liberalism. Edwards rejected traditional Christian teachings about the factuality of the biblical miracles, the substitutionary atonement of Christ, the immorality of homosexuality, and the reality of hell. His ultimate reason for rejecting these teachings was not that scripture does not support them, Stott observed, but that he found them unacceptable on intellectual and moral grounds. "Does this not mean that in the end you accord supremacy to your reason rather than to Scripture?" Stott asked. "We are back in the conflict between the Reformation and the Renaissance. As Luther said to Erasmus, 'The difference between you and me, Erasmus, is that you sit above Scripture and judge it, while I sit under Scripture and let it judge me.'"[10] Edwards was open to letting scripture inspire and even challenge him, but he was not willing to embrace whatever biblical teaching turned out to be without condition. This predisposition marked the limit of any serious dialogue between them, Stott concluded: "The final court of appeal for you is rationality and for me is Scripture."[11]

In the end, both pairs of theologians made a strong if inadvertent case for not bothering. Besides the example of greater civility that their dialogues presented, neither pair made any progress toward breaking the fundamental impasse between liberal and evangelical theologies. Both sides were quick to assert the unarguable necessity of their presuppositions. Both sides routinely attributed their disagreements to these rival premises. Though they were capable of speaking in similar ways about divine grace and the redeeming love of Christ, the rival complexes of reasons that they gave to justify their beliefs relativized even these agreements. Because evangelicals and liberals identify themselves with contrasting presuppositions about the epistemological basis of Christian claims, even the most well meaning attempts at dialogue that restrict themselves to doctrinal issues are doomed to produce little fruit.

This impasse is a symptom of the different relationships to modernity that theological liberalism and evangelicalism have customarily assumed. Liberal theology has been a straightforwardly modernizing project. It has sought to bring Christian claims into line with beliefs derived from the regnant critical consciousness of modernity. Theological liberalism embraces the Enlightenment-modernist wedge between reason and experience; for the most part, it accepts, or at least seeks to accommodate, the modernist valorization of objective, nonparticipatory knowledge over other ways of knowing; from Schleiermacher to Gordon Kaufman, it has carefully declined to dispute the naturalistic premises of modern historiography. For these reasons, liberal theologians have been poorly suited to expose or even recognize that evangelical theology is usually not as straightforwardly opposed to modernity as it claims to be. Most evangelical theologians since Warfield have presupposed their own peculiar forms of modernism in seeking to secure stable foundations for their religious claims; but from a liberal standpoint, evangelical theology is always remarkably deficient in acknowledging the authority of objective reason. This impression drives liberals to make evangelicals confront the irrationality of their creedal claims. Edwards responded to Stott's defense of biblical inerrancy by piling up a veritable mountain of biblical contradictions and problem texts, causing Stott to remark that he felt like a little evangelical peanut shattered beneath a "Mighty Liberal Steamroller."[12]

But this was ingratiating repartee. Stott could hardly have been surprised by Edwards's onslaught, and he gave no sign of being shattered by it. He doubted that Edwards's motivating concern was really intellectual integrity. He suggested that liberals always pile up arguments against biblical authority, not because they are more honest intellectually than evangelicals but because they assume that submission to biblical authority is incompatible with intellectual freedom. Stott's dialogue with Edwards broke down over this fundamental disagreement. Edwards equated evangelical biblicism with sacrifice of the intellect and judged that Stott was hiding from the plain implications of modern knowledge for Christian belief. Stott concluded that Edwards was unwilling to let scripture be the judge of modern knowledge and the ground of genuine intellectual freedom. From an evangelical standpoint, he argued, freedom is never in conflict with biblical authority; freedom derives from the submission of one's mind and heart to biblical authority. Having judged that the fatal defect of theological liberalism is its captivity to modernity, Stott was not disposed to acknowledge that evangelicalism has also been deeply affected by modernist tests for intellectual credibility. Having judged that evangelicalism fails to face up to modernity, Edwards was poorly suited to argue or even notice the vulnerability of evangelicalism on this point.

Just as the second generation of Reformers sought to defend the Reformation from Catholic criticism by adopting the scholastic outlook of their critics, the chief proponents of modern evangelicalism sought to defend their tradition from modernist criticism by adopting modernist tests of belief. The propositional character of evangelical belief was heightened to satisfy modernist tests of rationality, objectivity, and universalizability. Biblical inerrancy became the foundation of true Christianity, which was held to be truthful on account of its unsurpassed rationality. This strategy was probably unavoidable in a cultural context in which the intellectual and moral authority of the liberal achievement was overwhelming. Even the sworn opponents of modernity were forced to conform to it. In a cultural context in which the objectivizing consciousness of modernity no longer commands authority, however, some evangelical theologians have begun to consider what evangelicalism might be without its previously defining objectivism and individualism. What should evangelicalism be if it is no longer forced to fight off or accommodate a culturally triumphant modernism? Does the end of modernity open up better possibilities for evangelicalism?

EVANGELICALISM BEYOND MODERNITY: DONALD BLOESCH'S CATHOLIC (NEO)ORTHODOXY

Confessional differences aside, two broadly distinguishable kinds of evangelical theology are emerging today that explicitly seek to throw off the peculiar forms of modernism that evangelical teaching acquired during its fundamentalist phase. The first is a wide-ranging assortment of moderate evangelicals who propose to reestablish classical evangelical teaching and practices in ways that more faithfully reflect the heritage of catholic orthodoxy. This group includes Donald Bloesch, Robert Webber, Thomas C. Oden, Gabriel Fackre, and Alister McGrath.[13] According to Donald Bloesch, the group's most systematic thinker, the key dividing line in evangelicalism is between its rationalistic and biblical proponents. He observes that evangelical *rationalists* divide into two main groups—presuppositionalists and evidentialists. Both groups equate the Bible with divine revelation, but they pursue different strategies for establishing biblical truth. Evangelical presuppositionalists deduce conclusions from first principles set forth or implied within scripture, while evangelical evidentialists derive their truth-claiming principles from the facts recorded in scripture. The presuppositionalists identify the scripture principle with the idealistic rationalism of the early Enlightenment, while the evidentialists commit evangelicalism to the empirical rationalism of the later Enlightenment. In either case, Bloesch objects, conservative evangelicalism reduces the gospel faith to the logic of a modernist philosophical method: "The mystery and paradox in revelation are reduced to logical axioms capable of being understood by unbelievers as well as believers. The Word of God becomes a rational formula wholly in control of the theologian, and theology becomes the systematic harmonizing of rational truths."[14]

Bloesch counters that a truly *biblical* evangelicalism does not equate the scriptural text with revelation and does not commit the gospel faith to a philosophical method. Rather, it affirms the possibility of real knowledge of God, "but always knowledge given anew by the Spirit of God in conjunction with the hearing and reading of the biblical message." The difference between rationalistic and biblical evangelicalism is crucial, for in the second view, scripture is treated as "the divinely prepared medium or channel of divine revelation rather than the revelation itself." To recognize the divine authority and freedom of the Word is not to conceptualize theology as the systematic harmonization of rational truths, he insists. It is rather to conceive theology as "an incomplete and open-ended explication of revelational meaning that always stands in need of revision and further elucidation."[15]

Bloesch's carefully balanced outline of the biblical alternative restores the Reformers' emphasis on the dynamic correlation of Word and Spirit. "Theology needs to recover the paradoxical unity of Word and Spirit, for only on the basis of this unity can Scripture be made to come alive and be a transforming leaven in the life of the church," he urges. The truth of the Bible is not a datum determined by historical investigation or rationalistic deduction, for biblical truth is revealed truth. It can become known only through the action of its source, which is the Spirit of God. "Too often in evangelical and conservative circles the Word is viewed as something static and frozen, waiting to be analyzed and dissected," Bloesch observes. "But our ability to know the Word rests on the prior action of the Word."[16] The inscripturated Word becomes God's living Word only through the revelatory action of the Word of the Spirit.

Though he holds out for a decidedly un-Barthian infallible-teaching doctrine of biblical inerrancy, Bloesch's key arguments about the dynamic paradoxical relation between Word and Spirit are closely related to Barth's formulations.[17] In phrases that closely approximate Barth's, he argues that "the Bible in and of itself is not the Word of God—divine revelation—but it is translucent to this revelation by virtue of the Spirit of God working within it and within the mind of the reader and hearer."[18] As Bloesch explains, "Barth insisted that only when the written or proclaimed word is united with the revealed Word does it become revelation."[19] Bloesch adopts Barth's theory of "something like a perichoresis" between the forms of the Word revealed, written, and preached, adding that this threefold conception of the Word also needs to affirm the voice of conscience. Without making the Pietist mistake of subordinating the Word to the Spirit, Bloesch explains, evangelicalism must affirm the biblical teaching that the inner word of conscience also becomes "an infallible criterion for faith and practice" when joined by the Spirit with Jesus Christ. "The written Word and the proclaimed Word have no efficacy unless Christ makes his abode within us by his Spirit," he urges. Christians are engrafted into Christ's body not only by the light that comes to them from scripture and scriptural preaching but also by the light of the inner word "that shines within us by the indwelling Spirit."[20]

Central to Bloesch's evangelical reformulation of Barth's theology of the Word is his concept of scripture as a light-revealing channel or prism. Fundamentalist evangelicalism views the biblical text as itself the light of God's truth, Bloesch observes, while most forms of neoorthodoxy treat the text as merely a witness to God's saving acts in history. Modern theology features a kaleidoscope of other views that deal with scripture even less adequately. Mystical theologies treat the text as a window to a transcendent world of spiritual meaning; existentialist theologies view the text as a mirror of human existence; structuralist-oriented theologies conceive the text as a vortex of meaning that shapes reality; theologies guided by deconstructionist criticism treat the text as an interminable maze of unstable meanings.[21] In this crucial area, Bloesch observes, the fundamental impulse of the current school of postliberal "narrativist" theology, pioneered by Hans Frei and George Lindbeck, derives from structuralism. Though postliberals play up their kinship to neoorthodoxy and especially to Barth, they view the biblical text as a mosaic that redesigns reality and creates a followable worldview through the speaking of the text's distinctive grammar.[22]

Bloesch recognizes that many younger evangelicals have been attracted to Frei-style narrative theology in recent years, some of them because of its connections to Barth. With particular urgency, Bloesch warns that the kind of theology inspired by Frei's narrativist reading of scripture is not a good form of Barthian or even neoorthodox thinking, because it gives up the classical view of scripture as the mirror of God's ontologically normative truth. In Bloesch's reading, postliberal theology locates biblical theology in the narrative sequence itself, and nowhere else. Frei and his theological followers describe the biblical stories as truth bearing, he explains, but their conception of truth is not metaphysical or even historical but merely practical—the capacity to generate commitment and community. In this crucial respect, for all their talk about "postliberalism," the narrative theologians are still descendants of Kantian liberalism.[23] Narrative theologians assume that it is practical reason, not theoretical reason, that puts us in contact with reality. They conceive biblical truth as the capacity of the biblical text to draw readers into a new framework of meaning that makes sense of one's life and world. Bloesch objects that this strategy reduces Christian truth to evocative descriptions. Narrative theology casts aside the evangelical understanding of the biblical text "as the bearer of intrinsic, quasi-metaphysical meaning."[24] It does not look to the text for definitive information about God's being or historical acts but seeks merely for "sporadic illuminations of the human condition."[25]

Bloesch's alternative is a sacramental view of scriptural authority that sees the Bible as "an instrument or channel of divine activity." Evangelicalism should continue to uphold the doctrines of the verbal inspiration and infallibility of scripture, he urges, but it should uphold these doctrines in a way that acknowledges the material human dimension of the biblical text. Evangelicalism must continue to affirm that scripture discloses a divine message that contains metaphysical implications, but it is not obliged to uphold the traditional image of scripture as the mirror of God's truth. Bloesch commends the image of scripture as a prism as a more appropriate metaphor. In this image, the light of God is understood to shine on us through the prism of scripture, which is not itself the light but rather relays the light to us. If evangelicals begin to think of scripture in this way, he proposes, it should become possible to break with fundamentalism categorically while continuing to uphold the traditional evangelical belief that the meaning of scripture is located ultimately in the mind of its divine author. We cannot know what the biblical text means until we hear its author speaking to us through it.[26]

"I depart from some of my evangelical colleagues in that I understand the divine content of Scripture not as rationally comprehensible teachings but as the mystery of salvation declared in Jesus Christ," Bloesch remarks. "This mystery can be stated in propositional form, but it eludes rational comprehension." For him, as for Barth, Jesus Christ is the Word of God revealed, but the Word incarnate is not and has never been an empirically verifiable datum.[27] The Word of God who inhered in Jesus of Nazareth was not discernible to sense knowledge. Peter confessed his faith that Jesus was the Son of God, but Jesus told Peter that only the Father could have revealed this to him, not flesh and blood (Matt. 16:17). Thus, even in the very presence of the Word, Bloesch explains, the disciples were dependent on the movement of God's Spirit to see the Word in Jesus, which was hidden from their natural reason. This does not mean that revelation does not contain a "conceptual side," Bloesch cautions. What it does mean is that ultimate truth is not something that human beings can discover by their own reasoning. The Word of Christ is not an abstract theoretical truth, open to rational discovery. It is rather a "transrational" truth that claims us with its own conceptual content in the unity of the Spirit's interaction with the inscripturated or preached Word. Revelation is the speech of God "enveloped in mystery."[28]

This emphasis on the paradoxical unity of Word and Spirit contains the key to Bloesch's reformulation of evangelical teaching on scriptural infallibility. "I affirm that the message of Scripture is infallible and that the Spirit infallibly interprets this message to people of faith," he declares. "But the perfect accuracy of the letter or text is not an integral part of Christian faith. Because the term *inerrancy* is so often associated with the latter position, I agree with Clark Pinnock that it is not the preferable word to use in theological discussion today, even though it should not be abandoned, for it preserves the nuance of truthfulness that is necessary for a high view of Holy Scripture."[29]

Bloesch argues that because the term has become a barrier to theological communication, evangelicals should stop appealing to inerrancy on a persistent basis. At the same time, they must not relinquish their belief that scripture is inerrant in its union with the Spirit. This does not mean, he explains, that infallibility resides wholly in the text of scripture, as in fundamentalism. Nor does it mean that infallibility resides exclusively in the Spirit that speaks to Christians as they read the Bible or listen to the Word proclaimed. The kind of neoorthodoxy that makes the latter claim falls short of authentic evangelicalism, he cautions. The infallibility of scripture lies instead in the paradoxical unity of Word and Spirit. The scriptural text is infallible as the Holy Spirit speaks in and through it. The Bible employs modes of expression that are sometimes problematic, but the message that it conveys through its union with the Spirit transcends culture and history. It is infallible (*fallere*) by virtue of its certainty not to deceive. "While acknowledging innocent factual inaccuracies in the Bible, I hesitate to call these errors," Bloesch explains. "I readily grant that forms of expression in Scripture may conflict with science, but science is not the final norm, for scientific theories are constantly in flux. Because error does not touch what is truly divine in the Bible, it is more proper to speak of 'difficulties' than of errors, of chaff but not tares."[30]

Not all postfundamentalist evangelicals share Bloesch's high regard for Barthian theology or his emphasis on paradox. McGrath steers a path between evangelical fundamentalism and Barth's revelational fideism, arguing that evangelicals must defend traditional orthodoxy with the strongest historical and metaphysical arguments at their disposal.[31] Oden reaches back to the teaching of the early church fathers for the basis of his "paleoorthodoxy," arguing that all modern theologies are contaminated in some way by the influence of modernist individualism and secularism. He belongs to a group of "Great Tradition" evangelicals who are clearly more interested in pursuing dialogues with conservative Catholic and Orthodox theologians than with progressive evangelicals.[32] In key respects, Bloesch's affinity with Barth places him closer than McGrath or Oden to the new generation of progressivist-leaning evangelical thinkers. Bloesch's Barthian emphasis that the Spirit-illuminated Word is never possessed or fully comprehended by any orthodoxy gives his theology considerable resonance to evangelicals influenced by postmodern culture and criticism.

But even Bloesch's moderate evangelicalism is too stodgy and conservative for evangelicals influenced by the multiperspectival spirit of postmodern criticism. "We must never say" is a favorite Bloesch phrase. He admonishes evangelicals never to say that the Bible teaches any errors, that history is the arbiter of theological validity, that God's will is ever thwarted in history, that God is a Mother as well as a Father, or that homosexual relations can be morally permissible. He charges that Pinnock's creative love theism is closer to process theology than to the scriptural view of God as providential mystery.[33] On social issues, Bloesch is generally more moderate and less ideological than the politicized leadership of the Christian Right, but he nonetheless aligns himself with it: "I see no reason for not cooperating with Moral Majority and kindred groups in combating pornography, the abortion mills, no-fault divorce, incest, homosexuality, etc., because a society cannot long endure without a foundational moral code."[34] Though he opposes the patriarchalist sin of treating women as inferior to men, he also opposes modern feminism in the name of a "theonomous" biblical ideal in which wives submit themselves in "loving assistance" to their equally loving husbands. "Evangelicals must hold firm to the biblical principle that form and content are inextricably bound together," Bloesch warns. With regard to feminist criticism, this means that evangelicals are obliged to uphold the biblical concept of marriage as analogous to the relationship between Christ (the husband) and his church (the wife). It also means that evangelicals must not deviate from the biblical practice of using masculine metaphors almost exclusively to describe or refer to God.[35]

Notwithstanding his comparatively moderate politics and his important emphasis on the mystery of biblical truth and the paradoxical interaction of Word and Spirit, Bloesch remains a dogmatist in the older-style evangelical sense of the term. He assumes that scripture contains a stable core of doctrine, and that the purpose of theology is to explicate this normative doctrinal material. To determine what the Bible teaches on any matter of faith and practice is to find whatever it is that evangelicalism must teach on that subject. For him, evangelicalism remains a form of gospel faith that lives decidedly within the house of authority.

OPENING THE HOUSE OF AUTHORITY: PROGRESSIVE EVANGELICALISM

Bloesch's assumption rests less easily on many evangelicals who came of age in a decidedly post-Christian culture. Though it remains in question whether evangelicalism can teach or support a significantly different approach to biblical doctrine, today younger thinkers who do not share the defining generational experiences of the evangelical establishment are testing the borders of possible rethinking. The conservative evangelical dream of a re-Christianized America is alien to them, as is the conservative evangelical fear that airtight epistemological certainty must be secured at all costs. The theorists of new-model evangelicalism do not expect to find objective intellectual certainty or to create a new evangelical Christendom. Many of them are open to postmodern theory, not merely because it is intellectually fashionable but because they share much of the sensibility and experience behind it. Most of them urge that the end of the cultural authority of modernist consciousness could be a blessing for Christianity.

While recognizing that much so-called postmodern thinking is fragmenting and nihilistic, progressive evangelicals such as Stanley Grenz, Roger Olson, David Dockery, Rodney Clapp, Nancey Murphy, William Abraham, Brian J. Walsh, J. Richard Middleton, Philip D. Kenneson, Mark McLeod, Miroslav Volf, Steven J. Land, and Henry H. Knight III argue that evangelical theology should take advantage of the dethronement of modernism as a worldview and cultural ideal.[36] While seeking to rethink evangelical claims in the light of postmodern critiques of Enlightenment foundationalism and objectivism, some evangelicals also find the prospects for theological dialogue with "mainline" theologies improved by the presence of North American postliberal offshoots of Barthian theology.

Postmodern critiques of the Enlightenment rationalist claim to secure foundational universal knowledge are intriguing to progressive evangelicals. Much of the postmodern deconstructionist criticism that Jacques Derrida and Michel Foucault inspired is explicitly nihilistic, even in its religious forms, but Grenz observes that evangelical thinking nonetheless has much to gain by taking seriously the critique of epistemological foundationalism that postmodern theory has engendered.[37] Evangelicals since the fundamentalist reaction have usually embraced the modernist assumption that knowledge is certain, objective, and good, he notes; but on each point, the postmodern critical spirit is closer to the spirit of biblical faith. The deconstructionist tendency to view human reason as cunning and not wholly trustworthy is a *Christian* impulse. Scripture warns repeatedly that reason is deceitful and self-deceiving, and that certain aspects of saving truth lie beyond reason. Moreover, the modernist ideal of objective universal knowledge is a product of Cartesian anxiety; it builds on the model of a detached individual observing the world as an external object. The "postmodern" objection that no observer actually stands outside the historical process is a Christian theme, Grenz observes: "Postmodern epistemologists are actually echoing Augustine when they assert that our personal convictions and commitments not only color our search for knowledge but also facilitate the process of understanding."[38]

Reason is the servant of interest, and even the most objective search for knowledge is conditioned by our personal convictions and circumstances. Moreover, in the age of nuclear weapons, it would be absurd not to recognize that the attainment of knowledge is not necessarily good. Greater knowledge is often the precondition for new forms of evil. Postmodern theorists pay tribute to Nietzsche in explicating these themes, but all of them have deeper and truer roots in Christianity, especially in Paul, Tertullian, Athanasius, Augustine, Luther, Calvin, Kierkegaard, and Barth.[39] Grenz remarks that on all these counts, "the postmodern critique of modernity stands as a needed reminder that our humanity does not consist solely in our cognitive dimension."[40] This reminder is needed in evangelical theology, because evangelical leaders for the past century have exaggerated the rationalistic dimension of Christian belief.

Henry's six-volume apologetic epitomizes the problem for Grenz and other postconservative evangelicals. "In keeping with the rationalist tradition in theology, Henry elevates reason to the status of being the foundational dimension of the human person," he observes.[41] Evangelical rationalism is captive to the orientation of the detached individual seeker of objective knowledge. Grenz does not dispute that theology requires a cognitive dimension, but he explicitly charges that Henry's rationalistic evangelicalism presupposes a mistaken understanding of how the cognitive dimension of religious truth functions in the larger whole of revelation. That is, Grenz allows that no truly evangelical theology can write off the need for a grounding cognitive substance in Christian claims but he denies evangelicals are obliged to translate the cognitive substance in narrated scriptural testimony to the propositional language of an objectivist model of understanding. Conservative evangelicalism has long claimed to possess the universalistic epistemological foundation that its Enlightenment critics were seeking. "But this orientation is now beginning to lose its grip," Grenz observes. The Enlightenment dream of a rationalized world is no longer viewed as attainable or even desirable. In this situation, it would be absurd, if not perverse, for evangelicals to hold out for their own version of a dream that has done so much harm to the cause of Christianity in the modern age. Grenz therefore urges that "if our theology is to speak the biblical message in our contemporary situation, we must shed the cloak of modernity and reclaim the more profound community outlook in which the biblical people of God were rooted."[42]

Without claiming that evangelicalism should simply replace a rationalist model with a pure narrativist-communitarian model, Grenz and other postconservative evangelicals emphasize the primacy of narrative in scripture and the distinctive communal character of Christian speech. While cautioning that Christians must not give up their claim to an extracommunal religious truth, most progressive evangelicals embrace the defining postliberal emphasis on theology as the narrative-dependent grammar of a distinctive historical community, the Christian church. Grenz explains that all theological claims are necessarily historically conditioned because all theological reflection occurs within and for specific historical contexts. Theology is inherently contextual. If evangelicalism is to finally absorb the implications of this truism, he observes, it must give up its predisposition to translate the gospel message into some form of rationalistic abstraction.[43] The proper context of theology is the narrative of God's action within the same historical story in which we participate. In Grenz's words, "This means that the theological task can be properly pursued only 'from within'—that is, only from the vantage point of the faith community in which the theologian stands."[44]

REVELATORY NARRATIVE:
ENGAGING POSTLIBERAL THEOLOGY

Revelation comes to us fundamentally in the scriptural narrative of God's saving acts in history. The narratively disclosed truth of God forms the basic grammar of Christian speech through which the possibility of a Christian identity is established. Though Christian narrative is undoubtedly a product of historical experience when viewed from a historical standpoint, Grenz allows, the deeper truth for theology is that the retold narrative is experience creative. Revelatory narrative *creates* Christian experience. Moreover, it is not as individuated observers that we attain a Christian identity, for as Grenz observes, "our identity arises within a community—within the fellowship of God's people in the church."[45]

This evangelical turn toward a communitarian-narrativist understanding of Christianity has been influenced by the school of postliberal thinking pioneered by Yale theologians Hans Frei and George Lindbeck and developed by such theologians as William Placher, Stanley Hauerwas, James William McClendon Jr., Ronald Thiemann, George Stroup, Garrett Green, and George Hunsinger.[46] As a theological strategy, the postliberal narrativist approach generally shares with evangelicalism an emphasis on the unity of the biblical canon and the saving uniqueness of Jesus Christ. With the more progressive stream of evangelical theology, it also shares an emphasis on the community-forming centrality of scriptural narrative and a sense of the countercultural mission of the church.[47] For these reasons, even Bloesch and McGrath acknowledge that the kind of narrative-emphasizing theology that Frei pioneered offers a more promising basis for dialogue with evangelicalism than does conventional liberal theology.

Frei's epochal work, *The Eclipse of Biblical Narrative,* explicated the defining argument of this theological circle. In the eighteenth and nineteenth centuries, he observed, theologians undermined the authority of scripture and its formative function in cultivating Christian identity by locating the meaning of biblical teaching in some doctrine or worldview that was held to be more foundational than scripture itself. Both liberals and conservatives coped with modern challenges to Christian belief by looking past the narrative character of scripture. Liberals looked for the real meaning of the Bible in the eternal truths about God and humanity that it conveyed, while conservatives looked for the real meaning in the Bible's factual references. In both cases, Frei explained, the priority of scriptural narrative itself was overturned. Because scripture no longer defined in a normative way the world in which Christians lived, it was turned into a source of support for modern progress narratives or other doctrinal norms. "All across the theological spectrum the great reversal had taken place," he remarked. "Interpretation was a matter of fitting the biblical story into another world with another story rather than incorporating that world into the biblical story."[48]

With the loss of scripture as a grand formative narrative, the Bible became increasingly alien to the church. Its meaning became decipherable only to an academic elite. Liberal scholars looked for culture-affirming eternal truths in scripture and otherwise deconstructed the canonical text into historical-critical fragments.

Conservatives and fundamentalists turned the text into source material for propositions and developed highly artificial harmonizations of conflicting factual statements that created internal "solutions" not found in scripture at all. Frei gave most of his attention to the varieties of liberalism, but his verdict applied equally to modern liberal and conservative theologies. Though with opposing strategies, virtually all liberal and conservative theologians sought to cope with modernity by accommodating its presumption of superiority. "No one who pretended to any sort of theology or religious reflection at all wanted to go counter to the 'real' applicative meaning of biblical texts, once it had been determined what it was, even if one did not believe them on their own authority," he remarked. The "real" applicative meaning became all determinative. The explicative meaning of the narrative was subordinated to whatever choice one made about the real meaning. Conservatives therefore held out for the literal meaning of various factual references in scripture, and liberals countered that modern science and historical criticism negated literal meaning as an interpretive possibility. In both cases, the sense of scripture as canonical literary narrative was abandoned.[49]

This account of the modernist distortion of biblical interpretation has inspired a host of postliberal theologies that emphasize the primacy of scriptural narrative, the hermeneutical primacy of the world of scriptural narrative for theology, and the primacy of language over experience.[50] Drawing on Wittgensteinian language analysis and the cultural anthropology of Clifford Geertz, George Lindbeck presents an account of contemporary theological options that reinforces and amplifies much of Frei's argument. He argues that a third-way "cultural linguistic" approach is needed as an alternative to the "cognitive-propositional" and "experiential-expressive" approaches that have dominated theology during the modern age. In this account, liberal theologies are nearly always experiential-expressive; they seek to ground religious language on foundational claims about experiences of religious feeling, moral value, and the like. In contrast, most conservative theologies are cognitive-propositional; conservatives nearly always claim that doctrinal statements directly or "literally" refer to reality. Lindbeck observes that by virtue of their emphasis on the function of religious language as propositional information about objective realities, conservative theologians tend to confirm the approach to religion taken by most Anglo-American analytic philosophers. Analytic philosophy typically assumes that religious language is meaningful only if it makes universally valid statements about matters of fact in the form of propositions.[51]

Lindbeck counters that no religion can actually be understood on these terms. Religious traditions are historical, culturally encoded, and governed by internal rules of grammar. Any explanation of religious belief that disregards these factors will inevitably distort the religious tradition under examination. In the case of Christianity, he observes, it is scriptural narrative that shapes the cultural-linguistic world in which the corporate body of Christ expresses its meanings and seeks to follow Christ. Christian doctrines should not be understood as universalistic propositions or as interpretations of a universal religious experience. Doctrines are more like the rules of grammar that govern the way we use language to describe the world. Christian doctrine identifies the rules by which Christians use confessional language to define the social world that they dwell in. Like Wittgenstein, Lindbeck emphasizes the connection between "rationality" and the skillful use of acquired rules. Believers can prove the rationality or relevance of their religious tradition (or any tradition) only by skillfully using its internal grammar, he argues: "The reasonableness of a religion is largely a function of its assimilative powers, of its ability to provide an intelligible interpretation in its own terms of the varied situations and realities adherents encounter."[52]

This model of religious understanding does not rule out the possibility of an ad hoc apologetics; it rules out only the kind of apologetics that appeals to reasons prior to faith. The logic of coming to believe in Christianity is like that of learning a language, Lindbeck explains. Rational arguments on behalf of Christian claims become possible only after one has learned, through spiritual training, how to speak the language of Christian faith. Moreover, the question of relevance is analogous to the question of rationality. Relevance derives from meaning, and the meaning of Christian language can be found only in scripture. Postliberal narrativism "redescribes reality within the scriptural framework rather than translating Scripture into extrascriptural categories." In effect, Lindbeck translates Barth's theological realism of the Word into "textual" terms influenced by Wittgensteinian language philosophy. In this reading, "it is the text, so to speak, which absorbs the world, rather than the world the text."[53] If theologians would allow the story of the Bible to become their own story, he argues, they would not be so preoccupied with making Christianity relevant to the non-Christian world on non-Christian terms.

Does this mean that postliberal narrativism is committed to a fundamentally antirealist conception of Christian truth? Bloesch and McGrath reply that this is exactly the problem with the postliberal school. For all their laudable desire to make modern theology speak in the world-creating language of scripture, Bloesch judges, their epistemological antirealism drives Frei and Lindbeck to a merely occasionalist understanding of scripture as God's Word. It is wrong to reduce the gospel to a story or to treat the Bible as a collection of stories or to restrict the meaning of scripture to its stories: "Theology can ill afford to ignore the issue of truth, for it is truth that gives narrative its significance," Bloesch admonishes. Revelation discloses not only world-making insight into our condition but also foresight into God's purposes for all reality, in the present and in the future. Because God really acts in history, Bloesch insists, faithful Christian theology cannot shrink from offering an "excursus in ontology." The story of the Christian people has no meaning at all if it has no explicable metaphysical meaning. Theology must therefore be more than a generalized description of the faith of the Christian community; it must also probe the metaphysical truth about how this community is grounded in reality.[54]

McGrath emphasizes that genuinely Christian theology must include a historical account about how normative Christian language came into being. He observes that for all of his emphasis on theology as the regulative grammar of Christian speech, Lindbeck ignores the truth question about how this language came about. This is not a credible option for theology, McGrath contends. It is possible that

Christianity is based on a misunderstanding. It is possible that Christianity is based on a confused misrepresentation or even a deliberate falsification. Theology has a deep stake in whatever the truth may be on this matter. McGrath cautions that for this reason, theologians cannot simply take the language of faith as a given. Theologians must be willing to interrogate the historical and metaphysical credentials of Christian speech. While acknowledging that Lindbeck's obscure prose might be open to different readings on this point, McGrath judges that the postliberal project is fundamentally antirealist.[55]

"Postliberalism reduces the concept of 'truth' to 'internal consistency,'" he charges. Frei and Lindbeck subject the biblical narrative to the test of coherence, but this is not the only pertinent test of religious truth. Islam may be internally coherent, McGrath objects, but is it true? Evangelicalism dares to ask the same question about Christianity. It does not content itself with merely interpreting the narrated identity of Jesus; it also proclaims that Christian truth is knowable, credible, and defensible on both intratextual and extratextual grounds. "However the concept of truth may be stated, it is firmly understood to be located *outside* the language of Christianity, as well as within it," he explains. "Christianity aims to provide a systematic, regulated and coherent account of who God is and what God is like — that is to say, that there is an extrasystemic referent which functions as both foundation and criterion of the Christian language game."[56] To say that Christianity is true is to make a claim about a reality that sustains and transcends the language game of Christian faith. It is to avoid the abyss of epistemological relativism by allowing theology to ask *why* biblical narrative should be granted religious authority, apart from its capacity to inspire attractive religious communities.

These objections to the postliberal narrativist project are serious and generally well considered. Though McGrath and various others tend to overlook Frei's affirmative statements about the historicity of the resurrection, they have exposed the postliberal inclination to immunize Christian claims from historical criticism. Evangelicals are not the only observers to criticize Frei and Lindbeck for their apparent antirealism and confessional fideism, but their criticism in particular has prompted Lindbeck and other postliberals in recent years to clarify their position and to envision what a fully developed postliberal theology might look like.[57] At this point, the postliberal project has not advanced far beyond the level of a formal research program, and its dialogue with evangelicalism is still in an early stage. While evangelicals such as Bloesch and McGrath have made important critiques of postliberal theology, however, it is not clear that the postliberal project implies or requires a commitment to an explicitly antirealist epistemology. Moreover, many evangelicals today strongly contest the assumption that evangelicalism is necessarily wedded to epistemological realism.

Lindbeck clearly maintains that meaning is conceptually relative. He argues that there is no such thing as a concept-free experience of the world and therefore no such thing as "objective" knowledge, in the strict sense of the term. This claim is not necessarily antirealist, however. If there is no such thing as a "God's-eye" view or experience of the world, it does not necessarily follow that nothing exists independent of human cognition. That is, the claim that all experience is concept-laden does not necessarily imply the metaphysical view that existence itself is conceptually relative. One alternative possibility would be some form of critical realism, in which one emphasizes the relativity of knowledge from the standpoint of the knower while affirming the realist belief that reality must exist independent of cognition. Another possibility is to acknowledge the reality of the social construction of knowledge without committing oneself to any particular kind of realist or antirealist epistemology. Lindbeck implicitly takes the latter option, but his argument is not incompatible with critical realism.[58]

Jeffrey Hensley observes that it makes a considerable difference whether one views concepts as *instruments* by which we make the world of kinds and particulars or as *bridges* that link us to an existing world.[59] The former view is explicitly antirealist, but the latter view, though it acknowledges the social construction of knowledge, is still a type of realism. Hensley notes that Lindbeck's postliberalism is at least compatible with the notion of the concept as a bridge between one's search for reality and reality itself; Lindbeck's project does not preclude the possible viability of some kind of sociocritical realism. At the same time, Hensley recognizes that Lindbeck appears to take the neutrality option. Lindbeck's writings embrace no explicit metaphysical position on the realism-antirealism question. The important point is that despite the pronounced tendency of his critics to interpret postliberalism as a form of determined antirealism, Lindbeck's argument actually contains no commitment to metaphysical antirealism at all. He does argue that correspondence to reality is not a *sufficient* condition for truth, but he never denies that correspondence to reality may be a *necessary* condition for an adequate conception or account of truth. Whatever the case may be with regard to his implicit metaphysical position or lack of one, there is thus no basis for the conventional reading of Lindbeck as a determined opponent of realism or the correspondence theory of truth.

Much of the literature on postliberalism focuses on the realism issue, but this is not where Lindbeck and other postliberals have taken their stand. For them, the issue is epistemological foundationalism, not realism; and they *are* determined antifoundationalists. Modern philosophy since Descartes has sought to establish secure grounds of belief that comprise a universal foundation for all knowledge. Modern theology since Schleiermacher has adopted its own forms of this project, by translating Christian claims into the languages of presumably universal philosophies of existence, process, dialectic, and the like. Lindbeck-style postliberalism breaks entirely with this strategy of making foundational appeals to universal structures of thought or experience. It is explicitly antifoundationalist, but not irrationalist. "The issue is not whether there are universal norms of reasonableness, but whether these can be formulated in some neutral, framework-independent language," Lindbeck explains.[60] To give up the latter claim to objective rationality is not to leave science, philosophy, and theology without any standards of rationality. The rational norms that theologians should expect to employ and be judged by are the kinds of norms that Wittgenstein described with reference to philosophy and Thomas Kuhn with reference to science.[61] These norms are like the rules of depth grammar, which linguists search for and fallibly construct and reconstruct without ever quite grasping. In theology as in other fields, Lindbeck observes, reasonableness always contains aesthetic and performative aspects. Just as we define linguistic competence by the attainment of a certain kind of aesthetic character and performative skill, so should we judge arguments in other fields, for to be reasonable in any field is to be linguistically competent in its particular rules and idioms.

Lindbeck allows that this standard of rationality makes religious claims (like Kuhn's scientific paradigms) invulnerable to definite refutation or confirmation, but it does not make them impervious to the corrective discipline of critical discussion and examination. Reason is too contextual and framework-dependent to provide objective foundations for theology, but it is not too relative to censure bad arguments. Theology is like other disciplines in its lack of absolute standards, but it is also like other fields in being subject to pertinent norms of reasonableness that are developed through similar processes of testing and accumulative performance.[62] The fact that reason is always framework dependent does preclude the specific comparative judgments that many evangelicals want to make, however. If reason operates only within webs of field-specific assumptions and linguistic idioms, one cannot make definitive, objective judgments about the truth of one religion over another without doing violence to the religious claims in question. As Lindbeck explains, the notion that one should be able to determine rationally which religion (if any) is the true one is a product of the myth of pure reason. It assumes the possibility of a neutral epistemological standpoint from which one might objectively assess all religions without distorting their meanings. But this standpoint is a fantasy, he observes: "People are inevitably committed to working within a given conceptual cultural language system. We Christians think, look and argue from within the faith. There's no way of getting outside the faith to objectively compare different options."[63]

Evangelicals are prone to fret that everything will be lost if they have no ground of absolute certainty or no proof that Christianity is superior to Islam or Buddhism. This fear drives them to impose impossible tests on Christian belief. Inerrancy or the abyss! It also drives them to invest religious authority in a posited epistemological capacity that exists outside the circle of Christian faith. The truth of Christianity is then judged by rational tests that are not only external to Christian revelation but given authority over revelation. Under the influence of antifoundationalist criticism and the judgment that conservative evangelicalism unnecessarily jeopardizes Christian conviction, however, a new generation of evangelical thinkers is giving up the claim to objective foundational knowledge. "I think foundationalists need to admit that there is no such thing as safely and absolutely secured knowledge," Rodney Clapp declares. "Knowledge is particular and perspectival, and as such is always contestable." It is actually not safe at all to spend one's life at the top of a slippery slope, he observes, "which is why those who do so are obsessed with slippery slopes."[64] Evangelicalism will be healthier and less vulnerable to problems of its own making when it resolves to live in the real world, he argues. It is enough to claim the living Word of God, Jesus Christ, as our foundation in a lost and tormented world, without thinking that this claim has to be grounded in a deeper, universal foundation.

Fundamentalist thinking was forced on a conservative evangelical movement that felt obliged to ward off Enlightenment criticism, but evangelicals no longer live in a context in which the primary challenges to Christian belief come from the offshoots of Enlightenment rationalism. Few thinkers still criticize Christianity in the name of pure reason. Clapp argues that it is therefore time for evangelicals to relinquish their own peculiarly antimodernist forms of modernist foundationalism: "If we quit foundationalist rhetoric we can claim the specifics of the Christian tradition and forthrightly speak the name of Christ in any public forum. We can admit that our argument is contestable, as are the arguments of Marxists, Hindus, free-market capitalists and every other party, then speak unapologetically as Christians."[65]

The dominant forms of evangelical theology have operated within and been captive to the orientation of the objectivizing individual knower; but this orientation no longer rules academe or the larger cultural environment in which evangelicals seek to bear witness to Christ. In seeking to rethink how they should speak the gospel theologically under these circumstances, some evangelicals have turned to Barth's antifoundationalism, his triadic doctrine of the Word, and his emphasis on the dependent relationship between the Word of God written and the Word incarnate. Some have also followed Ramm in adopting Barth's insistence on the *diastasis* between the Word itself and the text of the inscripturated Word. Evangelicals such as Bloesch and Grenz do not invoke the latter distinction in order to deny or downplay the interrelation of revelation and scripture. Grenz explains that scripture is revelatory in derivative, functional, and intermediary senses of the term. As a witness to the revelatory acts of God in history, scripture is revelatory in a derivative sense; as the unique means by which the Holy Spirit brings us to saving knowledge of Christ, it is revelatory in a functional sense; in its capacity to bring us face to face with God through its testimony to Christ, it is revelatory in the sense of an intermediary. Scripture is holy because it is the unsubstitutable vehicle through which the Holy Spirit communicates the saving Word of God to us, he affirms.[66]

But the separation of Word and biblical words nonetheless marks a distinction that makes a qualitative difference for Christian belief. Scripture presupposes the reality of a logically prior revelation. As Grenz observes, to absorb this truism is to recognize that scripture is servant to revelation. That is, scripture is servant to revelation in the same way that it is servant to the work of the Holy Spirit. "The Spirit-energized message presented through Scripture takes primacy over the vehicle by means of which it is transmitted," he remarks. "The subservient character of the Bible to both revelation and the Spirit forms the context in which to set forth the authority of the Bible."[67] Bloesch warns that if the words of scripture are identified with God's Word, every command in scripture becomes absolute, including the command to put witches to death (Ex. 22:18). "I cannot accept James Packer's view that 'the biblical writers' thoughts' are, 'strictly and precisely, the communicated thoughts of God,'" he explains. "Not every idea expressed in Scripture is the 'mind of Christ,' but every idea can become the vehicle of the mind of Christ."[68]

This is precisely the claim that drove evangelicals to attack Barth for decades. Barth's subordination of the biblical text to revelation and the work of the Spirit was repeatedly denounced as a heresy. Conservative evangelical leaders were not mistaken in believing that Barth invested less significance than they did in the doctrine of biblical inspiration. They rightly noted that his theology contained none of the deductive inferences about factual inerrancy that they drew from the doctrine that scripture is inspired by God. In words very close to those of Grenz and other postconservative evangelicals, however, Barth affirmed that scripture is God's inspired Word and that it is nonetheless subordinate to God's logically prior revelation. "Scripture is holy and the Word of God, because by the Holy Spirit it became and will become to the Church a witness to divine revelation," he asserted.[69] This formulation provided the crucial corrective to the evangelicalism of his time. It will undoubtedly take more than a generation for Barth's reputation to recover from the critical pounding he took from evangelical leaders for decades, but today, the seeds of a new kind of evangelicalism are evident. In its protest against reading the Bible as source material for philosophical systems or worldviews, the project of postliberal theology is, among other things, a bridge that links Barth to this new evangelicalism. Lindbeck rightly observes that the future of postliberal theology as a communal enterprise of the church lies primarily in the hands of evangelicals.[70]

TAKING CULTURE SERIOUSLY: NEW HORIZONS IN HERMENEUTICS

It is too soon to speak of postconservative evangelicalism as the beginning of a fourth major evangelical paradigm. The kinds of evangelicalism that Grenz and even Bloesch represent still exist in a landscape dominated by the voices and institutions of fundamentalist evangelicalism. One sign that the progressive current within the larger postconservative trend is only in its beginning phase is the fact that it has spoken thus far almost entirely in a male voice. Twenty years after evangelical feminists such as Virginia Mollenkott and Nancy Hardesty first called for the development of an evangelical feminist theology, the promise of evangelical feminism as a systematically articulated theological perspective remains unfulfilled.[71] Mollenkott has moved away from evangelicalism itself, and very little of the theological rethinking that progressive evangelicals have carried out in recent years has been carried out by women committed to feminism. Postfundamentalist evangelical theology is dominated by nonfeminist academics such as Bloesch, and even the progressive current is dominated by male academics.

The lack of a developed feminist perspective in progressive evangelical theology is undoubtedly symptomatic of the serious difficulties that attend any attempt to reconcile feminist egalitarianism with a theological perspective that affirms the divinely secured infallibility of scriptural teaching. Feminism is about gender equality and the elimination of male privilege, but the link between biblical conservatism and male privilege is very tight. Most conservative evangelical leaders are determined not to relinquish male privileges (and responsibilities), which they regard as established by divine will. Many evangelical leaders continue to oppose even modest attempts to make English translations of the Bible more inclusive with reference to gender. Conservative evangelical leaders such as Wayne Grudem, James Dobson, and R. C. Sproul warn that gender-inclusive translations undermine the force of biblical teaching pertaining to the proper "headship" of males in their home and church relationships. In 1997, Grudem's Council for Biblical Manhood and Womanhood played a key role in a protest campaign that blocked plans for the publication of an inclusive-language edition of the New International Version of the Bible.[72] Evangelicals have waged similarly consuming battles in recent years over the gender politics of the popular men's Promise Keepers movement. Some Promise Keepers leaders uphold an ethic of gender equality in their teaching and practice, but a significant segment of the movement's leaders and much of its official literature insist on a "biblical" ethic of male headship and female subordination.[73]

The fact that much of the evangelical establishment is straightforwardly opposed to gender equality has undoubtedly impeded postconservative evangelicals from developing a theological ethic that makes gender a crucial category of analysis. Many moderate and progressive evangelicals are presently preoccupied with the need merely to establish that more than one viewpoint is hermeneutically possible within evangelicalism. Moreover, some postconservative evangelicals are clearly much less committed to gender equality than to narrative hermeneutics or epistemological nonfoundationalism. In contrast, the existence of numerous evangelical feminists in leadership positions in academe and the churches suggests that there is such a thing as a female-voice evangelical feminism that informs evangelicals, and which remains to be systematically articulated. The question of how evangelicalism should deal with the patriarchal character of scriptural narrative and teaching is a crucial issue for the future of evangelical theology as a whole. The importance of this question for any movement that seeks to effect a progressive turn in evangelical theology can hardly be overstated. Some advocates of progressive-model evangelicalism clearly recognize that their project needs to address and appropriate feminist criticism. Evangelicals such as Grenz (with Denise Muir Kjesbo), Rebecca Merrill Groothius, and Ruth A. Tucker have made noteworthy programmatic statements in this direction, and an activist organization, Christians for Biblical Equality, promotes gender equality in evangelical churches.[74] Very little systematic rethinking on this subject has occurred thus far, however. The kind of theological rethinking that Grenz and others like him represent is a novel departure in evangelicalism as a whole, in which certain crucial hermeneutical questions have barely begun to be asked.

Evangelical theologians discovered during their dialogues with Yale-school postliberals that postliberal narrativism has been long on formal discussions of method and short on theological substance. The very opposite has been true of evangelicalism. For decades, evangelical theologians plunged straight into the business of making biblical affirmations while paying little attention to the basic question of what it means to understand or seek to interpret the biblical text. "The evangelical tradition has not been nurtured to think methodologically," Richard

Lints remarks with understatement.[75] Evangelicals brushed aside hermeneutical problems while piling up proof texts that defended the literal factuality of "fundamental" doctrines. Though evangelical thinkers actually employed a considerable variety of interpretive strategies over the past century, the force of an exaggerated doctrine of biblical infallibility narrowed the field of legitimized hermeneutical discussion. Inerrancy doctrine functioned as a shield or immunity claim against a host of hermeneutical problems pertaining to the relativity of understanding and to historical-cultural context. It sharply limited the kinds of questions that could be asked in an evangelical context.

The trend in evangelical theology is clearly away from strict-inerrancy doctrine, however. Moreover, evangelicals increasingly recognize that no theology is actually immune from the problems of historical and cultural relativism and the instability of meaning. Even an infallible text provides no security against interpretive fallibility. The increasing recognition that modern evangelicalism is reductionist in this regard has prompted various proposals for an evangelicalism that is more deeply rooted in the idioms and interpretive strategies of classical orthodoxy. Robert E. Webber and Thomas C. Oden argue for an orthodox church theology in which scripture is read through the developing theology of the church fathers; J. I. Packer advocates a canonical approach that reads most of scripture through a typology derived from Paul, Luke, Matthew, and Hebrews; Charles J. Scalise appropriates Brevard Childs's theory of canonically shaped biblical doctrine; Bloesch advocates a christological hermeneutic that goes beyond the literal sense of the text to disclose how scripture everywhere reveals Christ to us; Russell Spittler holds out for a persistently exegetical approach that eschews all theological master concepts and patristic doctrines.[76]

Evangelicals from the Wesleyan and Pentecostal traditions make a significant challenge to these classically rooted "orthodoxies," arguing that most evangelical theologies subsume the role of the Holy Spirit under the category of scripture, tradition, or Christology. Spittler's strictly exegetical approach offers one way to restrain the influence of orthodox master concepts (in his case, from a Pentecostal perspective), but other Wesleyan and Pentecostal thinkers move explicitly from Spirit to Word, contending that theology must begin with the believer's actual encounter with God through God's Spirit. Numerous advocates of an explicitly progressive evangelicalism argue from this perspective, including Donald Dayton, Steven J. Land, Henry H. Knight III, and, with some equivocation, Clark Pinnock.[77]

Other progressive evangelicals advance liberationist, communitarian-narrativist, and interactionist models of interpretation. Having given up the expectation that a high enough doctrine of scripture should be able to ward off the contaminating influence of modern culture, evangelicals have begun to debate the limits of hermeneutical contextualization. One of the strongest cases for an evangelical liberationist hermeneutic is presented by Brian Walsh and J. Richard Middleton, who argue that normative scriptural narrative is defined most importantly by an emancipationist scriptural worldview, which finds the presence of God especially in the lives of oppressed and marginalized people. Biblical narrative is pervaded by the divine call to lift up the poor, set free the captives, treat the alien with kindness, and take care of widows and orphans. Walsh and Middleton propose that this scriptural theme amounts to a countercultural worldview that suffuses the heart of normative scriptural narrative. In response to the deconstructionist insistence that metanarrative is inevitably totalizing and oppressive, they emphasize the liberating character of biblical narrative. Scripture is undeniably grand in its narrative claims, but scripture subverts the usual logic of metanarrative by finding God at the margins of the world's story. With considerable boldness from an evangelical perspective, Walsh and Middleton acknowledge that some biblical texts do not advance or even fit into the Bible's redemptive plot. To be faithful to scripture is to embrace the meaning of its normative liberating story, they argue, which means that Christians must be willing to stand against the text when necessary.[78]

Under the various influences of social and cultural theory, postmodern criticism, postliberal theology, and the experiences of numerous missionaries, other postconservative evangelicals have begun to develop interactionist hermeneutical theories that conceptualize biblical interpretation as a circular process of narrative-framed understanding. Although conservative evangelicals such as David Wells contend that biblical doctrine must be protected from the relativizing hermeneutical process of moving from context to text, to an increasing number of evangelical thinkers, this requirement amounts to a form of intellectual suicide.[79] They note that the traditional evangelical opposition to hermeneutics sets evangelicalism against the conclusions of modern social science about the social character of all forms of understanding. Put differently, the stricture that we cannot bring anything from our situation into the interpretive process makes understanding impossible. We always come to the text from where we are. We cannot participate in a discussion or even a process of indoctrination that excludes our embodiment and situation.

Evangelical interactionists such as Grenz, William Dyrness, and Charles Kraft therefore urge that the message of scripture can be understood only by beginning with our embodied life in the world, not with a doctrine of scripture. "We must begin here because we simply cannot begin anywhere else," Dyrness remarks. That is, we cannot adopt a point of entry or standpoint that excludes our history and cultural environment. Against the charismatic position, however, we cannot open ourselves to the movement of God's Spirit in the inscripturated Word without some determinative understanding of the nature and purpose of scripture. "In our day particularly momentous and complex issues face us—diminishing resources, economic affluence and poverty, and arms escalation, to name only a few," Dyrness observes. "On a personal level many people carry heavy burdens of suffering or discouragement. These factors are surely relevant in the way we use Scripture." Just as God heard the cries of the Hebrews suffering under slavery in Egypt, so God hears the cries of those who suffer today: "It would be both inhuman and theologically deficient to fail to take such predispositions into account, for these are the particular openings which give opportunity for Scripture to speak with special power."[80]

Interactionist theory seeks to account for the different ways in which culture and other forms of personal and social difference influence how people hear the gospel. Mission strategists such as Kraft, C. René Padilla, and Harvie Conn have been leaders in this theological movement. They note from experience that communication of the Word is never a mere process of translation; it is always a two-way conversation that draws on and encodes distinctive cultural practices and meanings. Kraft criticizes the "extremely brittle conservative package" in which evangelical churches have traditionally wrapped the gospel. He observes that resistance to old-style North American monoculturalism is increasing within "the other six thousand cultural worlds" in which the gospel is preached and urges that it is harmful to all parties and to Christianity to impose a version of North American culture on the rest of the world in the name of a cross-cultural faith.[81] The need for a more contextual understanding of scriptural meaning was impressed on Dyrness during his mission experience in Asia. "While teaching in Asia I became aware how often Western readers tended to see the truth of Scripture in abstract terms, while Asian readers tended to focus on narrative and concrete images," he recalls. "They did not find it necessary, as we do, to isolate meanings and eliminate nuances and allusions."[82]

Dyrness and Kraft maintain that differences of this kind must be brought to consciousness if evangelicals are to avoid the pitfall of reading their own prejudices into scripture. To ignore the presuppositions and cultural predispositions individuals bring to the text, they caution, means we will inevitably derive meanings from scripture that have more basis in culture than in scripture. Interactionist interpretation helps readers of scripture become aware of their culturally influenced tendency to isolate particular themes or bring unacknowledged worldviews to the text. Its purpose is not to rationalize subjectivism but to enrich our understanding and appreciation of the multilayered polyphony of scripture, as well as to guard against narrow readings of it. "Our goal is progressively to interpret our vocations, our personal and family lives, in the light of God's program," Dyrness explains. "We come to see our unfolding story as a part of God's story." The chief purpose of scripture is not to inform us but to interpret us and our world. And it is emphatically for *this* world that scripture has been given, "for it is this world which Christ came to redeem and where we pray to see God's kingdom come."[83]

Grenz agrees that the historical-cultural context of the faith community plays a crucial role in shaping the church's understanding of what it means to follow Christ in the present moment. "The social community in which the people of God participate contains its own cognitive tools—language, symbols, myths and outlooks on the world—that facilitate identity formation and the experience of reality," he explains. The early Christian communities spoke of Christ not only as (Jewish) Lord and Son of God but as Logos; later, the church conceptualized Christ's incarnation and the divine Trinity by employing Greek ontological categories. This process of "listening to culture" is an indispensable task for Christian theology in every age, Grenz urges.[84] Its proper purpose is never to sacralize any particular worldview or cultural form but rather to be open to various cultural elements that help the church express the gospel message in a given situation. Calvin taught that "our constant endeavor, day and night, is not just to transmit the tradition faithfully, but also to put it in a form we think will prove best."[85] Grenz adds that evangelical theology fulfills this commitment whenever it holds fast to the gospel kerygma and consults the heritage of the church while keeping abreast of cultural developments that affect how the gospel is heard.

Interactive interpretation reaches its culminating stage when we see our stories as part of the same story told in scripture about God and the history of salvation. "The great culmination which God holds out for us involves both his story and ours in glorious interrelationship," Dyrness explains. The point of establishing an interaction between scripture and the Christian community is to allow the power of the Spirit-moved Word of God actually to operate in Christian communities. If God's story is to become known to us as our own story, he urges, we must allow scripture to function more like a musical score than a blueprint. A score gives guidance, but it is meant to be played in fresh ways. In a similar way, scripture is authoritative in Christian communities not merely when its authority is acknowledged but especially when its creative and redemptive power is manifest in the lives of Christian communities; "for it is the wisdom and maturity of the body of Christ as a whole that the Holy Spirit is working toward," Dyrness remarks. Understanding does not precede faithful experience but follows from it: "The light will grow; understanding will deepen within the community as we seek to engage ourselves in God's program." The process of equipping the saints begins anew with each generation, and it continues as a process of never-finished interaction between inscripturated Word and faithful community.[86]

Though many evangelicals worry that Grenz and other interactionists give too much interpretive authority to situated Christian communities, the debate in evangelical theology today is increasingly over the *degree* to which historical-cultural context should be taken seriously, not whether the issue is legitimate in evangelicalism. Though many evangelical leaders still oppose all forms of interactionist and other contextualizing hermeneutical strategies, the trend in evangelicalism is clearly away from errorless-claiming objectivism. Pinnock's career vividly illustrates this trend. Having begun as an ardent champion of Reformed-oriented Baptist fundamentalism, he has steadily relinquished various aspects of his doctrinal inheritance that obscure or conflict with his sense of scriptural meaning and the dynamic relation of Word and Spirit, becoming in the process an evangelical proponent of narrative theology.

"Even though the Bible is basically a storybook, theology has not bothered to orient itself in that way," he observes. Having assumed that theology is supposed to make the story make rational sense to educated modernists, theologians lost the biblical sense of truth as revelatory narrative. The truth of the gospel is primarily story truth, Pinnock argues. Propositions are needed in theology, but they derive their power from the primary story. For this reason, Christian theology "should not be primarily rational-propositional in form, even though it usually is, especially among evangelicals." To take story truth seriously is to give up the evangelical exaltation of the single interpretive voice, he observes. Stories are dynamic, participatory, and multivalent; they invite interpretation from many angles. Any theology that takes the story form of scriptural truth seriously must therefore call upon a "choir of workers" to capture the interplay of symbolic riches in scripture.[87]

The notion that Christianity is true primarily as true story is hardly new to Christian orthodoxy, but it is certainly new to modern evangelicalism. That Christian truth is therefore polyphonic and multivalent is also a new theme for evangelicalism, though not for orthodoxy. Evangelical theology in a postmodern mode is no longer threatened by the inexhaustible interplay of meaning that scriptural narrative contains. As Pinnock explains, the Word written is rich and complex because the story at its center bears these attributes inexhaustibly. "A rational theology simply cannot do justice to it," he remarks. "It will mistakenly try to create harmonies where there are tensions and unities where there are diversities. Narrative theology is required to handle unity within diversity. Each perspective can make a contribution, but none can tell the whole story. Each will enrich our understanding and need not be seen as necessarily in contradiction to the others."[88]

Evangelical theology increasingly speaks in this kind and tone of voice. It is a voice that reconnects modern evangelicalism to the polyphonic orthodox tradition of Irenaeus, Athanasius, Augustine, Chrysostom, Aquinas, Luther, Calvin, Hooker, Wesley, and Barth. Near the end of his life, Hans Frei told Carl Henry that his deepest theological desire was to witness the emergence of "a kind of generous orthodoxy" that blended and transcended elements of existing evangelicalism and liberalism.[89] Today, within a significant segment of evangelical theology, the conception of theology as polemic or tournament is receding. The confrontational spirit of fundamentalist evangelicalism is giving way to the discourse of a generous orthodoxy. If the quest for the kind of orthodoxy that Frei envisioned is to be fulfilled in the churches and seminaries of a new century, the evangelicals need to play a significant role in bringing it about.

Notes

INTRODUCTION: WHAT IS EVANGELICALISM?

1. James Davison Hunter, *American Evangelicalism: Conservative Religion and the Quandary of Modernity* (New Brunswick, NJ: Rutgers University Press, 1983), 7–9.
2. See Richard Quebedeaux, *The Young Evangelicals: Revolution in Orthodoxy* (New York: Harper & Row, 1974); Robert E. Webber, *Common Roots: A Call to Evangelical Maturity* (Grand Rapids: Zondervan Publishing House, 1979); Max L. Stackhouse, "Religious Right: New? Right?" *Commonweal* 29 (January 1982), 52–56; Donald W. Dayton, "The Use of Scripture in the Wesleyan Tradition," in *The Use of the Bible in Theology: Evangelical Options,* ed. Robert K. Johnston (Atlanta: John Knox Press, 1985), 121–26; Timothy P. Weber, "Premillennialism and the Branches of Evangelicalism," in *The Variety of American Evangelicalism,* ed. Donald W. Dayton and Robert K. Johnston (Downers Grove, IL: InterVarsity Press, 1991), 12–14.
3. See Donald W. Dayton, "Some Doubts about the Usefulness of the Category 'Evangelical,'" in Dayton and Johnston, eds., *Variety of American Evangelicalism,* 245–51; Dayton, "Use of Scripture in the Wesleyan Tradition," 125; Leonard I. Sweet, "The Evangelical Tradition in America," in *The Evangelical Tradition in America,* ed. Leonard I. Sweet (Macon, GA: Mercer University Press, 1984), 83–86.
4. William Ames, *The Marrow of Theology,* trans. John Dykstra Eusden (Durham, NC: Labyrinth Press, 1968), 78.11.
5. Philipp Jacob Spener, *Pia Desideria, or Heartfelt Desire for a God-Pleasing Reform of the True Evangelical Church, Together with Several Simple Christian Proposals Looking Toward This End* (1675), trans. Theodore G. Tappert (Philadelphia: Fortress Press, 1964), 112.
6. John Wesley, "Predestination Calmly Considered," in *John Wesley,* ed. Albert C. Outler (New York: Oxford University Press, 1964), 445.
7. See Weber, "Premillennialism and the Branches of Evangelicalism," 12–13.
8. See Ralph Reed, *Active Faith: How Christians Are Changing the Soul of American Politics* (New York: Free Press, 1996); Harvey Cox, "The Warring Visions of the Religious Right," *Atlantic Monthly,* no. 276 (November 1995), 59–69;

idem, *Fire from Heaven: The Rise of Pentecostal Spirituality and the Reshaping of Religion in the Twenty-first Century* (New York: Addison-Wesley Publishing Co., 1995), 287–95.

9. George Marsden, "The Evangelical Denomination," in *Evangelicalism and Modern America,* ed. George Marsden (Grand Rapids: Wm. B. Eerdmans Publishing Co., 1984), ix–x. See George Marsden, "From Fundamentalism to Evangelicalism: A Historical Analysis," in *The Evangelicals: What They Believe, Who They Are, Where They Are Changing,* ed. David F. Wells and John D. Woodbridge (Nashville: Abingdon Press, 1975), 122–42; and idem, "Fundamentalism as an American Phenomenon," in *Reckoning with the Past: Historical Essays on American Evangelicalism from the Institute for the Study of American Evangelicals,* ed. D. G. Hart (Grand Rapids: Baker Book House, 1995), 303–21.

10. Kenneth S. Kantzer and Carl F. H. Henry, eds., *Evangelical Affirmations* (Grand Rapids: Academie Books, 1990), 33.

11. John F. Walvoord, foreword to Robert P. Lightner, *Neoevangelicalism Today* (Schaumburg, IL: Regular Baptist Press, 1978), i. On this theme, see David F. Wells, *No Place for Truth: Or, Whatever Happened to Evangelical Theology?* (Grand Rapids: Wm. B. Eerdmans Publishing Co., 1993); and Millard J. Erickson, *The Evangelical Left: Encountering Postconservative Evangelical Theology* (Grand Rapids: Baker Book House, 1997).

12. See Rodney Clapp, *A Peculiar People: The Church as Culture in a Post-Christian Society* (Downers Grove, IL: InterVarsity Press, 1996); Stanley J. Grenz, *Revisioning Evangelical Theology: A Fresh Agenda for the Twenty-first Century* (Downers Grove, IL: InterVarsity Press, 1993); Henry H. Knight III, *A Future for Truth: Evangelical Theology in a Postmodern World* (Nashville: Abingdon Press, 1997); Nancey Murphy, *Beyond Liberalism and Fundamentalism: How Modern and Postmodern Philosophy Set the Theological Agenda* (Valley Forge, PA: Trinity Press International, 1996); Clark H. Pinnock, *Flame of Love: A Theology of the Holy Spirit* (Downers Grove, IL: InterVarsity Press, 1996); Miroslav Volf, *Exclusion and Embrace: A Theological Exploration of Identity, Otherness, and Reconciliation* (Nashville: Abingdon Press, 1996); J. Richard Middleton and Brian J. Walsh, *Truth Is Stranger than It Used to Be: Biblical Faith in a Postmodern Age* (Downers Grove, IL: InterVarsity Press, 1995).

CHAPTER 1: ANTIMODERNIST MODERNIZERS:
THE MAKING OF FUNDAMENTALIST EVANGELICALISM

1. Moody's and Torrey's responses appear in "What Was Christ's Attitude towards Error? A Symposium," *Record of Christian Work* (November 1899), 600, 602, quoted in Stanley N. Gundry, *Love Them In: The Proclamation Theology of D. L. Moody* (Chicago: Moody Press, 1976), 217–18.

2. George M. Marsden, *Fundamentalism and American Culture: The Shaping of Twentieth-Century Evangelicalism 1870–1925* (Oxford: Oxford University Press, 1980), 35–44, closing quote on 38. See D. L. Moody, *Glad Tidings: Sermons and Prayer Meeting Talks* (New York: Treat Press, 1876); William G. McLoughlin, *Modern Revivalism* (New York: Ronald Press, 1959), 3–64; Lyle W. Dorsett, *A Passion for Souls: The Life of D. L. Moody* (Chicago: Moody Press, 1997).

3. Moody once claimed that he would rather part with his entire library, "excepting

my Bible," than lose his collection of Mackintosh's writings: "They have been to me a very key to the Scriptures." Quoted in Ernest R. Sandeen, *The Roots of Fundamentalism: British and American Millenarianism 1800–1930* (Chicago: University of Chicago Press, 1970), 173. "Quit your fighting" quote in Marsden, *Fundamentalism and American Culture,* 33.

4. Ernest Sandeen's work emphasizes the influence of British and American pre-millennialism on the development of American fundamentalism; see *Roots of Fundamentalism,* esp. 59–80, 132–61. For a more nuanced assessment of the pre-millennialist roots of fundamentalism, see George M. Marsden, "Fundamentalism as an American Phenomenon," in *Reckoning with the Past: Historical Essays on American Evangelicalism from the Institute for the Study of American Evangelicals,* ed. D. G. Hart (Grand Rapids: Baker Book House, 1995), 303–21; and idem, *Fundamentalism and American Culture,* 4–5. On the dispensationalist takeover of most of the Bible conference movement, see Timothy P. Weber, *Living in the Shadow of the Second Coming: American Premillennialism, 1875–1982* (Chicago: University of Chicago Press, 1987), 26–28.

5. Marsden, *Fundamentalism and American Culture,* 117–18. For the text of the 1878 "Niagara Creed," see Sandeen, *Roots of Fundamentalism,* 273–77.

6. See Stewart G. Cole, *The History of Fundamentalism* (1931; reprint, Hamden, CT: Archon Books, 1963), 32–34; N. F. Furniss, *The Fundamentalist Controversy: 1918–31* (New Haven, CT: Yale University Press, 1954), 49; William Vance Trollinger Jr., *God's Empire: William Bell Riley and Midwestern Fundamentalism* (Madison: University of Wisconsin Press, 1990); Roger Nicole and J. Ramsey Michaels, eds., *Inerrancy and Common Sense* (Grand Rapids: Baker Book House, 1980), 49–70; Daniel B. Stevick, *Beyond Fundamentalism* (Richmond: John Knox Press, 1964), 17–22.

7. R. A. Torrey, A. C. Dixon, et al. *The Fundamentals: A Testimony to the Truth,* 4 vols. (1917; reprint, Grand Rapids: Baker Book House, 1993); see esp. George Frederick Wright, "The Mosaic Authorship of the Pentateuch," 1:43–54; William Caven, "The Testimony of Christ to the Old Testament," 1:201–27; James M. Gray, "The Inspiration of the Bible—Definition, Extent and Proof," 2: 9–43; Benjamin B. Warfield, "The Deity of Christ," 2:239–46.

8. On the development of an American fundamentalist subculture in the 1930s and 1940s, see Joel Carpenter, *Revive Us Again: The Reawakening of American Fundamentalism* (New York: Oxford University Press, 1997).

9. Charles Hodge, *Systematic Theology,* 3 vols. (1872; reprint, Grand Rapids: Wm. B. Eerdmans Publishing Co., 1993), 1:152; A. A. Hodge, *Outlines of Theology* (ca. 1860; reprint, Edinburgh: Banner of Truth Trust, 1991), 66.

10. Hodge, *Outlines of Theology,* 74–75; A. A. Hodge and Benjamin B. Warfield, "Inspiration," *Presbyterian Review* 2 (April 1881), 238–41, reprinted in A. A. Hodge and Benjamin B. Warfield, *Inspiration* (Grand Rapids: Baker Book House, 1979). See Benjamin B. Warfield, "Inspiration," in *The International Standard Bible Encyclopedia,* ed. James Orr, vol. 3 (Chicago: Howard-Severance Co., 1915), 1473–83, reprinted in Benjamin B. Warfield, *The Inspiration and Authority of the Bible* (1948; reprint, Philadelphia: Presbyterian and Reformed Publishing Co., 1964), 131–66.

11. Hodge and Warfield, "Inspiration" (Hodge's section), 238.

12. Warfield, *Inspiration and Authority of the Bible,* 421; see also 169–226; Hodge, *Systematic Theology,* 1:156–57.

13. Martin Luther, "Prefaces to the New Testament," in *Luther's Works,* ed. E. Theodore Bachmann, trans. Charles M. Jacobs and E. Theodore Bachmann (Philadelphia: Muhlenberg Press, 1960), 35:357–411, esp. 362, 394–99; idem, "Prefaces to the Old Testament," in *Luther's Works,* 35:236–37, 241–42, 277–78; idem, "The Meaning of Large Numbers in the Bible," *Luther's Works,* trans. and ed. Theodore G. Tappert (Philadelphia: Muhlenberg Press, 1960), 54:452; idem, "A Brief Instruction on What to Look for and Expect in the Gospels," in *Luther's Works,* 35:188–220; idem, "On the Councils and the Church," in *Luther's Works,* ed. Eric W. Gritsch (Philadelphia: Fortress Press, 1966), 41:27–29.

14. Martin Luther, "The Gospel for the Festival of the Epiphany," in *Luther's Works,* ed. Hans J. Hillerbrand (Philadelphia: Fortress Press, 1974), 52:205–6; idem, "Sermons on the Gospel of St. John," in *Luther's Works,* trans. Martin H. Bertram, ed. Jaroslav Pelikan (St. Louis: Concordia Publishing House, 1957), 22:218–21; idem, "Lectures on Galatians," in *Luther's Works,* ed. and trans. Jaroslav Pelikan (St. Louis: Concordia Publishing House, 1963), 26:294–96. See B. A. Gerrish, *Grace and Reason: A Study in the Theology of Luther* (Oxford: Clarendon Press, 1962), 43–56, 69–83; Paul Althaus, *The Theology of Martin Luther,* trans. Robert C. Schultz (Philadelphia: Fortress Press, 1966), 72–102.

15. John Calvin, *Genesis,* trans. John King (Carlisle, PA: Banner of Truth Trust, 1975), 86; idem, *Calvin's New Testament Commentaries,* vol. 1 of 12 vols: *A Harmony of the Gospels Matthew, Mark, and Luke,* trans. T. H. L. Parker (Grand Rapids: Wm. B. Eerdmans Publishing Co., 1972), 83, 139; idem, *Calvin's New Testament Commentaries,* vol. 2: *A Harmony of the Gospels Matthew, Mark, and Luke,* trans. T. H. L. Parker (Grand Rapids: Wm. B. Eerdmans Publishing Co., 1972), 55.

16. John Calvin, *Institutes of the Christian Religion,* trans. Ford Lewis Battles, ed. John T. McNeill (Philadelphia: Westminster Press, 1960), 1.7.4, 78. See Edward A. Dowey Jr., *The Knowledge of God in Calvin's Theology* (1952; reprint, Grand Rapids: Wm. B. Eerdmans Publishing Co., 1994), 106–24, 238–57; Roy A. Harrisville and Walter Sundberg, *The Bible in Modern Culture: Theology and Historical-Critical Method from Spinoza to Käsemann* (Grand Rapids: Wm. B. Eerdmans Publishing Co., 1995), 19–22; Hans-Joachim Kraus, "Calvin's Exegetical Principles," *Interpretation* 31 (1977), 8–18.

17. Philipp Melanchthon, "Apology of the Augsburg Confession" (1531), in *Concordia Triglotta,* ed. F. Bente and W. H. T. Daw (Milwaukee: Northwestern Publishing House, 1988), 123.

18. Johann Andreas Quenstedt, *Theologia didactico-polemica* (Wittenberg: Johannes Ludolph Quenstedt and Elerd Schumacher Haeredes [Matthaeus Henckel], 1685), 1:77; quoted and trans. Arthur Carl Piepkorn, "What Does 'Inerrancy' Mean?" *Concordia Theological Monthly* 36 (1965), 578. See Robert D. Preus, *The Theology of Post-Reformation Lutheranism,* vol. 1: *A Study of Theological Prolegomena* (St. Louis: Concordia Publishing House, 1970), 263–309; R. Schroder, *Johann Gerhards lutherische Christologie und die aristotelische Metaphysik* (Tübingen: J. C. B. Mohr (Paul Siebeck), 1983); Robert P. Scharlemann, *Thomas Aquinas and John Gerhard* (New Haven, CT: Yale University Press, 1964); Harrisville and Sundberg, *Bible in Modern Culture,* 22–24. On the differences between scholastic and monastic education, see Jean Leclercq, *The Love of Learning and the Desire for God: A Study of Monastic Culture,* trans. Catharine Misrahi (New York: Fordham University Press, 1961).

19. Francis Turretin, *Institutes of Elenctic Theology*, 3 vols., trans. George Musgrave Giger, ed. James T. Dennison Jr. (1679; reprint, Phillipsburg, NJ: Presbyterian and Reformed Publishing Co., 1992), 1:55–56, 62–63. See John W. Beardslee III, ed. and trans., *Reformed Dogmatics: J. Wollebius, G. Voetius, F. Turretin* (New York: Oxford University Press, 1965). Much of the literature on Protestant scholasticism bears an unfortunate partisan tendency either to exaggerate or to minimize the qualitative break between the Reformers and post-Reformation dogmatists. In my reading, the rationalizing process in Protestant orthodoxy was more gradual (especially in the Reformed tradition) than much of the literature about it suggests, but against the claims of its defenders, Protestant scholasticism did produce forms of orthodoxy that deviated profoundly from the spirit and claims of the Reformers. From this perspective, Francis Turretin is rightly viewed neither as a good Calvinist nor as the epitome of the scholastic break but as a highly significant architect and symbol of a rationalizing process that reached its logical culmination in the early eighteenth century. Among evangelical works that argue for a sharp break in the Reformed tradition, the most valuable study is by Jack B. Rogers and Donald K. McKim, *The Authority and Interpretation of the Bible: An Historical Approach* (San Francisco: Harper & Row, 1979), a major work that played a key background role in the evangelical debates over biblical inerrancy in the 1980s. While I differ with them on various historical points, the spirit of my argument is very close to that of Rogers and McKim. For a sharp polemic against their argument, see John D. Woodbridge, *Biblical Authority: A Critique of the Rogers/McKim Proposal* (Grand Rapids: Zondervan Publishing House, 1982). For important works that defend the continuity of Lutheran and Reformed orthodoxies with their respective Reformation traditions, see Preus, *Theology of Post-Reformation Lutheranism*, and Richard Miller, *Post-Reformation Reformed Dogmatics*, 2 vols. (Grand Rapids: Baker Book House, 1987, 1993). For a defense of Turretin's Calvinism that also describes the thoroughgoing rationalism of Turretin's son, see Timothy Ross Phillips, *Francis Turretin's Idea of Theology and Its Bearing upon His Doctrine of Scripture* (Ann Arbor: University Microfilms International, 1986).
20. Turretin, *Institutes of Elenctic Theology*, 1:106–7, 111.
21. For the text of the Helvetic Consensus Formula, see appendix 2 to Hodge, *Outlines of Theology*, 656–63; reprinted in John H. Leith, ed., *Creeds of the Churches* (Richmond: John Knox Press, 1973).
22. John Owen, *Biblical Theology, or, The Nature, Origin, Development, and Study of Theological Truth, In Six Books* (1661), trans. Stephen P. Westcott (Pittsburgh: Soli Deo Gloria Publications, 1994), 495–533; quote on 501. See Donald K. McKim, "John Owen's Doctrine of Scripture in Historical Perspective," *Evangelical Quarterly* (October–December 1973), 195–207.
23. Turretin, *Institutes of Elenctic Theology*, 1:114–16. See Jack Rogers, "The Church Doctrine of Biblical Authority," in *Biblical Authority*, ed. Jack Rogers (Waco, TX: Word Books, 1977), 29–39.
24. Calvin, *Institutes of the Christian Religion*, 1.7.5, 80.
25. The Westminster Confession of Faith (1647), par. 6.005, in *The Book of Confessions* (Louisville, KY: Office of the General Assembly, Presbyterian Church (U.S.A.), 1991); Rutherford quoted in Rogers and McKim, *Authority and Interpretation of the Bible*, 206. On Turretin's legacy at Princeton Theological Seminary, see James W. Alexander, *The Life of Archibald Alexander, D.D.* (New

York: Charles Scribner, 1854), 108–9; A. A. Hodge, *The Life of Charles Hodge, D.D., LL.D.* (New York: Charles Scribner's Sons, 1880), 323. The theology curriculum at Princeton Seminary was based on Turretin's *Institutes* until the publication of Hodge's *Systematic Theology* in 1872. Hodge continued afterward to base his upper-division classes on Turretin's text. The Westminster Assembly of Divines was called by the English Parliament from 1643 to 1649 for advice on religious reform. This group of seven Englishmen and four Scots included Rutherford, Thomas Gataker, Robert Harris, and Edward Reynolds.

26. Hodge, *Systematic Theology,* 1:16–17, 18–60; quote in Hodge, *Systematic Theology,* 3:60. See Thomas Reid, *An Inquiry into the Human Mind, on the Principles of Common Sense* (Edinburgh, 1764); Roger L. Emerson, "Science and Moral Philosophy in the Scottish Enlightenment," in *Studies in the Philosophy of the Scottish Enlightenment,* ed. M. A. Stewart (Oxford: Clarendon Press, 1990), 32–36; Theodore Dwight Bozeman, *Protestants in an Age of Science* (Chapel Hill: University of North Carolina Press, 1977); Mark A. Noll, *Princeton and the Republic, 1768–1822* (Princeton, NJ: Princeton University Press, 1989), 28–58; idem, "Common Sense Traditions and American Evangelical Thought," *American Quarterly* 37 (1985), 216–38; Rogers, "Church Doctrine of Biblical Authority," 39–40.

27. Charles Hodge, "What Is Christianity?" *Biblical Repertory and Princeton Review* (January 1860), 121.

28. Hodge, *Systematic Theology,* 1:1–2, 11–17, 364.

29. Hodge's "no theological novelty" remark cited in Claude Welch, *Protestant Thought in the Nineteenth Century,* vol. 1:*1799–1870* (New Haven, CT: Yale University Press, 1972), 201; Patton quoted in Ned B. Stonehouse, *J. Gresham Machen: A Bibliographical Memoir* (Grand Rapids: Wm. B. Eerdmans Publishing Co., 1954), 61–62. See Mark A. Noll, ed., *The Princeton Theology, 1812–1921: Scripture, Science, and Theological Method from Archibald Alexander to Benjamin Breckinridge Warfield* (Grand Rapids: Baker Book House, 1983).

30. In the 1820s, Hodge studied under Friedrich August Tholuck at the University of Halle and under Friedrich Schleiermacher and E. W. Hengstenberg at the University of Berlin. Between 1825 and 1875, he published nearly 150 articles in *Biblical Repertory and Princeton Review* (which he edited) on a wide range of religious, cultural, and political subjects. Many of these essays were reprinted in Charles Hodge, *Theological Essays: Reprinted from the Princeton Review* (New York: Wiley & Putnam, 1846), and in idem, *Essays and Review: Selected from the Princeton Review* (New York: Robert Carter & Brothers, 1856).

31. Quote from Warfield's 1888 inaugural lecture reprinted in Benjamin B. Warfield, *The Idea of Systematic Theology Considered as a Science* (New York: Anson Randolph & Co., 1888), 5–6; expanded version reprinted in idem, *Studies in Theology* (1932; reprint, Edinburgh: Banner of Truth Trust, 1988), 49–87. On Hodge's life, see Hodge, *Life of Charles Hodge;* and John W. Stewart, "Charles Hodge Revisited," *Princeton Seminary Bulletin* 18 (November 1997), 279–99.

32. See Hodge and Warfield, "Inspiration," 225–60; Charles Briggs, "Critical Theories of the Sacred Scriptures in Relation to Their Inspiration," *Presbyterian Review* 2 (April 1881), 550–79; idem, "A Critical Study of the Higher Criticism with Special Reference to the Pentateuch," *Presbyterian Review* 4 (April 1883), 69–130. On Warfield's debate with Charles Briggs, see Rogers and McKim, *Au-*

thority and Interpretation of the Bible, 348–61. The Northern Presbyterian church's 1892 "Portland Deliverance" statement on inerrancy is printed in the *Minutes* of the General Assembly of the Presbyterian Church in the U.S.A. (1892), 179–80.

33. On the Holiness and premillennialist movements, see Benjamin B. Warfield, *Studies in Perfectionism* (Philadelphia: Presbyterian and Reformed Publishing Co., 1958); idem, review of *What the Bible Teaches: A Thorough and Comprehensive Study of What the Bible Has to Say concerning the Great Doctrines of Which It Treats,* by Reuben A. Torrey, *Presbyterian and Reformed Review* 39 (July 1898), 562–64; idem, "The Gospel and the Second Coming," *Bible Magazine* 3 (1915), 300–309; idem, review of *He That Is Spiritual,* by Lewis Sperry Chafer, *Princeton Theological Review* 17 (April 1919), 322–27.

34. Nathan O. Hatch, "Millennialism and Popular Religion in the Early Republic," in *The Evangelical Tradition in America,* ed. Leonard I. Sweet (Macon, GA: Mercer University Press, 1984), 112–14; C. Norman Kraus, *Dispensationalism in America: Its Rise and Development* (Richmond: John Knox Press, 1958). On the Millerites, from whom the Seventh-Day Adventist movement later evolved, see Ruth A. Doan, *The Miller Heresy, Millennialism, and American Culture* (Philadelphia: Temple University Press, 1987); and Jonathan Butler, "The Making of a New Order: Millerism and the Origins of Seventh-Day Adventism," in *The Disappointed: Millerism and Millenarianism in the Nineteenth Century,* ed. Ronald Numbers and Jonathan Butler (Bloomington: Indiana University Press, 1987), 189–208.

35. See J. N. Darby, *The Collected Writings of J. N. Darby,* 35 vols., ed. William Kelly, Doctrinal No. 1 (reprint, Sunbury, PA: Believers Bookshelf, 1971), 3:1–43; Sandeen, *Roots of Fundamentalism,* 59–80; citation on 67.

36. C. I. Scofield, *Rightly Dividing the Word of Truth* (Westwood, NJ: Revell, 1896), 3; for Darby's discussion of the pretribulation rapture, see J. N. Darby, *The Collected Writings of J. N. Darby,* Prophetic No. 4 (reprint, Winschoten, The Netherlands: H. L. Heijkoop, 1971), 11:110–67. For a classic exposition of this eschatology, see Nathaniel West, *The Thousand Year Reign of Christ* (1899; reprint, Grand Rapids: Kregel Publications, 1993).

37. J. N. Darby, *The Collected Writings of J. N. Darby,* Prophetic No. 1 (reprint, Winschoten, The Netherlands: H. L. Heijkoop, 1971), 2:278–383. For discussions of the counting of the seventy weeks, see Weber, *Living in the Shadow of the Second Coming,* 18–19, 247–48; and idem, "Premillennialism and the Branches of Evangelicalism," in *The Variety of American Evangelicalism,* ed. Donald W. Dayton and Robert K. Johnston (Downers Grove, IL: InterVarsity Press, 1991), 9–11. For the most popular early formulation of dispensational theology, see William E. Blackstone, *Jesus Is Coming* (New York: Revell, 1908). See also James H. Brookes, *Israel and the Church* (St. Louis: Gospel Book and Tract Depository, n.d.); Samuel H. Kellogg, "Is the Advent Pre-Millennial?" *Presbyterian Review* 3 (1882), 475–502; idem, "Premillennialism: Its Relation to Doctrine and Practice," *Bibliotheca Sacra* 45 (1888), 234–74. On the postponement theory, see C. H. Mackintosh, *Papers on the Lord's Coming* (Chicago: Bible Institute Colportage Association, n.d.), 101–2.

38. For later elaborations of dispensational theology, see Lewis Sperry Chafer, *Dispensationalism* (Dallas: Dallas Theological Seminary Press, 1936); Henry C. Thiessen, *Introductory Lectures in Systematic Theology* (Grand Rapids: Wm. B.

Eerdmans Publishing Co., 1949); John Walvoord, *The Rapture Question* (Grand Rapids: Zondervan Publishing House, 1979). One of the best-selling books of all time is a dispensationalist primer, Hal Lindsey's *The Late Great Planet Earth* (New York: Bantam Books, 1973).

39. The number 1,000 represents absolute perfection and completeness in biblical symbolism, Warfield observed: "When the saints are said to live and reign with Christ a thousand years the idea intended is that of inconceivable exaltation, security and blessedness—a completeness of exaltation, security and blessedness beyond expression by ordinary language" (Benjamin B. Warfield, *Biblical Doctrines* [Edinburgh: Banner of Truth Trust, 1988], 643–64; quote on 655). On Holiness movements, see Warfield, *Studies in Perfectionism,* esp. 3–215, 216–311, 400–454; idem, *Counterfeit Miracles* (New York: Charles Scribner's Sons, 1918).

40. Warfield, review of *What the Bible Teaches,* 562.

41. Warfield, review of *He That Is Spiritual,* 327; *Biblical Doctrines,* 645–53. See Mark A. Noll, "B. B. Warfield," in *Handbook of Evangelical Theologians,* ed. Walter A. Elwell (Grand Rapids: Baker Book House, 1993), 32–33; Lewis Sperry Chafer, *Systematic Theology,* 8 vols. (Dallas: Dallas Theological Seminary Press, 1947–1948).

42. Hodge, *Systematic Theology,* 2:12–41; see Henry H. Beach, "The Decadence of Darwinism," and George Frederick Wright, "The Passing of Evolution," in Torrey et al., *The Fundamentals,* 4:59–71, 72–87.

43. See Warfield, *Studies in Theology,* 235–58; J. Gresham Machen, *The Christian View of Man* (London: Banner of Truth Trust, 1965), 114–20.

44. Machen's letters quoted in Ned B. Stonehouse, *J. Gresham Machen,* 106–7; and D. G. Hart, *Defending the Faith: J. Gresham Machen and the Crisis of Conservative Protestantism in Modern America* (Grand Rapids: Baker Book House, 1995), 19–27.

45. See Wilhelm Herrmann, *The Communion of the Christian with God: Described on the Basis of Luther's Statements,* trans. J. Sandys Stanyon and R. W. Stewart (4th German ed. 1903; reprint, Philadelphia: Fortress Press, 1971).

46. See Gresham Machen, "Christianity in Conflict," in *Contemporary American Theology: Theological Autobiographies,* ed. Vergilius Ferm (New York: Round Table Press, 1932), 252–64. For an interpretation that emphasizes Machen had doubts about Princeton orthodoxy before he went to Germany, see Hart, *Defending the Faith,* 22–26. For interpretations that portray his year in Germany as traumatizing and determinative, see George M. Marsden, "J. Gresham Machen, History, and Truth," *Westminster Theological Journal* 42 (1979), 167–68; and Bradley James Longfield, *The Presbyterian Controversy: Fundamentalists, Modernists and Moderates* (New York: Oxford University Press, 1991), 41–49. On the crisis of Christianity in modern higher education, see J. Gresham Machen, *What Is Christianity? and Other Addresses* (Grand Rapids: Wm. B. Eerdmans Publishing Co., 1951), 118–25.

47. Machen's letters on the war quoted in Hart, *Defending the Faith,* 45–46; and Stonehouse, *J. Gresham Machen,* 248. See J. Gresham Machen, "The Church in the War," in *What Is Christianity? and Other Addresses,* 213–16.

48. See Gary Dorrien, *Soul in Society: The Making and Renewal of Social Christianity* (Minneapolis: Fortress Press, 1995), 48–59; Marsden, *Fundamentalism and American Culture,* 141–53.

49. Machen quote in Stonehouse, *J. Gresham Machen,* 337. On Machen's cultural modernism, see D. G. Hart, "When Is a Fundamentalist a Modernist? J. Gresham Machen, "Cultural Modernism, and Conservative Protestantism," *Journal of the American Academy of Religion* 65 (fall 1997), 605–33.
50. Stonehouse, *J. Gresham Machen,* 310.
51. J. Gresham Machen, *The Origin of Paul's Religion* (Grand Rapids: Wm. B. Eerdmans Publishing Co., 1921).
52. Harry Emerson Fosdick, *The Living of These Days: An Autobiography* (New York: Harper & Brothers, 1956), 145; idem, "Shall the Fundamentalists Win?" reprinted in *American Protestant Thought: The Liberal Era,* ed. William R. Hutchison (New York: Harper & Row, 1968), 170–81.
53. Quoted in Stonehouse, *J. Gresham Machen,* 230–31.
54. J. Gresham Machen, *Christianity and Liberalism* (1923; reprint, Grand Rapids: Wm. B. Eerdmans Publishing Co., 1992), 119–20. The citation was from Fosdick's sermon, "Shall the Fundamentalists Win?"
55. Machen, *Christianity and Liberalism,* 120.
56. Ibid., 70.
57. Ibid., 74.
58. Ibid., 79.
59. Quoted in Hart, *Defending the Faith,* 122.
60. See Longfield, *Presbyterian Controversy;* Hart, *Defending the Faith,* 133–59; Lefferts A. Loetscher, *The Broadening Church: A Study of Theological Issues in the Presbyterian Church since 1869* (Philadelphia: University of Pennsylvania Press, 1954), 150–52.
61. On the schismatic legacy of Westminster Theological Seminary, see Harold J. Ockenga, "From Fundamentalism, through New Evangelicalism, to Evangelicalism," in *Evangelical Roots,* ed. Kenneth Kantzer (New York: Thomas Nelson, 1978), 35–46. Machen's "very serious heresy" quote in Mark A. Noll and Cassandra Niemczyk, "Evangelicals and the Self-Consciously Reformed," in Dayton and Johnston, eds., *Variety of American Evangelicalism,* 209.
62. For a helpful survey of fundamentalist evangelical literature produced by theologians in the mainline and traditionalist churches, see Roger Nicole, "Theology," in *Contemporary Evangelical Thought,* ed. Carl F. H. Henry (New York: Harper & Brothers, 1957), 85–101; for a more detailed narrative review of American evangelical biblical scholarship, see Mark A. Noll, *Between Faith and Criticism: Evangelicals, Scholarship, and the Bible in America* (Grand Rapids: Baker Book House, 1991).
63. See Gordon H. Clark, *God's Hammer: The Bible and Its Critics,* 2d rev. ed. (Jefferson, MD: Trinity Foundation, 1987); idem, "Special Divine Revelation as Rational," in *Revelation and the Bible,* ed. Carl F. H. Henry (Grand Rapids: Baker Book House, 1958), 25–42; Francis A. Schaeffer, *The Complete Works of Francis A. Schaeffer,* 5 vols. (Westchester, IL: Crossway Publications, 1982).
64. E. J. Young, *Thy Word Is Truth: Some Thoughts on the Biblical Doctrine of Inspiration* (1957; reprint, Edinburgh: Banner of Truth Trust, 1991), 48–49.
65. See Norman L. Geisler, ed., *Inerrancy* (Grand Rapids: Zondervan Publishing House, 1980); James Boice, ed., *The Foundation of Biblical Authority* (Grand Rapids: Zondervan Publishing House, 1979).
66. Harold Lindsell, *The Battle for the Bible* (Grand Rapids: Zondervan Publishing

House, 1976), 25. See idem, *The Bible in the Balance* (Grand Rapids: Zondervan Publishing House, 1979).

67. Lindsell, *Battle for the Bible,* 18–19.

68. James Orr, *The Christian View of God and the World* (1983; reprint, Grand Rapids: Kregel Publications, 1989), 9.

69. See Immanuel Kant, *Critique of Pure Reason* (1787), trans. Norman Kemp Smith (London: Macmillan Press, 1973); idem, *Religion within the Limits of Reason Alone* (1793), trans. Theodore M. Greene and Hoyt H. Hudson (Chicago: Open Court Publishing Co., 1934); Allen W. Wood, *Kant's Moral Religion* (Ithaca, NY: Cornell University Press, 1970).

70. Albrecht Ritschl, *The Christian Doctrine of Justification and Reconciliation,* ed. H. R. Mackintosh and A. B. Macaulay (Edinburgh: T. & T. Clark, 1902), 205. See idem, "Theology and Metaphysics," reprinted in idem, *Three Essays,* trans. and ed. Philip Hefner (Philadelphia: Fortress Press, 1972), 149–218.

71. See Gary Dorrien, *The Word as True Myth: Interpreting Modern Theology* (Louisville, Ky.: Westminster John Knox Press, 1997), 45–53.

72. James Orr, *Ritschlianism: Expository and Critical Essays* (London: Hodder & Stoughton, 1903), 16. See idem, *The Ritschlian Theology and the Evangelical Faith* (London: Hodder & Stoughton, 1897).

73. Orr, *Christian View of God and the World,* 30.

74. See James Orr, "The Holy Scriptures and Modern Negations," and "The Early Narratives of Genesis," in Torrey et al., eds., *The Fundamentals,* 1:94–110, 228–40; idem, "The Virgin Birth of Christ," in Torrey et al., eds., *The Fundamentals,* 2:247–60.

75. See James Orr, *The Problem of the Old Testament: Considered with Reference to Recent Criticism* (New York: Charles Scribner's Sons, 1911); idem, "Early Narratives of Genesis," 230–37.

76. James Orr, *The Faith of a Modern Christian* (London: Hodder & Stoughton, 1910), 7.

77. James Orr, *Revelation and Inspiration* (New York: Charles Scribner's Sons, 1910), 217–18; see idem, "Revelation and Inspiration," *Thinker* 6 (1894), 42–43.

78. Orr, *Revelation and Inspiration,* 197–214.

79. Hodge and Warfield, "Inspiration" (Warfield's section), 245; see Hodge, *Outlines of Theology,* 75–76.

80. Curtis Lee Laws, "The Old and New Theologies," *Watchman-Examiner* (February 1, 1917), 133–34. See Norman H. Maring, "Baptists and Changing Views of the Bible, 1865–1918," *Foundations* 1 (October 1958), 39, 55; idem, "Conservative but Progressive," in *What God Hath Wrought,* ed. Gilbert L. Guffin (Philadelphia: Judson Press, 1960), 16–17; Grant Wacker, *Augustus H. Strong and the Dilemma of Historical Consciousness* (Macon, GA: Mercer University Press, 1985), 142–47.

81. Denney quoted in A. B. Bruce, *Inspiration and Inerrancy* (London: James Clarke, 1891), 4.

82. Orr, *Revelation and Inspiration,* 197–98.

83. See John H. Leith, *Assembly at Westminster* (Richmond: John Knox Press, 1973); Jack Bartlett Rogers, *Scripture in the Westminster Confession* (Grand Rapids: Wm. B. Eerdmans Publishing Co., 1967).

84. On the early years of Fuller Theological Seminary, see Daniel P. Fuller, *Give the Winds a Mighty Voice: The Story of Charles E. Fuller* (Waco, TX: Word Books,

1972), 189–227; George M. Marsden, *Reforming Fundamentalism: Fuller Seminary and the New Evangelicalism* (Grand Rapids: Wm. B. Eerdmans Publishing Co., 1987), 13–82; Rudolph Nelson, *The Making and Unmaking of an Evangelical Mind: The Case of Edward Carnell* (Cambridge: Cambridge University Press, 1987),–73–106; Lindsell, *Battle for the Bible,* 106–16.

CHAPTER 2. "NEEDING PRESTIGE DESPERATELY": FUNDAMENTALISM REFORMED

1. See J. Elwin Wright, *The Old Fashioned Revival Hour and the Broadcasters* (Boston: Fellowship Press, 1940); Everett C. Parker, David W. Barry, and Dallas W. Smythe, *The Television-Radio Audience and Religion* (New York: Harper & Row, 1955); Quentin Schultze, "Evangelical Radio and the Rise of the Electronic Church, 1921–1948," *Journal of Broadcasting and Electronic Media* 32 (summer 1988), 295–99.

2. See Daniel P. Fuller, *Give the Winds a Mighty Voice: The Story of Charles E. Fuller* (Waco, TX: Word Books, 1972); Wilbur M. Smith, *A Voice for God: The Life of Charles E. Fuller, Originator of the Old Fashioned Revival Hour* (Boston: W. A. Wilde, 1949); Joel A. Carpenter, *Revive Us Again: The Reawakening of American Fundamentalism* (New York: Oxford University Press, 1997), 135–39.

3. Quoted in Fuller, *Give the Winds a Mighty Voice,* 108–9.

4. Ibid., 189, 197.

5. See Harold Lindsell, *Park Street Prophet: A Life of Harold John Ockenga* (Wheaton, IL: Van Kampen Press, 1951), 127–32; George M. Marsden, *Reforming Fundamentalism: Fuller Seminary and the New Evangelicalism* (Grand Rapids: Wm. B. Eerdmans Publishing Co., 1987), 16–17.

6. Fuller, *Give the Winds a Mighty Voice,* 198.

7. Ibid.; Harold J. Ockenga, foreword to Harold Lindsell, *The Battle for the Bible* (Grand Rapids: Zondervan Publishing House, 1976), 10. See Carpenter, *Revive Us Again,* 193–94; "An Evangelical Manifesto, Issued by the Plymouth Conference for the Advancement of Evangelical Scholarship, Plymouth, Mass., August 18," *United Evangelical Action* (September 15, 1945), 4.

8. See Wilbur Smith, *Before I Forget* (Chicago: Moody Press, 1971), 65–88; George Marsden, "Perspectives on the Division of 1937," in *Pressing toward the Mark: Essays Commemorating Fifty Years of the Orthodox Presbyterian Church,* ed. Charles G. Dennison and Richard C. Gamble (Philadelphia: Orthodox Presbyterian Church, 1986), 295–328; Marsden, *Reforming Fundamentalism,* 25–26, 36; Carpenter, *Revive Us Again,* 196–97.

9. See Wilbur Smith, *The Atomic Age and the Word of God* (Boston: W. A. Wilde, 1948); idem, *World Crises and the Prophetic Scriptures* (Chicago: Moody Press, 1951).

10. See Marsden, *Reforming Fundamentalism,* 72.

11. Wilbur Smith, *Therefore Stand: A Plea for a Vigorous Apologetic in the Present Crisis of Evangelical Christianity* (Chicago: Moody Press, 1945), 502–6; see idem, "The Urgent Need for a New Evangelical Literature," *United Evangelical Action* (June 15, 1946), 3–5.

12. Harold John Ockenga, "Can Fundamentalism Win America?" *Christian Life* (June 1947), 13–15.

13. Carl F. H. Henry, *The Uneasy Conscience of Modern Fundamentalism* (Grand Rapids: Wm. B. Eerdmans Publishing Co., 1947), 18–19, 29–30.

14. Ibid., 29–34, 52–57; closing quote on 54.

15. Harold John Ockenga, introduction to Henry, *Uneasy Conscience of Modern Fundamentalism,* 13.

16. Carl F. H. Henry, *Remaking the Modern Mind* (Grand Rapids: Wm. B. Eerdmans Publishing Co., 1946).

17. Carl F. H. Henry, *Confessions of a Theologian: An Autobiography* (Waco, TX: Word Books, 1986), 114–15; Carl F. H. Henry and Kenneth Kantzer, "Standing on the Promises," *Christianity Today* 40 (September 16, 1996), 29–31.

18. Marsden, *Reforming Fundamentalism,* 34; Machen quote in Lindsell, *Park Street Prophet,* 35.

19. See Edwin H. Rian, *The Presbyterian Conflict* (Grand Rapids: Wm. B. Eerdmans Publishing Co., 1940), 97–99; Marsden, "Perspectives on the Division of 1937," 295–328; Carpenter, *Revive Us Again,* 189.

20. Harold J. Ockenga, "The Challenge to the Christian Culture of the West" (convocation address, Fuller Theological Seminary, Pasadena, California, October 1, 1947), quoted in Carpenter, *Revive Us Again,* 195; closing quote in Ockenga, foreword to Lindsell, *Battle for the Bible,* 10–11.

21. See Henry, *Confessions of a Theologian,* 279–87.

22. Ockenga, foreword to Lindsell, *Battle for the Bible,* 11.

23. See Harold Lindsell, "The Bible and Race Relations," *Eternity* (August 1956), 43–44; Edward J. Carnell, "A Christian Social Ethics," *Opinion* (November 1962), 1–2; Marsden, *Reforming Fundamentalism,* 252–55.

24. Quoted in Rudolph Nelson, *The Making and Unmaking of an Evangelical Mind: The Case of Edward Carnell* (Cambridge: Cambridge University Press, 1987), 70.

25. See Henry, *Confessions of a Theologian,* 60–76.

26. Edward John Carnell, "Post-Fundamentalist Faith," *Christian Century* 76, (August 26, 1959), 971.

27. See Carl F. H. Henry, "A Wide and Deep Swath," in *The Philosophy of Gordon H. Clark: A Festschrift,* ed. Ronald N. Nash (Philadelphia: Presbyterian and Reformed Publishing Co., 1968), 16; idem, *Confessions of a Theologian,* 67–71; Nelson, *Making and Unmaking of an Evangelical Mind,* 36–37.

28. See Paul M. Bechtel, *Wheaton College: A Heritage Remembered, 1860–1984* (Wheaton, IL: Harold Shaw, 1984), 144–53, 207–9; Henry, *Confessions of a Theologian,* 64–68.

29. See Gordon H. Clark, *Religion, Reason and Revelation* (Nutley, NJ: Craig Press, 1961), 108–10; idem, "Special Divine Revelation as Rational," in *Revelation and the Bible: Contemporary Evangelical Thought,* ed. Carl F. H. Henry (Grand Rapids: Baker Book House, 1958), 27–41; idem, "Apologetics," in *Contemporary Evangelical Thought,* ed. Carl F. H. Henry (New York: Harper & Brothers, 1957), 137–61.

30. Gordon H. Clark, "The Nature of the Physical Universe," in *Christian Faith and Modern Theology: Contemporary Evangelical Thought,* ed. Carl F. H. Henry (New York: Channel Press, 1964), 143.

31. Nelson, *Making and Unmaking of an Evangelical Mind,* 39–40.

32. Ibid., 46.

33. The only professor of theology at Harvard during Carnell's period was Johannes

Abraham Cristoffel Fagginger Auer, a religious humanist and Parkman professor, who agreed in 1942 to direct the Divinity School's graduate program in theology in the absence of a theologian on the faculty.

34. See Edward John Carnell, "The Concept of Dialectic in the Theology of Reinhold Niebuhr" (Th.D. diss., Harvard Divinity School, 1948); rev. ed. published in idem, *The Theology of Reinhold Niebuhr* (ca. 1950; reprint, Grand Rapids: Wm. B. Eerdmans Publishing Co., 1960); and idem, "The Problem of Verification in Søren Kierkegaard" (Ph.D. diss. Boston University, 1948). Near the end of his life, Carnell published a substantially toned-down edition of this work as *The Burden of Søren Kierkegaard* (Grand Rapids: Wm. B. Eerdmans Publishing Co., 1965). The later version emphasized Kierkegaard's psychological insight and was dedicated to Carnell's psychiatrist.

35. Henry, *Confessions of a Theologian,* 121–22.

36. Carnell, "Concept of Dialectic," 417.

37. Edward John Carnell, preface to the 4th ed., *An Introduction to Christian Apologetics: A Philosophic Defense of the Trinitarian-Theistic Faith* (Grand Rapids: Wm. B. Eerdmans Publishing Co., 1952), 7.

38. Ibid., 7–8.

39. Ibid., 82.

40. J. Gresham Machen, *What Is Faith?* (New York: Macmillan Co., 1925), 94. For a generally discerning interpretation of Carnell's apologetic that nonetheless fails to capture the dialectical quality of his understanding of the relation between faith and knowledge, see Gordon R. Lewis, *Testing Christianity's Truth Claims* (Lanham, MD: University Press of America, 1990).

41. Carnell, *Introduction to Christian Apologetics,* 113.

42. James Orr, *The Christian View of God and the World* (1887; reprint, Grand Rapids: Kregel Publications, 1989), 20.

43. Carnell, *Introduction to Christian Apologetics,* 119.

44. Ibid., 117.

45. Thomas Aquinas, *Summa Theologica* 1, q. 12: "How God Is Known By Us," in *Basic Writings of Saint Thomas Aquinas,* ed. Anton C. Pegis (New York: Random House, 1944), 91–111. See Brian Davies, *The Thought of Thomas Aquinas* (Oxford: Clarendon Press, 1993), 21–39.

46. Carnell, *Introduction to Christian Apologetics,* 150.

47. See Gordon H. Clark, *A Christian Philosophy of Education* (Grand Rapids: Wm. B. Eerdmans Publishing Co., 1946), 177.

48. Carnell, *Introduction to Christian Apologetics,* 150.

49. Ibid., 158–59.

50. Benjamin B. Warfield, *Studies in Tertullian and Augustine* (Grand Rapids: Baker Book House, 1930), 138–39.

51. Anselm, *Basic Writings: Proslogium,* trans. S. N. Deane (LaSalle, IL: Open Court Publishing Co., 1962), 47–80. See John H. Hick and Arthur C. McGill, eds., *The Many-Faced Argument: Recent Studies on the Ontological Argument for the Existence of God* (New York: Macmillan Co., 1967).

52. Carnell, *Introduction to Christian Apologetics,* 159.

53. John Calvin, *Institutes of the Christian Religion,* trans. Ford Lewis Battles, ed. John T. McNeil (Philadelphia: Westminster Press, 1960), 1.1.3, 38–39.

54. Carnell, *Introduction to Christian Apologetics,* 174.

55. Ibid., 175.

56. Ibid.
57. Ibid., 196.
58. Ibid., 198–99.
59. Ibid., 203.
60. Charles Hodge, *Systematic Theology,* 3 vols. (1872; reprint, Grand Rapids: Wm. B. Eerdmans Publishing Co., 1993), 1:1.
61. Carnell, *Introduction to Christian Apologetics,* 208.
62. Ibid., 238–42.
63. Ibid., 354–55.
64. See Rudolph Nelson, "Fundamentalism at Harvard: The Case of Edward John Carnell," *Quarterly Review: A Scholarly Journal for Reflection on Ministry* (summer 1982), 79–98; idem, *Making and Unmaking of an Evangelical Mind,* 55–56.
65. William Hordern, *A Layman's Guide to Protestant Theology* (New York: Macmillan Co., 1960), 67; Roger Shinn, review of *Christian Commitment,* by Edward John Carnell, *Theology Today* 15 (July 1958), 278. See John Murray, *The Collected Writings of John Murray,* 4 vols. (Edinburgh: Banner of Truth Trust, 1976–1983).
66. See Gordon H. Clark, "The Answer to a Complaint against Several Actions and Decisions of the Presbytery of Philadelphia Taken in a Special Meeting Held on July 7, 1944" (unpublished defense paper, Philadelphia Orthodox Presbyterian Church); idem, "The Bible as Truth," *Bibliotheca Sacra* 114 (April 1957), reprinted in idem, *God's Hammer: The Bible and Its Critics* (Jefferson, MD: Trinity Foundation, 1987), 24–38; idem, "Apologetics," 152–61; idem, "Special Divine Revelation as Rational," 29–41.
67. Cornelius Van Til, *Christian Apologetics* (Phillipsburg, NJ: Presbyterian and Reformed Publishing Co., 1976), 6–7; idem, *The Defense of the Faith* (Philadelphia: Presbyterian and Reformed Publishing Co., 1955), 35–41; idem, *Introduction to Systematic Theology* (Nutley, NJ: Presbyterian and Reformed Publishing Co., 1974).
68. For pro–Van Til discussions of his debate with Clark, see Fred H. Klooster, *The Incomprehensibility of God in the Orthodox Presbyterian Conflict* (Franeker: T. Wever, 1951); and John M. Frame, *The Doctrine of the Knowledge of God* (Phillipsburg, NJ: Presbyterian and Reformed Publishing Co., 1987), 21–40. "Proof" quote from "At the Beginning, God: An Interview with Cornelius Van Til," *Christianity Today* (December 30, 1977), 19; closing quote from Van Til, *Defense of the Faith,* 121.
69. Edward John Carnell, *Christian Commitment: An Apologetic* (New York: Macmillan Co., 1957), 40; see Cornelius Van Til, *A Christian Theory of Knowledge* (Nutley, NJ: Presbyterian and Reformed Publishing Co., 1969); idem, *Common Grace and the Gospel* (Nutley, NJ: Presbyterian and Reformed Publishing Co., 1964).
70. "Response by C. Van Til," in *Jerusalem and Athens: Critical Discussions on the Theology and Apologetics of Cornelius Van Til,* ed. E. R. Geehan (Nutley, NJ: Presbyterian and Reformed Publishing Co., 1971), 361–68. Several contributors to Geehan's volume make the same charge against Van Til's approach, notably John Warwick Montgomery and Clark Pinnock. The question of whether Van Til was an absolute or exclusive presuppositionalist has sustained a vigorous debate about his work among critics and different schools of followers. Apologetic evidentialists such as Montgomery and Pinnock tend to read him as an absolute pre-

suppositionalist, though Van Til rarely used the term in a technical sense. One problem that pervades the entire debate is that Van Til was not a clear or especially consistent thinker. His writing style was opaque and jargon-filled, he refused to define key terms, and he made little effort to defend the idealist epistemology that undergirded his apologetic. For many years, much of his work circulated in unpublished form among his students and followers. For a defense of his approach that emphasizes his negative method of apologetics and his belief in general revelation, see John M. Frame, *Cornelius Van Til: An Analysis of His Thought* (Phillipsburg, NJ: Presbyterian and Reformed Publishing Co., 1995).

71. See Clark, "Apologetics," 152–59; idem, *Religion, Reason and Revelation,* 28–110; idem, "Special Divine Revelation as Rational," 39–41.

72. See Edward John Carnell, "Niebuhr's Criteria of Verification," in *Reinhold Niebuhr: His Religious, Social, and Political Thought,* ed. Charles W. Kegley and Robert W. Bretall (New York: Macmillan Co., 1956), 380–90; idem, "Reinhold Niebuhr's View of Scripture," in *Inspiration and Interpretation,* ed. John F. Walvoord (Grand Rapids: Wm. B. Eerdmans Publishing Co., 1957), 239–52; idem, "Karl Barth as Inconsistent Evangelical," *Christian Century* 79 (June 6, 1962), reprinted in idem, *The Case for Biblical Christianity* (Grand Rapids: Wm. B. Eerdmans Publishing Co., 1969), 153–56.

73. Edward J. Carnell, letter to Gordon Clark, January 5, 1953; quoted in Nelson, *Making and Unmaking of an Evangelical Mind,* 153.

74. Edward John Carnell, *A Philosophy of the Christian Religion* (Grand Rapids: Wm. B. Eerdmans Publishing Co., 1954), 26–27.

75. Ibid., 38.

76. Ibid., 184.

77. Carnell, letters to Clark, January 5, 1953, and February 23, 1953; quoted in Nelson, *Making and Unmaking of an Evangelical Mind,* 153.

78. Carnell, *Philosophy of the Christian Religion,* 494.

79. Ibid., 494–95.

80. Søren Kierkegaard, *Concluding Unscientific Postscript,* trans. David F. Swenson (Princeton, NJ: Princeton University Press, 1941), 528; see idem, *Philosophical Fragments: or, A Fragment of Philosophy,* trans. David F. Swenson and Howard V. Hong (Princeton, NJ: Princeton University Press, 1962), 46–60.

81. Kierkegaard, *Concluding Unscientific Postscript,* 30.

82. Søren Kierkegaard, *Works of Love,* trans. David F. Swenson and Lillian Marvin Swenson (Princeton, NJ: Princeton University Press, 1946), 162–63; see idem, *Attack upon "Christendom,"* trans. David F. Swenson (Princeton, NJ: Princeton University Press, 1944).

83. Søren Kierkegaard, *For Self-Examination and Judge for Yourselves!* trans. Walter Lowrie (New York: Oxford University Press, 1941), 88.

84. Carnell, *Philosophy of the Christian Religion,* 485, 489.

85. Ibid., 506.

86. Quoted in Nelson, *Making and Unmaking of an Evangelical Mind,* 87.

87. Ibid., 88.

88. Ibid., 89.

89. See Henry, *Confessions of a Theologian,* 139–40; Marsden, *Reforming Fundamentalism,* 142–43.

90. Quoted in Nelson, *Making and Unmaking of an Evangelical Mind,* 91.

91. See Edward J. Carnell, "The Glory of a Theological Seminary" (inaugural presidential speech, May 17, 1955; Fuller Theological Seminary Alumni Association, Pasadena, California).

92. Woodbridge told Ockenga that he was offended by Carnell's "sweet, forgiving *appeasement* toward heretics" and demanded that he either retract his inaugural speech or resign from the presidency. See Marsden, *Reforming Fundamentalism,* 148–49; Hubbard quoted in Nelson, *Making and Unmaking of an Evangelical Mind,* 96. For Woodbridge's account, see Charles Woodbridge, "Reaping the Whirlwind," *Christian Beacon* (May 5, 1977), 7.

93. Fuller Seminary creedal statement quoted in Marsden, *Reforming Fundamentalism,* 150. See David Hubbard, "The Strange Case of Fuller Seminary," *Theology News and Notes,* special issue (1976), 9.

94. George E. Ladd, *The Blessed Hope* (Grand Rapids: Wm. B. Eerdmans Publishing Co., 1956), 140–55; see idem, *A Theology of the New Testament* (1974; reprint, Grand Rapids: Wm. B. Eerdmans Publishing Co., 1994), 610–11; Robert A. Guelich, ed., *Unity and Diversity in New Testament Theology: Essays in Honor of George E. Ladd* (Grand Rapids: Wm. B. Eerdmans Publishing Co., 1978).

95. Quoted in Henry, *Confessions of a Theologian,* 137.

96. Carnell, *Christian Commitment,* 2–3.

97. Ibid., 14–16.

98. Ibid., 10–12.

99. Ibid., 12.

100. See Friedrich Schleiermacher, *On Religion: Addresses in Response to Its Cultured Critics,* trans. Terrence N. Tice (Richmond: John Knox Press, 1969), 114–28; idem, *The Christian Faith,* ed. H. R. Mackintosh and J. S. Stewart (1928; reprint, Edinburgh: T. & T. Clark, 1968), 12–18.

101. Carnell, *Christian Commitment,* 13.

102. Ibid., 20–21.

103. See Immanuel Kant, *Critique of Practical Reason,* trans. Lewis White Beck (Indianapolis: Bobbs-Merrill Co., 1956), 128–36; idem, *Lectures on Philosophical Theology,* trans. Allen W. Wood and Gertrude M. Clark (Ithaca, NY: Cornell University Press, 1978), 109–31; Allen W. Wood, *Kant's Moral Religion* (Ithaca, NY: Cornell University Press, 1970).

104. Carnell, *Christian Commitment,* 121.

105. Ibid., ix, 109.

106. See Anselm, *Basic Writings: Proslogium,* 54–55; *Monologium,* 81–85.

107. Carnell, *Christian Commitment,* 130–31.

108. Ibid., 249–83.

109. Ibid., 286.

110. Edward John Carnell, "Fundamentalism," in *A Handbook of Christian Theology,* ed. Marvin Halverson and Arthur A. Cohen (Cleveland: World Publishing Co., 1958), 142–43.

111. Quoted in Nelson, *Making and Unmaking of an Evangelical Mind,* 105; see Marsden, *Reforming Fundamentalism,* 177–80.

112. Nelson, *Making and Unmaking of an Evangelical Mind,* 112.

113. Carnell was forced to switch to ethics because Jewett held his former theology position.

114. See William Hordern, *The Case for a New Reformation Theology* (Philadelphia:

Westminster Press, 1959); L. Harold DeWolf, *The Case for Theology in Liberal Perspective* (Philadelphia: Westminster Press, 1959).

115. Edward John Carnell, *The Case for Orthodox Theology* (Philadelphia: Westminster Press, 1959), 13.

116. Abraham Kuyper taught that "by faith you are sure of all those things of which you have a *firm conviction,* but which conviction is *not* the outcome of observation or demonstration" (*Principles of Sacred Theology,* trans. J. Hendrik De Vries [1898; reprint, Grand Rapids: Wm. B. Eerdmans Publishing Co., 1954], 131).

117. Carnell, *Case for Orthodox Theology,* 33–34.

118. Ibid., 93–95.

119. James Orr, *The Bible under Trial* (London: Marshall Brothers, 1907), 9–10; see idem, *The Problem of the Old Testament* (New York: Charles Scribner's Sons, 1911), 4–10.

120. Benjamin B. Warfield, "Professor Henry Preserved Smith on Inspiration," *Presbyterian and Reformed Review* 5 (1894), 652–53; see idem, *The Inspiration and Authority of the Bible* (1948; reprint, Philadelphia: Presbyterian and Reformed Publishing Co., 1964), 419–42.

121. Carnell, *Case for Orthodox Theology,* 98.

122. Henry Preserved Smith, *Inspiration and Inerrancy: A History and a Defense* (London: Robert Clarke & Co., 1893), 120–35, 265–70; Warfield, *Inspiration and Authority of the Bible,* 420.

123. Quoted in Carnell, *Case for Orthodox Theology,* 102.

124. Warfield, *Inspiration and Authority of the Bible,* 226.

125. Warfield, "Professor Henry Preserved Smith on Inspiration," 646.

126. Carnell, *Case for Orthodox Theology,* 106.

127. Ibid., 58, 106. On the hermeneutical primacy of Romans and Galatians, see Edward John Carnell, "Orthodoxy: Cultic vs. Classical," *Christian Century* 77 (March 30, 1960), reprinted in Edward J. Carnell, *The Case for Biblical Christianity,* ed. Ronald N. Nash (Grand Rapids: Wm. B. Eerdmans Publishing Co., 1969), 40–45.

128. Benjamin B. Warfield, "Reviews of Recent Theological Literature," *Presbyterian and Reformed Review* 4 (1893), 499; see idem, *Inspiration and Authority of the Bible,* 99–348.

129. See James Orr, *The Faith of a Modern Christian* (London: Hodder & Stoughton, 1910), 7–17; idem, *Revelation and Inspiration* (New York: Charles Scribner's Sons, 1910), 197–218.

130. Orr, *Revelation and Inspiration,* 163–65.

131. Ibid., 165.

132. Carnell, *Case for Orthodox Theology,* 110.

133. Ibid., 111.

134. Ibid., 114.

135. Ibid., 114–20.

136. Ibid., pp. 115–16.

137. Carnell, "Post-Fundamentalist Faith," 971; reprinted in Carnell, *Case for Biblical Christianity,* 45–47.

138. Ibid.; idem, "Orthodoxy: Cultic vs. Classical," 41–42. For his subsequent reflections on the law of love, see Edward John Carnell, *The Kingdom of Love and the Pride of Life* (Grand Rapids: Wm. B. Eerdmans Publishing Co., 1960).

139. Rice quoted in Nelson, *Making and Unmaking of an Evangelical Mind,* 109. For other negative reviews of Carnell from the evangelical right, see Cornelius Van

Til, *The Case for Calvinism* (Grand Rapids: Baker Book House, 1964), 61–105; Charles J. Woodbridge, *The New Evangelicalism* (Greenville, SC: Bob Jones University Press, 1969), 7–33.

140. Carnell, *Case for Orthodox Theology,* 14; Ockenga quoted in Nelson, *Making and Unmaking of an Evangelical Mind,* 111–12.

141. Carnell, "Orthodoxy: Cultic vs. Classical," 42.

142. See Marsden, *Reforming Fundamentalism,* 195, 207–8; Harold Lindsell, letter to the editor, *Christianity Today* 6 (June 8, 1962), 19–20.

143. See Gleason L. Archer, "Alleged Errors and Discrepancies in the Original Manuscripts of the Bible," in *Inerrancy,* ed. Norman L. Geisler (Grand Rapids: Zondervan Publishing House, 1980), 57–82; idem, *Encyclopedia of Bible Difficulties* (Grand Rapids: Zondervan Publishing House, 1982); idem, *A Survey of Old Testament Introduction* (Chicago: Moody Press, 1964).

144. Everett F. Harrison, "The Phenomena of Scripture," in Henry, ed., *Revelation and the Bible,* 249.

145. See Marsden, *Reforming Fundamentalism,* 213; Lindsell, *Battle for the Bible,* 108–11.

146. Marsden, *Reforming Fundamentalism,* 211.

147. See Daniel Fuller, "Benjamin B. Warfield's View of Faith and History: A Critique in the Light of the New Testament," *Journal of the Evangelical Theological Society* 2 (spring 1968), 75–83; idem, "The Resurrection of Jesus and the Historical Method," *Journal of Bible and Religion* 34 (January 1966), 18–24; idem, *Easter Faith and History* (Grand Rapids: Wm. B. Eerdmans Publishing Co., 1965).

148. Quoted in Marsden, *Reforming Fundamentalism,* 212.

149. Nelson, *Making and Unmaking of an Evangelical Mind,* 190; Marsden, *Reforming Fundamentalism,* 212.

150. See Gordon H. Clark, "Special Report: Encountering Barth in Chicago," *Christianity Today* 6 (May 11, 1962), 35–36.

151. See Nelson, *Making and Unmaking of an Evangelical Mind,* 112, 187–89.

152. See Carnell, "Karl Barth as Inconsistent Evangelical," 154–56.

153. Edward John Carnell, "The Penny or the Cake," *Christianity Today* 7 (October 14, 1966), 23.

154. On Hubbard's early presidency, see Marsden, *Reforming Fundamentalism,* 215–33.

155. Hubbard quoted in Lindsell, *Battle for the Bible,* 115.

156. Quoted in Nelson, *Making and Unmaking of an Evangelical Mind,* 190.

157. Quoted in Henry, *Confessions of a Theologian,* 137.

CHAPTER 3.
THE EVANGELICAL CROSSROADS: RETHINKING INFALLIBILITY

1. Carl F. H. Henry, *Evangelicals at the Brink of Crisis* (Waco, TX: Word Books, 1967); idem, *Evangelicals in Search of Identity* (Waco, TX: Word Books, 1976), 96.

2. See Carl F. H. Henry, *Christian Countermoves in a Decadent Culture* (Portland, OR: Multnomah Press, 1986); idem, *The Christian Mindset in a Secular Society: Promoting Evangelical Renewal and National Righteousness* (Portland, OR: Multnomah Press, 1984).

3. Carl F. H. Henry, *Confessions of a Theologian: An Autobiography* (Waco, TX: Word Books, 1986), 141–43. For a similar assessment of the state of mainline Protestantism, from an insider, see Charles Clayton Morrison, *Can Protestantism Win America?* (New York: Harper & Brothers, 1948), 1–16.

4. Unsigned editorial, "*Why Christianity Today?*" *Christianity Today* 1 (October 15, 1956), 1.

5. See Henry, *Confessions of a Theologian,* 182–84.

6. Ibid., 276, 281.

7. Ibid., 402; see idem, *Christian Mindset in a Secular Society,* 9–25.

8. Carl F. H. Henry, *Frontiers in Modern Theology: A Critique of Current Theological Trends* (Chicago: Moody Press, 1964), 12–13.

9. Ibid., 24.

10. Ibid., 40.

11. Ibid., 103.

12. Ibid., 154–55.

13. Carl F. H. Henry, *God, Revelation and Authority,* vol. 1: *God Who Speaks and Shows* (Waco, TX: Word Books, 1976), 10.

14. Ibid., 95.

15. Ibid., 215.

16. Ibid., 222–23.

17. Ibid., 223.

18. See R. C. Sproul, John Gerstner, and Arthur Lindsley, *Classical Apologetics: A Rational Defense of the Christian Faith and a Critique of Presuppositional Apologetics* (Grand Rapids: Zondervan Publishing House, 1984), 183–338; Gordon R. Lewis, *Testing Christianity's Truth Claims: Approaches to Christian Apologetics* (Chicago: Moody Press, 1976), 100–150, 176–209; Ronald H. Nash, *The New Evangelicalism* (Grand Rapids: Zondervan Publishing House, 1963), 131–43.

19. Henry, *God, Revelation and Authority,* 1:226–27.

20. Ibid., 229.

21. Karl Barth, *Church Dogmatics,* vol. 1: *The Doctrine of the Word of God,* part 1, trans. G. T. Thomson (1936; reprint, Edinburgh: T. & T. Clark, 1969), 1–11.

22. Henry, *God, Revelation and Authority,* 1:233.

23. Cornelius Van Til, *The Defense of the Faith* (1955; reprint, Phillipsburg, NJ: Presbyterian and Reformed Publishing Co., 1967), 126.

24. See John Warwick Montgomery, "Once upon an A Priori," in *Jerusalem and Athens: Critical Discussions on the Philosophy and Apologetics of Cornelius Van Til,* ed. E. R. Geehan (1971; reprint, Phillipsburg, NJ: Presbyterian and Reformed Publishing Co., 1980), 380–92; Sproul, Gerstner, and Lindsley, *Classical Apologetics,* 212–40.

25. Clark H. Pinnock, "The Philosophy of Christian Evidences," in Geehan, ed., *Jerusalem and Athens,* 421.

26. John Calvin, *Institutes of the Christian Religion,* trans. Ford Lewis Battles, ed. John T. McNeil (Philadelphia: Westminster Press, 1960), 7.5, 1:80–81.

27. The Westminster Confession of Faith (1647), 6.004, in Office of the General Assembly, *The Constitution of the Presbyterian Church (U.S.A.),* part 1: *Book of Confessions* (Louisville, KY: Office of the General Assembly, Presbyterian Church (U.S.A.), 1991).

28. Abraham Kuyper, *Principles of Sacred Theology,* trans. J. Hendrik De Vries

(1898; reprint, Grand Rapids: Wm. B. Eerdmans Publishing Co., 1968), 365; Herman Bavinck, *Gereformeerde Dogmatiek* (Kampen: Bos, 1895), 1:559; John Murray, "The Attestation of Scripture," in *The Infallible Word: A Symposium,* ed. N. B. Stonehouse and Paul Woolley (Grand Rapids: Wm. B. Eerdmans Publishing Co., 1946), 7–10; E. J. Young, *Thy Word Is Truth: Some Thoughts on the Biblical Doctrine of Inspiration* (1957; reprint, Edinburgh: Banner of Truth Trust, 1991), 31; Gordon Clark et al., *Can I Trust My Bible?* (Chicago: Moody Press, 1963), 28.

29. Clark H. Pinnock, *Biblical Revelation: The Foundation of Christian Theology* (Chicago: Moody Press, 1971), 42.

30. Pinnock, "Philosophy of Christian Evidences," 423–25.

31. Henry, *God, Revelation and Authority,* 1:241.

32. Gordon H. Clark, *Karl Barth's Theological Method* (Philadelphia: Presbyterian and Reformed Publishing Co., 1963), 69; Henry, *God, Revelation and Authority,* 1:240.

33. Henry, *God, Revelation and Authority,* vol. 3: *God Who Speaks and Shows* (Waco, TX: Word Books, 1979), 283.

34. Ibid., 457.

35. Ibid., 430.

36. Gordon H. Clark, *Religion, Reason and Revelation* (Philadelphia: Presbyterian and Reformed Publishing Co., 1961), 87.

37. See Emil Brunner, *Truth as Encounter,* trans. Amandus W. Loos and David Cairns (Philadelphia: Westminster Press, 1964), 18–30.

38. Karl Barth, *Church Dogmatics,* vol. 1: *The Doctrine of the Word of God,* part 2, trans. G. T. Thomson and Harold Knight (Edinburgh: T. & T. Clark, 1956), 499.

39. Henry, *God, Revelation and Authority,* 3:468; Clark, *Karl Barth's Theological Method,* 130.

40. Austin Farrer, *The Glass of Vision* (London: Dacre Press, 1948); idem, *A Rebirth of Images* (London: Dacre Press, 1949), 21; L. S. Thornton, *The Dominion of Christ: The Form of the Servant* (London: Dacre Press, 1952).

41. Henry, *God, Revelation and Authority,* vol. 4: *God Who Speaks and Shows* (Waco, TX: Word Books, 1979), 107.

42. Ibid., 3:468.

43. Clark, *Karl Barth's Theological Method,* 150.

44. Henry, *God, Revelation and Authority,* 3:480.

45. See Daniel P. Fuller, "The Nature of Biblical Inerrancy," *Journal of the American Scientific Affiliation* 24, 2 (June 1972), 47–51; George Eldon Ladd, *The New Testament and Criticism* (Grand Rapids: Wm. B. Eerdmans Publishing Co., 1967); Donald G. Bloesch, *Essentials of Evangelical Theology,* vol. 1: *God, Authority, and Salvation* (San Francisco: Harper & Row, 1978), 64–74; Dewey M. Beegle, *Scripture, Tradition, and Infallibility* (Grand Rapids: Wm. B. Eerdmans Publishing Co., 1973), 264–312.

46. Gleason L. Archer, *A Survey of Old Testament Introduction* (Chicago: Moody Press, 1964), 17; see idem, *An Encyclopedia of Biblical Difficulties* (Grand Rapids: Zondervan Publishing House, 1982).

47. Henry, *God, Revelation and Authority,* 4:192.

48. Pinnock, *Biblical Revelation,* 77–78.

49. Henry, *God, Revelation and Authority,* 4:180.

50. Ibid., 178–81.

51. See George M. Marsden, *The Soul of the American University: From Protestant Establishment to Established Nonbelief* (New York: Oxford University Press, 1994); idem, "The Collapse of American Evangelical Academia," in *Reckoning with the Past: Historical Essays on American Evangelicalism from the Institute for the Study of American Evangelicals,* ed. D. G. Hart (Grand Rapids: Baker Book House, 1995), 221–66.

52. See George M. Marsden, *Reforming Fundamentalism: Fuller Seminary and the New Evangelicalism* (Grand Rapids: Wm. B. Eerdmans Publishing Co., 1987), 214.

53. See Charles Augustus Briggs, *Biblical Study: Its Principles, Methods and History* (New York: Charles Scribner's Sons, 1883); idem, *Whither? A Theological Question for the Times* (New York: Charles Scribner's Sons, 1889); Benjamin B. Warfield, *The Westminster Assembly and Its Work* (New York: Oxford University Press, 1931); Jack B. Rogers and Donald K. McKim, *The Authority and Interpretation of the Bible: An Historical Approach* (San Francisco: Harper & Row, 1979), 348–69.

54. Henry, *God, Revelation and Authority,* 4:178.

55. James Barr, *Fundamentalism* (Philadelphia: Westminster Press, 1978), 40–89.

56. Henry, *God, Revelation and Authority,* 4:362.

57. John W. Haley, *An Examination of the Alleged Discrepancies of the Bible* (1874; reprint, Grand Rapids: Baker Book House, 1958), 284.

58. Harold Lindsell, *The Battle for the Bible* (Grand Rapids: Zondervan Publishing House, 1976), 174–76.

59. Henry, *God, Revelation and Authority,* 4:363.

60. Ibid., 205.

61. See Ronald Youngblood, ed., *Evangelicals and Inerrancy: Selections from the Journal of the Evangelical Theological Society* (Nashville: Thomas Nelson Publishers, 1984).

62. See Francis A. Schaeffer, *The God Who Is There* (Chicago: InterVarsity Press, 1968); idem, *Escape from Reason* (Chicago: InterVarsity Press, 1968); idem, *Genesis in Space and Time* (Downers Grove, IL: InterVarsity Press, 1972); J. I. Packer, "Thirty Years' War: The Doctrine of Holy Scripture," in *Practical Theology and the Ministry of the Church,* ed. H. Conn (Phillipsburg, NJ: Presbyterian and Reformed Publishing Co., 1990), 25–44.

63. Lindsell, *Battle for the Bible,* 210.

64. Henry, *Evangelicals in Search of Identity,* 67; J. I. Packer, *The Evangelical Anglican Identity Problem,* Latimer Study No. 1 (Oxford: Latimer House, 1978), 4–5; idem, *God Has Spoken* (1965; rev. ed., Grand Rapids: Baker Book House, 1988), 149–72; Alister McGrath, "A Peacemaker in the Battle for the Bible," *Books and Culture: A Christian Review* 3 (November–December 1997), 22–25.

65. Carl F. H. Henry, "Whose Battle for the Bible?" (Evangelical Press Association syndicated article), cited in Harold Lindsell, *The Bible in the Balance* (Grand Rapids: Zondervan Publishing House, 1979), 32–33.

66. Henry, *Evangelicals in Search of Identity,* 55.

67. Henry quote from December 16, 1977, issue of *Evangelical Newsletter,* cited in Lindsell, *Bible in the Balance,* 32.

68. Lindsell, *Bible in the Balance,* 20.

69. Ibid., 32.

70. Henry, *Evangelicals in Search of Identity,* 53.

71. See Benjamin B. Warfield, *The Inspiration and Authority of the Bible* (Phillipsburg, NJ: Presbyterian and Reformed Publishing Co., 1948), 71–226.
72. See G. C. Berkouwer, *Holy Scripture,* trans. Jack B. Rogers (Grand Rapids: Wm. B. Eerdmans Publishing Co., 1975); Beegle, *Scripture, Tradition, and Infallibility.*
73. See Lindsell, *Battle for the Bible,* 81–82, 204–6.
74. Carl F. H. Henry, "The War of the Word," *New Review of Books and Religion* (September 1976), 7; see "The Battle for the Bible: An Interview with Dr. Carl F. H. Henry," *Scribe* (spring 1976), 4.
75. E. J. Young, *Thy Word Is Truth: Some Thoughts on the Biblical Doctrine of Inspiration* (Grand Rapids: Wm. B. Eerdmans Publishing Co., 1957), 219; Lindsell, *Bible in the Balance,* 301.
76. Lindsell, *Bible in the Balance,* 300–301.
77. See Kurt E. Marquart, *Anatomy of an Explosion* (St. Louis: Concordia Publishing House, 1977); Grady C. Cothen, *What Happened to the Southern Baptist Convention? A Memoir of the Controversy* (Macon, GA: Smyth & Helwys Publishing, 1993); Paul G. Bretscher, *After the Purifying* (River Forest: Lutheran Education Association, 1975); Robert S. Alley, *Revolt against the Faithful* (Garden City, NY: Doubleday & Co., 1970); William E. Hull, *The Integrity of the Theological Curriculum* (Louisville, KY: Southern Baptist Theological Seminary, 1969).
78. George M. Marsden, *Fundamentalism and American Culture: The Shaping of Twentieth-Century Evangelicalism, 1870–1925* (New York: Oxford University Press, 1980), 186–87; Lindsell, *Bible in the Balance,* 342.
79. Bernard Ramm, *The Christian View of Science and Scripture* (Grand Rapids: Wm. B. Eerdmans Publishing Co., 1954), 46–48.
80. See Marsden, *Reforming Fundamentalism,* 158–59.
81. See Bernard L. Ramm, *Protestant Biblical Interpretation: A Textbook of Hermeneutics for Conservative Protestants* (Boston: Wilde Publications, 1950); idem, "The Three Levels of the New Testament," *Watchman-Examiner* 37 (January 6, 1949), 11–12; idem, "Can I Trust My Old Testament?" *King's Business* 40 (February 1949), 8–9; idem, "The Word and the Spirit," *Watchman-Examiner* 41 (July 9, 1953), 678–79.
82. See Bernard L. Ramm, *Problems in Christian Apologetics* (Portland, OR: Western Baptist Theological Seminary, 1949); idem, *Protestant Christian Evidences: A Textbook of the Evidences of the Truthfulness of the Christian Faith for Conservative Protestants* (Chicago: Moody Press, 1953); idem, *Types of Apologetic Systems: An Introductory Study to the Christian Philosophy of Religion* (Wheaton, IL: Van Kampen, 1953); idem, "The Catholic Approach to Bible and Science," *Bibliotheca Sacra* 111 (July 1954), 204–12.
83. Bernard Ramm, *After Fundamentalism: The Future of Evangelical Theology* (San Francisco: Harper & Row, 1983), 1.
84. Bernard Ramm, "Helps from Karl Barth," in *How Karl Barth Changed My Mind,* ed. Donald K. McKim (Grand Rapids: Wm. B. Eerdmans Publishing Co., 1986), 121.
85. Bernard Ramm, *The Pattern of Religious Authority* (1st ed., *The Pattern of Authority,* 1957; reprint, Grand Rapids: Wm. B. Eerdmans Publishing Co., 1958); idem, *The Witness of the Spirit: An Essay on the Contemporary Relevance of the Internal Witness of the Holy Spirit* (Grand Rapids: Wm. B. Eerdmans Publishing

Co., 1959); idem, *Special Revelation and the Word of God* (Grand Rapids: Wm. B. Eerdmans Publishing Co., 1961).

86. Calvin, *Institutes of the Christian Religion,* vol. 2, bk 4, 14.8, 1284.

87. See Karl Barth, *Church Dogmatics,* vol. 2: *The Doctrine of God,* part 1, trans. T. H. L. Parker, W. B. Johnston, Harold Knight, and J. L. M. Haire (Edinburgh: T. & T. Clark, 1957), 257–350.

88. Ramm, *Witness of the Spirit,* 64.

89. Ibid., 126–27.

90. Bernard Ramm, *Protestant Biblical Interpretation: A Textbook of Hermeneutics,* 3d rev. ed. (Grand Rapids: Baker Book House, 1970), 201–14.

91. Cornelius Van Til, *Has Karl Barth Turned Orthodox?* (Philadelphia: Presbyterian and Reformed Publishing Co., 1954), 181; idem, *The New Modernism* (1946; reprint, Phillipsburg, NJ: Presbyterian and Reformed Publishing Co., 1973); Karl Barth, *Church Dogmatics,* vol. 3: *The Doctrine of Creation,* part 4, trans. A. T. Mackay, T. H. L. Parker, Harold Knight, Henry A. Kennedy, and John Marks (Edinburgh: T. & T. Clark, 1961), xiii; idem, *Church Dogmatics,* vol. 4: *The Doctrine of Reconciliation,* part 2, trans. G. W. Bromiley (Edinburgh: T. & T. Clark, 1958), xii; G. C. Berkouwer, *The Triumph of Grace in the Theology of Karl Barth,* trans. Harry R. Boer (Grand Rapids: Wm. B. Eerdmans Publishing Co., 1956). See Hans Urs von Balthasar, *The Theology of Karl Barth,* trans. John Drury (New York: Holt, Rinehart & Winston, 1971); Henri Bouillard, *Karl Barth,* vol. 1: *Genèse et évolution de la théologie dialectique* (Aubier: Editions Montagne, 1957); Hans Küng, *Theology for the Third Millennium: An Ecumenical View,* trans. Peter Heinegg (New York: Doubleday, 1988), 259–84.

92. Bernard L. Ramm, *The Evangelical Heritage* (Waco, TX: Word Books, 1973), 114; see Eberhard Busch, *Karl Barth: His Life from Letters and Autobiographical Texts,* trans. John Bowden (London: SCM Press, 1976), 381.

93. Barth, *Church Dogmatics,* vol. 1, part 2, 532–33.

94. Ramm, *Evangelical Heritage,* 118.

95. Ibid., 154, 165.

96. Bernard Ramm, "Misplaced Battle Lines," *Reformed Journal* 26 (July–August 1976), 37.

97. Bernard Ramm, "Is 'Scripture Alone' the Essence of Christianity?" in *Biblical Authority,* ed. Jack Rogers (Waco, TX: Word Books, 1977), 116.

98. Lindsell, *Bible in the Balance,* 48.

99. Ramm, "Is 'Scripture Alone' the Essence of Christianity?" 122.

100. See Clark H. Pinnock, *A Defense of Biblical Infallibility* (Philadelphia: Presbyterian and Reformed Publishing Co., 1967); idem, *A New Reformation* (Tigerville, SC: Jewel Books, 1968); idem, *Evangelism and Truth* (Tigerville, SC: Jewel Books, 1969).

101. Pinnock, *New Reformation,* 6–10.

102. Clark H. Pinnock, *Set Forth Your Case: An Examination of Christianity's Credentials* (1967; reprint, Chicago: Moody Press, 1971), 100–101.

103. Pinnock, *Defense of Biblical Infallibility,* 28–29.

104. See Robert D. Preus, "Notes on the Inerrancy of Scripture," in *Crisis in Lutheran Theology,* ed. John Warwick Montgomery (Grand Rapids: Baker Book House, 1967), 1:133, 136; idem, *The Inspiration of Scripture: A Study of the Theology of the Seventeenth Century Lutheran Dogmaticians* (London: Oliver & Boyd, 1955).

105. James Orr, *Revelation and Inspiration* (Grand Rapids: Wm. B. Eerdmans Publishing Co., 1952), 156–74.
106. Ramm, *Special Revelation and the Word of God,* 63–69; quote on 68–69.
107. Pinnock, *Biblical Revelation,* 192.
108. Ibid., 193.
109. Pinnock, *Set Forth Your Case,* 132.
110. Clark H. Pinnock, *Three Keys to Spiritual Renewal* (Minneapolis: Bethany House Publishers, 1985), 18; see idem, "I Was a Teenage Fundamentalist," *Wittenberg Door* (December 1982–January 1983), 18; idem, "Baptists and Biblical Authority," *Journal of the Evangelical Theological Society* 17 (1974), 193.
111. Clark H. Pinnock, "From Augustine to Arminius: A Pilgrimage in Theology," in *The Grace of God and the Will of Man,* ed. Clark H. Pinnock (1989; reprint, Minneapolis: Bethany House Publishers, 1995), 17.
112. Pinnock, *Set Forth Your Case,* 44.
113. Pinnock, *Three Keys to Spiritual Renewal,* 51–52; see Robert K. Johnston, "Clark H. Pinnock," in *Handbook of Evangelical Theologians,* ed. Walter A. Elwell (Grand Rapids: Baker Book House, 1993), 428–29.
114. See Pinnock, "From Augustine to Arminius," 17–23; idem, "Responsible Freedom and the Flow of Biblical History," in *Grace Unlimited,* ed. Clark H. Pinnock (Minneapolis: Bethany House Publishers, 1975), 105–6.
115. See Clark H. Pinnock, "A Pilgrimage in Political Theology: A Personal Witness," in *Liberation Theology,* ed. Ronald H. Nash (Milford, MI: Mott Media, 1984), 103–20; idem, "Fruits Worthy of Repentance: The True Weight of Biblical Authority," *Sojourners* (December 1977), 29–30.
116. See Clark H. Pinnock, "God Limits His Knowledge," in *Predestination and Free Will,* ed. David Basinger and Randall Basinger (Downers Grove, IL: InterVarsity Press, 1986), 141–62; idem, "The Arminian Option," *Christianity Today* (February 19, 1990), 15; idem, "The Need for a Scriptural, and Therefore a Neo-Classical Theism," in *Perspectives on Evangelical Theology,* ed. Kenneth S. Kantzer and Stanley N. Gundry (Grand Rapids: Baker Book House, 1979), 37–42.
117. Clark H. Pinnock, "The Inerrancy Debate among the Evangelicals," *Theology, News and Notes,* special issue (1976), 11–13; see idem, "Inspiration and Authority: A Truce Proposal," *Other Side* (May 1976), 61–65.
118. Clark H. Pinnock, foreword to Stephen T. Davis, *The Debate about the Bible: Inerrancy versus Infallibility* (Philadelphia: Westminster Press, 1977), 11.
119. Pinnock, *Biblical Revelation,* 78.
120. Pinnock, "Inerrancy Debate among the Evangelicals," 12.
121. Ibid., 11–12.
122. Lindsell, *Bible in the Balance,* 36.
123. See Benjamin B. Warfield and A. A. Hodge, "Inspiration," *Presbyterian Review* 6 (April 1881), 245: "No objection [to inerrancy] is valid which overlooks the prime question: what was the professed or implied purpose of the writer in making this statement?"
124. Clark H. Pinnock, "Three Views of the Bible in Contemporary Theology," in Rogers, ed., *Biblical Authority,* 64.
125. Ibid., 65–66.
126. Ibid., 66.
127. Ibid., 67.
128. Ibid., 68.

129. Ibid.; see idem, "The Ongoing Struggle over Biblical Inerrancy," *Journal of the American Scientific Affiliation* 31, 2 (June 1979), 69–74.
130. Clark H. Pinnock, "Evangelicals and Inerrancy: The Current Debate," *Theology Today* 35 (April 1978), 67.
131. See Barr, *Fundamentalism,* 304–44.
132. Pinnock, "Evangelicals and Inerrancy," 67.
133. Vatican II, *Verbum Dei,* Dogmatic Constitution on Divine Revelation, chap. 3, in *Documents of Vatican II,* ed. Austin P. Flannery (Grand Rapids: Wm. B. Eerdmans Publishing Co., 1975), 756–57. See James T. Burtchaell, *Catholic Theories of Biblical Inspiration since 1810: A Review and Critique* (Cambridge: Cambridge University Press, 1969); Bruce Vawter, *Biblical Inspiration: Theological Resources* (Philadelphia: Westminster Press, 1972).
134. See Harry R. Boer, *The Bible and Higher Criticism* (Grand Rapids: Wm. B. Eerdmans Publishing Co., 1981); Herman N. Ridderbos, *Studies in Scripture and Its Authority* (Grand Rapids: Wm. B. Eerdmans Publishing Co., 1978).
135. Pinnock, "Evangelicals and Inerrancy," 67.
136. See Rogers and McKim, *Authority and Interpretation of the Bible,* 457–61; John D. Woodbridge, *Biblical Authority: A Critique of the Rogers/McKim Proposal* (Grand Rapids: Zondervan Publishing House, 1982). Though he rejected Woodbridge's fundamentalism, Pinnock was influenced by his historical rejoinder to Rogers and McKim. On the theme of classical Christian theology as a project done within the "house of authority," see Edward Farley, *Ecclesial Reflection: An Anatomy of Theological Method* (Philadelphia: Fortress Press, 1982), 3–168. Pinnock was also influenced by Farley's work.
137. Clark H. Pinnock, *The Scripture Principle* (San Francisco: Harper & Row, 1984), xii.
138. Ibid., xviii.
139. Ibid., xviii–xix.
140. Ibid., xix.
141. Ibid., 24.
142. Ibid., 26.
143. Barth, *Church Dogmatics,* vol. 1, part 1, 123–24. See Emil Brunner, *Revelation and Reason: The Christian Doctrine of Faith and Knowledge,* trans. Olive Wyon (Philadelphia: Westminster Press, 1946), 20–32; William Temple, *Nature, Man and God* (1934; reprint, London: Macmillan & Co., 1964), 301–25.
144. Pinnock, *Scripture Principle,* 21.
145. Clark H. Pinnock, "Parameters of Biblical Inerrancy," in *Proceedings of the Conference on Biblical Inerrancy, 1987* (Nashville: Broadman Press, 1987), 96.
146. Pinnock, *Scripture Principle,* 62, 78.
147. Ibid., 78; see Clark H. Pinnock, "What Is Biblical Inerrancy?" in *Proceedings of the Conference on Biblical Inerrancy, 1987,* 74.
148. Pinnock, *The Scripture Principle,* 122–123.
149. Ibid., 123.
150. Ibid., 121.
151. See Warfield, *Inspiration and Authority of the Bible,* 419–42.
152. See Westminster Confession, chap. 3: "Of God's Eternal Decrees," 6.014–21.
153. Pinnock, *Scripture Principle,* 101.
154. See Pinnock, "God Limits His Knowledge," 141–62; idem, "Arminian Option," 15; Clark H. Pinnock, "Between Classical and Process Theism," in

Process Theology, ed. Ronald H. Nash (Grand Rapids: Baker Book House, 1987), 309–27.

155. Pinnock, *Scripture Principle,* 102–3.

156. Ibid., 103–4.

157. Ibid., 104–5.

158. Ibid., 112–15.

159. Paul K. Jewett, *Man as Male and Female: A Study in Sexual Relationships from a Theological Point of View* (Grand Rapids: Wm. B. Eerdmans Publishing Co., 1975), 49–61, 111–28.

160. Pinnock, *Scripture Principle,* 67.

161. Ibid., 147, 224–25.

162. Ramm, *After Fundamentalism,* 27.

163. Barth, *Church Dogmatics,* vol. 2, part 1, 195.

164. Ramm, *After Fundamentalism,* 90.

165. Barth, *Church Dogmatics,* vol. 1, part 1, 111–24, 150–62.

166. Ramm, *After Fundamentalism,* 91.

167. See Karl Barth, *Church Dogmatics,* vol. 3: *The Doctrine of Creation,* part 1, trans. J. W. Edwards, O. Bussey, and Harold Knight (Edinburgh: T. & T. Clark, 1958), 61–94.

168. See esp. Clark, *Karl Barth's Theological Method,* 160–225; Klaas Runia, *Karl Barth's Doctrine of Holy Scripture* (Grand Rapids: Wm. B. Eerdmans Publishing Co., 1962), 116–88.

169. Karl Barth, *Church Dogmatics,* vol. 3: *The Doctrine of Creation,* part 3, trans. G. W. Bromiley and R. J. Ehrlich (Edinburgh: T. & T. Clark, 1961), 200–204.

170. Ramm, *After Fundamentalism,* 94.

171. Cornelius Van Til, *Christianity and Barthianism* (Grand Rapids: Baker Book House, 1962), 213–16, 438–46; quote on 214.

172. Barth, *Church Dogmatics,* vol. 4, part 2, 143.

173. Ibid., 209–10.

174. Karl Barth, *Church Dogmatics,* vol. 4: *The Doctrine of Reconciliation,* part 3, trans. G. W. Bromiley (Edinburgh: T. & T. Clark, 1961), 298.

175. On the history of the distinction between *Historie* and *Geschichte,* see Gary Dorrien, *The Word as True Myth: Interpreting Modern Theology* (Louisville, KY: Westminster John Knox Press, 1997), 109–12.

176. Karl Barth *Die Auferstehung der Toten* (Munich: Chr. Kaiser Verlag, 1924), 143; Karl Barth, *The Epistle to the Romans,* 6th ed., trans. Edwyn C. Hoskyns (London: Oxford University Press, 1928), 30.

177. See Martin Kähler, *The So-Called Historical Jesus and the Historic Biblical Christ,* trans. Carl E. Braaten (Philadelphia: Fortress Press, 1988), 63, 131.

178. Karl Barth, *Church Dogmatics,* vol. 3: *The Doctrine of Creation,* part 2, trans. G. W. Bromiley and R. J. Ehrlich (Edinburgh: T. & T. Clark, 1961), 445–47.

179. See Van Austen Harvey, *The Historian and the Believer: The Morality of Historical Knowledge and Christian Belief* (New York: Macmillan Co., 1966).

180. Barth, *Church Dogmatics,* vol. 3, part 2, 446.

181. Ramm, *After Fundamentalism,* 199–204.

182. See Barth, *Church Dogmatics,* vol. 3, part 2, 441–56.

183. Ramm, *After Fundamentalism,* 61.

184. See John D. Godsey, ed., *Karl Barth's Table Talk* (Scottish Journal of Theology Occasional Papers, No. 10; Edinburgh: Tweeddale Court, 1963), 59–60.

185. Ramm, *After Fundamentalism,* 61–62.
186. See Edward Dobson, *In Search of Unity: An Appeal to Fundamentalists and Evangelicals* (Nashville: Thomas Nelson Publishers, 1985), 84; Fred H. Klooster, review of *After Fundamentalism,* by Bernard Ramm, *Westminster Theological Journal* 47 (1985), 301; John D. Woodbridge, "Some Misconceptions of the Impact of the 'Enlightenment' on the Doctrine of Scripture," in *Hermeneutics, Authority, and Canon,* ed. D. A. Carson and John D. Woodbridge (Grand Rapids: Zondervan Publishing House, 1986), 237–70; Harold Lindsell, *The New Paganism: Understanding American Culture and the Role of the Church* (San Francisco: Harper & Row, 1987), 185–90.
187. See Thomas F. Torrance, *Theological Science* (London: Oxford University Press, 1969); Otto Weber, *Foundations of Dogmatics,* vol. 1, trans. Darrell L. Guder (Grand Rapids: Wm. B. Eerdmans Publishing Co., 1981); Helmut Thielicke, *The Hidden Question of God,* trans. G. W. Bromiley (Grand Rapids: Wm. B. Eerdmans Publishing Co., 1977).
188. See Berkouwer, *Triumph of Grace in the Theology of Karl Barth;* G. W. Bromiley, "Karl Barth," in *Creative Minds in Contemporary Theology,* ed. Philip Edgcumbe Hughes (Grand Rapids: Wm. B. Eerdmans Publishing Co., 1969), 27–62; Donald G. Bloesch, *The Evangelical Renaissance* (Grand Rapids: Wm. B. Eerdmans Publishing Co., 1973), 80–100.
189. Bloesch, *Evangelical Renaissance,* 90.

CHAPTER 4. ARMINIAN AND CATHOLIC OPTIONS: OPENING UP EVANGELICALISM

1. See Ronald J. Sider, *Rich Christians in an Age of Hunger* (1977; rev. ed., Downers Grove, IL: InterVarsity Press, 1984); idem, "An Evangelical Theology of Liberation," in *Piety and Politics: Evangelicals and Fundamentalists Confront the World,* ed. Richard John Neuhaus and Michael Cromartie (Washington, DC: Ethics and Public Policy Center, 1987), 145–60; Virginia Ramey Mollenkott, *Women, Men and the Bible* (Nashville: Abingdon Press, 1977); idem, "Evangelicalism: A Feminist Perspective," *Union Seminary Quarterly Review* 32 (winter 1977), 95–103; Nancy Hardesty, *Women Called to Witness: Evangelical Feminism in the Nineteenth Century* (Nashville: Abingdon Press, 1984); Letha Scanzoni and Nancy Hardesty, *All We're Meant to Be* (Waco, TX: Word Books, 1974).
2. See John Oliver, "A Failure of Evangelical Conscience," *The Post-American* (May 1975), 26–30; Donald W. Dayton, *Discovering an Evangelical Heritage* (New York: Harper & Row, 1976), 2–3.
3. David O. Moberg, *The Great Reversal: Evangelism versus Social Concern* (Philadelphia: J. B. Lippincott Co., 1972), 42–43.
4. Dayton's articles were published under the title "Recovering a Heritage" in ten consecutive issues of *The Post-American* between June 1974 and July 1975. This material is reprinted in Dayton, *Discovering an Evangelical Heritage,* 7–98.
5. See V. Raymond Edmon, *Finney Lives On: The Secret of Revival in Our Time* (Wheaton, IL: Scripture Press, 1951); Dayton, *Discovering an Evangelical Heritage,* 15–24.
6. Dayton, *Discovering an Evangelical Heritage,* 121–35.
7. William S. Barker, "The Social Views of Charles Hodge (1797–1878): A Study in

Nineteenth-Century Calvinism and Conservatism," *Presbyterian* (spring 1975), 1–22; Ronald W. Hogeland, "Charles Hodge, the Association of Gentlemen and Ornamental Womanhood: A Study of Male Conventional Wisdom, 1825–1855," *Journal of Presbyterian History* (fall 1975), 239–55; J. W. Stewart, *Mediating the Center: Charles Hodge on American Science, Language, Literature and Politics,* Studies in Reformed Theology and History 3 (Princeton, NJ: Princeton Theological Seminary, 1995), 71–87; Dayton, *Discovering an Evangelical Heritage,* 129–31.

8. Charles Finney, *Finney's Systematic Theology* (1878; new exp. ed. Minneapolis: Bethany House Publishers, 1994), 478–79.

9. Ibid., 479.

10. Ibid., 390–91.

11. Donald W. Dayton, "The Radical Message of Evangelical Christianity," in *Churches in Struggle: Liberation Theologies and Social Change in North America,* ed. William K. Tabb (New York: Monthly Review Press, 1986), 213.

12. On the transdenominational ethos of American evangelicalism, see George Marsden, "The Evangelical Denomination," in *Evangelicalism and Modern America,* ed. George Marsden (Grand Rapids: Wm. B. Eerdmans Publishing Co., 1984), ix–x. For Dayton's later judgment that evangelicalism is too diffuse to make any use of the term meaningful, see Donald W. Dayton, "Some Doubts about the Usefulness of the Category 'Evangelical,'" in *The Variety of American Evangelicalism,* ed. Donald W. Dayton and Robert K. Johnston (Downers Grove, IL: InterVarsity Press, 1991), 245–51.

13. William J. Abraham, *The Coming Great Revival: Recovering the Full Evangelical Tradition* (San Francisco: Harper & Row, 1984), ix–x.

14. Ibid., 36–37.

15. Ibid., 37.

16. William J. Abraham, *The Divine Inspiration of Holy Scripture* (Oxford: Oxford University Press, 1981), 118, 28–29; see Abraham, *Divine Revelation and the Limits of Historical Criticism* (Oxford: Oxford University Press, 1982).

17. Abraham, *Coming Great Revival,* 85.

18. Ibid., 47.

19. See Jack B. Rogers and Donald K. McKim, *The Authority and Interpretation of the Bible: An Historical Approach* (San Francisco: Harper & Row, 1979); John D. Woodbridge, *Biblical Authority: A Critique of the Rogers/McKim Proposal* (Grand Rapids: Zondervan Publishing House, 1982).

20. Abraham, *Coming Great Revival,* 34.

21. See John Wesley, "A Plain Account of Christian Perfection as Believed and Taught by the Reverend Mr. John Wesley, from the Year 1725, to the Year 1777," in *The Works of John Wesley,* 14 vols. (1872; reprint, Grand Rapids: Baker Book House, 1996), 11:366–449; idem, "A Clear and Concise Demonstration of the Divine Inspiration of the Holy Scriptures," 11:484; idem, "Remarks on the Limits of Human Knowledge," 13:488–98.

22. See John Wesley, "Thoughts upon Slavery," in *Works of John Wesley,* 11:59–79; idem, Sermon 1, "Salvation by Faith," 5:7–16; idem, Sermon 4, "Scriptural Christianity," 5:37–52; idem, Sermon 10, "The Witness of the Spirit," 5:111–22; idem, Sermon 18, "The Marks of the New Birth," 5:212–22.

23. Abraham, *Coming Great Revival,* 54–59.

24. Miner Raymond, *Systematic Theology,* 3 vols. (New York: Nelson & Phillips,

1877); Thomas Ralston, *Elements of Divinity; Or, A Concise and Comprehensive View of Bible Theology; Comprising the Doctrines, Evidences, Morals and Institutions of Christianity* (1847; 3d ed., Nashville: A. H. Redford, 1871); William Burt Pope, *Compendium of Christian Theology; Being Analytical Outlines of a Course of Theological Study, Biblical, Dogmatic, Historical*, 3 vols. (New York: Phillips & Hunt, 1880); Amos Binney, *Binney's Theological Compend, Improved; Containing a Synopsis of the Evidences, Doctrines, Morals, and Institutions of Christianity* (New York: Eaton & Mains, 1874); Luther Lee, *Elements of Theology; Or, An Exposition of the Divine Origin, Doctrines, Morals, and Institutions of Christianity*, 2d ed. (Syracuse, NY: S. Lee, 1859).

25. John Miley, *Systematic Theology*, 2 vols. (New York: Hunt & Eaton, 1893; reprint, Peabody, MA: Hendrickson Publishers, 1989); see 2:357–58, 479–89.

26. Paul Merritt Bassett, "The Theological Identity of the North American Holiness Movement," in Dayton and Johnston, eds., *Variety of American Evangelicalism*, 90. I am indebted to Bassett's perceptive discussion throughout this section.

27. A. M. Hills, *Fundamental Christian Theology*, 2 vols. (Pasadena, CA: C. J. Kinne, 1934); R. R. Byrum, *Christian Theology* (Anderson, IN: Gospel Trumpet Company, 1924).

28. H. Orton Wiley, *Christian Theology*, 3 vols. (Kansas City, MO: Beacon Hill Press, 1940), 1:141–42.

29. Ibid., 142.

30. Ibid., 143.

31. H. Orton Wiley and Paul T. Culbertson, *Introduction to Christian Theology* (Kansas City, MO: Beacon Hill Press, 1946), 27. This work condensed Wiley's three-volume dogmatics into a single volume.

32. See Arthur C. Cochrane, *Reformed Confessions of the Sixteenth Century* (Philadelphia: Westminster Press, 1966); *The Book of Confessions* (Louisville, KY: Office of the General Assembly, Presbyterian Church (U.S.A.), 1991).

33. The pertinent Lutheran texts are especially the Augsburg Confession (1530), the Smalcald Articles (1537), and the Large Catechism (1529). See *The Book of Concord: The Confessions of the Evangelical Lutheran Church*, ed. Theodore G. Tappert (Philadelphia: Fortress Press, 1959). On the significance of Wesley's Anglicanism in this regard, see Bassett, "Theological Identity of the North American Holiness Movement," 76–78.

34. "Articles of Religion," reprinted in the "Historical Documents" section of the Episcopal Church's *The Book of Common Prayer* (New York: Church Hymnal Corporation, 1979), 867–76; Richard Hooker, *Of the Laws of Ecclesiastical Polity* (New York: E. P. Dutton & Co., 1958), 1.14.1–5, 1:276–82.

35. See Paul Elmer More and Frank Leslie Cross, eds., *Anglicanism: The Thought and Practice of the Church of England, Illustrated from the Religious Literature of the Seventeenth Century* (London: SPCK, 1935), 89–120; H. R. McAdoo, *The Spirit of Anglicanism* (London: SPCK, 1965); Paul Avis, *Anglicanism and the Christian Church: Theological Resources in Historical Perspective* (Philadelphia: Fortress Press, 1989), 79–96.

36. John Wesley, "Preface to Collected Sermons," in *Works of John Wesley*, 5:3.

37. John Wesley, *Explanatory Notes upon the New Testament* (1755; London: Epworth Press, 1950). See Bassett, "Theological Identity of the North American Holiness Movement," 81–82.

38. See John Wesley, Sermon 70, "The Case of Reason Impartially Considered," in

Works of John Wesley, 6:350–60; idem, "Remarks on the Limits of Human Knowledge," 13:488–98.

39. See H. Ray Dunning, *Grace, Faith, and Holiness* (Kansas City, MO: Beacon Hill Press, 1988), 55–76; J. Kenneth Grider, *A Wesleyan-Holiness Theology* (Kansas City, MO: Beacon Hill Press, 1994), 63–85.

40. See Gordon D. Fee, *God's Empowering Presence: The Holy Spirit in the Letters of Paul* (Peabody, MA: Hendrickson Publishers, 1994); idem, *Paul, the Spirit, and the People of God* (Peabody, MA: Hendrickson Publishers, 1996); Scott A. Ellington, "Pentecostalism and the Authority of Scripture," *Journal of Pentecostal Theology* 9 (1996), 16–38; Steven J. Land, *Pentecostal Spirituality: A Passion for the Kingdom* (Sheffield: Sheffield Academic Press, 1993), 74. See also Donald W. Dayton, *The Theological Roots of Pentecostalism* (Grand Rapids: Zondervan Publishing House, 1987); D. William Faupel, *The Everlasting Gospel: The Significance of Eschatology in the Development of Pentecostal Thought* (Sheffield: Sheffield Academic Press, 1996).

41. See John Wesley, "Predestination Calmly Considered," in *Works of John Wesley,* 10:256–59; idem, "Some Remarks on Mr. Hill's 'Review of All the Doctrines Taught by Mr. John Wesley,'" 10:374–414; idem, "An Answer to Mr. Rowland Hill's Tract, Entitled, 'Imposture Detected,'" 10:446–54.

42. Wiley, *Christian Theology,* 2:441.

43. John Wesley, "The Question, 'What Is an Arminian?,' Answered by a Lover of Free Grace," in *Works of John Wesley,* 10:358.

44. Ibid., 359–60. See James Arminius, *The Works of James Arminius,* trans. James Nichols and William Nichols, 3 vols. (Grand Rapids: Baker Book House, 1996); Carl Bangs, "Arminius as a Reformed Theologian," in *The Heritage of John Calvin,* ed. John H. Bratt (Grand Rapids: Wm. B. Eerdmans Publishing Co., 1973), 209–22; Richard A. Muller, *God, Creation, and Providence in the Thought of Jacob Arminius: Sources and Directions of Scholastic Protestantism in the Era of Early Orthodoxy* (Grand Rapids: Baker Book House, 1991).

45. John Wesley, "A Dialogue between a Predestinarian and His Friend," in *Works of John Wesley,* 10:259–66; quote on 260. See idem, "Serious Thoughts upon the Perseverance of the Saints," 10:284–98; idem, "Thoughts on the Imputed Righteousness of Christ," 10:312–15; idem, "Thoughts upon God's Sovereignty," 10:361–63.

46. Abraham, *Coming Great Revival,* 9.

47. Ibid., 15.

48. Robert E. Webber and Donald Bloesch, eds., *The Orthodox Evangelicals: Who They Are and What They Are Saying* (Nashville: Thomas Nelson Publishers, 1978), 11.

49. Ibid., 12.

50. Robert E. Webber, *Common Roots: A Call to Evangelical Maturity* (Grand Rapids: Zondervan Publishing House, 1979), 16.

51. See Richard Lovelace, "A Call to Historic Roots and Continuity," 43–67; Roger Nicole, "A Call to Biblical Fidelity," 68–76; Thomas Howard, "A Call to Sacramental Integrity," 118–45, all in Webber and Bloesch, eds., *Orthodox Evangelicals.*

52. Howard, "Call to Sacramental Integrity," 122.

53. On the anti-Protestantism of the Oxford Movement, see John Henry Newman, "The Nature and Ground of Roman and Protestant Errors," in *The Oxford Move-*

ment, ed. Eugene R. Fairweather (New York: Oxford University Press, 1964), 114–27; Perry Butler, "From the Early Eighteenth Century to the Present Day," in *The Study of Anglicanism,* ed. Stephen Sykes and John Booty (Philadelphia: Fortress Press, 1988), 34–35; Avis, *Anglicanism and the Christian Church,* 220–36.

54. David F. Wells, "Reflections about Catholic Renewal in Evangelicalism," in Webber and Bloesch, eds., *Orthodox Evangelicals,* 214.

55. Ibid., 214, 220.

56. Webber, *Common Roots,* 231.

57. Abraham, *Coming Great Revival,* 46.

58. Ibid., 47–48.

59. See Robert Brow, "Evangelical Megashift," *Christianity Today* 34 (February 19, 1990), 12–14.

60. See Clark H. Pinnock, *Three Keys to Spiritual Renewal: A Challenge to the Church* (Minneapolis: Bethany House Publishers, 1985), 64–78; idem, "A Pilgrimage in Political Theology: A Personal Witness," in *Liberation Theology,* ed. Ronald H. Nash (Milford, MI: Mott Media, 1984), 103–20.

61. C. S. Lewis, *The Problem of Pain* (1962; reprint, New York: Simon & Schuster, 1996), 105–14, quote on 114; idem, *The Great Divorce* (1946; reprint, New York: Simon & Schuster, 1996); Brow, "Evangelical Megashift," 12.

62. C. S. Lewis, *Mere Christianity* (1952; reprint, New York: Simon & Schuster, 1996), 57–61; idem, *The Lion, the Witch, and the Wardrobe* (1950; reprint, New York: Simon & Schuster, 1996); idem, *Problem of Pain,* 129–38; idem, *God in the Dock: Essays on Theology and Ethics* (Grand Rapids: Wm. B. Eerdmans Publishing Co., 1970), 63–67; idem, *Surprised by Joy: The Shape of My Early Life* (1956; reprint, San Diego: Harcourt Brace Jovanovich, 1984), 234–37.

63. On Lewis's conception of Christ as true myth, see Gary Dorrien, *The Word as True Myth: Interpreting Modern Theology* (Louisville, KY: Westminster John Knox Press, 1997), 236–38.

64. See John Kenneth Mozley, "The Incarnation," in *Essays Catholic and Critical: By Members of the Anglican Communion,* ed. Edward Gordon Selwyn (London: SPCK, 1926), 179–202; A. E. J. Rawlinson, ed., *Essays on the Trinity and the Incarnation: By Members of the Anglican Communion* (London: Longmans, Green & Co., 1932), 23–46, 361–402.

65. Brow, "Evangelical Megashift," 12.

66. Clark H. Pinnock, "The Arminian Option," *Christianity Today* 34 (February 19, 1990), 15.

67. Clark H. Pinnock and Robert C. Brow, *Unbounded Love: A Good News Theology for the Twenty-first Century* (Downers Grove, IL: InterVarsity Press, 1994), 8.

68. Clark H. Pinnock, "From Augustine to Arminius: A Pilgrimage in Theology," in *The Grace of God and the Will of Man,* ed. Clark H. Pinnock (Minneapolis: Bethany House Publishers, 1989), 18.

69. Arminius, *Works of James Arminius,* 3:66.

70. Jack W. Cottrell, *What the Bible Says about God the Ruler* (Joplin, MO: College Press, 1984); idem, "The Nature of the Divine Sovereignty," in Pinnock, ed., *Grace of God and Will of Man,* 97–119.

71. See Richard Rice, "Divine Foreknowledge and Free-Will Theism," in Richard Rice, *God's Foreknowledge and Man's Free Will* (Minneapolis: Bethany House

Publishers, 1985); idem, "Biblical Support for a New Perspective," in Clark Pinnock, Richard Rice, John Sanders, William Hasker, and David Basinger, *The Openness of God: A Biblical Challenge to the Traditional Understanding of God* (Downers Grove, IL: InterVarsity Press, 1994), 11–58.

72. Clark H. Pinnock, "Systematic Theology," in Pinnock et al., *Openness of God,* 114–15. For other representative works, see David Basinger and Randall Basinger, eds., *Predestination and Free Will* (Downers Grove, IL: InterVarsity Press, 1986); David Basinger, *Divine Power in Process Theism: A Philosophical Critique* (Albany: State University of New York Press, 1988); William Hasker, *God, Time and Knowledge* (Ithaca, NY: Cornell University Press, 1989); John E. Sanders, "God as Personal," in Pinnock, ed., *Grace of God and Will of Man,* 165–80; Rice, *God's Foreknowledge and Man's Free Will.*

73. Pinnock, "Systematic Theology," 115.

74. Ibid., 118.

75. Pinnock and Brow, *Unbounded Love,* 9.

76. Karl Barth, *The Humanity of God* (Atlanta: John Knox Press, 1960), 61–62.

77. Karl Barth, *Church Dogmatics,* vol. 2: *The Doctrine of God,* part 2, trans. G. W. Bromiley, J. C. Campbell, Iain Wilson, J. Strathearn McNab, Harold Knight, and R. A. Stewart (Edinburgh: T. & T. Clark, 1957), 145–81.

78. Clark H. Pinnock, "Fire, Then Nothing," *Christianity Today* 31 (March 20, 1987), 40.

79. Pinnock and Brow, *Unbounded Love,* 90.

80. Clark H. Pinnock, *A Wideness in God's Mercy: The Finality of Jesus Christ in a World of Religions* (Grand Rapids: Zondervan Publishing House, 1992), 160–61.

81. Clark H. Pinnock, "An Inclusivist View," in *Four Views on Salvation in a Pluralistic World,* ed. Dennis L. Okholm and Timothy R. Phillips (Grand Rapids: Zondervan Publishing House, 1996), 95–123; quotes on 100. See Karl Rahner, "Christianity and the Non-Christian Religions," in *Theological Investigations,* 23 vols. (London: Darton, Longman & Todd, 1966), 5:121–31; "Dogmatic Constitution on the Church," in *The Documents of Vatican II,* ed. Austin P. Flannery (Grand Rapids: Wm. B. Eerdmans Publishing Co., 1975), art. 16.

82. "Dogmatic Constitution on the Church," par. 18.

83. Origen, *On First Principles* 1.6.2.

84. Clark H. Pinnock, "Acts 4:12—No Other Name under Heaven," in *Through No Fault of Their Own? The Fate of Those Who Have Never Heard,* ed. William V. Crockett and James G. Sigountos (Grand Rapids: Baker Book House, 1991), 113–14.

85. Pinnock, "Fire, Then Nothing," 40.

86. Pinnock and Brow, *Unbounded Love,* 92.

87. David Edwards and John R. W. Stott, *Evangelical Essentials: A Liberal-Evangelical Dialogue* (Downers Grove, IL: InterVarsity Press, 1988), 316. For the argument that the biblical use of *eternal* admits no distinctions, see David F. Wells, "Everlasting Punishment," *Christianity Today* 31 (March 20, 1987), 41–42.

88. Edwards and Stott, *Evangelical Essentials,* 312–320; see John R. W. Stott, "God on the Gallows: How Could I Worship a God Immune to Pain?" *Christianity Today* 31 (January 16, 1987), 28–30.

89. See Basil F. C. Atkinson, *Life and Immortality* (Taunton, England: Goodman, 1962); Harold E. Guillebaud, *The Righteous Judge: A Study of the Biblical Doctrine of Everlasting Punishment* (Taunton, England: Goodman, 1964); Edward

W. Fudge, *The Fire That Consumes* (Houston: Providential, 1982); John W. Wenham, *The Goodness of God* (Downers Grove, IL: InterVarsity Press, 1974), 34–41; Stephen H. Travis, *I Believe in the Second Coming of Jesus* (Grand Rapids: Wm. B. Eerdmans Publishing Co., 1982), 197–98.

90. Pinnock and Brow, *Unbounded Love,* 92; Pinnock, "Fire, Then Nothing," 40; Edwards and Stott, *Evangelical Essentials,* 316.
91. Pinnock, "Systematic Theology," 125.
92. Pinnock, "From Augustine to Arminius," 27.
93. Ibid.

CHAPTER 5. POSTCONSERVATIVE EVANGELICALISM: DIALOGUES IN SEARCH OF A GENEROUS ORTHODOXY

1. Richard J. Coleman, *Issues of Theological Warfare: Evangelicals and Liberals* (Grand Rapids: Wm. B. Eerdmans Publishing Co., 1972), 7. Coleman's second edition (1980) was more hopeful and less combatitive, as reflected in the revised title, *Issues of Theological Conflict: Liberals and Conservatives.*
2. Mark Ellingsen, *The Evangelical Movement: Growth, Impact, Controversy, Dialog* (Minneapolis: Augsburg Publishing House, 1988), 24; Gabriel Fackre, *Ecumenical Faith in Evangelical Perspective* (Grand Rapids: Wm. B. Eerdmans Publishing Co., 1993), 205.
3. Roger E. Olson, "Whales and Elephants Both God's Creatures, but Can They Meet? Evangelicals and Liberals in Dialogue," *Pro Ecclesia* 4 (spring 1995), 165–68.
4. David L. Edwards and John Stott, *Evangelical Essentials: A Liberal-Evangelical Dialogue* (Downers Grove, IL: InterVarsity Press, 1988).
5. Clark H. Pinnock and Delwin Brown, *Theological Crossfire: An Evangelical/Liberal Dialogue* (Grand Rapids: Zondervan Publishing House, 1990). For discussions of both dialogues, see Olson, "Whales and Elephants Both God's Creatures," 171–73; and Stanley J. Grenz, *Revisioning Evangelical Theology: A Fresh Agenda for the Twenty-first Century* (Downers Grove, IL: InterVarsity Press, 1993), 28–29.
6. Pinnock and Brown, *Theological Crossfire,* 9.
7. Ibid., 21.
8. Ibid., 258.
9. Ibid., 133.
10. Edwards and Stott, *Evangelical Essentials,* 104–5.
11. Ibid., 333.
12. Ibid., 83.
13. See Donald G. Bloesch, *Essentials of Evangelical Theology,* 2 vols. (New York: Harper & Row, 1982); Thomas C. Oden, *Systematic Theology,* 3 vols. (San Francisco: HarperCollins, 1992–1994); Alister McGrath, *Evangelicalism and the Future of Christianity* (Downers Grove, IL: InterVarsity Press, 1995).
14. Donald G. Bloesch, *The Future of Evangelical Christianity: A Call for Unity amid Diversity* (Colorado Springs: Helmers & Howard, 1988), 89–90.
15. Donald G. Bloesch, *Holy Scripture: Revelation, Inspiration and Interpretation* (Downers Grove, IL: InterVarsity Press, 1994), 18; closing quote in idem, *Future of Evangelical Christianity,* 90. See idem, *A Theology of Word and Spirit: Authority and Method in Theology* (Downers Grove, IL: InterVarsity Press,

1992), 67–142; idem, *Essentials of Evangelical Theology,* vol. 1: *God, Authority, and Salvation,* 51–78; idem, *The Ground of Certainty: Toward an Evangelical Theology of Revelation* (Grand Rapids: Wm. B. Eerdmans Publishing Co.,
1971).

16. Bloesch, *Holy Scripture,* 25–26.

17. See Donald G. Bloesch, *The Evangelical Renaissance* (Grand Rapids: Wm. B.
Eerdmans Publishing Co., 1973), 80–100; idem, *Jesus Is Victor! Karl Barth's
Doctrine of Salvation* (Nashville: Abingdon Press, 1976); idem, *Theology of
Word and Spirit,* 149–55.

18. Bloesch, *Holy Scripture,* 27.

19. Ibid., 62.

20. Bloesch, *Theology of Word and Spirit,* 190–91.

21. See Anthony C. Thiselton, *The Two Horizons: New Testament Hermeneutics and
Philosophical Description with Special Reference to Heidegger, Bultmann,
Gadamer and Wittgenstein* (Grand Rapids: Wm. B. Eerdmans Publishing Co.,
1980); Grant R. Osborne, *The Hermeneutical Spiral: A Comprehensive Introduction to Biblical Interpretation* (Downers Grove, IL: InterVarsity Press, 1991).

22. See Daniel Patte, *What Is Structural Exegesis?* (Philadelphia: Fortress Press,
1976); Art Berman, *From the New Criticism to Deconstruction: The Reception
of Structuralism and Post-Structuralism* (Urbana: University of Illinois Press,
1988), 114–70; Bloesch, *Holy Scripture,* 210–13.

23. Bloesch, *Holy Scripture,* 209.

24. Bloesch, *Theology of Word and Spirit,* 17, 30.

25. Bloesch, *Holy Scripture,* 210.

26. Ibid., 40, 114–20, 211–13.

27. Ibid., 114, 297.

28. Bloesch, *Theology of Word and Spirit,* 19–20. See Donald G. Bloesch, *Jesus
Christ: Savior and Lord* (Downers Grove, IL: InterVarsity Press, 1997), 53–57.

29. Bloesch, *Holy Scripture,* 114.

30. Ibid., 116–17.

31. Alister McGrath, *A Passion for Truth: The Intellectual Coherence of Evangelicalism* (Downers Grove, IL: InterVarsity Press, 1996), 53–118, 149–56.

32. Thomas C. Oden, *After Modernity . . . What? Agenda for Theology* (Grand
Rapids: Academie Books, 1990), 21–70; idem, *Requiem: A Lament in Three
Movements* (Nashville: Abingdon Press, 1995), 33–79.

33. Donald G. Bloesch, *God the Almighty: Power, Wisdom, Holiness, Love* (Downers Grove, IL: InterVarsity Press, 1995), 254–60.

34. Bloesch, *Future of Evangelical Christianity,* 139.

35. Ibid., 141–45.

36. See Roger E. Olson, "Postconservative Evangelicals Greet the Postmodern Age,"
Christian Century 112 (May 3, 1995), 480–83; David S. Dockery, ed., *The Chal-
lenge of Postmodernism: An Evangelical Engagement* (Wheaton, IL: Victor
Books, 1995); Nancey Murphy, "Textual Relativism, Philosophy of Language,
and the Baptist Vision," in *Theology without Foundations: Religious Practice
and the Future of Theological Truth,* ed. Stanley Hauerwas, Nancey Murphy, and
Mark Nation (Nashville: Abingdon Press, 1994), 245–72; Philipp D. Kenneson,
"There's No Such Thing as Objective Truth, and It's a Good Thing, Too," in
Christian Apologetics in the Postmodern World, ed. Timothy R. Phillips and
Dennis L. Okholm (Downers Grove, IL: InterVarsity Press, 1995), 155–70;

Mark McLeod, "Making God Dance: Postmodern Theorizing and the Christian College," *Christian Scholar's Review* 21 (March 1992), 275–81; Steven J. Land, *Pentecostal Spirituality: A Passion for the Kingdom* (Sheffield: Sheffield Academic Press, 1993).

37. See Thomas J. J. Altizer, Max A. Myers, Carl A. Raschke, Robert P. Scharlemann, Mark C. Taylor, and Charles E. Winquist, *Deconstruction and Theology* (New York: Crossroad, 1982); Philippa Berry and Andrew Wernick, eds., *Shadow of Spirit: Postmodernism and Religion* (New York: Routledge & Kegan Paul, 1992).

38. Stanley J. Grenz, *A Primer on Postmodernism* (Grand Rapids: Wm. B. Eerdmans Publishing Co., 1996), 165–66.

39. See Carl A. Raschke, "The Deconstruction of God," in Altizer et al., *Deconstruction and Theology*, 1–33.

40. Grenz, *Primer on Postmodernism*, 169.

41. Grenz, *Revisioning Evangelical Theology*, 69.

42. Ibid., 73.

43. Stanley J. Grenz, *Theology for the Community of God* (Nashville: Broadman & Holman Publishers, 1994), 10.

44. Grenz, *Revisioning Evangelical Theology*, 72.

45. Grenz, *Theology for the Community of God*, 8.

46. See William C. Placher, *Unapologetic Theology: A Christian Voice in a Pluralistic Conversation* (Louisville, KY: Westminster/John Knox Press, 1989); James William McClendon Jr., *Systematic Theology*, 2 vols. (Nashville: Abingdon Press, 1986, 1994); Ronald F. Thiemann, *Revelation and Theology: The Gospel as Narrated Promise* (Notre Dame, IN: University of Notre Dame Press, 1985); George W. Stroup, *The Promise of Narrative Theology: Recovering the Gospel in the Church* (Atlanta: John Knox Press, 1981); Stanley Hauerwas, *A Community of Character: Toward a Constructive Christian Social Ethic* (Notre Dame, IN: University of Notre Dame Press, 1981); Stanley Hauerwas and L. Gregory Jones, eds., *Why Narrative? Readings in Narrative Theology* (Grand Rapids: Wm. B. Eerdmans Publishing Co., 1989).

47. On the theme of realistic narrative, see Hans W. Frei, "Theology and the Interpretation of Narrative: Some Hermeneutical Considerations" and "The 'Literal Reading' of Biblical Narrative in the Christian Tradition: Does It Stretch or Will It Break?" in idem, *Theology and Narrative: Selected Essays*, ed. George Hunsinger and William C. Placher (New York: Oxford University Press, 1993), 94–152; and William C. Placher, "Hans Frei and the Meaning of Biblical Narrative," *Christian Century* 105 (May 24–31, 1989), 556–59.

48. Hans W. Frei, *The Eclipse of Biblical Narrative: A Study in Eighteenth and Nineteenth Century Hermeneutics* (New Haven, CT: Yale University Press, 1974), 130.

49. Ibid., 130–31.

50. See William C. Placher, "Paul Ricoeur and Postliberal Theology: A Conflict of Interpretations," *Modern Theology* 4 (1987), 35–52.

51. George A. Lindbeck, *The Nature of Doctrine: Religion and Theology in a Postliberal Age* (Philadelphia: Westminster Press, 1984), 16. For a classic statement of the analytical approach, see A. J. Ayer, *Language, Truth and Logic* (New York: Dover Publications, 1946); for influential theological responses, see William Hordern, *Speaking of God: The Nature and Purpose of Theological*

Language (New York: Macmillan Co., 1964); and Langdon Gilkey, *Naming the Whirlwind: The Renewal of God-Language* (Indianapolis: Bobbs-Merrill Co., 1969).

52. Lindbeck, *Nature of Doctrine,* 131.
53. Ibid., 118. On Lindbeck's Lutheran confessionalism, see "A Panel Discussion: Lindbeck, Hunsinger, McGrath and Fackre," in *The Nature of Confession: Evangelicals and Postliberals in Conversation,* ed. Timothy R. Phillips and Dennis L. Okholm (Downers Grove, IL: InterVarsity Press, 1996), 246–47.
54. Bloesch, *Theology of Word and Spirit,* 133.
55. McGrath, *Passion for Truth,* 148–54.
56. Ibid., 153–55.
57. For critiques of postliberal antirealism, see Ian Barbour, *Religion in an Age of Science* (San Francisco: HarperCollins, 1990), 14–15; C. John Sommerville, "Is Religion a Language Game? A Real World Critique of the Cultural-Linguistic Theory," *Theology Today* 51 (1995), 594–99; Mark Wallace, *The Second Naivete: Barth, Ricoeur and the New Yale Theology* (Macon, GA: Mercer University Press, 1990) 104–10; Brevard S. Childs, *Biblical Theology of the Old and New Testaments: Theological Reflection on the Christian Bible* (Minneapolis: Fortress Press, 1992), 21–22.
58. See Crispin Wright, *Realism, Meaning and Truth* (Oxford: Basil Blackwell Publisher, 1993); Hilary Putnam, *The Many Faces of Realism* (LaSalle, IL: Open Court, 1987); Roy Wood Sellars, *Critical Realism: A Study of the Nature and Conditions of Knowledge* (New York: Russell & Russell, 1969).
59. Jeffrey Hensley, "Are Postliberals Necessarily Antirealists? Reexamining the Metaphysics of Lindbeck's Postliberal Theology," in Phillips and Okholm, eds., *Nature of Confession,* 77–78.
60. Lindbeck, *Nature of Doctrine,* 130. On this argument, see George Lindbeck, "Theologische Methode und Wissenschaftstheorie," *Theologische Revue* 74 (1978), 267–80.
61. See Thomas S. Kuhn, *The Structure of Scientific Revolutions* (Chicago: University of Chicago Press, 1962); idem, "Logic of Discovery or Psychology of Research," in *Criticism and the Growth of Knowledge,* ed. Imre Lakatos and Alan Musgrave (Cambridge: Cambridge University Press, 1970), 1–23; Ludwig Wittgenstein, *Philosophical Investigations,* trans. G. E. M. Anscombe (New York: Macmillan Co., 1953).
62. Lindbeck, *Nature of Doctrine,* 130–32.
63. "A Panel Discussion," 252.
64. Rodney Clapp, "How Firm a Foundation: Can Evangelicals Be Nonfoundationalists?" in Phillips and Okholm, eds., *Nature of Confession,* 89.
65. Ibid., 91.
66. Grenz, *Revisioning Evangelical Theology,* 133–34.
67. Ibid., 132.
68. Bloesch, *Holy Scripture,* 58.
69. Karl Barth, *Church Dogmatics,* vol. 1: *The Doctrine of the Word of God,* part 2, trans. G. T. Thomson and Harold Knight (Edinburgh: T. & T. Clark, 1956), 457.
70. "A Panel Discussion," 252–53.
71. See Virginia Ramey Mollenkott, *Women, Men and the Bible* (Nashville: Abingdon Press, 1977); Nancy Hardesty, *Women Called to Witness: Evangelical Feminism in the Nineteenth Century* (Nashville: Abingdon Press, 1984); Letha

Scanzoni and Nancy Hardesty, *All We're Meant to Be* (Waco, TX: Word Books, 1974).

72. See Wayne Grudem, "Do Inclusive Language Bibles Distort Scripture? Yes," *Christianity Today* 41 (October 27, 1997), 26–32; John Piper and Wayne Grudem, eds., *Recovering Biblical Manhood and Womanhood: A Response to Evangelical Feminism* (Wheaton, IL: Crossway, 1991). Grudem's Council on Biblical Manhood and Womanhood (located in Libertyville, Illinois) works with James Dobson's Focus on the Family organization and R. C. Sproul's Ligonier Ministries to promote male headship in church and home gender relationships.

73. See Joe Maxwell, "Will the Walls Fall Down?" *Christianity Today* 41 (November 17, 1997), 62–65; Mary Stewart Van Leeuwen, "Servanthood or Soft Patriarchy? A Christian Feminist Looks at the Promise Keepers Movement," *Journal of Men's Studies* 5 (February 1997), 233–61; idem, "Weeping Warriors," *Books and Culture: A Christian Review* 3 (November–December 1997), 9–11; idem, "Mixed Messages on the Mall," *Christian Century* 114 (October 22, 1997), 932–34.

74. Stanley J. Grenz, with Denise Muir Kjesbo, *Women in the Church: A Biblical Theology of Women in Ministry* (Downers Grove, IL: InterVarsity Press, 1995); Rebecca Merrill Groothius, *Good News for Women: A Biblical Picture of Gender Equality* (Grand Rapids: Baker Book House, 1997); Ruth A. Tucker, *Women in the Maze: Questions and Answers on Biblical Equality* (Downers Grove, IL: InterVarsity Press, 1992). See Alvera Mickelsen, ed., *Women, Authority and the Bible* (Downers Grove, IL: InterVarsity Press, 1986). Christians for Biblical Equality is located in Minneapolis, Minnesota.

75. Richard Lints, *The Fabric of Theology: A Prolegomenon to Evangelical Theology* (Grand Rapids: Wm. B. Eerdmans Publishing Co., 1993), 259.

76. Oden, *Systematic Theology,* 1:319–74; James I. Packer, "In Quest of Canonical Interpretation," in *The Use of the Bible in Theology: Evangelical Options,* ed. Robert K. Johnston (Atlanta: John Knox Press, 1985), 35–55; Charles J. Scalise, *From Scripture to Theology: A Canonical Journey into Hermeneutics* (Downers Grove, IL: InterVarsity Press, 1996); Bloesch, *Holy Scripture,* 171–222; Russell P. Spittler, "Scripture and the Theological Enterprise: View from a Big Canoe," in Johnston, ed., *Use of the Bible in Theology,* 56–78.

77. Donald W. Dayton, *The Theological Roots of Pentecostalism* (Grand Rapids: Zondervan Publishing House, 1987); Steven J. Land, *Pentecostal Spirituality: A Passion for the Kingdom* (Sheffield: Sheffield Academic Press, 1993); Henry H. Knight III, *A Future for Truth: Evangelical Theology in a Postmodern World* (Nashville: Abingdon Press, 1997); Clark H. Pinnock, *Flame of Love: A Theology of the Holy Spirit* (Downers Grove, IL: InterVarsity Press, 1996); Helmut Thielicke, *The Evangelical Faith,* vol. 1, trans. Geoffrey W. Bromiley (Grand Rapids: Wm. B. Eerdmans Publishing Co., 1974).

78. J. Richard Middleton and Brian J. Walsh, *Truth Is Stranger than It Used to Be: Biblical Faith in a Postmodern Age* (Downers Grove, IL: InterVarsity Press, 1995).

79. David F. Wells, "The Nature and Function of Theology," in Johnston, ed., *Use of the Bible in Theology,* 175–99.

80. William A. Dyrness, "How Does the Bible Function in the Christian Life?" in Johnston, ed., *Use of the Bible in Theology,* 160–61.

81. See Charles H. Kraft, *Christianity in Culture: A Study in Dynamic Biblical*

Theologizing in Cross-Cultural Perspective (Maryknoll, NY: Orbis Books, 1979), 3, 13–16. See C. René Padilla, "Hermeneutics and Culture—A Theological Perspective," in *Down to Earth: Studies in Christianity and Culture,* ed. John R. W. Stott and Robert Coote (Grand Rapids: Wm. B. Eerdmans Publishing Co., 1980), 63–78; Harvie M. Conn, "Contextualization: Where Do We Begin?" in *Evangelicals and Liberation,* ed. Carl E. Armerding (Grand Rapids: Baker Book House, 1977), 97–98.

82. Dyrness, "How Does the Bible Function in the Christian Life?" 162, 164.
83. Ibid., 170.
84. Grenz, *Revisioning Evangelical Theology,* 97–102; quote on 97.
85. Quoted in B. A. Gerrish, *Tradition and the Modern World* (Chicago: University of Chicago Press, 1977), 13; quoted in Grenz, *Revisioning Evangelical Theology,* 100–101.
86. Dyrness, "How Does the Bible Function in the Christian Life?" 171–73.
87. Clark H. Pinnock, *Tracking the Maze: Finding Our Way through Modern Theology from an Evangelical Perspective* (San Francisco: Harper & Row, 1990), 182–85.
88. Ibid., 185.
89. Hans Frei, "Response to 'Narrative Theology: An Evangelical Appraisal,'" *Trinity Journal* 8 (spring 1987), 21–24; reprinted in Frei, *Theology and Narrative,* ed. Hunsinger and Placher, quote on 208.

Index

Abbott, Lyman, 35
abolitionism: early evangelicals and, 155–59
Abraham, William J., 159–63, 168–69, 173, 194; Arminianism and, 173
adiaphora concept: political conservatism of evangelicals and, 156
Alexander, Archibald, 25–26
Alexander, John, 153
allegorical exegesis: Luther and Calvin on, 19–21
Allis, Oswald T., 40, 42
American Council of Christian Churches, 47, 52
Ames, William, 5
Amish: Anabaptist evangelicalism and, 2
Anabaptist theology: classification of, 2–3; fundamentalism and, 41, 133
Andover Seminary, 116
Anglican theology: classification of, 2–3; Henry on, 113; of Lewis, 174–75; Oxford Movement and, 171; Wesleyan tradition and, 166
Anglican Thirty-Nine Articles of Religion, 166
annihilationism: neoevangelicalism and, 181–83
"anonymous Christianity" theory, 179
Anselmian theology: Carnell and, 82–83
anti-intellectualism: fundamentalist theology and, 53
antipoverty movement: evangelicalism and, 154–55

any-moment secret rapture: Darby dispensationalism and, 28–29
apocalyptic millennialist movements: emergence of, 28–32
apologetics theology: biblical inerrancy and, 139; of Carnell, 62–68; Fuller Theological Seminary and, 52; limits of, 68–71; personalization of, 78–85; postliberal theology and, 198; rationality and, 71–75
Apology of the Augsburg Confession, 21
Aquinas, St. Thomas, 21, 63, 83, 209; Arminian tradition and, 176
Archer, Gleason, 42, 68, 78, 95–99, 114
Aristotelian logic: apologetics theology and, 68–70; Protestant theology and, 21; Reform orthodoxy and, 86–87
Arminianism: Calvinism and, 157, 159; evangelicalism and, 153–59; Methodist theology and, 163–64; modern evangelicalism and, 168–69, 173–77
Arminius, Jacob, 41, 168
Armstrong, William Park, 34
Athanasius, 179, 195, 209
Atkinson, Basil F. C., 181
Auer, Johann Abraham Cristoffel Fagginger, 222 n.33
Augsburg Confession, 171
Augustine, 195, 209; Arminian tradition and, 176; Carnell influenced by, 63–64; second chance doctrine, 179; Wesleyan tradition and, 169

Authority and Interpretation of the Bible: An Historical Approach, The, 215 n.19

Awakening movement: Pietists and, 6

Baptist Church: classification of, 2–3; Darby dispensationalism and, 31; roots of evangelicalism and, 153

Barker, Glenn, 58, 68

Barr, James, 117, 136

Barth, Karl, 7, 33, 71, 85, 95, 96–99, 106; Henry and, 107–10, 113; neoorthodoxy and, 139–40, 146–52, 190–93; postliberal theology and, 195, 198, 202–3, 209; Ramm and, 124–27; universalism of, 178

Bassett, Paul Merritt, 164

Battle for the Bible, The, 118–20, 128, 133

Bauer, P. T., 173

Baur, Ferdinand Christian, 6

Bavinck, Herman, 110

Beegle, Dewey, 114, 129, 137, 145

Bell, Nelson, 104–5

Berkouwer, G. C., 106, 114, 119, 122, 153; on Barth, 126; biblical inerrancy doctrine and, 137, 151

Bertocci, Peter, 60

Bible Presbyterian Church, 40

biblical criticism: Carnell on, 66, 86–95; Catholic Church and, 136–37; fundamentalist protest of, 16; modernist theology and, 27–28

biblical inerrancy doctrine: Abraham's critique of, 160–63; Barthian theology and, 146–52; Carnell on, 66–68, 86–95; catholic neoorthodoxy and, 189–93; classification of evangelicalism based on, 3, 6–9; cultural context of, 188–89; Darby dispensationalism and, 29–30; epistemological reasoning and, 26–27; evangelical orthodoxy and, 114–23; evolution theory and, 33; Fuller Theological Seminary schism over, 95–101; Helvetic Consensus Formula, 22–23; hermeneutics and, 204–9; historical consciousness and, 6; modern fundamentalism and, 42–43; modernist theology and, 27–28; myth and, 141–46;

narrativist theology and, 196–97; new evangelicalism and rethinking of, 138–46; Ockenga's belief in, 55; panevangelicalism and, 172–73; Pinnock and, 133–39; Protestant fundamentalism and, 17–18; Protestant scholasticism and, 19–24; Ramm on science and, 123–29; rejection of, in fundamentalism, 43–47; revelational fideism and, 108–14; Turretin on, 22–23; Wesleyan traditions and, 163–69

Biblical Seminary, 41

Binney, Amos, 163

Blackstone, W. E.: Darby dispensationalism and, 29

Blanchard, Jonathan, 155

Blessed Hope, The, 78

Bloesch, Donald, 114, 126, 151–52, 170, 172; Catholic neoorthodoxy and, 189–93; postliberal theology and, 196, 198, 203

Boer, Harry, 137

Boice, James, M., 42

Boston University, 60, 85

Briggs, Charles, 27, 116

Brightman, Edgar S., 57, 60

Bromiley, Geoffrey, 98, 126, 151

Brookes, James H.: Darby dispensationalism and, 29

Brooks, James H., 15

Brow, Robert, 174–76, 178

Brown, Delwin, 185–86

Brown, Robert McAfee, 100

Bruce, F. F., 114, 119, 131, 137

Brunner, Emil, 106; on evangelicalism, 2; Henry and, 107

Bryan, William Jennings, 17, 39–40, 49, 122; populism of, 155

Bultmann, Rudolf, 33, 106

Buswell, J. Oliver, 41, 55, 58–59

Byrum, R. R., 164

Caird, Edward, 43

Calvinism: biblical inerrancy and, 20–21, 110; dispensationalism and, 28; on gospel message, 4; on knowledge and theology, 63–64; orthodoxy of Christianity in, 171; Pinnock influenced by, 132–33, 142–46; progressive evangelicalism and, 195, 209; Protestant scholasticism and, 19–24; Reform orthodoxy and, 19, 86–87; roots of evangelicalism and, 153, 182–83; social activism and, 157; waning influence of, 159; Wesleyan tradition and, 169; on witness of the Spirit, 24

Cameron, Robert, 30

Campbellite restorationists, 3

Campus Crusade for Christ, 94

Cappel, Louis, 23

Carnell, Edward John, 7, 45, 47, 153; addiction problems of, 81, 84–85; apologetics theology and, 68–71; biblical inerrancy doctrine and, 85–95, 98–99, 111, 114–16; emotional breakdown, 84–85; on faith and knowledge, 62–68, 223 n.40; Fuller Theological Seminary and, 56–58; graduate dissertations of, 60–61, 223 n.34; new evangelicalism and, 85–95, 100–101, 104–5, 108, 153; Pinnock and, 134; presidency of Fuller, 75–78, 226 n.92; on rationality, 71–75; reform of fundamentalism and, 52; "sackful of arguments" defense of Christianity, 61–68; seminary education of, 60–61; on threat of secularism, 116; at Wheaton College, 59–60; writings of, 78–85

Case for Orthodox Theology, The, 85–86, 95, 97

categorical imperative: Carnell on, 81–82

Catholic Church: alleged distortion of gospel by, 4; biblical inerrancy doctrine and, 136–37; evangelicalism and, 153–59, 169–73, 179–80; neoorthodoxy in, 189–93; Protestant scholasticism and, 21–24

Caven, William, 16

Chafer, Lewis Sperry, 32

Chalcedon, 171

Chicago Call conference, 170–73

Chicago Tribune, 57

Childs, Brevard, 205

Christian America, ideology of, 35

Christian Century, 85, 93–95, 104

Christian Coalition: political partisanship in, 8–9

Christian Commitment, 75, 78–85

Christian democracy: social gospelism and, 35

Christianity and Liberalism, 37–39

Christianity Today, 56, 129; biblical inerrancy debate in, 98–99; Henry's editorship tenure at, 103–7; new evangelicalism and, 173; opposition to civil rights in, 154, 159

Christian Reformed Church, 110; fundamentalism and, 8; fundamentalism within, 41

Christians for Biblical Equality, 204

Christian Theology, 164

Christian View of God and the World, The, 43

Christian View of Science and Scripture, The, 123–29

Chrysostom, 209

Church Dogmatics, 126, 148

Church of God, 164

Church of the Bretheren: Anabaptist evangelicalism and, 2

Church of the Nazarene, 164

Civil Rights movement: evangelicalism and, 153–54

Clapp, Rodney, 194, 201–2

Clark, Gordon, 42, 153; apologetics and, 68–71; biblical inerrancy and, 148; Carnell influenced by, 57–63, 68, 77, 98–99; evangelical epistemology and, 107, 110, 114; rationalism of, 72–74

classical theology: apologetics and, 75; Carnell on, 63; defined, 2–3; evangelicalism's return to, 205–9; gospel message in, 4–5

Clowney, Edmund P., 42, 58

cognitive-propositional approach: postliberal theology and, 197–98

Coleman, Richard, 185

College of New Jersey: epistemological realism and, 25

Common Roots, 172–73

"common sense" philosophy (Scottish school), 24–25

Communion of the Christian with God, The, 33

communitarianism: postliberal evangelicalism and, 196–203

Compendium theologiae Christianae, 22

conditional immortality: neoevangelicalism and, 182–83

confessional evangelicalism: classification of, 2; Protestant fundamentalism and, 17

Conn, Harvie, 207

Constitution on Divine Revelation, 136–37

Consultation on Evangelical Affirmations, 11

Cottrell, Jack, 176

Council for Biblical Manhood and Womanhood, 204, 247 n.72

Council of Trent: biblical infalliblity doctrine and, 21

Counter-Reformationist criticism: biblical infalliblity doctrine and, 21

Covenant Seminary, 41

creative love theism: neoevangelicalism and, 175–83, 193

Critique of Pure Reason, 44

Crum, Terelle, 68

cultural linguistics: postliberal theology and, 197–98

cultural relativism: biblical inerrancy and, 145–46, 204–9

Cyprian, 171

Dallas Theological Seminary, 50, 52

damnation doctrine: neoevangelicalism and, 179–83

Darby, John Nelson, 14; dispensationalism movement of, 28–32, 47, 159

Darrow, Clarence, 122

Darwinism. *See* evolution

Davis, Clair, 58

Davis, Stephen, 129

Dayton, Donald W., 2–4, 153, 155–59, 170, 205

deconstructionism: progressive evangelicalism and, 194–95

Denney, James, 46, 91, 119, 130

Derrida, Jacques, 194

DeWolf, Harold, 57, 85

diastasis: evangelicalism and, 147–48, 202

dictation theory: biblical inerrancy doctrine and, 118; Helvetica Consensus and, 22–23

dispensationalism: Carnell's critique of, 92–95; Darby movement and, 28–32, 47; Fuller's fundamentalism and, 50, 52–53, 78; reform of fundamentalism and, 52–53; social activism and, 155

Divine Inspiration of Holy Scripture, The, 160–61

Divino Afflante Spiritu, 136–37

Dixon, A. C., 15–16

Dobson, James, 204, 247 n.72

Dockery, David, 194

dogmatist theology: Protestant scholasticism and, 22–24

Dunning, H. Ray, 167

Dutch Calvinists: Barth and, 126

Dyrness, William, 206–8

Eastern Orthodox Church: evangelism and, 170

ecclesial separatism: fundamentalism and, 41

Eclipse of Biblical Narrative, The, 196

ecumenical movement: Henry's opposition to, 104–7; Machen's opposition to, 36–37

Edwards, David L., 185–89

Eerdmans Evangelical Book Award Competition, 61

either-or theology: Carnell's development of, 62–68

Ellingsen, Mark, 185

Ellington, Scott A., 167

Elmer Gantry, 49

Enlightenment: catholic neoorthodoxy and, 189; evangelicalism and, 167, 202–3; liberal theology and, 187–89; progressive evangelicalism and, 194–95

epistemological realism: Princeton theology and, 25–28; rejection of biblical inerrancy and, 43

Erdman, William J., 15

evangelical epistemology: emergence of, 107–14

evangelicalism: Abraham's critique of, 159–63; biblical inerrancy and, 114–23, 131–38; Catholic Church and, 169–73; classification of, 2–9; definitions of, 4, 8–9; liberal theology and, 184–89; mainstream dismissal of, 1–2; political conservatism and, 153–59; postliberal theology and, 200–203; role of knowledge in, 200–203; scripture principle and, 10–11; *vs.* fundamentalism, 1–2, 9
Evangelicals at the Brink of Crisis, 103
Evangelicals in Search of Identity, 103
Evangelical Theological Society (ETS), 42, 118, 120
evidentialist ideology: evangelical epistemology and, 109–10
evolution, theory of: Carnell on, 67; fundamentalist campaign against, 17; Princeton orthodoxy and, 32–33
Examination of the Alleged Discrepancies of the Bible, An, 117
experiential-expressive approach: postliberal theology and, 197–98

Fackre, Gabriel, 185, 189
faith: Carnell's apologetic on, 62–68
Faith Seminary, 41
Faith Theological Seminary, 58
Falwell, Jerry, 8
Farrer, Austin, 113
Federal Council of Churches, 47, 49–51
Fee, Gordon D., 167
feminist movement: evangelicalism and, 154–55, 203–4
Finney, Charles G., 13–14, 27, 155–59; Hodge and, 157
Finney-style perfectionism, 27
First Helvetic Confession, 165
"five points" of fundamentalism: reaffirmation of, 1916–1923, 17
Focus on the Family, 247 n.72
Fosdick, Harry Emerson, 37–40, 50
Foucault, Michel, 194
foundationalism: postliberal theology and, 200–203
Fourth Lateran Council, 171
Free Methodist Church, 163
Frei, Hans, 190–91, 196–99, 209

Frontiers in Modern Theology, 106
Fudge, Edward William, 181
Fuller, Charles, 47, 50–51, 85, 99; financial investments of, 84; reform of fundamentalism and, 52–61
Fuller, Daniel: biblical inerrancy doctrine and, 114, 129; Fuller Theological Seminary and, 78, 95, 97–99
Fuller Theological Seminary, 4; administrative problems at, 75–78; bibilical inerrancy doctrine at, 114–23; founding of, 7, 17, 47, 51; fundamentalist attacks on, 94–95; ideological split in, 95–101; reform of fundamentalism and, 49, 52–61; threat of secularism and, 116
Fundamental Christian Theology, 164
fundamentalism: Carnell's criticism of, 92–95; classification of, 9; Darby dispensationalism and, 29; evangelicalism and, 3, 9; founders of reform in, 52–61; historical consciousness and, 6; lack of respect for, 49–50; marginalization in 1930s, 40; negative images of, 56; partisan politics and, 8–9; postliberal theology and, 200–203; postwar reform of, 7–8; Princeton theology and, 32–40; reform movement within, 49–101; rejection of biblical inerrancy in, 43–47; revolt against modernism by, 16; roots of, 1–2; scripture principle and, 10–11; subcultural network, 17
Fundamentals, The, 16, 45

Gaebelein, Arno C.: Darby dispensationalism and, 29–30
Gaebelein, Frank, 76
Gataker, Thomas, 216 n.25
Geertz, Clifford, 197
Geisler, Norman, 42
gender equity: evangelicalism and, 203–4
General Association of Regular Baptists, 59
Gerhard, Johan, 21, 162
Gerstner, John, 42, 68; evidentialist ideology and, 109
Geschichte, 149–50
God, Revelation and Authority, 107

Goddard, Burton, 51, 68
Gordon, A. J., 15, 155
Gordon College, 61, 155; Divinity School, 68
Gordon-Conwell Seminary, 155
gospel message: evangelicalism's roots in, 4–9; Luther on, 20; Moody's theology rooted in, 14
Graf-Wellhausen documentary hypothesis, 16, 45
Graham, Billy: *Christianity Today* and, 104–5; Clark's influence on, 58; Fuller Theological Seminary and, 85, 100; integrated crusades of, 56; modern evangelicalism and, 153; political conservatism of, 159; Ramm's views on science and scripture and, 124–29; Smith's influence on, 53
Granberg, Lars, 58
Gray, James M., 15
Great Divorce, The, 174
Green, Garrett, 196
Grenz, Stanley, 194–96, 202–4, 206–8
Grider, J. Kenneth, 167
Groothuis, Rebecca Merrill, 204
Grudem, Wayne, 204, 247 n.72
Guillebaud, Harold E., 181

Haley, John, 117
Handbook of Christian Theology, 84
Hardesty, Nancy, 154, 203
Harris, Robert, 216 n.25
Harrison, Everett F., 51–52, 78, 96–97
Harvard Divinity School, 116
Harvard University, 60, 68, 116, 222 n.33
Hauerwas, Stanley, 196
Hebrew punctuation in scripture: Helvetica Consensus Forum, 22–23
Hegel, G. W. F., 44
hell, evangelical concept of, 179–83
Helvetic Consensus Formula, 22–23
Henry, Carl F. H., 7, 45, 47, 51; apologetics of, 159–60; biblical inerrancy doctrine and, 114–23, 148; Carnell and, 60–61, 79; as *Christianity Today* editor, 56, 99–101, 103–7, 154; on cultism of evangelicalism, 103, 153; evangelical epistemology and, 107–14; as evangelicalism's intellectual

leader, 101, 103; Fuller Theological Seminary and, 53–54, 56–57, 76–77; Pinnock influenced by, 132; progressive evangelicalism and, 195, 209; at Wheaton College, 59
Henry, Matthew, 90–91
Hensley, Jeffrey, 200
Hermann, Wilhelm, 106
Hermeneutics: postconservative evangelicalism and, 204–9
hermeneutics: biblical inerrancy and, 129–30
Herrmann, Wilhelm, 33–34, 37, 44
heterodoxy, threat of, 116
Higher Life movement, 27
Hills, A. M., 164
historical consciousness: of Catholic and Orthodox traditions, 170–73; fundamentalist evangelicalism and, 6, 148–52, 204–9
historical criticism: biblical inerrancy doctrine and, 136–37, 196–97
Hodge, A. A., 17–19, 22, 216 n.25; on biblical inerrancy, 46, 89; dogmatic system of, 24–25; modernization fought by, 26
Hodge, Charles, 17–18; abolitionism denouced by, 156; biblical criticism and, 89, 121; condemnation of evolution by, 32; epistemological realism of, 24–26, 31; Finney and, 157; on knowledge and theology, 63, 68; on liberal theology, 26, 216 n.30; personality of, 26–27; on systematic theology, 66
Hodges, A. A.: Wesleyan tradition and, 169
Hodges, Charles: Wesleyan tradition and, 169
Holiness movements: classification of, 2–3; fundamentalism and, 41; fundamentalism's origins and, 16; gospel message in, 5–6; neoevangelicalism and, 7; ordination of women, 155; social activism and, 158–59; Warfield and, 27–28, 32; Wesleyan tradition and, 164, 166–69
Holmes, Arthur, 114

Holy Spirit, as guardian of orthodoxy, 165–69
Hooker, Richard, 166, 209
Horder, William, 68
Hordern, Willam, 85
Howard, Thomas, 170–71
Hubbard, David, 77, 99–100
Hume, David: philosophical skepticism of, 26
Hunsinger, George, 196
Hunter, James Davison, 2–3

incarnation doctrine: Carnell on, 73–75
Independent Fundamental Churches of America, 41
inerrancy doctrine. *See* biblical infalliblity
inspiration, doctrine of: Pinnock on inerrancy and, 134–39; Protestant fundamentalism and, 18; *vs.* liberal theology, 39–40, 126–29
Institutes of Elenctic Theology, 22
interactionist theory: postconservative evangelicalism and, 206–9
International Council on Biblical Inerrancy, 42
Inter-Varsity Christian Fellowship, 94, 159
Introduction to Christian Apologetics, An, 61
Irenaeus, 195, 209

Jewett, Paul, 58, 68, 77–78, 95, 97–99, 114, 144–45
Jones, Bob, 41
Jülicher, Adolf, 33

Kähler, Martin, 149–50
Kant, Immanuel: liberal theology and, 111–12; moral philosophy of, 81–83; philosophical skepticism of, 26
Kantzer, Kenneth S., 42, 68
Kaufman, Gordon, 188
Kenneson, Phillip D., 194
Keswick Holiness (Pietism), 27, 31
Kierkegaard, Søren, 60, 71–74, 80, 195, 223 n.16
King, Henry Churchill, 35
King, Martin Luther Jr., 56, 154, 158
Kjesbo, Denise Muir, 204

Knight, Henry H. III, 194, 205
knowledge: narrativist theology and, 199–203; spiritual *vs.* formal knowledge, debate concerning, 164–65
knowledge-before-faith apologetics, 62–68
Kraft, Charles, 206–7
Kuhn, Harold, 68
Kuhn, Thomas, 200–201
Kummel, Werner Georg, 106
Kuyper, Abraham, 86, 110, 227 n.116

Ladd, George E., 68, 78, 95, 97, 114, 119; biblical inerrancy doctrine and, 114, 119, 137
Land, Steven J., 167, 194, 205
Lane Seminary, 27
LaSor, William, 95
Laurin, Robert, 99
Laws, Curtis Lee, 46
"layman's revival," 13
L'Engle, Madeleine, 175
Lewis, C. S., 173–74, 178
Lewis, Jack, 68
liberal theology. *See also* postliberal theology: biblical inerrancy and, 115–23, 131; Carnell on, 60, 81, 83–84; *Christianity Today,* 104; dismissal of fundamentalism by, 49–50; ecumenical movement and, 36–37; epistemological realism and, 26–27; evolution theory and, 33; fundamentalism and, 37–40; Kant and, 111–12; Orr's epistemological realism and, 44–47; Pinnock on, 139–40; postconservative evangelicalism and, 186–89; Princeton orthodoxy and, 33–36; rift with evangelicalism, 185–89; secularism and, 116; *vs.* Paulist theology, 37
libertarianism: Protestant fundamentalism and, 35
Ligonier Ministries, 247 n.72
Lindbeck, George, 190–91, 196–203
Lindsell, Harold, 42–43; biblical inerrancy doctrine, 117–23, 128–29; Fuller Theological Seminary and, 77–78, 95–99; Pinnock and, 131, 133–34; reform of fundamentalism and, 52, 54, 58; scripture-science debate and, 124

Lints, Richard, 204–5
literary form: biblical inerrancy and, 140–42, 145–46
Loci theologici, 21–22
Logos Christology, 174
Lovelace, Richard, 170
Lutheran Church. *See also* Missouri Synod; Wisconsin Synod: Biblical inerrancy, 19–24; emphasis on salvation by, 5; evangelicalism in, classification of, 2; on gospel message, 4; orthodoxy of, 171; progressive evangelicalism and, 195, 209; Protestant scholasticism and, 19–24; Wesleyan tradition and, 169
Lutheran tradition: pietistic evangelicalism and, 3

MacArthur, Robert Stuarty, 46
Macartney, Clarence, 42, 55
Machen, J. Gresham, 7; Carnell influenced by, 62, 68, 108, 223 n.40; Carnell's critique of, 93, 98–99; Darby dispensationalism and, 31–32; Fosdick and, 37–39; Fuller Theological Seminary and, 52; liberal theology and, 33–34, 38–39; Northern Presbyterian schism and, 58, 60; Ockenga and, 54–55; politics and cultural background of, 35–36; Princeton orthodoxy and fundamentalism, 32–41
Mackintosh, C. H., 14, 213 n.3; Darby dispensationalism and, 29
MacRae, Allan, 51
mainstream theology: dismissal of evangelicalism by, 1, 7; fundamentalism in midst of, 41–42; fundamentalism overlooked by, 1–2, 49–50, 56
male privilege: evangelicalism and, 203–4, 247 n.72
Marburg Articles, 171
Marrow of Theology, The, 5
Marsden, George, 9
Marshall, I. Howard, 129, 137
Mathews, Shailer, 35
McClendon, James William Jr., 196
McGrath, Alister, 189, 192–93, 196, 198–99
McIntyre, Carl, 47, 49, 52; Northern Presbyterian Church and, 40–41, 55, 58
McKim, Donald K., 129, 137, 145, 215 n.19, 235 n.136
McLeod, Mark, 194
McMaster Divinity College, 133
Melanchthon, Philipp, 21
Mencken, H. L., 36
Mennonites: Anabaptist evangelicalism and, 2
Mere Christianity, 174
Meredith, James, 154
metaphysics: Carnell on, 81–85; Ritschlian theology and, 44
Metaphysics, 70
Methodist evangelicalism: classification of, 3; social activism and, 155, 158–59; Wesleyan evangelicalism and, 163–69
Metzger, Bruce, 119
Meyer, Louis, 16
Middleton, J. Richard, 194, 205–6
Miley, John, 163
Millerites: millennialism and, 28
Missouri Synod. *See also* Lutheran Church: biblical inerrancy and, 122; fundamentalism and, 8; fundamentalism within, 41
Moberg, David, 154–56
modernist theology: epistemological realism and, 26; fundamentalist influence and, 41–42; Henry's attack on, 110–14; liberal theology and, 187–89; North Presbyterian Church and, 18; Princeton theology and, 26–28
Mollenkott, Virginia Ramey, 154, 203
Montgomery, John Warwick: evidentialist ideology and, 109
Montogomery, John Warwick, 224 n.70
Moody, Dwight L., 52, 155, 159; theology of, 13–14
Moody Bible Institute, 52; fundamentalism and, 14
morality: Carnell on Kant's moral philosophy and, 82; God as law of, 157
Moral Majority movement, 8
Mosaic authorship: evangelicalism and, 16, 162

Murphy, Nancey, 194
Murray, 132
Murray, John, 42, 60, 110
Mutual Broadcasting System, 50–51
myth: biblical inerrancy and, 141–46; Pinnock's discussion of, 140–41

narrativist theology, 190–91; postliberal evangelicalism and, 196–203
National Association of Evangelicals (NAE), 11, 47, 51–52, 55
"natural revelation," Carnell's theology of, 65–68
Needham, George, 15
neo-Aristotelianism: Princeton theology and, 19
neoevangelicalism: Arminianism and, 174–77; biblical inerrancy and, 139–46; Carnell's biblical criticism and, 61, 84–95; in Catholic Church, 189–93; emergence of, 7; evangelical dispute with, 126–27; Henry's evangelical epistemology and, 107; neoevangelicalism and, 7, 10; Ockenga and, 56; Ramm's views on science and scripture and, 124–29; scripture principle and, 9
New International Version of the Bible, 204
Newman, John Henry, 171
New-school Presbyterians: classification of, 3
Newsweek, 103, 142
Niagara Bible Conference, 15; tribulationist party split and, 30–31
Nicene Creed, 171
Nicole, Roger, 68, 170
Niebuhr, Reinhold, 60; Carnell's rejection of, 60–61, 223 n.33
Nietzsche, Friedrich, 195
non-Western Christianity: evangelicalism and, 171–73
Norris, J. Frank, 15
North American Karl Barth Society, 151–52
Northern Baptist Church: fundamentalism and, 17, 39; modernist control of, 40; split within, 37
Northern Baptist Theological Seminary, 53

Northern Presbyterian Church: fundamentalism and, 15–17, 39, 56; fundamentalist-modernist split in, 27, 37, 40, 55, 58; Machen and, 27, 37, 93
Novak, Michael, 173

Oberlin College, 155–56
Oberlin revivalism, 3, 156
Ockenga, Harold J., 7, 40, 42, 47; Christianity Today and, 105; Fuller Theological Seminary and, 51–53, 51–57, 75–76, 84–85, 94–99; reform of fundamentalism and, 52–61, 68
Oden, Thomas C., 189, 192–93; on classical orthodoxy, 205
Old Fashioned Revival Hour, 50–51
Olson, Roger, 185, 194
Origenist theology, 171, 179–80
Origin of Paul's Religion, The, 37
Orr, James, 16; on biblical inerrancy and criticism, 87–92, 97–98, 119, 130, 133; "English school" evangelicalism, 43–47, 90; on liberal theology, 62–63
Orthodox Presbyterian Church (OPC), 40, 42; schism within, 68–69
Other Side, The, 154
Outlines of Theology, 17–18
Owen, John, 23, 162
Oxford Movement, 171
Oxford Tractarians, 171

pacificism: evangelicalism and, 153–59
Packer, J. I., 119, 205
Packer, James I., 42
Padilla, C. René, 207
"paleoorthodoxy," 192–93
panevangelical commonality: Chicago Call conference and, 171–73
Pannenberg, Wolfhart, 106
parachurch organizations: fundamentalist development of, 50
Park Street Congregational Church, 55, 57
Parsons, Henry M., 15
partisan politics: evangelicalism and conservatism, 153–59; fundamentalism and, 8–9

Pascal, Blaise, 80
patriotism: Protestant fundamentalism and, 35
Patton, Francis, 26, 34
Paulist theology: Barth and, 178; Finney and, 157–58; Machen on, 37; Pinnock and, 144–46; progressive evangelicalism and, 195
penal substitution, doctrine of, 38–39
Pentateuch: critical scholarship concerning, 16, 162–63
Pentecostalism: classical theology and, 205; partisan politics and expansion of, 8–9; social activism and, 159; Warfield and, 27
perfect autographs concept: biblical inerrancy doctrine and, 46, 87–89, 115–16, 133
perfect errorlessness doctrine: fundamentalism and, 42
Pew, J. Howard, 104–5
Pharisaism: modern evangelicalism and, 135–36
Philosophy of the Christian Religion, A, 71–75, 79
Pietism: biblical inerrancy and, 166; defined, 3; gospel message in, 5–6; social activism and, 158–59
Pinnock, Clark, 224 n.70; Arminianism and, 133–38, 175–77; biblical inerrancy doctrine and, 114–15, 120, 122, 129–38, 148, 235 n.136; on conservativism of evangelicals, 153; creative love theism of, 175–83, 193; evidentialist ideology and, 109–11; on liberalism and evangelicalism, 186; on neoevangelicalism, 139–46, 173, 174–83; on postconservative evangelicalism, 185–86, 205, 209; second chance doctrine, 179–83; universal inclusivism doctrine, 179–83
Pius XII (Pope), 136
Placher, William, 196
Plan of Union, 36–37
Plato, 65
Platonism: evangelicalism and, 182–83
Plymouth Brethren, 28–29
Plymouth Conference for the Advancement of Evangelical Scholarship, 51
Point Breeze Presbyterian Church, 55

political conservatism: evangelicalism and, 153–59
Pope, William Burt, 163–64
Post-American, The, 133, 154
postconservative evangelicalism: Arminian roots of, 173–77; cultural context of, 203–9; emergence of, 185–209; gender equity and, 203–4; origins of, 6–7
postliberal theology: catholic (neo)orthodoxy and, 190–93; revelatory narrative and, 196–203
postmodern theory: progressive evangelicalism and, 193–95
"postponement theory": dispensationalism and, 30
Post-Reformation orthodoxy: gospel message and, 5
Pound, Ezra, 36
premillennialism: dispensationalism's emergence and, 28–32; Fuller Theological Seminary's commitment to, 77–78; fundamentalism and, 14–16, 213 n.5; fundamentalist splits and, 41; Henry's critique of fundamentalism and, 53–54; social activism and, 155–59; Warfield and, 27–28
prenes concept: biblical inerrancy doctrine and, 117
Presbyterian Church: Darby dispensationalism and, 31; Machen's expulsion from, 40; Niagara Bible conference and, 15–16; reform of fundamentalism and, 52
presuppositionalism: catholic neoorthodoxy and, 189; evangelical epistemology and, 108
pretribulationalism: Fuller Theological Seminary and, 78
Preus, Robert D., 42, 130
Princeton Theological Seminary, 6, 17, 25; Machen's career at, 32–35, 40
Princeton theology: Darby dispensationalism and, 31; development of, 18–19; dictation theory, 23; epistemological realism and, 24–28; fundamentalist movement and, 32–40; Protestant fundamentalism and, 17–18; Turretin and, 22–24, 216 n.25

Princeton University, 116

Problem of Pain, The, 174

progressive evangelicalism, 6, 193–95, 205–9

Prohibition: fundamentalist support for, 17

Promise Keepers, 204

propositional truth: apologetics theology and, 79–85

Protestant Biblical Interpretation, 126

Protestant evangelicalism: countercultural schools, 17; gospel faith and, 4; history of biblical inerrancy, 116; importance of gospel message in, 2; mid-century changes in, 17

Protestant scholasticism: *vs.* evangelicalism, 164–69; intellectual certainty and, 24–28; Luther and Calvin and, 19–24; Orr's critique of, 45–46; Princeton theology and, 18–19; Reformation/post-Reformation split and, 215 n.19

"protracted meeting" evangelism, 13

Puritans: gospel message and, 5; premillennialist dispensationalism and, 28

"purity crusade," 156

Quebedeaux, Richard: classification of evangelicalism, 2

Quenstedt, Johann Andreas, 21–22

racism: postwar fundamentalism and, 56, 153–54

Rahner, Karl, 179

Ramm, Bernard, 101, 114, 122–23; biblical inerrancy and, 130, 137, 145; evangelical reform and, 146–52, 202; on literary forms, 140–41; religion-science problem and, 123–29

"rapture" doctrine: Darby dispensationalism and, 28–32; Warfield and, 27–28

rationality: apologetics theology and, 68–71; Carnell on faith and, 62–68; catholic neoorthodoxy and, 189; postliberal theology and, 200–203; reform of fundamentalism and, 59–61, 71–75; Wesleyan tradition and, 167

Rauschenbusch, Walter, 35

Raymond, Miner, 163

reason: progressive evangelicalism and, 194–95; Ritschlian theology and, 44

Record of Christian Work, 13

Reformation: classical evangelicalism and, 3; slogans of gospel message during, 4

Reformational-Confessional evangelicalism: classification of, 2

Reformed Episcopal church: fundamentalism within, 41

Reform orthodoxy: Carnell and, 86; Catholic and Orthodox traditions and, 170–73; classification of evangelicalism and, 2–3, 9; Darby dispensationalism and, 31–32; dispensationalism and, 31–32; modernist theology and, 27–28; perfect errorlessness doctrine, 42; pietistic evangelicalism and, 3; Pinnock's theology and, 132–33; post-Reformation break with, 21–22, 215 n.19; presuppositionalism and, 111; Protestant fundamentalism and, 17–18; salvation as theme of, 5; scholastic certainty and Princeton realism, 24–28; Wheaton College curriculum and, 58

Reid, Thomas, 24

Religionsgeschichtliche Schule (History of Religions School), 33

Remaking the Modern Mind, 54

revelational fideism: biblical inerrancy and, 96–98, 108–14, 139–52, 192–93

revelatory narrative: postliberal theology, 196–203

Revised Standard Version of the Bible, 66

revivalism: Carnell on orthodox Protestantism and, 67; legacy of, 13–14

Reynolds, Edward, 216 n.25

Rice, John R., 41, 94

Rice, Richard, 176–77

Ridderbos, H. N., 137

Riley, William B., 15–16

Ritschl, Albrecht, 44

Ritschlian theology, 44

Riverside Church, 40

Roberts, David, 59–60

Robertson, Pat, 8–9
Rockefeller, John D. Jr., 40
Rogers, Jack B., 129, 137, 145, 215 n.19, 235 n.136
Roos, Joe, 133
Rudolph, Robert, 58
Runia, Klaus, 148
Rutherford Samuel, 24, 216 n.25

Salvation Army, 155, 164
salvation ideology: biblical inerrancy and, 148–49; Lutheran emphasis on, 5
Sandeen, Ernest, 28, 156
Scalise, Charles J., 205
Schaeffer, Francis, 42, 118, 131
Schleiermacher, Friedrich, 26, 37, 44, 46, 81, 83, 188, 200, 216 n.30
Schultz, Samuel, 68
science: biblical inerrancy doctrine and, 122–23, 197; Carnell on theology and, 62–68, 86–87; Ramm on scripture and, 123–29; Ritschlian theology and, 44–45; study of scripture and, 25
Scofield, C. I., 15, 29–32
Scofield Reference Bible, 31
Scopes evolution trial, 17, 33, 40, 49, 122–23
Scottish Reform theology: biblical criticism and, 91
scriptural schematic: Darby dispensationalism and, 29–32
scripture principle: fundamentalism and, 10; Ramm on science and, 123–29
Scripture Principle, The, 134
second chance doctrine, 179–83
Second Helvetic Confession, 165
sectarianism: fundamentalism and, 17
secularism: liberal theology and, 116
self-awareness, faith and, 64–68
separatism: reform of fundamentalism and, 52–53, 58–59
Set Forth Your Case, 131
Shakers: millennialism and, 28
"Shall the Fundamentalists Win?" (Fosdick sermon), 37
Sheppard, Gerald, 167
Shinn, Roger, 68

Sider, Ron, 154
slavery: evangelicalism and, 156
Smith, Henry Preserved, 27, 88–89
Smith, Wilbur: Fuller Theological Seminary and, 76–78, 84, 95–96, 99; reform of fundamentalism and, 52–53; on threat of secularism, 116
social activism: evangelicalism and, 154–59
social gospel theology: Protestant fundamentalism and, 35–40
Socrates, 80
Sojourners magazine, 133, 154
sola motifs: of Reformation, 4, 6
Southern Baptist Convention, 41; biblical inerrancy doctrine, 118, 122, 129; fundamentalism and, 8; Pinnock and, 131–32
Southern Presbyterians: slavery supported by, 156
Spener, Philip Jacob, 5
Spitler, Russell, 205
Sproul, R. C., 42, 204, 247 n.72
Stackhouse, Max: classification of evangelicalism, 2
Stevenson, J. Ross, 40
Stewart, Lyman, 16
Stewart, Milton, 16
Stonehouse, Ned, 40
Stott, John, 181, 185–89
Strong, Augustus H., 46, 119
Stroup, George, 196
Sunday, Billy, 49
Sword of the Lord, 94
Systematic Theology, 18, 25, 163–64

temperance movement: evangelicalism and, 156
Tenney, Merrill, 51, 68
Tertullian, 195
testimonium ideology: biblical inerrancy and, 125–29, 166
theistic evolution: Darwinian evolution and, 32–33
Theologia didactitico-polemica, 21
theological liberalism. See liberal theology
Therefore Stand, 53
Thielicke, Helmut, 151

Thiemann, Ronald, 196
Tholuck, Friedrich August, 216 n.30
Thornton, Lionel, 113
Thornwell, James Henley, 156
Thy Word Is Truth, 42
Time, 142
Tompkins, James, 58
Torrance, Thomas, 151
Torrey, Reuben A., 7, 13, 15–16; Darby dispensationalism and, 29, 31; Fuller as student of, 50; Smith influenced by, 52
transdenominational evangelical movement, 42
Trinity Evangelical Divinity School, 11, 99, 119
Triumph of Grace in the Theology of Karl Barth, The, 126
Troeltsch, Ernst, 33, 115
truth: apologetic dialogue on, 68–71; apologetics and objectivity of, 71–75; apologetics theology and ontology of, 79–85; fundamentalist preoccupation with, 125–29; postliberal theology and, 198–203
Tübingen School, 6
Tucker, Ruth A., 204
Turretin, Francis, 22–23, 162, 215 n.19; Hodge and, 26; Wesleyan tradition and, 169
Turretin, Jean-Alphonse, 22

Uneasy Conscience of Modern Fundamentalism, The, 53
Union Theological Seminary, 27
United Churches of Christ in America, 36–37
universal inclusivism doctrine: neoevangelicalism and, 179–83
universalism: neoevangelicalism and, 178–79
University of Chicago, 116
University of Chicago Divinity School, 98

Van Til, Cornelius, 40, 42, 51, 60, 62, 153; apologetics and, 68–71, 224 n.70; attacks on Barth, 126–27, 148; Pinnock influenced by, 132; presuppositionalism and, 108–11

Vatican Council II, 136–37, 179
Veitch, John, 43
Vietnam War: evangelicalism and, 153–55
Volf, Miroslav, 194
von Harnack, Adolf, 44

Wallis, Jim, 133, 153, 155
Walsh, Brian J., 194, 205–6
Walton, Brian, 23
Walvoord, John F., 11
Warfield, Benjamin B., 7; atonement theory, 31, 218 n.39; on biblical inerrancy, 46, 87–89, 116, 120–21, 134, 142–43, 234 n.123; conservative Protestants and, 27–28, 36; Darby dispensationalism and, 31–32, 218 n.39; on knowledge and theology, 63–64, 68; Machen and, 35–36; modernization fought by, 26–27; Princeton theology and, 16, 18–19, 22, 26, 32, 34; Wesleyan tradition and, 169
Webber, Robert E.: catholic neoorthodoxy and, 189; Chicago Call conference, 170–73; on classical orthodoxy, 205; classification of evangelicalism, 2–3
Weber, Otto, 106, 151
Weber, Timothy P.: classification of evangelicalism, 2, 6
Weld, Theodore, 155
Wells, David F., 3, 171–72, 206
Wenham Conference, 118
Wesley, John, 5, 158–59, 162–63, 165–69, 209
Wesleyan evangelicalism: classical theology and, 205; classification of, 2–3; neoevangelicalism and, 7; postfundamentalist differences in, 159–63; roots of, 163–69; social activism and, 155–56, 158–59
West, Nathaniel, 15
Western philosophy: Carnell on, 80
Westminster Assembly of Divines, 47, 216 n.25
Westminster Confession of Faith, 24, 110, 171; biblical inerrancy and, 142; modernist theology and, 27
Westminster Press, 85

Westminster Theological Seminary: formation of, 40; Fuller and, 52; Ockenga at, 54; schisms in, 41; Wheaton College and, 58–60

Wheaton College, 55, 57–59, 155, 158–59

Whitefield, George, 5

Wiley, H. Orton, 164–65

Wilson, Robert Dick, 40

Wilson, Woodrow: World War I and, 34–35

Wisconsin Synod. *See also* Lutheran Church: fundamentalism and, 8; fundamentalism within, 41

Witherspoon, John, 25

Wittgenstein, 197–200

Wollebius, Johannes, 22

Woodbridge, Charles, 55, 76–78, 84, 94, 226 n.92

Works of Love, 74

World's Christian Fundamentals Association, 16

World Vision International, 103

World War I: Protestant fundamentalism and, 34–35

Wright, George Frederick, 16

Wyrtzen, Jack, 94

Yale University, 116

Young, E. J., 42, 110, 121

Young Life, 94

Young Men's Christian Association (YMCA): Machen and, 34–3